Between Worlds

SUNY Series in Judaica:
Hermeneutics, Mysticism, and Religion

Michael Fishbane, Robert Goldenberg,
and Arthur Green, Editors

Between Worlds

The Life and Thought of
Rabbi David ben Judah Messer Leon

Hava Tirosh-Rothschild

State University of New York Press

Published by
State University of New York Press, Albany

© 1991 State University of New York
All rights reserved

Printed in the United States of America

For information, address State University of New York
Press, State University Plaza, Albany, N.Y. 12246

Library of Congress Cataloging in Publication Data

Tirosh-Rothschild, Hava, 1950-
    Between worlds: the life and thought of Rabbi David ben Judah
    Messer Leon/Hava Tirosh-Rothschild.
        p. cm. — (SUNY series in Judaica: Hermeneutics, mysticism,
    and religion)
    Includes bibliographical references.
    ISBN 0-7914-0447-1 (alk. paper). — ISBN 0-7914-0448-X (pbk.
alk. paper)
    1. Judah ben Jehiel, 15th cent. 2. Rabbis — Italy — Biography.
3. Rabbis — Turkey — Biography. 4. Philosophers, Jewish — Biography.
5. Judaism — Doctrines — History — 16th century. I. Title.
II. Series: SUNY series in Judaica.
BM755.K784T57
909'.0492404'092 — dc20   89-26341
[B]   CIP
10 9 8 7 6 5 4 3 2 1

Contents

v

Acknowledgments

This study originated in my Ph.D. dissertation at the Hebrew University written under the guidance of the late Prof. Shlomo Pines. I thank Prof. Pines for initiating me into medieval Jewish philosophy. His impeccable scholarship will always remain my ideal. My original dissertation focused on the relationship between Aristotelian philosophy and Kabbalah in the writings of R. David ben Judah Messer Leon. This book, however, reflects my own methodological shift from the history of ideas to intellectual history which took place during my years at Columbia University. I am grateful to Prof. Yosef Yerushalmi of Columbia University for the opportunity to learn from his historical insight and to teach the inquisitive students of Columbia University. As a person who herself stands "between worlds" (i.e., the academic communities of Israel and America), I am thankful to several colleagues from Israel with whom I have kept in touch over the years, in particular, Prof. Moshe Idel of the Hebrew University, who kindly shared with me his immense knowledge of Kabbalah and Renaissance culture and extended warm support over the years. Prof. Robert Bonfil and Prof. Joseph Hacker of the Hebrew University also shared their knowledge with me in several private conversations. To my colleagues in America, Prof. Aryeh Leo Motzkin of Boston University and Prof. Yael Feldman of New York University, many thanks for being such good friends and offering much needed insight. Special thanks is given here as well to Zeev Gries of Hebrew College who helped with his vast bibliographical knowledge. Last, but not least, I am indebted to William L. Rothschild, who laboriously edited the manuscript with utmost care and dedication. I take full responsibility for the remaining mistakes.

Most of R. David's writings are extant only in manuscript. I have viewed these manuscripts in the National and University Library of the Hebrew University in Jerusalem. I would like to thank the following libraries for permission to cite from manuscripts in their possession: Jews' College, in London,[8] the Bodleian Library of Oxford University, and the Biblioteca Medicea Laurenziana in Firenze, Italy. Most of Chapter Three already appeared in an article published in *Jewish History,* Vol. III (1988), no. 2. I thank Haifa University Press for allowing me to reprint that article in this book. I also thank the Rabbinical Assembly for allowing me to reprint sections from my article "Maimonides and Aquinas: The Interplay of Two Masters in Medieval Jewish Philosophy," published in *Conservative Judaism,* Vol. XXXIX (Fall 1986), no. 1. Likewise, I thank the *AJS Review* for permission to incorporate selections from my article "Sefirot as the Essence of God in the Writings of David Messer Leon," published in the *AJS Review* 7-8 (1982-83). Situated in the context of this book, the previously published material receives a new nuance.

Introduction

The turn of the sixteenth century was a period of upheaval and transition in Jewish history. Persecutions culminating in local and general expulsions virtually ended the presence of professing Jews in Western Europe. The map of Jewish diaspora was redrawn. Jews migrated eastward to the Ottoman Empire and Eastern Europe. A major transformation of thought accompanied these individual journeys: Jewish philosophy declined; and in its stead Kabbalah emerged as the dominant mode of thought among Jewish intellectuals.

This study sheds light on that period through one man and his journeys: Rabbi David ben Judah Messer Leon (ca. 1470-ca. 1535). He is known by many labels: Italian Jew, Talmudist, biblical exegete, philosopher, theologian, Kabbalist, physician, poet, and orator. His life and thought illustrate the culture of Renaissance Italian Jewry, Ottoman Jewry after the expulsion from Spain, and the transition from philosophy to Kabbalah in Jewish intellectual history.

Although modern Jewish historians have paid considerable attention to Renaissance Italian Jewry, there is no consensus about the meaning of the Renaissance in Jewish history. Scholars debate such questions as: What was the status of Jews in Italian society? Does the Renaissance constitute a meaningful category in Jewish history? Did Jews undergo Renaissance parallel to and coterminous with the Italian Renaissance? Did the culture of Italian Jewry during the Renaissance differ from other Jewish subcultures? Did the Renaissance account for the distinct features of Judeo-Italian culture? If the

Renaissance did exert some impact on Jewish culture, what was the nature and scope of this impact? What was the relevant cultural context of Italian Jewry? Elsewhere I suggested that the answer to these questions depends both on one's conception of the Renaissance and on one's understanding of Jewish history.[1] Here I respond through case study.

The period from 1300 to 1600 was a distinct chapter in the history of Italian Jewry. After the devastation of Jewish communities in Southern Italy, Jews migrated northward to establish new settlements that would absorb immigrants from Germany, France, Provençe and Spain. In ethnic make-up and geographic location, Italian Jewry during the Renaissance differed from its medieval antecedents. But economically, politically, and socially most medieval patterns persisted throughout the Renaissance. The Renaissance exhibited direct continuity, rather than a break, with the Middle Ages.

Moneylending was the economic foundation of tiny Jewish communities comprised of the bankers' family, business associates, and associated religious functionaries. The economic needs of Italian society made the activities of Jewish bankers a success despite clerical opposition and popular animosity. A class of affluent Jewish bankers linked through blood lines and business interests emerged as the backbone of Italian Jewry. Modeling itself after the Italian patriciate, this class shaped Italian culture during the Renaissance.

Jewish status in Renaissance Italy was as precarious as it was during the Middle Ages. Jews were generally tolerated but often harassed. Their very presence in Christian society was never taken for granted and was secured through temporary charters that could be easily revoked. By the mid-sixteenth century papal policies challenged the very theoretical premise of Christian toleration, and intensified missionary pressures. The exclusive association of Jews with moneylending exacerbated their marginal existence in Italian society. Clerical pressures, popular hatred, changing needs of ruling parties, and competition from Italian bankers undermined the stability of Jewish life. Local expulsions were a constant threat offtimes realized.

The social relations between Jews and Christians were essentially *functional*. A small number of outstanding Jewish individuals rendered services to Christians that facilitated several Renaissance activities. When Christians deemed the function no longer worthwhile — whether it was fulfilled, the need for it ceased, or it was considered detrimental to Italian society — the relationship was terminated. We should therefore discard the romantic notion that Jews and Christians freely socialized with each other or that they experienced open and egalitarian relationship. The Renaissance was not an epoch of tolerance, secularism, and individualism as Jewish historians from the late nineteenth century to the 1960s portrayed it. Neither did the Renaissance anticipate the Emancipation or the beginning of modernity for Jews.[2]

The Renaissance posed a challenge for Italian Jews. As a group they remained a marginal minority in Italian society separated from the majority culture. But as individuals Jewish moneylenders, physicians, printers, and scholars had access to, and were informed of, the achievements of Renaissance art, letters, and thought. These Jews could no longer simply regard the surrounding culture as inferior to their own. They responded to the challenge of the Renaissance in a variety of ways ranging from outright rejection to voluntary conversion.[3] We may therefore talk about the impact of the Renaissance on elite Jewish culture. Italian Jews of the upper classes not only expressed interest in Italian letters, music, dance, and theatre, but also grafted Italian aesthetic conventions into their own rabbinic culture, thereby transposing them for the purpose of expressing distinctly Jewish needs. During the sixteenth and seventeenth centuries, certain social institutions within the Jewish community also attest to the impact of majority society.[4]

To some extent such interaction is integral to Jewish diaspora existence. Jews have always conversed with their surrounding cultures, though the nature of the conversation varied from one locality to another and from one period to another. This process of adoption and adaptation was indeed common during the medieval period; it existed not only among Sepharadic and Provençal Jewries but even to some extent among Ashkenazic Jewry. In Italy, this process of cultural interaction with the majority culture began in earnest in the thirteenth century, and increased continually throughout the fifteenth and sixteenth centuries, even during the period of ghettoization. Consequently Italian Jewry developed characteristics distinct from those of other Jews.

The very interest of Italian humanists in Hebrew letters, rabbinic literature, and, above all, Kabbalah, enhanced the traffic of ideas between Jews and non-Jews in Renaissance Italy. In some unique cases we find that Jewish scholars in fact influenced the views of their Italian patrons. Nonetheless, the functional, and often polemical, basis of Jewish-Christian relations remained unchanged. While Renaissance humanists accorded an unprecedented respect to Judaism and collaborated with a few Jewish scholars, Renaissance humanism was a thoroughly Christian phenomenon. Jewish scholars could not partake in it qua Jews; they were expected to convert. Humanism continued to assert the spiritual superiority of Christianity over Judaism, so that the relationship between the two religions remained unchanged: hostility and rivalry.

R. David ben Judah Messer Leon serves us as a case study of Jewish culture in Renaissance Italy. He was born in Venice to Stella, the daughter of R. Benjamin of Fano, and to R. Judah ben Yehiel Messer Leon (ca. 1425-ca.1495). R. David's family belonged to the social and intellectual elite of fifteenth century Italian Jewry. His father was related to the richest Jewish banker in Tuscany—Yehiel da Pisa—and had business ties with another important Jewish banking family—the Norsas of Mantua. An outstanding Aristotelian philosopher, R. Judah Messer Leon was beyond doubt the most prominent Jewish scholar in fifteenth century Italy. He also achieved the highest social status available to Jews in medieval and Renaissance Italy. He received a doctoral degree in philosophy and medicine from the German emperor, Frederick III.

Chapter One of this book presents R. David ben Judah Messer Leon's roots. It first describes Italian Jewry in the fifteenth century: the emergence of small Jewish communities in central and northern Italy, their legal status, economic sources, patterns of leadership, and ties to non-Jewish society. The chapter concludes with a brief biography of R. David's father, R. Judah Messer Leon, whose influence upon R. David was profound.

R. David's education reflected a fusion of rabbinic Judaism and secular studies unique to native Italian Jews. It was a peculiar blend of four traditions: Halakhah; medieval philosophy; Renaissance humanism; and Kabbalah. Fully aware of their differences, R. David tried to integrate them all into a coherent whole. That attempt marks R. David as a syncretist thinker and reflects the prevailing syncretism of the Italian Renaissance. Chapter Two discusses R. David ben Judah's childhood and education and contains a reconstruction of the varied texts that David read and studied. The chapter delineates R. David's mastery of diverse scholarly disciplines and charts his intellectual growth in the academies of Naples and Padua. The chapter focuses on R. David's preoccupation with the potential conflict between religion and philosophy that would become a *leitmotif* throughout his life.

In his twenties R. David ben Judah was already accomplished

in several disciplines, among them Jewish law, biblical exegesis, philosophy, medicine, poetry, rhetoric and music. But his promising career ended abruptly in 1495 when the French armies of King Charles VIII conquered the Kingdom of Naples. Neopolitan Jews suffered immensely during the French conquest and the ensuing battles with the armies of the Spanish ruler, King Ferdinand of Aragon. The Spanish king expelled the Jews, an extension of earlier expulsions from Spain, Sicily, and Sardinia. R. David ben Judah joined hundred of thousands of Jewish exiles who had found their way to the Ottoman Empire.

Within several decades after the expulsion from Spain, the Sephardim came to dominate Ottoman Jewry. Though R. David was an outspoken defender of Judeo-Italian culture, he was forced to contend with rising prominence of Judeo-Hispanics, and his later works show their unmistakable impact: he mastered their legal and philosophic literature, he imitated their literary style, and he shared their intellectual concerns. While in Italy R. David had attempted to reconcile rabbinic Judaism and Renaissance culture, in the Ottoman Empire he tried to fuse Judeo-Italian and Judeo-Hispanic cultures into one universe of discourse.

Despite important advances of the last two decades, modern research in Ottoman Jewry after the expulsion from Spain is still in its early stages. This case study advances that research, because R. David ben Judah illustrates the trauma of relocation and adjustment, the diversity and fragmentation of Jewish community, the intellectual concerns of the exiles, and the strategies Jewish thinkers employed to overcome their spiritual anguish.

Two factors make R. David's experience particularly interesting. First is his Renaissance Italian origin; R. David is among the very few Italian scholars who achieved prominence in the Ottoman Empire and whose writings survive. Second is R. David's propensity for controversy; he fell, or pushed himself, into four major disputes within the Ottoman Jewish communities in which he resided. Two controversies were overtly political, concerning the scope of rabbinic authority within Jewish communities. The other two were more academic, concerning the legitimacy of cultivating secular studies. Analysis of these controversies clarifies both the nature of intercommunal tensions in Ottoman Jewry and negative reactions among some Jews to Judeo-Italian culture.

Chapter Three portrays the emergence of Ottoman Jewry in the postexpulsions era and focuses on the difficulties R. David experienced in Constantinople in 1496-97. Opposition to his Renaissance Italian preaching style essentially cost him his rabbinic position, so he requested financial support from a former patroness in Italy by writing a book entitled *Shevah ha-Nashim (Praise of Women)*, which was ostensibly a commentary on Proverbs 31, known then and now as the Hymn to the Woman of Valor. However, before praising the ideal woman (with strong influence of Petrarch), R. David describes his difficulties in Constantinople, defends in detail his Italian education (especially the humanist program), and justifies the integration of that Renaissance education into rabbinic Judaism.

The expulsion from Spain and its dominions irrevocably changed the ethnic make up, communal organization and cultural orientation of Ottoman Jewry. Immigrants differed from the indigenous Greek-speaking Jewish population, known as Romanyots, in their legal status, language, religious customs, halakhic traditions, political institutions, and education. Jews in the Ottoman Empire were organized in autonomous communities according to their land of origin, so Ottoman Jewry became highly fragmented, culturally diverse, and prone to frequent intercommunal disputes.

Chapter Four discusses R. David's public controversies in the Ottoman Empire: his support for the Romanyot leader Moses Capsali (Constantinople, 1496-97), his defense of Maimonides (Salonika, ca. 1506), and his dispute with the Sephardim in Valona (1510). The chapter highlights R. David's stormy relationship with the immigrants from Spain, who emerged as the dominant subgroup in Ottoman Jewry by the first third of the sixteenth century. R. David describes these controversies in his responsa (one in manuscript, the other printed under the title *Kevod Hakhamim (The Honor of Scholars)*, and his commentary to Maimonides *The Guide of the Perplexed*, entitled *'Ein ha-Qore (The Eye of the Reader)*.

R. David ben Judah Messer Leon became one of the outstanding Jewish scholars in Ottoman Jewry at the turn of the sixteenth century. His writings are important not only because they help us reconstruct two Jewish subcultures, but also because they clarify a major paradigm shift in Jewish intellectual history: the transition from Aristotelian philosophy to Kabbalah. Lasting from the mid-fifteenth to the mid-sixteenth century, this transition from one mode of thought to another symbolically ended with the publication of Moses de Leon's *Sefer ha-Zohar* in Italy in 1558-1559.

Modern scholarship has only begun to explore this complex process, and much research is still necessary before it can be properly understood. To date, most of the pertinent primary sources are still extant only in manuscript and await critical editions; only a handful of monographs are available; and there are very few comprehensive studies of general trends in Jewish intellectual life during this period. To some extent, this unfortunate state of affairs reflects the low esteem in which modern historians of Jewish philosophy hold the quality of Jewish philosophy during this period.[5] Jewish thinkers of the period under consideration are usually dismissed as unoriginal, mediocre, and overly concerned with non-philosophical problems such as polemics against Christianity. Compared with Jewish philosophers of previous centuries (e.g., Saadia Gaon, ibn Gabirol, Moses Maimonides, Gersonides, and Crescas), these thinkers are considered mere epigones who made little, if any, original contribution. As a result, the transition from Aristotelian philosophy to Kabbalah has received too little attention.

R. David ben Judah Messer Leon was essential to that transition. He was among the first Italian Jewish Aristotelian philosophers to study Kabbalah at all. He maintained that Aristotelian philosophy and Kabbalah are not mutually exclusive, because Kabbalah can be interpreted philosophically. His philosophization of Kabbalistic theosophy was crucial to the dissemination of Kabbalah both in Italy and in the Ottoman Empire. He not only made Kabbalah more palatable to philosophically trained scholars, but also articulated a theoretical model in which Kabbalah and Aristotelian philosophy could coexist as components of one Jewish theology.

R. David thus reflects a turning point in the evolution of Jewish culture in Renaissance Italy: he remained loyal to his Jewish tradition while attempting to take part in the cultural wealth of the Renaissance. He perpetuated many of his father's cultural patterns, but also inaugurated new trends. Jewish thinkers during the sixteenth century would follow the son rather than his father. This study assesses R. David's interaction with the three dominant intellectual traditions in Renaissance Italy—namely, scholasticism, humanism, and Neoplatonism—and explains the theory that R. David devised to legitimize that interaction.

Chapter Five shifts the focus from R. David's public career to his intellectual endeavors, and presents him as the embodiment of the Renaissance ideal of *homo universalis,* or in Hebrew, *hakham kolel,* namely the scholar who is versed in all branches of knowledge, human and divine. The key to the attainment of this lofty scholarly ideal lies in the synthesis of reason and faith. I analyze R. David's position in reference to Maimonides and Thomas Aquinas. The chapter explains the influence of Aquinas on Jewish conception of theology as the science of divine revelation. Most of the material for R. David's position comes from *Magen David (Shield of David)*, composed soon after his settlement in the Ottoman Empire. This text attests to a fusion of Judeo-Italian and Judeo-Hispanic materials in R. David's universe of discourse.

The key to the transition from Aristotelianism to Kabbalah is the conceptualization of theology as a science of divine revelation formally distinct from philosophy; whereas theology is grounded in the infallible truths of revelation, philosophy is grounded in the discoveries of natural human reason. Delineating the relationship between theology and philosophy can best be understood in the broader context of medieval and Renaissance attempts to resolve the so-called conflict of reason and faith. From the thirteenth to the fifteenth centuries, Jewish scholars followed Maimonides' harmonization of reason and faith, or philosophy and religion, but by the second half of the fifteenth century Jewish scholars followed Aquinas instead.

Aquinas deeply influenced R. David ben Judah, although R. David's treatment of Aquinas ultimately remained polemical. R. David attempted to refute Christian claims and strengthen the allegiance of Jews to their faith by co-opting certain Thomistic themes to Judaism. The modern reader might wonder about such Christian influence, especially in a period when Christianity emerges victorious from its age-old feud with Judaism. The mass apostasy of Iberian Jews and the expulsions of the Jews from Western Europe appeared to have vindicated Christian claims for superiority. But to the medieval historian the influence of Christianity upon a Jewish thinker is not peculiar at all. Rather, it reflects a Jewish response to Christianity in a period when the Jews have finally completed their shift from the orbit of Islam to the orbit of Christendom. The very polemical encounter between Judaism and Christianity brought growing Jewish familiarity with Christian scholasticism and ability to answer Christianity in that very language.

Theology is premised on dogmas, that is, beliefs axiomatic to Judaism that reason could not ultimately prove and that accordingly must be accepted on faith. The last work of R. David ben Judah Messer Leon is *Tehillah le-David (Glory to David)*. It is a summary of Jewish theology on encyclopedic scope, typical of Sephardic works in the postexpulsion era. As a *summa* of Jewish theology, this work consolidates existing knowledge by reviewing and responding to previous authoritative scholars. Chapter Six derives its material from the first two sections of *Tehillah le-David,* in which the author outlines his conception of Jewish dogmas. The chapter situates R. David's position in the context of medieval Jewish dogmatism, especially its fifteenth century phase, then presents R. David's defense of Maimonides' Thirteen Principles, and finally analyzes R. David's own formulation of the dogmas of Judaism. R. David reduces them to three: creation *ex nihilo,* prophecy, and miracles.

As a Jewish theologian, R. David ben Judah Messer Leon was ultimately concerned with the knowledge of God. The last chapter analyzes R. David's concept of God: God's existence, God's attributes, God's essence, and divine knowledge and providence. This chapter is based primarily on the last section of *Tehillah le-David,* which R. David left unfinished due to his unexpected death. By analyzing R. David's position, we can best understand his indebtedness to previous Jewish and non-Jewish thinkers, and his importance in the evolution of Jewish intellectual history. The chapter highlights the reconciliation of Kabbalah and Aristotelian philosophy as well as the unmistakable impact of Thomas Aquinas.

The book concludes with a note on the decline of the house of Messer Leon and discussion of R. David's place in Jewish intellectual history. R. David fused Halakhah, medieval philosophy, Renaissance humanism, and Kabbalah. That rabbinic Judaism produced such a figure is in itself fascinating; that this man sheds light on the evolution of Jewish intellectual history makes him even more important.

No label fits R. David ben Judah Messer Leon well. He was an observant Jew, indeed a renowned rabbi, but his culture developed through strong interaction with the Italian Renaissance. He was typically Italian, but he lived most of his adult life in Ottoman Turkey. He was both a brilliant Halakhist and an erudite philosopher. His Halakhic training reflects fusions of Italian, Ashkenazic and Sephardic traditions, and his philosophic training reflects both the medieval Judeo-Arabic and the Christian-Scholastic traditions. Although an ardent student of philosophy, R. David also studied and respected Kabbalah. And while an heir of medieval patterns of thought, R. David accepted innovations of Renaissance humanism.

The title of this book — *Between Worlds* — tries to capture R. David ben Judah Messer Leon's life and his place in Jewish intellectual history. He stood between Renaissance Italy and Ottoman Turkey, between rabbinic Judaism and philosophy, between medieval scholasticism and Renaissance humanism, between Aristotelianism and Kabbalah, between Judaism and Christianity.

Between Worlds is a study in Jewish intellectual history. My approach to intellectual activity is contextual; namely, I maintain that intellectual activity cannot be fully understood apart from its historical context.[6] Ideas are always thought by people who live at certain times and places, and who struggle with specific existential concerns. Historical conditions mold the questions intellectuals ask, the categories they employ to answer these questions, and the answers they consider satisfactory or not. This does not mean that intellectual activity may be reduced to specific social conditions. In fact, interpretations over time of ideas attributed to particular scholars themselves constitute intellectual traditions (for example, Aristotelianism, Neoplatonism, Averroism, Maimonideanism and Thomism) that take on lives of their own. But these intellectual traditions also do not develop in a social or intellectual vacuum; rather, they reflect the changing concerns of scholars whose works give rise to intellectual traditions.

I thus believe that accurate interpretation of culture requires consideration of individual and community, text and context, specific ideas and intellectual traditions. I have asked: What kind of life could R. David have led as a Jew at that time and place? Which issues were important to him? Which problems did he attempt to address? How did he address them? What could have motivated him to adopt one position over another? Answering these questions clarifies the complex Jewish history of the turn of the sixteenth century.

Like all attempts to interpret the past, intellectual history must overcome not only the distance which separates the modern researcher from his or her subject matter but also the very limitations of language. Deconstruction has exacerbated modern scepticism concerning the feasibility and desirability of reconstructing the past, leaving intellectual historians to ponder the methodological pitfalls of their discipline.[7] Despite the perils of language, this study assumes that an understanding of the past *on its own terms* is both possible and worthwhile. With appreciation to Rabbi Tarfon, (Mishnah, Avot, 2:19) our inability to complete the task with absolute certainty is no excuse for refusing to begin at all.

1

The Italian Setting

Fifteenth Century Italian Jewry

Italian Jewry underwent a major transformation at the close of the thirteenth century. In 1291 the Church launched a two-year campaign for the total conversion of the Jews in Apulia.[1] About half the Jews were forcibly converted, and many were killed. Study in the distinguished academies of Bari and Otranto was brought to a standstill. Thus the Jewry of Southern Italy—an old Jewish community whose origins date back to the first century C.E.—was practically destroyed.[2] Survivors migrated northward, first toward Rome, where the Jewish community enjoyed some papal protection. From Rome Jews later migrated to other provinces in central and northern Italy, where they met refugees fleeing persecution and expulsions in France and Germany.

The Jewish population of Italy increased until the Black Death struck in the mid-fourteenth century, killing Jews as well as Christians, but then began to rise again when the mass destruction of Spanish Jewry in 1391, and the total expulsion of French Jewry in 1394, brought another wave of Jewish refugees to Italy.[3] As a result, Italian Jewry of the fifteenth century comprised three diverse ethnic subgroups: the native Italian Jews, the Ashkenazic Jews of France and Germany, and the Sephardic Jews of the Iberian Peninsula. Meanwhile Italian city-states tried to overcome an economic stagnation that had begun even before the Black Death. Land prices and land profits reached their lowest point in the late fourteenth century, land reclamation and colonization had come to a virtual standstill, and the demand for Italian exports such as wool had diminished considerably. The capital of major banks such as the Medici family's reached an unprecedented low, and industrial and commercial expansion of many city-states came to a halt. The lavish lifestyle of the ruling classes, and their constant engagement in military campaigns, drained capital even further, and expenditures in those areas reflected the widening gap between rich and poor.[4]

These Jewish immigrants to Italy did not come empty-handed or empty-headed. They brought capital, and they brought important financial skills either as moneylenders—the primary occupation open to them in France, Germany, and Provençe—or as fiscal administrators and tax framers—typical occupations in Spain. Communes and princes turned to them. Jews were allowed to settle in locations from which they were previously either barred or expelled.[5] Moneylenders were welcomed despite prior and longstanding opposition. Ecclesiastical authorities devised appropriate "dispensations" from canonic legislation to permit Jewish moneylending. Ironically, the major focus of anti-Jewish sentiment and legislation in Western Europe—moneylending—became the catalyst for the growth and creativity of Jews in fifteenth century Italy.

A new chapter in the history of Italian Jewry began. Population growth, geographical expansion, economic prosperity and cultural creativity during the fifteenth century reversed the decline this Jewry had experienced since 1291. Jewish settlements developed in a typical pattern: local authorities permitted individual Jews to settle and open a bank or pawn shop. Jews were legally considered aliens, so their right of residence was affirmed in special charters known as *condotti*.[6] A *condotta* granted its holder a monopoly on moneylending in a specified region, spelled out the precise terms of his approved financial transactions, and defined the personal status of the recipient. The *condotta* also afforded a wide range of privileges to the Jewish banker: it extended protection over life and property, exempted the banker from local and regional taxes, permitted the holder to observe his Jewish faith both in private and in public, and allowed him to buy land for assembly (i.e., synagogues) and burial.

These combination business charters and residence permits reflect the underlying insecurity of Jewish life in Italy. *Condotti* were granted for a term of only three to seven years and could be easily revoked on the ruler's whim. City-states ruled by strong princes (e.g., Florence under the Medicis, Ferarra under the Este family, and Mantua under the Gonzagas) usually accorded Jews some stability and long-term protection. In short, Jews were tolerated in Italian city-states as long as the rulers deemed them financially beneficial — a typical medieval phenomenon. Yet changes in the power structure of a given city, the rising political influence of the clergy, and the impact of international politics on Italy, could undermine the very existence of the tiny Jewish settlement. Throughout the fifteenth and sixteenth centuries, Jews lived under the fear of popular hostility, ecclesiastical missionizing, and expulsion.

Jewish settlements in Italy during the fifteenth century were extremely small: extended households consisting of the banker, his immediate family, his business associates, and other professionals — such as teachers, butchers, and physicians — essential to Jewish life. In Florence, for example, where four Jewish banks operated in the mid-fifteenth century, the entire settlement consisted of only 75-100 Jews. Similarly, the Jewish population of Mantua in this period did not exceed two hundred people, with another hundred Jews in the city's outskirts.[7] The minute size of Jewish settlements accounts for the close proximity between Jews and non-Jews, and the difficulties of maintaining Jewish life. Offtimes Jews had to depart from strict tradition and law to facilitate ritual observance itself. For example, women and children occasionally performed ritual slaughtering to provide meat for the dinner table.[8]

The development of the Jewish settlement in Arezzo after 1398-99 suggests that the Jews were originally invited to provide funds for the lower strata of Italian society.[9] Their business, however, quickly extended upward, from paupers residing in rural outskirts of urban centers to dukes and princes of the city-states. As a result, the Jewish bankers succeeded in amassing considerable wealth, which soon fueled hatred and animosity. Franciscan friars established charity funds *(monti di pieta)* to replace private moneylending and openly called for Jewish expulsion.[10] But neither widespread hatred, Franciscan harassment, nor even competition from Italian bankers could halt the success of the Jewish bankers.

The financial power of the Jewish bankers, coupled with their privileged status with the ruling power, served as the source of the banker's authority within Italian Jewry. Concomitantly, the wealth accrued from moneylending enabled the Jewish bankers to live luxuriously, with the lifestyle and social norms of the Italian patriciate.[11] They built palaces and furnished them dearly, invested in luxuries such as cosmetics and high fashion, or retreated to country villas to relax from the oppressive conditions of the congested, small towns.[12]

Still, material opulence and sensual pleasures were not the major vehicle or self-expression among the Jewish elite. No less central was the celebration of Jewish festivals and life-cycle events within the extended households, inspired by the newly developed tastes and aesthetic norms of the Italian ruling classes. New Jewish creativity was fostered in the social arts—dance, music, theater—initially intended for the exclusive entertainment of Jewish audiences, and later for Christian rulers.[13] Thus we find Jewish musicians and actors employed by the Gonzagas in Mantua, and Jewish dancers teaching Christian nobles.[14]

During the fifteenth century bankers played an important role in the development of Italian Jewish culture. Personally committed to the cultivation of Jewish learning and creativity, they established libraries of considerable size for their own use and extended financial support to rabbinic scholars, philosophers, artists, and poets. Employment in the household of a Jewish banker, either as a private tutor or as a manuscript copyist, was a highly lucrative and well-paid position, often secured by fierce competition.

The patron-client relationship between the Jewish banker and the scholar was fashioned according to the model of the Christian Renaissance humanists and their patrician and princely patrons.[15] Renaissance humanism was a cultural, literary, and scholarly movement associated with the rise of the *studia humanitatis,* a well-defined cycle of academic disciplines consisting of grammar, rhetoric, poetry, history, and moral philosophy.[16] Its overarching concern was an "effective expression in speech and in writing, in verse and in prose, in Latin and in the vernacular languages, of any content of ideas, images, feelings or events."[17] Renaissance humanists derived their model of elegant expression from the literary sources of classical antiquity which they rediscovered, copied, and edited. They read classical authors directly in their original tongues and urged that such studies of primary sources be made the core of the art curriculum. Their approach to education emphasized a text-oriented, individual scholarship in contrast to the established tradition of interpretation typical of the Middle Ages.

The humanist cultural program was not a mere academic matter, but rather an ideal for practical application in civic life. Its pursuit of eloquence had concrete purposes: to move, to persuade, to excite, and to educate listeners and readers. Humanism, in other words, was intended for the public domain. Leonardo Bruni, the Florentine humanist-historian, expressed this view when he said that the *studia humanitatis* made the complete man. Likewise, Ermolao Barbaro, a Venetian noble, diplomat, humanist, Aristotelian philosopher, and cardinal, asserted that "*humanitas* is not a matter simply of externals, of ornament, it is a spiritual entity which produces in man the true man, the citizen, the man in his totality."[18] Renaissance humanism was thus an educational program to raise the moral and intellectual quality of the citizen (i.e., ruling) class. It attempted to turn citizens into statesmen and statesmen into moral men.[19]

Eloquence became an ideal for a way of life of the Renaissance gentleman—the *homo universalis*. He was expected to be versatile, sociable, well versed in classical letters, and ready to apply the lessons of the past to current problems. The education of the gentleman was entrusted to humanists, who earned their living as secretaries, librarians, and tutors of princes and patricians, thereby helping their patrons to assume responsibility in the civic life of Italy's factious city-states. Nevertheless, the cult of elegant speech was not confined only to the ruling classes, but was cultivated as well among those townspeople responsible for welding the newly entered masses within the city walls into a genuine community.

W. Bouwsma describes this development as follows:

Rhetoric provided the cultural foundation for the new urban culture of 15th century Italy. It operated on every level of human interaction, both private and public. Businessmen had to learn to communicate persuasively with their customers, suppliers and associates; lawyers had to argue their conflicts of interests in courts; citizens conversed and corresponded with their friends in personal matters and sought agreement with their peers on questions of public interest; rulers had to maintain the support of their subjects; and governments corresponded with one another. Rhetoric was undoubtedly the core of humanist education and moral interpretation.[20]

In Renaissance Italy humanism first competed and later coexisted with scholasticism, which had been introduced into Italy from France in the mid-thirteenth century. The scholastic tradition was a systematic, reasoned attempt to reconcile Greek philosophy with the Christian faith. From the thirteenth century onward, the major trend within scholasticism was Aristotelianism. Aristotle's philosophico-scientific corpus determined the curriculum, analytic methods, philosophical vocabulary, and conceptual framework of the newly established universities in Naples, Salerno, Bologna, and Padua.[21] Aristotelianism remained strong well into the sixteenth century, invigorated in part by new translations of Aristotle's works guided by humanist philology. While humanists and scholastics continued to debate their ideological differences in the realm of education and authoritative texts, most Italian scholars integrated the two programs to some extent.[22]

By the second half of the fifteenth century, Italian Jews began to absorb Renaissance humanism, which provided the literary genres, the textual methods, and the educational aspirations for a movement of Jewish humanism.[23] Notable differences between Jewish humanism and its Italian paradigm still remained. Unlike their Italian counterparts who witnessed ideological and academic struggle between humanists and scholastics, Italian Jews did not consider humanism antithetical to scholasticism. Rather, they adopted the *studia humanitatis* as an integral expansion of an already existing curriculum of the secular studies which they inherited from Provençe and Spain.

The study of philosophy and science began among medieval Jews already in the tenth century. Under the influence of Muslim culture, the Jews of Andalusia (Muslim Spain) cultivated secular studies including medicine, mathematics, biology, physics, astronomy, alchemy, and astrology. The scientific outlook influenced all literary activity of Jews in Muslim Spain. It inspired the study of philology and grammar, biblical and Talmudic commentaries, the writing of secular poetry, and the philosophical defense of Judaism. The crowning achievement of the rationalist tradition was systematic theology: the reasoned analysis of Jewish beliefs with an attempt to harmonize religious claims with the dictates of human reason. In this regard, scholasticism emerged in Judaism (and Islam) two centuries prior to its rise in the Latin West. With the Christian reconquest of Iberia, Jews brought with them the rationalist tradition to northern kingdoms of Iberia (Catalonia, Castile, and Aragon), and from there rationalism spread to Jewish communities in Provençe and Italy.

Italian Jews began to engage in the study of the sciences by the end of the twelfth century. This new scholarly interest is associated with R. Abraham ibn 'Ezra, the Spanish biblical exegete, philosopher, astronomer, and mathematician (1089-1164) who was active in Italy during the 1160s.[24] Italian Jewry was further drawn into the cultural orbit of Spain and Provençe during the thirteenth century, when Provençal and Spanish scholars, among them Jacob Anatoli and Zerahya b. Isaac Shealtiel, settled in Italy (especially in Rome and in Naples) and spread the knowledge of philosophy.[25] They taught Maimonides' *The Guide of the Perplexed,* composed philosophical biblical commentaries, and collaborated with Christian scholars in translating Hebrew and Arabic philosophic texts into Latin. Collaboration between Jewish and Christian scholars further enhanced the impact of rationalism on the education of Italian Jews. By the late thirteenth century, the secular curriculum became an integral part of Italian Jewish education. Consequently, Italian Jewry became embroiled in the Maimonidean controversy that had recently engulfed world Jewry.[26]

In Italy the Jewish curriculum of secular studies integrated two educational systems: the Judeo-Arabic, and the Christian-Latin. From the Christian-Latin schooling, Italian Jews adopted the seven liberal arts—the *trivium* (grammar, logic, and rhetoric)—and the *quadrivium* (arithmetics, geometry, music, and astronomy).[27] However, Italian Jews culled their knowledge of these sciences from Hebrew texts written by either Jews or Muslim authors. The seven liberal arts were preparatory to the study of philosophy—divided into practical philosophy (economics, ethics, and politics) and speculative philosophy (physics, metaphysics, and theology). The few students who excelled in the study of the secular disciplines and could afford the study of medicine pursued this study as well. By the early sixteenth century, some exceptional Jewish students were allowed to study medicine in Italian universities.[28] Italian Jews grafted onto this scholastic curriculum the humanist program consisting of grammar, rhetoric, poetry, history, and moral philosophy.

Renaissance Humanism gave Judeo-Italian culture a flavor distinguishing it from its Jewish counterparts in Spain and Provençe, although they also cultivated the secular sciences. For example, Jewish scholars in fourteenth century Provençe studied rhetoric through Todros Todrosi's Hebrew translation of Averroës' commentary to Aristotle's *Rhetoric;* in Italy they studied not only that text but also Cicero's orations, which the Italian humanists regarded as the most perfect human speech. Similarly, while in Provençe and Spain Jews studied Hebrew grammar, in Italy they studied Latin grammar as well, and practiced the art of epistolography to cultivate eloquent prose. The ideal of elegant speech was equally cultivated through the art of poetry. Italian Jews absorbed the literary innovations of Dante (1265-1321) already in the early fourteenth century and composed Hebrew poems imitating his innovative verse written in the Tuscan dialect. In style, themes, and literary convention, Hebrew secular poetry in Italy arose as a fusion between the Spanish-Provençal and the Italian traditions.[29] Under the impact of humanism, Italian Jewish scholars also cultivated Hebrew poetics, by studying Aristotle's *Poetics*, thus replacing the Arabic poetics adapted into Hebrew modes in Muslim Spain by Dunash ibn Labrat (tenth century) and Moses ibn 'Ezra (d. ca. 1135).[30] Most noticeably, Renaissance humanism affected Jewish culture in the rise of new literary genres: histories of foreign nations, biographies, and Jewish historiography.[31]

Although stimulated by Renaissance humanism, Jewish humanism developed independently to serve specific Jewish needs. By enlarging the scope of Jewish education, Italian Jews could propose their own version of the Renaissance ideal *homo universalis.* For Jews, the *hakham kolel* (literally, the comprehensive scholar) was the wise man who was well versed in the liberal arts, the *studia humanitatis,* philosophy and medicine, as much as he was erudite in the rabbinic tradition. Similarly, Jewish humanism differed from its Italian counterpart in its attitude toward the past. Jews did not share the disdain of their contemporaries toward the immediate medieval past. Nor did they revel in the rebirth of classical Rome—the destroyer of Jerusalem.[32] Indeed, Jewish humanists read classical literature with interest and enjoyed its literary merits. But to counter the appeal of classical antiquity, Jewish humanists praised the biblical past as a desirable model for emulation. The return to the glorious biblical era was the best Jewish, polemical retort to the cult of the ancients. Anti-Christian polemics also guided a Jewish humanist such as 'Azaria de Rossi to reexamine rabbinic chronology by employing humanist textual methods.[33]

Humanist pursuit of eloquence was most evident in the emphasis of Italian Jews on the mastery of Latin and Italian; wealthy bankers often employed Christian tutors to instruct their children in these languages. Italian Jews practiced the art of rhetoric by writing model letters. Several collections of such model texts are still extant and recently published in critical editions.[34] They give us an excellent glimpse into the daily realities of Italian Jews and show that humanist ideals were widespread among Italian Jews regardless of their social status.[35]

Native Italian Jews of the fifteenth century had a well-established tradition of harmonizing rabbinic Judaism with secular studies. Such openness toward the so-called "alien disciplines" contrasted with Ashkenazic Jewry's long-standing hostility toward the secular sciences. By the second half of the fifteenth century, Ashkenazic Jews constituted a significant portion of the Jewish communities in Northern Italy. Their legal tradition spread rapidly, helped by the printing of the legal code *Arba'ah Turim (Four Columns)* by R. Jacob b. Asher.[36] Gradually the native Italian Jews adopted the Ashkenazic method of Talmud study and regarded the Ashkenazic legal authorities as their masters in addition to such Sephardic authorities as R. Isaac Alfasi and Moses Maimonides. Nevertheless, the opposition of Ashkenazic Jews toward secular studies necessarily resulted in communal conflicts and personal disputes.

In fact, the very ethnic diversity of fifteenth century Italian Jewry caused communal controversies. There were three major components: the native Italian Jews, concentrated in the Papal States and the north-central provinces; the Ashkenazic Jews from Germany and France, settled primarily in the northern and north-central regions; and the Sephardic Jews in the kingdom of Naples. Each group possessed its unique customs and rituals, traditions of learning, and political institutions, and each established separate synagogues. Encounters among the three groups brought personal conflict and ideological dispute.

Individualism inherent in the patronage system impeded communal organization and fueled incessant personal controversies among Italian Jewish intellectuals. Fifteenth century Italian Jewry was only beginning to consolidate its collective identity and to establish its own forms of communal organization. This process would gain momentum only by the early sixteenth century with the massive influx of refugees from Spain and Portugal after the expulsions of 1492 and 1497, the flight of Marrano Jews from the Inquisition, and the immigration of Jewish traders from North Africa and the Ottoman Empire. More population growth, and particularly the rise of the strong middle class of merchants and artisans, would minimize the political strength of the Jewish banking oligarchy and give rise to a more complex communal structure.[37]

Rabbis, Scholars, and Community Organization

Both David and his father Judah bore the title "rabbi," and each became embroiled in controversies over the scope of his rabbinic authority. It is well known that the title carried a different job description in pre-Emancipation Europe than it does today. "Rabbi" signified not only scholarship and communal leadership in areas we consider "religious"—for example, life cycle functions and public worship—but judicial authority as well. Less well known but no less important was the rift between Ashkenazim and Sephardim. It arose from differences in the two groups' communal structure: who bestowed the title "rabbi"; what authority did it convey; and how far did that authority extend? The debate about the meaning and scope of the rabbinate emerged repeatedly throughout the life of R. David ben Judah. To understand it a brief history of the rabbinate is in order.

The rabbinate evolved in the Second Temple era or shortly thereafter.[38] In the Land of Israel the Sanhedrin granted the title "rabbi" (*rabi*) and with it judicial authority.[39] In Babylonia each yeshivah granted the title "rav" (*rab*); judicial authority apparently depended upon the recognition given the individual rav and his yeshivah. Both titles acknowledge mastery of halakhah and mark the rise of rabbinic scholars as successors to the priesthood. Authority in Judaism ultimately stems from the revelation at Mount Sinai; the rabbinate was legitimized by tracing that authority up the generational chain through each who granted it to a successor, all the way back to Moses.[40] The granting of the title was called *semikhah*, usually translated as "ordination," and the ceremony involved a laying on of the hands to symbolize the transmission of authority. Thus did rabbinic ordination convey legal, religious, and even sacramental import.

After the demise of the Sanhedrin, ordination in the Land of Israel fell to the Nasi and the rabbis of his yeshivah. The status of ordained rabbis then declined along with political and economic conditions in the Land of Israel,[41] until the fourth century, when Jewish political autonomy ended and rabbis were no longer ordained there. The rabbinate continued and changed in Babylonia through the rise of the Gaonate in the seventh century, when a Gaon would ordain rabbis to offices with specific, well-drained authority.[42]

The proliferation of Jewish communities in the Mediterranean basin and Western Europe during the tenth and eleventh centuries complicated the status of rabbis. They could no longer base their authority upon personal contact with accepted political or educational institutions in Babylonia or the Land of Israel, and no new institutions with such universal recognition had yet arisen. Furthermore, rabbis now had to contend with the rise of nonrabbinic leadership, including lay courts.[43]

Nevertheless, there is some evidence that rabbis continued to be ordained in Western Europe in the eleventh century. R. Judah ben Barzilay of Barcelona mentions a writ of ordination *(ketav masmikh)*.[44] Unlike the Palestinian ordination, this ceremony did not involve laying on of the hands, and the writ could be conferred by the city elders or the synagogue elders. The ordinee gained the title *rabbi*, assumed the social and legal obligations of the scholarly class, and became a judge *(dayyan)*; but his authority did not exceed what the community was willing to bestow upon him in light of his scholarship. Alongside this practice, isolated cases of individual ordination continued to occur; for example, R. Isaac Alfasi ordained R. Joseph ibn Megash, who in turn ordained his own student.

The rabbinate then took different turns among the Sephardim and the Ashkenazim. Jews in Spain quickly developed strong communal organizations. Rabbis then became salaried community officials, whom community leaders selected from among the local scholars.[45] During the reign of Alfonso X (1221-84) a new position evolved, called *el rab* (the rav), with authority over all Jewish judicial matters in a given province. That title thereafter "designated crown-appointed chief rabbis or justices who enjoyed great social and political prestige."[46]

Each individual Sephardic congregation would employ not a rabbi but a *Marbiz Torah* (literally, teacher of Torah).[47] Paid handsomely and accountable directly to the congregation, the *Marbiz Torah* served as its judicial, spiritual, pedagogical, social, and moral guide. He enjoyed a wide range of authority: he adjudicated all civil suits between his congregants, arranged marriages, divorces, *yibbum* (levirate marriage), and *halizah* (the dispensation from levirate marriage), and supervised lay leaders in congregational administration. Most importantly, the *Marbiz Torah* taught Torah—to school children in the day school or Talmud Torah, to adolescents and young adults in the Yeshivah, and to the entire congregation through regular Sabbath and Holiday sermons. In fact, preaching was the *Marbiz Torah's* major vehicle to disseminate his views, exhibit his knowledge, and even rebuke his congregants for improper conduct. The *Marbiz Torah* was accorded profound respect even after his death.

In France and Germany, by contrast, Jews did not develop strong communal organization. Local communities and congregations would individually consult outstanding scholars according to daily need. As in talmudic times, rabbis dispensed their rabbinic services without pay, deriving their income from other sources. Scholars who performed the functions of the Sephardic *Marbiẓ Torah* were called "rabbi."

During the twelfth and thirteenth centuries, scholars customarily bestowed the title of rabbi upon those students whom they deemed worthy. Ordination enabled the student to open his own yeshivah, but the authority it conveyed was informal: it depended upon public recognition of the knowledge and wisdom of both the ordaining rabbi and, increasingly over time, the ordinee. In the fourteenth century the decline of Jewish status in France and Germany, particularly the persecutions and expulsions following the Black Death, necessitated the institutionalization of rabbinic ordination to ensure the quality of scholars.[48] The formal ordination of scholars by other reputable scholars was one attempt to safeguard against the decline of Jewish leadership. Rabbinic authority came to be secured through formal bestowal of the title *morenu* (our teacher).

Ashkenazic rabbinic ordination was evidenced by a certificate (also called a *semikhah*), signed by one or more rabbis, which served to introduce the ordinee's credentials in each politically isolated community and to permit him to exercise a degree of authority dependent upon the community's recognition of the signers' reputations. That physical evidence was less needed in Iberia where on the one hand a rabbi's authority had more limited and better defined geographic boundaries, and on the other hand that authority was upheld by the local civil authorities. In time a metonymy occurred: *semikhah* or "ordination" began to designate a rabbi according to the Ashkenazic method, as distinct from a rabbi according to the Sephardic method. Rabbinic ordination within this definition of terms stopped in Spain and was afterwards known there only by hearsay.[49] In contrast, ordination never fully disappeared in France and Germany, and began to reemerge in the twelfth century. By the fourteenth century, it again became a common formal procedure,[50] and when Ashkenazic Jews fled persecutions in fourteenth century Germany and France, they brought this institution with them to Sephardic communities.

Ashkenazic Jews migrated to Italy in increasing numbers during the fifteenth century.[51] There the formal, public art of ordination developed under the influence of the Christian doctoral degree.[52] Two Jewish degrees became common. The first was *Semikhah me-rabbanut* (ordination of rabbinate), which bestowed the title *Morenu ha-Rav* (Our Teacher, the Rav) and empowered the recipient to teach halakhah. Once ordained, rabbis could also adjudicate legal issues involving the full range of halakhah, from torts to contracts to family law. They could perform life cycle ceremonies, and even (at least in theory) excommunicate. The community honored ordained rabbis with reserved seats in synagogue and yeshivah, presents on special occasions, tax breaks, and exemption from other communal obligations.[53] The second Jewish degree was *Semikhah me-Haverut* (ordination of membership), which bestowed the title *Haver* (member or colleague) of the group on scholars with the lesser rank of *talmid hakham* (literally, student of a scholar). The *Haver* could not teach halakha but did enjoy some social honors.

Sephardic talmudic scholars challenged Ashkenazic ordination. R. Isaac ben Sheshet (Ribash) disputed its claim to descendence from ancient rabbinic ordination in the Land of Israel.[54] Other Sephardic scholars, for example Don Isaac Abravanel, ridiculed ordination for imitating the Christian doctorate.[55] Unable to eradicate the Ashkenazic practice entirely, R. Isaac ben Sheshet limited its significance to the relationship between teacher and student: ordination permitted the ordinee to teach halakhah in public without the specific permission of his teacher.

Rabbinic ordination in the Ashkenazic tradition became common in Italy during the fourteenth and fifteenth centuries under the influence of French and German rabbis.[56] By the second half of the fifteenth century, Italian scholars still debated the prerequisites for ordination, the halakhic rationale for it, and the privileges and benefits it bestowed.

In Florence, R. Benjamin of Montalcino, although himself ordained, advocated a narrow interpretation of rabbinic ordination, namely, that it accords no political authority whatsoever.[57] He argued as follows: First, ordination accorded political authority only in the Land of Israel when Jews had their own political government, which they did not currently have. Second, since ordination accords no political authority per se, authority must arise either from public (Jewish) consent or from the civil government. Third, the ordinee's jurisdiction can therefore extend no farther than the boundaries of the community or government granting him that authority.[58] The formal act of rabbinic ordination is but a public ceremony evidencing the competence of the ordinee to teach halakhah. This position reflected the current views among the French rabbis in Italy, including R. Joseph Colon, who was otherwise no great supporter of the Florentine rabbi.[59]

R. Judah Messer Leon, R. David's father, took a different view, namely, that rabbinic ordination per se grants political authority wherever the ordained rabbi may find himself. (See below in this chapter R. Judah's confrontation with R. Benjamin of Montalcino over this issue.) R. David inherited his father's view, and became involved in two public controversies, one concerning Moses Capsali, then the chief rabbi of the Romanyot community in Constantinople, and the other concerning R. David's rabbinate in Valona. Both are discussed below in Chapter Four.

R. Judah ben Yehiel Messer Leon

During the second half of the fifteenth century, the political climate of Italian Jewry was extremely unstable. Privileged members of the Jewish oligarchy with strong personalities and outstanding merits attempted to impose their personal authority upon all Italian Jewry, giving little consideration to the consent of the public at large. These assertions of power were not unusual in fifteenth century Italy but followed those of Renaissance Italy, in which princes and patricians ruthlessly pursued their personal ends regardless of the means. These assertions of power among Jews were also encouraged by the sharp differences in legal and social status within the Jewish community itself between privileged bankers, on the one hand, and their dependents on the other.

A most notable example of this civic individualism among Italian Jews was R. Judah ben Yehiel Messer Leon (ca. 1425-ca. 1495). "Messer Leon" is a title. "Messer" is a short form of *mio serro* ("my lord"). "Leon," meaning "lion," alludes to "Judah" through the well-known biblical reference of the lion as the metaphor for the tribe of Judah. R. Judah possessed a superb intellect, a strong personality, familial ties within the Jewish oligarchy, and widespread recognition in non-Jewish society. He was not only the foremost Jewish philosopher of fifteenth century Italy but also a rabbi, physician, poet, and orator. R. Judah thus came closest to embodying the Renaissance ideal of *homo universalis*.

Scholars have devoted attention to R. Judah ben Yehiel Messer Leon over the last twenty years. Daniel Carpi,[60] Robert Bonfil,[61] Isaac Rabinowitz,[62] and Abraham Melamed[63] have greatly increased our knowledge of R. Judah's life in general, his ties to the Italian scholarly community, his literary productivity, and his political philosophy. Yet much remains to be done. Many biographical details remain unknown, unreliable, or disputed. Much of what is known comes only from R. Judah's son R. David, and his highly stylized language raises questions of hyperbole. Similarly, R. Judah Messer Leon's immense literary legacy has been studied only superficially and still awaits systematic research. In fact, modern scholars have often confused father and son; one of the R. David's compositions, *Shevah ha-Nashim*, has been incorrectly attributed to his father, and its crucial importance in the son's life has thus been completely ignored.[64]

R. Judah so influenced his son R. David that a short survey of R. Judah's life is in order. R. Judah was born to an Italian Jewish family in the town of Montecchio sometime between 1420 and 1425.[65] His father, Yehiel, was a physician, from which we infer that the family was financially secure. No direct information exists concerning R. Judah's upbringing, but it is likely that he received a typical Italian Jewish education combining thorough rabbinic training and the secular disciplines.

R. Judah ben Yehiel distinguished himself at an early age. Before reaching his thirties he was ordained as a rabbi and most likely obtained a diploma in medicine in one of Italy's universities. His competence as a physician gained him fame among Christians as well as Jews. He was awarded the honorary title "Messer" in 1452 by the German emperor Frederick III during Frederick III's first visit to Italy.[66] Only two other Jews, also physicians, are known to have held the title "Messer" in medieval and Renaissance Italy, although many Jewish physicians entered the personal service of Italian dignitaries.[67] The title probably granted R. Judah Messer Leon some legal privileges; although their specific content is not known, it is reasonable to assume that R. Judah was exempted from the humiliating Jewish badge, as were other prominent Jewish physicians and the wealthy bankers. R. Judah Messer Leon apparently also held the knightly title *miles,* the highest social status held by a Jew in Renaissance Italy.[68] These accomplishments inevitably instilled in him a strong aristocratic consciousness.

In the early 1450s, R. Judah Messer Leon was invited to head a yeshiva, a Jewish academy, in the Adriatic seaport town of Ancona. There he began to write, ostensibly for the education of his students, but also for personal political reasons. R. Judah Messer Leon's early works, *Livenat ha-Sappir (The Sapphire Stone)* and *Mikhlal Yofi (Perfection of Beauty)*, are entirely within the medieval scholastic tradition: not original, but commentaries on authoritative texts. The first is a grammar book based on Abraham ibn 'Ezra's work on Hebrew grammar;[69] the second is a compilation of excerpts from popular scholastic books on Aristotelian logic, primarily *Logica Magna* by Paul of Venice.[70]

R. Judah composed *Livenat ha-Sappir* and *Mikhlal Yofi* to teach the first two arts of the *trivium*, namely, grammar and logic. The introduction to *Mikhlal Yofi* clearly demonstrates that R. Judah Messer Leon was concerned, perhaps even obsessed, with the ramifications for Jewish communities of the study of logic. R. Judah Messer Leon was familiar with the intense activity in fourteenth century Provençe of Jewish logicians such as R. Levi ben Gerson (Gersonides), R. Calonimus ben Calonimus and R. Todros Todrosi. During this so-called Golden Age of Jewish logic, Jewish Provençal logicians produced numerous summaries, commentaries, and paraphrases of Aristotle. They knew of Aristotle primarily through the Muslim philosopher Averroës, whose commentaries on Aristotle were translated into Hebrew by the early fourteenth century.[71]

R. Judah Messer Leon was trained by Christian logicians. In the fifteenth century they criticized Averroës' interpretation of Aristotle and abandoned it for the *via moderna* in logic. R. Judah Messer Leon was convinced, moreover, that the Jewish Provençal logicians and their Italian followers had misused the art of logic to propagate heretical beliefs, contrary to the explicit words of a divinely revealed Torah. Therefore, R. Judah defended Judaism against "the philosophers among the people of our Law" not by banning the study of logic but by teaching it correctly. R. Judah reasoned that, properly grasped, Aristotle's philosophy, and particularly his logic, did not contradict the teaching of Torah, but actually proved the absolute superiority of divinely revealed Law over all other human wisdom.[72] For forty years, R. Judah Messer Leon campaigned against those whom he accused of propagating subversive views and thereby corrupting the integrity of Jewish traditional society.

R. Judah Messer Leon's preoccupation with education as a preventive measure against heresy was only one manifestation of his efforts to influence the views and practice of Italian Jews. In 1455, while still in Ancona, he issued two decrees applicable not only to his local community but to other Jewish settlements as well. The first was addressed to the Italian Jews in the central and southern regions. It attempted to change the established ritual of female purity.[73] The second, addressed to the Ashkenazic academies of the northern regions, banned the study of both Gersonides' *Perush 'al ha-Torah (Commentary on the Pentateuch)*, which R. Judah considered too philosophical and thus religiously subversive, and Kabbalah in general, which he considered both logically unsound and a nonrabbinic, and therefore inappropriate, innovation.[74] By these decrees R. Judah

Messer Leon attempted to establish his personal authority over all Italian Jewry. They provoked fierce opposition from his rabbinic colleagues who correctly surmised his attempt.

In order to understand R. Judah Messer Leon's initiative, we must place it in historical context. As noted above, Italian Jewry began to consolidate its collective identity in the second half of the fifteenth century through clashes between major ethnic subgroups. R. Judah Messer Leon was an Italian rabbi committed to the legal and theological heritage of Maimonides. Still, in his legal decisions he was increasingly influenced by Ashkenazic, non-Maimonidean, legal traditions. And R. Judah Messer Leon also understood the technological/cultural advances of the Italian Renaissance, such as the invention of movable type, and recognized the enormous potential of the printing press to influence Jewish culture.

The significance of R. Judah's two decrees now becomes evident. The first, based on the Ashkenazic legal codes and in particular R. Jacob ben Asher's *Arba'ah Turim (Four Columns)*—a code comprising Ashkenazic as well as Sephardic legal traditions—was intended to disseminate Ashkenazic rituals among the Italian and Sephardic Jews of southern and central Italy, and thus to secure the supremacy of R. Judah Messer Leon's position as a jurist, since he authored the decree. The second decree was directed to the northern Jewish communities, composed of immigrants from France and Germany, in which the study of either Gersonides' biblical commentary or Kabbalah was not yet common. However, R. Judah Messer Leon understood that the printing press could quickly change this state of affairs. Indeed, as R. Bonfil has noted, Gersonides' *Commentary on the Pentateuch* was published in 1476 and was then more accessible to these communities. So R. Judah engaged in a preemptive strike, with the ulterior motive of establishing himself as the supreme authority in Italian Jewry in terms of Jewish beliefs.

The very issuance of these decrees showed an immense sense of self-worth; R. Judah believed himself qualified to influence the destiny of Italian Jewry.[75] Those feelings were nurtured not only by R. Judah's formal recognition in Italian society but also by R. Judah's rabbinic ordination. Although we do not know who taught R. Judah or who ordained him, we do know that R. Judah held a distinct conception of rabbinic ordination: not merely as a formal act which publicized an already established communal consent to the candidate's juridical/political authority, but rather as the act of granting that authority regardless of communal consent.[76]

The most critical response to Messer Leon's decrees came from Rabbi Benjamin ben Joab of Montalcino (then residing in Florence) who urged the elders of Ancona not to comply with the first decree.[77] R. Benjamin asserted that R. Judah's ordination granted only local jurisdiction, and criticized Messer Leon for not consulting with the authorities in the communities to which his decrees were directed. Finally, R. Benjamin doubly criticized R. Judah's method. R. Judah could have strengthened his political base by allying himself with wealthy members of each community, "since they can bestow benefits, keep their promises, and truly abide by them."[78] And R. Judah should have employed education rather than an outright ban which was effectively a form of curse.

Only one extant manuscript records the decrees of R. Judah Messer Leon and the opposition of R. Benjamin of Montalcino.[79] If the controversy occurred in 1455, as that manuscript suggests, then R. Judah Messer Leon correctly interpreted the impact of the printing press on Jewish culture, and followed Benjamin ben Joab's advice. In the next few years R. Judah allied himself closely with the most influential families in Italian Jewry, the Da Pisa and the Norsa, and invested time and effort in educating a generation of students. The large number of extant manuscripts of R. Judah Messer Leon's works attests to his popularity as a teacher of the *trivium*.

This controversy suggests that R. Judah Messer Leon perceived himself the leader of Italian Jewry. So does the title he bestowed upon himself: *Meor Hagolah* (Light of the Exile). R. David inherited that aristocratic consciousness. He referred to his father as *Rosh Golat Ariel* (The Head of the Diaspora of Ariel, "Ariel" being a synonym for the People of Israel), and to himself as the "son of the Light of the Exile." Titles like these do not designate any formal office; Ashkenazic rabbis customarily invented them to honor distinguished colleagues.[80]

Like many scholars of the Italian Renaissance—both Jewish and Christian—R. Judah Messer Leon often relocated in order to pursue intellectual challenges and opportunities. Although interpretations of sparse data differ, it appears that R. Judah did not remain long in Ancona. He apparently lived in Bologna in the early 1460s, where his academy attracted students from other Italian city-states.[81] One student, David ben Joab of Tivoli,[82] later became the son-in-law of Yehiel ben Isaac of Pisa, the most important Jewish banker in Tuscany, a patron of scholars, an associate of Lorenzo de Medici, and a friend of Isaac Abravanel, and the Jewish financier and advisor to the royal houses of Portugal and Aragon. Although the precise family tie is not known, the marriage of R. David ben Joab to the daughter of Yehiel of Pisa, Hanna, linked R. Judah Messer Leon with the most prominent Jewish family in Italy, further enhancing his social and political standing within Italian Jewry. R. Judah Messer Leon thus became a member of a closely knit Jewish oligarchy which guarded its integrity through planned marriages.

In Bologna, R. Judah Messer Leon wrote *Perush Mavo-Maamarot-Melizah (Supercommentary on Isagoge-Categories-De Interpretatione),* continuing his activities as an Aristotelian commentator of the Averroistic tradition. As an Aristotelian philosopher, he may have hoped to draw upon the resources of the renowned University of Bologna, a center of Christian theology and canon law.[83] But that university was hostile to foreigners, which may have prompted R. Judah's move to Padua by the mid-1460s. The University of Padua,[84] outstanding in the natural sciences and medicine, welcomed foreign students and teachers. After 1517 the University of Padua would formally open its gates to Jews as members of different "nations," along with Italians, Germans, Spaniards, or Poles.

In Padua R. Judah Messer Leon fully integrated the Aristotelian/scholastic tradition with Ashkenazic halakhah, a synthesis he would later transmit to his son R. David. R. Judah's scientific career reached its zenith on 21 February 1469, when Holy Roman Emperor Frederick III, during his second visit to Italy, bestowed upon R. Judah doctoral degrees in philosophy and medicine.[85] These degrees granted R. Judah all the customary honors and privileges, including the titles of *dignitas* and *nobilitas,* and two unique privileges as well: R. Judah was permitted to treat non-Jewish patients and to award doctoral degrees in philosophy and medicine to his Jewish students. He later awarded at least two degrees in philosophy: to Yohanan ben Isaac Alemanno of Mantua in February 1470 and to Baruch ben Jacob de Galis of Parma in June of the same year.[86]

R. Judah Messer Leon's success as a physician may have limited the time available for biblical exegesis, but it did not minimize his allegiance to Judaism. On the contrary, R. Judah deepened his commitment to Ashkenazic traditionalism through his association with the famous Ashkenazic jurist, R. Judah Minz, who immigrated to Padua in 1467.[87]

From Padua R. Judah Messer Leon moved to Venice for a short time, despite Venice's prohibition on Jewish settlement that remained in effect until 1509.[88] There R. Judah's second wife, Stella, the daughter of Benjamin ben Joab of Fano, gave birth to their son

David. (R. Judah already had a daughter, Belladona, from his first marriage to a woman whose name is no longer known.)

By 1473 we find R. Judah Messer Leon in Mantua, where he continued teaching through his academy and also began the formal education of his son R. David. R. Judah's relationship with the wealthy Mantuan Jewish bankers and textile merchants, R. Judah and Jacob Norsa, may have motivated the move. They were typical Jewish patrons of learning, ardent students of rabbinic tradition and secular studies. They highly esteemed R. Judah Messer Leon's work on grammar and logic and employed a young Provençal scribe, Abraham ben Mordecai Farissol, to copy these works for their personal library.[89] R. Judah also became involved in the family's textile business, apparently investing in it.[90] These ties further drew R. Judah into the small Italian Jewish oligarchy.

Another public controversy, this time in Mantua, shows R. Judah's continued fight against what he viewed as the misuse of philosophic knowledge. In R. Judah's employ was someone known to us only as R. David the Spaniard, apparently of Spanish origin. He taught Moses Narboni's translation and commentary of Alghazali's *The Intention of the Philosophers*, one of the popular texts for the study of logic, physics, and metaphysics among the Jews of the late middle ages.[91] R. Judah grew increasingly dissatisfied with R. David the Spaniard, claimed that the teacher misused philosophy to propagate heretical views, and ultimately dismissed him from the academy. In retaliation R. David the Spaniard accused R. Judah Messer Leon of plagiarism and other intellectual dishonesty. R. Judah then found need to defend himself through a public letter to the elders of Bologna, where the accusations had spread.[92]

R. Judah Messer Leon enjoyed a brilliant career in Mantua. He continued to write supercommentaries to the Averroist-Aristotelian corpus and completed a supercommentary on four books of Aristotle's physics.[93] In 1475-76 he published a manual on Hebrew rhetoric, *Nofet Zufim (The Book of the Honeycomb's Flow)*, which became the first Hebrew book to be printed while his author was still alive. R. Judah's decision to publish *Nofet Zufim* demonstrates his openness toward Renaissance humanism as well as his unique political sensitivity, which we can appreciate by recognizing the political import of rhetoric.

Rhetoric, T. Todorov recently wrote

is a double discourse. It presents itself first as an inventory of the forms of language, thus an extension of grammar—as a description of all the possible ways of deploying words. At the same time, however, it has a didactic function; it teaches us how to produce effective discourse and, more specifically, discourse that engages the conviction of the listener. Rhetoric is simultaneously a form of knowledge and a norm; it prescribes even as it describes.[94]

Plato understood that rhetoric can influence the convictions of the listeners. Therefore he opposed rhetoric (and its practitioners, the Sophists) on the ground that it is antagonistic to true wisdom. Cicero addressed Plato's fears when he insisted on integrating rhetoric and wisdom. Cicero's maxim was, "Wisdom without eloquence has been of little help to states, but eloquence without wisdom has often been a great obstacle and never an advantage." Cicero's view of rhetoric as *civilis ratio* was inextricably linked to politics and other branches of knowledge.[95] R. Judah Messer Leon understood the political power of rhetoric in shaping the communal life of Italian Jewry. Therefore he published *Nofet Zufim*.

As an inventory of linguistic forms, *Nofet Zufim* is not original; it is rather a compilation of forms derived from two distinct rhetorical traditions: the Averroist-Aristotelian, which R. Judah knew through Todros Todrosi's Hebrew translation of Averroës' *Middle Commentary on Aristotle's Rhetoric*;[96] and the Ciceronian-Quintilian, which reflected the renewed interest of the Italian humanists in classical rhetoric. Though both in structure and style *Nofet Zufim* is clearly a medieval scholastic work, its author's conception of rhetoric reflects the influence of Renaissance humanism. A public debate then raged among Italian intellectuals over the proper relationship between philosophy and rhetoric. Like the Venetian humanist Ermolao Barbaro, R. Judah recognized the potentially dangerous use of rhetoric as an end in itself. So R. Judah adopted the Ciceronian view: eloquence was beneficial only insofar as it complemented both the moral and the intellectual perfection of the individual.[97] A good orator, therefore, first had to be a good man and a good philosopher in order to make the best use of his rhetorical skills.

R. Judah Messer Leon wrote this manual on Hebrew rhetoric for his students. In a period when Italian Jewry was struggling to define the function of the rabbi in growing communities, a knowledge of rhetoric had definite political significance. R. Judah thus gave his students the latest techniques for influencing the conduct and views of Italian Jewry.[98] *Nofet Zufim* served a polemical purpose as well. R. Judah Messer Leon shared the longstanding medieval Jewish view of divinely revealed Torah as the source of all human wisdom, including the art of rhetoric. That view legitimized the study of pagan and Christian orators by Jewish students on the one hand and argued for the superiority of biblical oratory over all expression of human eloquence on the other.[99] It thereby enhanced Jewish self-esteem and substantiated claims for Jewish spiritual superiority as solace for the suffering and humiliation which most Renaissance Italian Jews endured.

R. Judah Messer Leon's views on rhetoric undoubtedly reflect his familiarity with and receptiveness to Renaissance civic humanism. Yet humanism remained peripheral to his overall literary enterprise, and he was more attuned to Renaissance scholasticism as practiced in the Italian universities than to contemporary humanist thought. His commitment to humanistic education is indirectly evident, however, for the extant writings of his son R. David, discussed in Chapters Two and Three below, reveal the undeniable influence of a humanistic program of study and educational ideals.

The length of R. Judah Messer Leon's stay in Mantua is not known for sure. Gedaliah ibn Yahya's *Shalshelet ha-Kabbalah (The Chain of Tradition)* fosters the view that Messer Leon's departure was related to a major controversy with the French jurist, Rabbi Joseph Colon. The Duke of Mantua is said to have resolved the controversy in part by expelling them both. However, recent scholarship has discredited this story.[100] In any event, R. Judah then moved his family and his academy to Naples, although there is some evidence that R. Judah spent some time in Lucca along the way.[101]

R. Judah Messer Leon probably chose Naples because of the extensive privileges which the king of Naples, Ferrante I (1458-1494) of Aragon, accorded to Jews. Ferrante I attempted to establish himself as a major political force in Italy both through military campaigns in alliance with the de Medici House in Florence, and by attracting artists and scholars to his magnificent court in Naples. At least since 1443, when Alfonso V took control, the House of Aragon in Naples competed for power with the local landed aristocracy. Ferrante I sought to free himself from indebtedness to the barons by developing a strong middle class whose industry and commerce were completely under his control.[102] So Ferrante I invited Jewish bankers and their entourages to settle in Naples.

By the early 1480s R. Judah's academy, now in Naples, experienced unprecedented prosperity, employing "twenty two ordained rabbis ... from France, Germany and other countries."[103] Their origins indicate R. Judah Messer Leon's continued commitment to disseminate Ashkenazic traditions among the Italian and Sephardic Jews of southern Italy. R. Judah Messer Leon died in Naples no later than 1497.[104] His death is probably related to the destruction of Naple's Jewry in the wake of the French invasion by Charles VIII in 1495, and Ferdinand of Aragon's subsequent reconquest. The possibility that R. Judah Messer Leon could be identified with a certain physician named Leon who was reportedly executed in Moscow in 1499 is very remote.

R. Judah Messer Leon was a prolific author. In addition to the works already mentioned, R. Judah composed supercommentaries to Aristotle's *Prior Analytics, On the Soul, Metaphysics, Nicomachean Ethics,* and possibly the *Topics.* In philosophy he composed *Perush 'al ha-Torah (Commentary on the Pentateuch),* a commentary on Maimonides' *The Guide of the Perplexed* entitled *Moreh Zedeq (Teacher of Righteousness),* and a commentary on Yedayah Bedersi's *Behinat 'Olam (Examination of the Universe),* one of the most popular Jewish philosophic texts among the Jews of fifteenth century Italy. In medicine R. Judah composed a commentary to the first and second sections of Avicenna's *Qannon,* the standard medical text book in most European universities until the late seventeenth century. He wrote other medical treatises on various aspects of human physiology.[105]

R. Judah Messer Leon apparently did not hold an official teaching position in any Italian university, although some modern scholars disagree. Most, if not all, of R. Judah's students were Jews. For them R. Judah Messer Leon composed summaries *(Sefeqot)* to the scholastic *questiones* debated by the Italian academic community. The summaries consisted of statements of debated problems, potential difficulties, and resolution of these difficulties in accordance with the customary method of medieval universities still in practice in Renaissance Italy. He also composed liturgical pieces, sermons, and one halakhic treatise. He delivered the sermons either at the conclusion of a study period or of a given Talmudic tractate.

R. Judah Messer Leon lived traditionally (i.e., according to Jewish law), yet was thoroughly at home in both Judeo-Muslim and Christian medieval philosophy. Through his deeds and his writing he synthesized four distinct trends: Ashkenazic talmudism; Maimonidean rationalism; medieval scholasticism; and Renaissance humanism. He also taught them to his son. R. Judah Messer Leon was R. David's chief teacher, authority figure, and spiritual guide.

2

Educating an Italian
Jewish Gentleman

R. David was born in Venice to R. Judah ben Yehiel Messer Leon and his second wife, Stella, the daughter of Benjamin ben Joab of Fano.[1] Most scholars fix R. David's date of birth at about 10 December 1471, calculating from a legal decision that R. David rendered as a rabbi in Valona.[2] There R. David states three separate times that he was forty years old when the controversy that provoked the decision began,[3] which is generally thought to be in 1512.[4] That controversy is discussed in Chapter Four below. However, Daniel Carpi asserts that this birth year conflicts with other information known about R. David and his father R. Judah, and suggests antedating R. David's birth by at least ten years.[5] Carpi's suggestion, however, conflicts with other data.[6] So without more conclusive evidence, one can reasonably assert that R. David was born sometime between 1469 and 1471, and leave the matter open for further debate.

A Student of R. Judah Messer Leon

R. David probably began his formal education at home as early as three or four years of age, when wealthy Italian Jews would customarily hire a private tutor for their sons under the following system. The tutor would be hired for a year at a time by written contract. The family provided room, board, and all material needs. In addition to teaching, the tutor would perform other tasks on request such as writing letters, supervising accounts, or even running errands. The job, although coveted for its prestige and material comfort, was difficult. Turnover was high, and many tutors left before their contracts expired.[7]

R. David's elementary education consisted first of basic language skills (reading, writing, and grammar) in Hebrew and Italian. Torah — the Five Books of Moses — was the first subject taught to Jewish children. The language of Bible instruction was Italian; that is, children would translate biblical verses into the vernacular and the teacher would explain the verse in the vernacular.[8] At this early stage children studied the *peshat*, or simple, literal, meaning of the verse. Upon completion of their first reading of the Torah, children would repeat the cycle once more, this time adding the Prophets and some medieval commentaries.

David also studied the Mishnah with Maimonides' Commentary and some Talmudic tractates with Rashi's Commentary. David probably studied arithmetic as well. His elementary education lasted until the age of eight or ten, when he enrolled in his father's academy, then in Naples.[9]

No official schedule of the curriculum of R. Judah Messer Leon's academy is extant. However, one of R. Judah Messer Leon's most celebrated students, Yohanan Alemanno, did leave a program of study which survives.[10] It probably approximates that of R. Judah's academy not only because Alemanno studied there but also because R. David ben Judah's extant writings cite most of the texts and authors which Alemanno listed.

According to Alemanno, from the age of thirteen to twenty-one the student should gain proficiency in the Oral Law and in the liberal arts. Students were to devote three hours in the morning, for four days a week, to the study of Talmud, Tosafot and Codes. Other sources also confirm that students in Italian academies spent their mornings studying rabbinic subjects and their afternoons and evenings in secular studies.[11] Alemanno specifies ten tractates of the Babylonian Talmud as required texts: *Berakhot, Shabat, Pesahim, Yom*

Tov, Baba Meẓi'a, Sanehedrin, Ketubot, Gittin, Hullin, and *Niddah.*[12] The Talmud was studied with Rashi's commentary and the *Tosafot,* the glosses of the German and French medieval halakhists. Alemanno refers to the Tosafot as a generic term, but we may assume that he used the Tosafot of R. Pereẓ ben Isaac then prevalent in Italy.[13] Alemanno lists by name the codes of the Sephardic R. Isaac Alfasi, the Italian R. Isaiah Trani the Younger, and the Ashkenazic R. Asher ben Yehiel. This sample reflects the fusion of three legal traditions in the rabbinic training of Italian Jews, which the young R. David ben Judah inherited.

The secular curriculum consisted of the *trivium*—grammar, rhetoric, and logic—and most of the *quadrivium*—arithmetic, geometry, astronomy. (Alemanno did not mention the fourth *quadrivium* art, music, but R. David studied it as well).[14] Alemanno recommends the study of the *quadrivium* during the months of Nisan and Tishrei when it was not customary to study Talmud and Codes.

These liberal arts were studied in Hebrew, through texts written in Spain, Provençe, and Italy from the twelfth to the fifteenth centuries. Alemanno cites *Sefer ha-Mikhlol,* by R. David Qimhi, *Sefer Ma'aseh Efod,* by Profiat Duran, and *Sefer Even Bohan,* by 'Immanuel of Rome, as required texts for Hebrew grammar.[15] Rhetoric was taught through Aristotle's *Rhetoric,* R. Judah Messer Leon's *Nofet Ẓufim,* and contemporary humanist texts in Ciceronian rhetoric.[16] Logic was taught through Aristotle's *Organon,* with the commentaries of R. Judah Messer Leon, Averroës, and R. Joseph ibn Caspi.[17] Arithmetic was studied through the works of R. Levi ben Gerson (Gersonides) and R. Abraham ibn 'Ezra, and from practices common among Italian Jews.[18] Geometry was taught through Euclid's *Elementa* and the teachings of Abraham ibn 'Ezra dispersed through his various writings.[19] Astronomy was taught through R. Jacob Anatoli's translations of Ptolemy's *Almagest,* Averroës' paraphrase to this text, Alfragani's *Sefer Yesodot ha-Tekhunah,* R. Abraham Bar Hiyya's *Sefer Ẓurat ha-Areẓ ve-Tavnit ha-Shamayim,* and his astronomical tablets, Profiat Duran's *Heshev ha-Efod,* and Isaac Israeli's *Sefer Yesod 'Olam.*[20]

Students who mastered the liberal arts and wished to enrich their secular training would continue with philosophy and medicine. Since Alemanno received his doctoral degrees in medicine and philosophy from R. Judah Messer Leon, we may assume that the texts he listed were actually taught to advanced students at R. Judah's academy. Alemanno states that during his first seven years of philosophical training (from the age of twenty-one to twenty-eight), the student should study Aristotle's *Physics* and *Metaphysics,* with Averroës' commentaries, and Alghazali's *The Intention of the Philosophers.*[21] Evenings were devoted to ethics and politics through Averroës' Commentary on Plato's *Republic,* Aristotle's *Ethics,* Alghazali's *Sefer Mozney Zedeq,* and Solomon ibn Gabirol's *Tiqqun Middot ha-Nefesh.*[22]

From the ages of twenty-eight to thirty-five the student should consult the works of Jewish and Muslim (medieval) philosophers. Alemanno refers specifically to works of Moses Narboni, Isaac Albalag, Judah Halevi, Moses Maimonides, Joseph ibn Caspi, Shem Tov Falaqera, Profiat Duran, Hasdai Crescas, Judah of Rome, Levi ben Abraham, Isaac ibn Latif and Averroës.[23] Their texts should be studied in conjunction with the biblical commentaries of Rashi, Moses ben Nahman, and Abraham ibn 'Ezra. Finally, the academy taught Latin grammar and epistolography. Stimulated by the humanist preoccupation with eloquence, Italian Jews cultivated these arts to achieve an elegant prose style.[24]

Alemanno also recommends the study of Kabbalah as an integral part of Jewish theology, citing R. Menahem Recanati's *Commentary on the Torah,* the anonymous *Ma'arekhet ha-Elohut,* and the works of Abraham Abulafia.[25] Though Alemanno tended to interpret Kabbalah philosophically, he considered it a science along with magic, alchemy, and astrology.[26] Undoubtedly, R. Judah Messer Leon did not allow Kabbalah, alchemy, magic, or astrology in his academy. These subjects reflect the intellectual bent of the mature Alemanno, which he cultivated in Florence under the influence of the famous humanist Pico Della Mirandola.[27]

Through all this, David continued to study Bible, Mishnah, and Aggadah—as was the Italian custom—alongside the study of Jewish law in accordance with both Italian and Ashkenazic traditions. Consequently, R. David was introduced to the legal compilations and Talmudic analyses of the German and French Tosafists and acquired proficiency in the Ashkenazic method of *pilpul* (Talmudic dialectic).[28]

David was undoubtedly one of the most distinguished students in his father's academy. Before the age of eighteen he apparently studied not only the rabbinic subjects and the liberal arts but also some philosophy as well—thus compressing an education that Alemanno suggested should continue until age thirty-five.

Evidence of David's early scholarship and the breadth of study at his father's academy is found in an exchange of letters between

David ben Judah, then about thirteen years old, and his relative R. David ben Joab of Tivoli, a wealthy banker in Lucca, and himself a renowned poet and a patron of scholars.[29] R. David ben Joab wrote young David, praising his scholarly versatility and intellectual prowess—particularly in integrating "Bible, Mishnah, and Aggadah" with "science, philosophy, and logic"[30]—and his mastery of logic, physics, metaphysics, grammar, and rhetoric.[31] David ben Judah wrote back on the twenty-fourth day of the Omer in 5244 (i.e., 4-5 May 1484).[32] In an ordered and polished style, he modestly shifted attention from his own achievements to those of his celebrated father, relating his father's literary accomplishments, correctly portraying him as a scholar who harmonized Torah studies and secular disciplines. David admiringly refers to his father as the spiritual leader of the Jews of Naples, and depicts the academy as an intellectually stimulating place.[33] David ben Judah then urges R. David ben Joab to send his own son, Joab (ben R. David), to study in R. Judah Messer Leon's academy and promises to take good care of him there.

That invitation was not a rhetorical nicety. Rather, it was a response to the difficult conditions R. David ben Joab faced during the mid-1480s. As the major Jewish moneylender in Lucca, he was particularly subject to the attacks of Bernadino de Feltre, the Franciscan friar, against the Jews of Lucca. Though he was not expelled from the town, R. David ben Joab was fined by the council of Lucca for his banking activities.[34]

David ben Judah Messer Leon remained at his father's academy until he received the highest formal recognition of his intellectual prowess: ordination as a rabbi at the unprecedented age of eighteen. The customary age of ordination was forty.[35] Like the doctoral degree awarded in Italian universities, rabbinic ordination not only publicly recognized the academic excellence of the recipient but also granted him political privileges and social honors, and allowed him to assume a position of authority in communal administration.[36] As noted above, R. Judah Messer Leon in particular viewed rabbinic ordination as the source of political authority within the Jewish community. For that reason and because of David's age, R. Judah refused to ordain his son himself and insisted that David be ordained by the other rabbis in the academy. The ordaining rabbis cited both talmudic precedents supporting ordination at an early age and the outstanding qualifications of the ordinee.[37] R. David later wrote that he was married on the very day of his ordination, but we know nothing about the identity of his wife.[38]

For Italian Jews the *hakham kolel* was the Jewish counterpart of the Renaissance ideal of *homo universalis,* the "universal (i.e., complete) man."[39] R. David's broad education epitomized these ideals, and combined contradictory traditions without apparent tension. He was trained in both rabbinic Judaism and the secular sciences, reflecting the impact of Sephardic and Provençal Jewry on native Italian Jews. His halakhic training integrated traditions common among native Italian Jews with Ashkenazic legal traditions that his father fostered. His training in the secular sciences also reflects diversity: medieval Judeo-Arabic philosophy, Christian scholasticism, and Renaissance humanism.

R. David's outstanding erudition is evident in his extant writing which are a rich tapestry woven from citations and paraphrases of other literary sources. His eclectic style of writing reflects the syncretist nature of the Italian Renaissance. On the one hand, Renaissance syncretism exhibited itself in the coexistence of many intellectual currents—Aristotelianism, Platonism, Thomism, Augustinianism, Stoicism and Hermeticism—and on the other hand, individual Renaissance thinkers borrowed freely from all these schools of thought and attempted to harmonize them into a coherent system. However, not all Italian humanists succeeded, or even attempted, to construct a coherent philosophical system. Many of them, lacking professional philosophic skills, did not adhere to standards of terminological precision or consistent argumentation. Humanist compositions often comprised contradictions either within the various literary sources collected by the author, or in the presentation of the author's own views. Even though R. David ben Judah was a systematic philosopher, his breadth of scholarship reflects the very richness of the Italian Renaissance.

In short, R. David ben R. Judah Messer Leon was born and raised as a Jewish, Renaissance gentleman—a man of privilege, culture, tradition, and authority, well versed in a broad range of scholarly disciplines. At the age of eighteen, his reputation was already established.

Tensions in Padua

In 1489 or 1490, immediately after R. David's ordination, his father sent him to Padua to study with the German halakhist, R. Judah Minz, and to receive a second ordination.[40] R. Judah Messer

Leon perhaps hoped to avoid any dispute arising from the circumstances of R. David's first ordination and to solidify R. David's commitment to the Ashkenazic legal tradition. In R. Judah Minz's academy, R. David sharpened his legal and rhetorical skills through *pilpul* and expanded his knowledge of Ashkenazic legal compendia and codes.

Elija Capsali's *Seder Eliyahu Zuta* provides a detailed description of R. Judah Minz's academy,[41] as follows: the Ashkenazic community in Padua provided R. Judah Minz with a house and an annual salary of a hundred florins to support him and his students, who resided with him. During the morning, R. Judah Minz would go first to the academy to engage in *pilpul* with the other rabbis. He would then go home to teach Talmud to the less stellar students, and in the evening he would teach Tosafot to the brighter ones. Wealthy Jews who could afford a rabbi to teach them privately would also follow this order of study, devoting their mornings to the Talmud and afternoons to Tosafot.

The members of R. Judah Minz's yeshivah and other Jews in Padua would gather together for at least an hour of study a day. Minz began these sessions by stating the legal issue arising from the talmudic text under consideration; the members of the academy, working in pairs and without consulting the written text, would then attempt to resolve the difficulties through *pilpul*. After lively and at times vociferous exchange, the Ashkenazic rabbi would conclude the debate and assign the next day's text, which the students would then prepare with their teachers either privately or at the academy. This rigorous schedule lasted five days a week. Students would study individually during the Sabbath eve and day, and they would reconvene with their rabbis or with Minz after evening prayers marking the end of the Sabbath.

R. David gained proficiency in the Tosafot and the Ashkenazic codes during his sojourn in Padua, and followed his father's allegiance to Ashkenazic halakhah. R. David would later write, "We accept the authority of our French and German rabbis from whom Torah shall come forth and according to whom we live."[42] Through the vast Ashkenazic legal literature, R. David also became acquainted with German Hasidism. R. David mentions citations from *Sefer Hasidim* by R. Judah He-Hasid, found in the *Mordecai,* and from *Seder Teshuvah* by R. Eleazar of Worms.[43] These two references suggest that R. David viewed German Hasidism as one of the sources of Ashkenazic customs and legal practices closely related to the legacy of the Tosafot, and that R. David could have gained access to German Hasidic quasi-mystical esoteric works, even though his extant writings contain no direct reference to them.[44]

R. David's encounter with the Ashkenazic culture was significant. A circumstantial link appears between his study in Padua and his interest in Kabbalah, which is discussed in Chapter Seven below. In the opening of *Magen David,* composed later in Constantinople, R. David confesses that, despite his father's opposition:

> ... I engaged in this study (of Kabbalah) for many years, and I have seen its mysterious and difficult books ever since I was a young lad, eighteen years of age, the year of my marriage. I have studied this discipline in secret, because my master, my father, may God guard him and protect him, did not let me study it for my young age. Nevertheless, since I greatly desired it, I did not rest and did not calm down until my eyes opened up by virtue of its mysteries; and the blessing of my father, my master, may he rest in peace, would come upon me. Though most philosophers and physicians, whose wisdom we study every day, rejected this science, I do not share their view. For all sciences, to those who understand their fundamentals and principles, are compatible with one another.[45]

It is highly unlikely that R. David studied Kabbalah at home in Naples, and more probable that he studied it in Padua, away from his father's eye and in an entirely different intellectual climate from that of Naples.

We are left to wonder how R. David studied Kabbalah and who was his teacher, for even in Padua during the last decades of the fifteenth century, the study of Kabbalah was not yet taken for granted. In fact, while in Padua R. David undoubtedly witnessed the controversy concerning the Jewish philosopher from Crete, Elijah del Medigo, whose critical attitude toward Kabbalah presents an interesting counterpoint to R. David's embrace of it and refinement of it into philosophy.

Del Medigo lived in Italy for only ten years, from 1480 to 1490, but his knowledge of Aristotelian-Averroian philosophy made him a significant influence on Christian scholars there.[46] Such Venetian scholars as Girolamo Donato, Domenico Grimani and Antonio Pizzamano employed del Medigo to teach and to translate Averroës' works, originally written in Arabic, from Hebrew into Latin.[47] Del

Medigo prepared original treatises and translations for the Florentine scholar Pico della Mirandola and held two extensive discussions on a variety of philosophical subjects. Del Medigo was associated with Pico from 1481 to 1486, first in Padua and later in Florence, where the association between the Jewish scholar and his Christian patron came under severe strain. Pico was gradually being swayed by Platonism and was more interested in Kabbalah than in rationalist philosophy. He employed the aged Jewish scholar Yohanan Alemanno and the new convert Flavius Mithridates (alias Raymondo Moncada) to teach him Kabbalah and to translate Kabbalistic texts into Latin.

Elijah del Medigo did not share Pico's enthusiasm for Platonism and Kabbalah but continued to insist on the substantive difference between Aristotelianism and Platonism. In contrast to Alemanno, del Medigo regarded Kabbalah not as ancient wisdom but as a recent Midrash. In 1486 del Medigo wrote Pico of his reservations about both Kabbalah and Platonism in a letter that accompanied his translation into Latin of the Kabbalistic biblical commentary by Menahem Recanati.

In 1485, while still in Pico's service in Florence, del Medigo was forced to defend Judaism in a public disputation, which we know about from Marsilio Ficino's letter to Domenico Benivieni.[48] Del Medigo joined with another Jewish philosopher and physician, Abraham Farissol, himself an excellent choice to defend Judaism against Christianity because he had already done so in the court of Ercole I in Ferrara. Del Medigo would later include his own anti-Christian polemics in the theological work *Behinat ha-Dat (Examination of Religion)*, which he composed in Crete in 1490, after he left Italy.

Del Medigo returned to Venice after parting ways with Pico in 1486. He spent the end of the decade in several cities of the Venetian Republic, including Padua, and abruptly left Italy under the cloud of controversy. The details of the controversy and del Medigo's departure are not clear, but the most plausible is the one suggested by D. Geffen.[49] It is very likely that the Ashkenazim in Padua rejected either del Medigo's preoccupation with philosophy or his rationalist position on the relationship of reason and revelation, which developed under the influence of Averroës.[50] The Ashkenazim apparently made the climate in the Jewish community in Padua so inhospitable that del Medigo left. Other conjectures erroneously relate the departure of Elijah del Medigo either to the ecclesiastical opposition to Averroist teaching on the unity of the human intellect,[51] or to the death of Pico della Mirandola in 1494.[52] In any event, del Medigo returned to his native Crete, where he could cultivate his rationalist philosophy with little opposition.

R. David ben R. Judah was in Padua while this controversy raged, and must have known Elijah del Medigo, particularly because the two shared a knowledge of the Aristotelian-Averroian corpora. Perhaps R. David even studied privately with the Cretan philosopher.

The del Medigo controversy provoked another response as well. Sometime in 1489-1490 R. David wrote a formal query to Rabbi Jacob ben R. David Provenzali of Naples concerning the status of secular sciences within traditional Judaism.[53] We do not know why R. David chose to write R. Jacob, but Jacob's Provençal origin makes it possible that R. David exemplified him as a pious rabbi who was also immersed in the secular sciences. The young and perplexed R. David wanted to know whether any talmudic support existed for the hostility that, at least under the interpretation of the Ashkenazic rabbis in Padua, talmudic Judaism exhibited toward philosophy and the secular disciplines. R. David asked, "Were they (the secular disciplines) desired or rejected by our venerable sages, may they rest in peace, since, in principle, it appears that the Talmudic sages opposed philosophy?"[54]

R. Jacob Provenzali's response strongly reflects the cultural climate of Italian Jews during the second half of the fifteenth century. His first letter assured R. David, "Undoubtedly each one of the seven arts (literally, wisdoms) was praised and appreciated by our sages who embraced them wholeheartedly."[55] However, R. Jacob Provenzali then made a clear distinction between the liberal arts and medicine on the one hand, and what he called "the demonstrations of Aristotle" on the other hand. Whereas he endorsed the former and claimed that most talmudic sages were "erudite in at least one or two secular disciplines," he rejected the latter, that is, the rationalist demonstration of religious truths, calling it "deception" and "vanity devoid of any benefit." Thus R. Jacob Provenzali encouraged R. David ben Judah to continue his study of secular disciplines, while affirming the superiority of Torah study over all other intellectual pursuits.

R. Jacob Provenzali was concerned that his letter would be wrongly interpreted as unequivocal approval of the study of philosophy. He therefore wrote a second letter, stating that the pursuit of secular studies had more complex ramifications for Italian Jews than he had first acknowledged. He then conceded that the recent admission of Jews to Italian universities and the custom of wealthy Jews to hire private Christian tutors had caused a widespread neglect of Torah and Talmud studies.[56] He lamented that Jewish students had no respect for rabbinic scholars, who, as a result, could hardly find adequate employment. Jewish youth preferred "to listen to Christian scholars who could teach them wisdom for little money" rather than hire more expensive Jewish scholars. Humanists could hire themselves out for less because they were normally subsidized by the Italian rulers or wealthy patricians, whereas rabbinic scholars, by contrast, depended on teaching as their sole source of income.[57]

Given this unfortunate state of affairs, R. Jacob Provenzali could hardly voice enthusiasm toward the study of the secular disciplines. He continued to praise the material benefits to be derived from the sciences, especially medicine, in which he urged R. David to excel. Nevertheless, the Provençal rabbi stressed the ultimate superiority of Torah and Talmud above all other subjects, and urged R. David to make them his top priority. Provenzali ended his elaborate second response by praising R. David as "a very venerable scholar" and expressing utter confidence in R. David's ability to reconcile the pursuit of secular knowledge with steadfast allegiance to Judaism. Jacob Provenzali entrusted R. David "to make fruits above, and not to relinquish the root in order to hold the bark." With this charge the older rabbi expressed his assurance that the study of secular sciences, including metaphysics, would not lead R. David to embrace Aristotelian philosophy at the expense of Judaism.

R. David would later confirm R. Jacob Provenzali's faith in him. While continuing to study Aristotelian philosophy, R. David would insist that such knowledge does not impinge upon the superiority of divinely revealed Judaism. As shown below, R. David would maintain that Aristotelian philosophy serves only to demonstrate the superiority of Judaism, whose techniques are grounded in the infinitely perfect divine reason. R. David's life and literary career would be devoted to the harmonization of the secular sciences (i.e., truths obtained through human reasoning) with the ultimate truths revealed by God at Sinai.

A Visit to Florence

The precise length of R. David's stay in Padua is no longer known for sure. There is evidence that by 1492 he had already returned to Naples, where he began his literary career. R. David stopped in Florence on the way home.[58] Although short, that visit strongly influenced R. David's intellectual development. In Padua he had sought to harmonize Jewish traditionalism with the scientific pursuits of medieval scholasticism. In Florence he was further exposed to Renaissance humanism, and added yet another dimension to his multifaceted education.

Florence was ruled by a small oligarchy of rich merchants, led by the Medici family. Though greed and envy governed much of Florence's political and financial life, the city-state enjoyed a strong tradition of civic patronage.[59] During the thirteenth and fourteenth centuries, Florentine oligarchy funded monasteries, beautified churches, and established charities. Florence's civic pride suffered greatly in its desperate war with Milan in 1343. Out of this political failure evolved a new civic consciousness: not only to oppose tyranny at home but also to protect the liberty of neighboring city-states. The Florentines began to see themselves as the true heirs of republican Rome. Their governing families, among them Salutati, Bruni, and Bracciolini, found their inspiration in Cicero's belief that the full life, indeed the good life, could only be lived if a man dedicated himself to civic virtues.[60]

Florence's struggle with Milan gave strong impetus to the peculiar qualities of the Florentine Renaissance. The convictions that classical learning molds the citizen's character and that great moral value could be derived from the study of philosophy became deeply embedded in the Florentine tradition. Florence's civic humanism, though rooted in its civic life, rapidly developed into a full-fledged scholarly and cultural movement. Her humanists dedicated themselves to the classics through new textual and philological techniques. Their preoccupation with style, grammar, and the minutiae of textual criticism was inspired by the ideal of eloquence.[61] In their search for elegant speech, Florentine humanists also cultivated fine poetry and prose written in the exemplary Latin of classical poetry. Classical studies and other scholarly activity in Florence enjoyed the patronage of the ruling family and other patricians. The Medicis founded and encouraged the Platonic Academy, patronized handsomely the greatest philosophers—Ficino, Pico and others—and invested heavily in the arts. Thus Florence produced the greatest artists of the fifteenth century whose paintings, sculptures, and architecture graced Rome, Venice, Milan, and the lesser cities of Italy.[62] Florence dominated the intellectual and artistic life of Italy during the fifteenth century.

Jews partly financed Florence's art, architecture, and classical scholarship, as well as its sumptuous life of pageants, tournaments and carnivals. Although few Jews were in Florence, their banking activities were crucial to its economy and foreign policy, especially after 1437. On October 17, 1437 the Commune of Florence officially allowed Jewish bankers residing in San Miniato to conduct business in Florence.[63] Until the Medicis fell from power in 1496, Jewish money-lenders were protected from popular animosity and ecclesiastical hostility. The richest Jewish banking family in Tuscany—the da Pisas—resided in Florence and was closely associated with the Medicis.

Florence's prominence as the most dynamic and creative center of Renaissance Italy probably prompted R. David's visit. He must have understood that role; we know that other Italian Jews did.[64] At his father's yeshivah, R. David had already been instructed in the *studia humanitatis,* and was acquainted with the current debates between scholastics and humanists in the Italian scholarly community—for instance, the debate between Pico della Mirandola and Ermolao Barbaro.[65] A visit to Florence could only solidify R. David's mastery of the humanist curriculum. Indeed, R. David's extant works exhibit his profound indebtedness to Renaissance humanism, far beyond the initial openness of R. Judah Messer Leon to this cultural trend.

Lacking the legal right to reside in Florence on his own account, R. David could have remained there only under the auspices of a privileged Jew, probably one of the da Pisa family. Its *paterfamilias,* the celebrated banker Yehiel da Pisa, died in 1490 and was succeeded by his son Isaac.[66] One of the daughters of Yehiel da Pisa was married to R. David ben Joab of Tivoli (R. David ben Judah's relative through his father), with whom R. David ben Judah had corresponded as a child. Isaac's brother, Samuel, married a woman named Laura, who most likely was the addressee and subject of R. David's letter/essay *Shevah ha-Nashim* discussed in Chapter Three below. R. David wrote poems in the early 1490s in defense of women and probably dedicated them to Laura as well.[67] We may surmise that R. David stayed in the da Pisa household while in Florence and he may have been employed as a private tutor and manuscript copier.

The da Pisas typified the wealth, glamour and scholarly interests of the Italian Jewish patriarchy; their home was known as "the assembly house for scholars," who would gather to exchange academic information and to enjoy the fine arts.[68] R. David Reubeni, the Messianic contender, depicted them as a highly cultivated and refined family. He was particularly impressed with the ladies, who

studied the secular sciences, played musical instruments, and participated in scholarly conversations.[69]

During the late 1480s and early 1490s the da Pisas employed
Yohanan Alemanno as a scholar-in-residence,[70] which may have pro-
vided R. David another incentive to visit. Although forty years R.
David's senior, Alemanno had similar intellectual interests. As noted
above, Alemanno too was trained in R. Judah Messer Leon's acad-
emy; R. Judah had awarded him a doctoral degree in philosophy.[71]
And Alemanno also ignored R. Judah's ban on the study of
Kabbalah. In fact, Alemanno acquired immense erudition in
Kabbalah, magic, alchemy, and astrology, all culled from Jewish and
Muslim Neoplatonic texts.

R. David probably knew of Alemanno's pursuit of Kabbalah;
other Jews in Naples did. The Sephardic Kabbalist Isaac Mar
Hayyim, residing in Naples in 1489, wrote a letter to Isaac ben Yehiel
da Pisa warning him against Alemanno's intellectualist approach to
Kabbalah, through which he allegedly "interpreted the words of
Kabbalah so as to agree with philosophy."[72] Yet precisely this
approach made Alemanno a suitable candidate to instruct R. David
in Kabbalah. R. David viewed Kabbalah a speculative science,
indeed an integral part of Jewish theology, explicable by means of
philosophic categories.

Alemanno's erudition in Kabbalah was especially valued by the
Florentine humanist Pico della Mirandola, who employed the aged
Jew to teach him Kabbalah, to translate Kabbalistic texts into Latin,
and to guide him in the mysteries of the occult sciences.[73] Thus
Alemanno became instrumental in the development of Christian
Hebraism, Christian Kabbalah, and the flourishing of the occult sciences in the Italian Renaissance. Pico's interests in Jewish learning,
inspired first in Padua where he met Elijah del Medigo, derived their
theoretical justification from the theories of Marsilio Ficino, who
developed the notion of *prisca theologica,* or ancient theology,
according to which there is one universal truth in which various
schools of thought participate.[74] Ficino argued that the ancient pagan
thinkers, Plato, Zoroaster, Hermes Trismegistus, Orpheus, and
Pythagoras, all represent different aspects of an underlying universal
truth. Within this universal scheme, Ficino and Pico could find room
to include Judaism as a true religion.

According to Marsilio Ficino and Pico della Mirandola, Mosaic
Law consists of an esoteric, eternal, spiritual truth. Since all spiritual
truths participate in the one universal truth, the inner truth of Juda-

ism enjoys the same status as the mysteries of Orphic hymns, Christ's revelations to Paul, and the Neoplatonic writings of the pseudo-Dionysius. According to Pico, the inner, spiritual truth of Mosaic Law was known to an exclusive elite among the Jews—the Kabbalists—both in antiquity and in Pico's own day.[75] Hence, in order to understand fully the divine mysteries embedded in ancient theology, Christian humanists had to study Kabbalah under contemporary Jews, which Pico did through Alemanno. By regarding Kabbalah as eternal truth, Italian humanists such as Pico went beyond the traditional Christian view of *hebraica veritas*.[76] For the first time in Western intellectual history, a Christian scholar validated Judaism as intrinsically worthy even in his own day, rather than legal tradition superseded by the coming of Christ.

Unfortunately the humanists' interest in Kabbalah did not mean accepting contemporary Jews as equals or renouncing claims of Christian superiority. Ultimately Pico attempted to dissociate Kabbalah from Judaism and to appropriate it completely to Christianity.[77] Pico identified the esoteric teachings of Kabbalah with the mysteries of Christianity, and hence expected his Jewish associates to convert to Christianity. His missionary attempts were not without success: among the intellectuals surrounding Pico were two recent Jewish converts: Flavius Mithridates and Paulus Ricci. Both instructed Pico in Kabbalah and even fabricated Kabbalistic texts to satisfy the intellectual thirst of the young Christian humanist.[78] Jewish scholars such as Abraham Farissol and Elija del Medigo had to engage in polemical exchanges to defend Judaism against the claims of Pico and the new converts.[79]

It is possible that this misuse of Kabbalah for Christian missionizing prompted R. Judah Messer Leon to ban it. Nevertheless R. David must have known of this Jewish/Christian collaboration while in Florence, because just a few years later R. David would contribute to the on-going Jewish polemic against Christian Kabbalah, at the request of R. David ben Joab of Tivoli, by writing *Magen David*.[80]

R. David's exposure to Florentine culture left him with the unmistakable influence of Renaissance humanism. He cultivated the *studia humanitatis* and viewed them as disciplines necessary for the attainment of human perfection.[81] Like the Italian humanists, R. David highly valued the study of grammar as the foundation of clear thinking and correct reasoning, and applied it to the study of Jewish Law, both Written and Oral.[82] Most notably, R. David shared the humanists' interest in classical rhetoric and poetry. He avidly studied the works of Cicero, Seneca, Quintilian, Virgil, and Ovid, to mention just a few, and as will become clear later, integrated excerpts from their writings into his exegetical and philosophical works.[83] From classical orators and poets, R. David derived literary conventions and aesthetic sensibilities which he applied to all his intellectual pursuits. In particular, R. David would use the humanist preoccupation with eloquence in his biblical exegesis either as a preacher or as a commentator.

R. David further endorsed the humanist ideal of eloquence by composing poetry. Like other contemporary Italian humanists, he admired Petrarch's poetry (both in the Tuscan dialect and in Latin), memorized Petrarch's sonnets, and imitated them in his own verse, which, unfortunately, is no longer extant. We know of it from R. David's discussion of Petrarch and defense of poetry in *Shevah ha-Nashim*.[84]

R. David's interest in music is another example of the impact of Renaissance culture. R. David composed a work on music theory, also no longer extant, and several comments in his extant works attest to knowledge of singing.[85] R. David held the humanist view that music had theurgic power through which humans can affect the supernal world and in return receive divine effluence (*shefa'*). Music enables man to "draw spirituality" from the heavenly spheres, thereby overcoming the corporeal limits of human existence. R. David's comments suggest that he was versed not only in musical theory but also in musical performance. He discusses the production of sound from a stringed instrument, probably the lute, as well as vocal techniques. Only a scholar of music or a practicing musician could have written these comments.[86] Yohanan Alemanno was the first Jew to articulate that approach to music[87] and may have introduced R. David to it.

Viewing music as a means of human spiritualization went hand-in-hand with humanist interest in talismatic magic, astrology, and alchemy. The major sources instructing Florentine humanists in these disciplines were Neoplatonic texts composed in Egypt about 100-300 C.E. and attributed to the ancient Egyptian sage Hermes Trismegistus (Hermes the Thrice-Blessed).[88] Hermetic literature was known to some of the early Church Fathers; for example, Lactantius considered Hermes a major historical figure who gave the Egyptians their letters and laws, founded a great city, was skilled in all arts, wrote many books of wisdom, and was a monotheist. Lactantius also praised Hermes for his prophecy of the coming Son of God and for his prediction of the Christian religion.

Augustine was another Church Father who referred to the Hermetic tradition, though he disapproved of Hermes' reported practice of infusing life into statues of Egyptian gods. During the Middle Ages, excerpts from Hermetic writings became known to the Latin West either through these Church Fathers or through some Arabic translations. In the Byzantine East, the philosopher Michael Pselus studied Hermetic writings in the original Greek during the twelfth century. It is his work which would later facilitate the revival of Hermeticism in fifteenth century Italy.

Renaissance Hermeticism emerged in the 1460s after a monk employed by Cosimo de Medici the Elder to collect Greek manuscripts brought to Florence an incomplete copy of the *Corpus Hermeticum,* a collection of Hermetic treatises. Cosimo, the patron of Marsilio Ficino, ordered Ficino to translate the new find. Ficino's translation and commentary, entitled *Pimander,* was published in 1471 and enjoyed immense popularity; sixteen editions were published before 1500.[89] Ficino followed Augustine and Lactantius in the belief that Hermes was a historic figure. Ficino dated Hermes as living only two generations after Moses and considered him the author of Egyptian theology which had passed on to the Greek sage Orpheus and then successively to Pythagoras, Philolaus, and finally to Plato. On this basis Ficino considered the Hermetic tradition an older form of Platonism, and hence more authentic than Plato's teachings. Given the Neoplatonic nature of Hermetic literature, Ficino had no problem fusing Platonism and Hermeticism.[90]

There is evidence that R. David was aware of the interest of Florentine humanists in Hermetic literature. He cites Hermes Trismegistus once in his *Shevah ha-Nashim* as an ancient sage who, along with other pagan, Christian, biblical, and rabbinic scholars, advocated a life-long pursuit of wisdom.[91] As Idel has shown, similar references to Hermes are found in the works of R. David's contemporaries Isaac and Judah Abravanel, Sephardic exiles who settled in Naples in 1492.[92] Isaac Abravanel even identified Hermes with the biblical figure Hanoch. R. David did not go that far, but did view Hermetic knowledge as an integral part of classical wisdom.

The revival of Hermeticism in Florence was but one aspect of the Platonic orientation of Florentine humanism. R. David's attitude toward Plato should be understood in the context of the Platonic revival in Renaissance Italy. Although primarily an Aristotelian, R. David talked about Plato with profound admiration, referring to him as *Aplaton ha-Elohi* ("the divine Plato"), whose views R. David claimed were identical with "the true Kabbalah."[93] The very association of Plato and Kabbalah reflects both the prevailing search for *prisca theologica* among Renaissance humanists as well as the need to provide a Jewish response to the humanist claim. Like Isaac Abravanel, Abraham Farissol and Yohanan Alemanno, R. David justified the compatibility of Plato and Kabbalah by resorting to an "historical" argument, namely, that Plato was a disciple of the Prophet Jeremiah in Egypt.[94] By forging this historical link between Plato and Jeremiah, R. David and his Jewish contemporaries rationalized and justified Jewish preoccupation with Renaissance Platonism; since the origin of Plato's teaching was Jewish, there should be no barrier to the study of Platonism. Furthermore, by "Judaizing" Platonism, R. David could provide a Jewish version of *prisca theologica* through which the origins of both Hermeticism and Platonism are found in Judaism, grounded in divine revelation to Moses.

The impact of Renaissance humanism is evident in R. David's interest in history, one of the *studia humanitatis*. Renaissance humanists developed a new historical awareness, departing from medieval typological thinking.[95] They denigrated the immediate past as the "Dark Ages" and extolled classical antiquity as the model for emulation. Italian humanists paid particular attention to Roman historiography, biography, and epistolography as records of human exemplary conduct. Like his Italian contemporaries, R. David was fascinated with the writings of the Roman historians Plutarch, Pliny the Younger, and Livy. He cited them in his *Shevah ha-Nashim* and derived from them an ability to understand the past in concrete terms.[96]

Fascination with classical antiquity, cultivation of the *studia humanitatis,* openness to Platonism and Hermeticism, and refined aesthetic sensibilities all reflect the impact of Renaissance humanism. R. David integrated Renaissance humanism with other dimensions of his intellectual universe: traditional Judaism and medieval scholasticism. R. David regarded Renaissance humanism not as a *weltanschauung* but rather as a literary, or aesthetic, cultural trend. Medieval Jewish rationalism molded R. David's world view, as we shall see in later chapters of this book; Renaissance humanism determined R. David's literary conventions and aesthetic sensibilities. It was precisely these which were foreign to other Jewish subcultures which R. David encountered after his departure from Italy. The full scope of R. David's humanism becomes clear when he defends it, discussed in Chapter Three below.

Abrupt Departure from Naples

R. David returned to Naples by 1492 and remained until his flight in 1495. Little is known of his activities there; his later works indicate that he arbitrated Jewish disputes and taught in his father's academy.[97] Apparently R. David derived no income from his rabbinic activity. In *Magen David* he noted that only in the Ottoman Empire did he start to charge for his rabbinic services, due to the low demand for his medical expertise.[98] So R. David probably supported himself in Italy primarily from his medical practice, and perhaps received something as well from his patroness, Laura, to whom he would later write *Shevah ha-Nashim*.[99] In any event, R. David's financial security explains in part his literary productivity. In a very short period he composed an impressive array of works exhibiting versatility in halakhah, theology, philosophy, grammar, poetry, and music.

None of R. David's Italian works remains extant. We know of their titles and subjects from R. David's references to them in his extant works, all written later in the Ottoman Empire. R. David's Italian works include a talmudic treatise entitled *Migdal David (Tower of David)*;[100] two works in theology, *Mizmor le-David (A Hymn to David)*, and *Menorat ha-Zahav (The Golden Lantern)*;[101] a work on ethics, *Nahal 'Adanim (A River of Delights)*;[102] a work on Hebrew grammar, *Segulat Melakhim (The Virtue of Kings)*;[103] a collection of sermons, *Tiferet Adam (The Glory of Man)*;[104] a collection of tercets *(terza rima)* on the subject of female merits to which he refers as *Halazah Gimel*;[105] and a book on music theory, *Abir Ya'acov (The Mighty One of Jacob)*.[106] R. David thus followed his father, R. Judah Messer Leon, in integrating Torah and secular studies.

R. David's only public act in Naples was his support for the publication of the Ashkenazic halakhist R. Jacob Landau's *Sefer ha-Aggur,* a compendium of Ashkenazic legal practices and customs.[107] R. David's signature appeared in the *haskamah* (affidavit of approval) his father wrote to this book alongside the names of other Ashkenazic and Italian rabbis in Naples.[108] R. Jacob Landau compiled the book to counter what he considered the religious ignorance and laxity rampant among Neapolitan Jews. The book reflects the response of an Ashkenazic rabbi to the culture of Sephardic Jews who were expelled from the Iberian Peninsula in 1492 and Sicily in 1493. In supporting the publication of *Sefer ha-Aggur*, R. Judah and R. David Messer Leon probably sought to solidify their own communal authority among the Jews of Naples and to diminish the spread of Sephardic customs.

The traumatic destruction and exile of Spanish Jewry in 1492 had far-reaching implications for the Jews of Naples. The Kingdom of Naples under Ferrante I was one of the few Italian city-states that welcomed the empty-handed, fatigued, and disease-ridden Spanish refugees.[109] Ferrante not only allowed them to settle in his kingdom, but accorded the refugees from Spain and Sicily the same legal status enjoyed by the local Jews. He did not retreat from his pro-Jewish policies even after the newcomers brought a plague that killed more than twenty thousand Neapolitans in 1493. The shrewd Aragonese ruler was even instrumental in organizing relief efforts to the stricken Jews, establishing separate camps for them and offering the best available medical treatment.

Ferrante's unique favor toward Spanish Jewish immigrants is epitomized in his relationship with the most distinguished among them — Don Isaac Abravanel — the famous financier, statesman, and scholar.[110] A royal Aragonese, Ferrante was aware of the outstanding diplomatic and financial career of Isaac Abravanel, first in Portugal and later in the service of Ferdinand and Isabelle in Aragon. Abravanel's talents and reputation quickly secured him a position as advisor at the Neapolitan court and enabled him to regain his wealth, vitality, and productivity within two years of his arrival.

The established Neapolitan Jewish leadership, among them R. Judah and R. David Messer Leon, did not welcome Abravanel's meteoric rise. Over a decade later, R. David expressed strong resentment in 'Ein ha-Qore, written in Salonika about 1508.[111] Ostensibly disputing Abravanel's critique of Maimonides, R. David launched a most virulent ad hominem attack against Abravanel, accusing him of arrogance, political manipulation, greed, and philosophic incompetence. For example, Abravanel "almost made himself a Messiah when he purported to be a noble and great prince of the seed of David."[112] R. David compares this arrogance to the modesty exhibited by R. Judah the Prince (the Redactor of the Mishnah), notwithstanding that R. Judah "truly was from the seed of David."[113]

The internal squabbles of Naples' Jewish community paled to insignificance when compared to the devastation that befell from without as a result of political changes in the Appenine Peninsula. The death of Ferrante I in February 1494 caused the Angevin ruler of France, Charles VIII, to renew his old geopolitical claims. Encouraged by Ludovico Sforza—the Duke of Milan and Ferrante's rival for Milan—Charles VIII invaded Italy in September 1494. Over the next few years most of the Peninsula would become a battleground for French, Spanish, German, and Swiss armies.

Charles VIII swept through most of Italy with little resistance. By the time he approached Naples, the conditions of the Jews had already deteriorated considerably. Many fled Naples, most likely in fear of the syphilis epidemic spread by the invading armies, leaving their estates and wealth behind in the hope of regaining them later. Those hopes were in vain. On 22 February 1495, the city of Naples was conquered without a single battle, and the invaders, assisted by the local inhabitants, attacked the Jews. Houses were looted, women raped, youths captured and sold into slavery, and many simply killed indiscriminately.[114] The king, Alfonso VI, fled to Messina with his loyal advisor, Isaac Abravanel, whose household was also destroyed. (Abravanel's entire library was lost except the books he had already shipped to Salonika). Thus did the French invasion of Naples destroy a newfound haven for Iberian Jews, who once again were forced to flee.

Most of the Neapolitan exiles eventually found their way to Ottoman Turkey, where Bayezid II actively encouraged Jewish settlement. R. David was apparently among them, leaving Jews of Naples who fled the city, either before the French invasion or after, when Naples was recaptured by Ferdinand of Aragon and a decree issued expelling the remaining Jews. Though the decree was not seriously enforced until 1510, most of Naples' Jews had already left by then. We have no knowledge of the circumstances under which R. David departed from his beloved Italy, when he left, his route to Ottoman Turkey, or his experiences en route.

We next find R. David in Constantinople about 1496 as a rabbi and a physician. In a responsum written about 1497 he alludes to his exodus from Italy,[115] lamenting in highly stylized language the destruction of his home and especially of his library, which forced him to quote from memory. In his *Magen David,* written before this responsum, R. David used the expression *zarot ha-gerush* (the woes of expulsion) to explain his difficulties in Ottoman Turkey.

3

Italian Exile in the Ottoman Empire

R. David ben Judah Messer Leon, the privileged and well-connected Italian rabbi and gentleman, arrived in Constantinople in 1495-96 an uprooted exile, forced to struggle for his public stature and even his livelihood. He left Constantinople for Salonika some time before 1504 and went on to Valona in 1510. R. David became embroiled in at least four major public debates while in the Ottoman Empire. The first, in Constantinople, concerned the legitimacy of humanism within Jewish life and studies; this chapter is devoted to it. The second, also in Constantinople, concerned a ruling by Moses Capsali, the chief rabbi of the Romanyot community. The third arose in Salonika and was another skirmish in the Maimonidean controversy that had engulfed medieval Jewry ever since Maimonides' death. The fourth, in Valona, was the most personal; it arose from R. David's assertion of rabbinic authority over a congregation other than the one he was serving at the time. Chapter Four below discusses the last three controversies.

Ottoman Jewry after the Expulsion from Spain

R. David met a fate typical of the hundreds of thousands of Jews in Western Europe at the close of the fifteenth century. They were forcibly expelled—from Spain and its dominions in 1492, from Provençe in 1493, from Naples in 1495, and from Portugal in 1497. Numerous local expulsions also occurred in Germany and northern Italy.

The map of Jewish diaspora was redrawn. By the dawn of the sixteenth century, Western Europe became virtually devoid of professing Jews, and new centers of Jewish life emerged in the Ottoman Empire and Poland. Jewish refugees had to withstand the turmoil of relocation and adjustment, reorganize their communal institutions, and respond to the theological challenge wrought by the trauma of expulsion. Indeed, the last decade of the fifteenth century and the first three decades of the sixteenth century were fraught with societal and personal tragedy. Yet despite the hardships, the new centers of Jewish life would achieve unprecedented economic productivity and cultural vitality by the mid-sixteenth century.

The oldest Jewish community in Constantinople was Romanyot, the designation of those Jews who had lived in the Byzantine Empire, which comprised the Balkans, Greece, and Turkey. The Romanyots gradually came under the rule of the Ottomans, a process consolidated with the fall of Constantinople in 1453.[1] After conquering Constantinople, Sultan Mehmet II embarked on an ambitious campaign to repopulate the city and turn it into the capital of his empire. Toward this goal, the Sultan enacted a policy of compulsory resettlement of various ethnic groups, among them Jews, Greeks, and Armenians.

Thus Romanyots from Anatolia, Rumelia, and some Balkan towns were forcefully deported to Constantinople to participate in the comprehensive rebuilding efforts. This policy bred deep resentment toward the Ottoman rulers, not only because people were uprooted but also because their freedoms were restricted in their new home.[2] Legally, they were now *sürgün* (literally, deported) and as such subject to laws limiting their movement and levying special taxes.[3] Over the years many such Jews (mostly traders) obtained permission to settle elsewhere. Yet their legal status did not change; they and their descendants were still registered as residents of Constantinople and had to pay taxes there.

Despite deportation, most Romanyot Jews benefited from Ottoman policies in the long run. As a whole, Jews under the Ottomans were recognized as *dhimmi* (literally, dependent) in accordance with Muslim law. As such they were accorded considerable religious and judicial autonomy, but paid a head tax and a host of occasional taxes.[4]

The sultan preserved the integrity of the various ethnic and religious units under his rule, a policy referred to as the "millet system,"[5] according to which a subject of the Ottoman Empire had no legal status except as a member of a designated group. Religious and ethnic minorities were allowed to conduct their affairs according to their traditional laws and customs. To facilitate the self-rule of Romanyot Jews in Constantinople, the authorities approved an official position of chief rabbi for the Romanyot Jews of the capital only—which demanded a special tax, *Rav ackcesi* (the Rabbi's tax). This tax should not imply that the jurisdiction of the chief rabbi in Constantinople extended over all the Jews of the Ottoman Empire;[6] other Jews communities apparently paid it as well to support their own rabbis.

The first chief rabbi of Constantinople was R. Moses Capsali (d. 1497), the political and spiritual head of the Romanyot community. Much scholarly controversy surrounds the nature of his position. Following the seminal work of Heinrich Graetz, most scholars accepted the view that Capsali, as the chief rabbi of *Hakham Baschi,* was appointed by the Ottoman government to serve as the official representative of the entire Ottoman Jewish community and to enforce governmental policies throughout the Empire. According to Graetz, the position was both religious and secular: the chief rabbi collected taxes, guaranteed law and order within the Jewish community, adjudicated among Jewish litigants, and participated in the policy-making process of the Ottoman council.

Recent research discounts this view. J. Hacker concludes that R. Moses Capsali was accepted as the Jewish leader only of Romanyots in Constantinople, based on Capsali's position as *Ab Beth Din* of the largest Jewish court in Constantinople. No one else was under his jurisdiction. Further, the imperial government did not appoint him but merely adopted the Jewish perception of him. Finally, Capsali's leadership extended only to matters completely within the Jewish community and did not embrace any function between the community and the imperial government, such as taxation. According to Hacker, Graetz based his inaccurate description on two major sources: *Seder Eliyahu Zuta* by Elijah Capsali, the sixteenth century Cretan historian and close relative of Moses Capsali, and *Divrey Yosef* by Joseph Sambari, the seventeenth century Egyptian chronicler. Both sources embellished Moses Capsali's position, either out of familial loyalty or in order to mold Capsali's position in accordance with the Nagidate of Egyptian Jewry.

Mehmet II's deportations and the consequent resentment of Romanyot Jews are recorded in the Responsa of Romanyot rabbis. Surprisingly, these painful memories did not leave a lasting impression on Jewish perceptions of Ottoman rule. Criticism was soon overshadowed by the praise and admiration Jews accorded to Sultan Bayezid II, who succeeded Mehmet II in 1481. Bayezid II's response to the expulsion of the Jews from Spain eleven years later was a watershed in the history of Byzantine and Ottoman Jews: he welcomed them.[7] As a result, Jewish chroniclers, such as Elijah Capsali and Joseph Sambari, preserved for posterity a very positive image of Ottoman rulers, and even portrayed Bayezid II's pro-Jewish policies in messianic terms.[8]

This second massive immigration of Jews within 40 years, now mostly Spanish and Portuguese, still disrupted the Romanyot community and ultimately altered the structure and cultural orientation of Ottoman Jewry. Although the Romanyot leaders, particularly R. Moses Capsali, were instrumental in ransoming Spanish refugees and helping to resettle them, there was an unbridgeable rift between the native Romanyots and the Iberian newcomers.

Bayezid II showed a shrewd recognition of the economic and cultural advantages that the sophisticated, well-educated, and productive Jews could offer to his administration. In an apocryphal but fictional story, he is reported to have doubted the wisdom of the Spanish king, Ferdinand of Aragon, who in expelling the Jews "impoverished his country and enriched my kingdom."[9] Accurate or not, the story reflects the economic prosperity that Jews would enjoy in the Ottoman Empire.

The Spanish and Portuguese newcomers brought great prosperity to Ottoman economy. Many of them had well-established international trading ties throughout the Mediterranean basin and as far north as the Netherlands, where Marranos and their descendants settled. Ottoman Jews were major traders for a variety of commodities such as wool, leather, tobacco, grain, textiles, perfumes, and precious stones. Spanish immigrants also helped develop crafts and small industry, primarily in textiles.[10] Introducing the illustrious achievements of Spanish textile industry to Ottoman markets, they made Salonika, and later Safed, major textile centers. Other industries benefiting from Spanish immigration were the mining of precious metals, jewelry-making, and printing. Spanish Jews introduced the printing press to the Ottoman Empire, and throughout the sixteenth century they were active in printing Hebrew books of past and contemporary authors.[11]

Medicine was the other contribution of Spanish Jews to their new host country. Many Jews had served as private physicians to Spanish rulers, first in Muslim, and later in Christian, Spain. The Ottoman sultans also permitted Jews (including Marranos) to treat non-Jewish patients. Moreover, the sultans exploited the political talents and international connections of these cultured refugees, employing them both as court physicians and as political advisors and diplomatic envoys.[12] The Ottoman government thus facilitated the creation of a Jewish aristocracy which imported to the East the lifestyle, cultural orientation, and atmosphere of a sophisticated Judeo-Spanish aristocracy.[13]

The emergence of a Sephardic aristocracy with ties to the Ottoman court was one reason for the eventual dominance of Sephardic culture in Ottoman Jewry. Wealthy and cultured Sephardic Jews were convinced of their cultural superiority, both within Jewish society and with respect to their Muslim host country, and vowed to restore their lost glory to the heights it once knew. Lay and religious leaders of the Sephardic community devoted their efforts to massive educational and cultural renewal.[14] They reinstituted in the Ottoman Empire the patronage system that accounted for much of the creativity of Jews in Muslim and Christian Spain. Rich patrons financed the printing of Hebrew books, founded private libraries, and supported the copying of manuscripts. Although their own children were educated by private tutors, wealthy families contributed to extensive public education.

A broad-based, Jewish lay intelligentsia thus arose alongside the rabbinic scholars based in the academies or yeshivot. Its existence explains both the immense literary output of Sephardic scholars and the nature of their work. They responded to popular demand by composing works of either encyclopedic or homiletical nature, undistinguished in originality or depth, written primarily to preserve and expand the illustrious Sephardic heritage. The scholars succeeded in their goal.[15] The numerical superiority of Sephardic immigrants, their economic prosperity and close ties to Ottoman administration, and above all, their relentless educational campaign account for Sephardic dominance among Ottoman Jews by the mid-sixteenth century.

The fundamental diversity of Ottoman Jewish society remained nonetheless, in part because Jews were organized by congregations, as was Ottoman society at large. The congregation—*qahal* in Hebrew—was an autonomous unit administratively, economically, and socially.[16] Taxation and legal representation flowed through the congregation.[17] Membership in a congregation was based on place of birth or country of origin, so different Jewish groups remained separate and did not assimilate into a unified, dominant Jewish culture. This pattern had developed during the resettlement of Romanyot Jews in Constantinople, but it is not clear whether the Jews had initiated it or Ottoman authorities had imposed it. In any case, the early sixteenth century immigrants followed this pattern, and Ottoman Jewry remained fragmented.

Early in the sixteenth century a particular congregation usually occupied a distinct neighborhood, and thus constituted both a geographic and administrative unit. Ottoman authorities also divided cities into administrative districts or neighborhoods (*mahale* in Turkish). As more newcomers arrived, congregational divisions correlated less and less to administrative divisions; one neighborhood could have more than one Jewish congregation.

Membership in a given congregation entailed payment of taxes that found their way both to the congregation itself and to the central government. Membership also entailed prayer in the congregational synagogue. The synagogue was the heart of congregational life. It was not only the center of Jewish public worship, but also the focus of congregational self-government. Institutions such as schools, public bath and charitable societies were organized through the congregation at the synagogue, and most life-cycle functions were addressed by synagogue administration. Each congregation had a lay administration, financed and run by elected *parnasim* and treasurers. Religious administration consisted of a rabbi, who was usually the head of the yeshivah, a *Marbiz Torah* (religious teacher), and a *Dayyan* (judge). Offtimes one individual filled all three roles.

The congregation exercised extensive control over its members' lives through ordinances (*taqqanot*) instituted by the rabbi, the *Dayyan*, scholars, and communal leaders. Violators could be placed under a ban or even excommunicated. With an influx of immigrants and dissension within the congregations, disgruntled congregants often seceded, founded new congregations, and thus further fragmented Ottoman Jewry.

Friction among congregations was exceptionally strong in Constantinople, where the highly organized Romanyot community clashed with the Sephardic immigrants.[18] Constantinople also harbored a strong Karaite community, which maintained an amicable relationship with the Romanyots,[19] and a few Ashkenazic and Italian congregations as well.

The points of friction were numerous, beginning with a legal distinction. The Romanyots had long been *sürgün* (deported), but the newer Sephardim enjoyed the status of *kendi gellen,* that is, immigrants of their own free will. Romanyots paid governmental taxes from which the newcomers were exempt. According to Muslim practice, the legal distinctions of different communities were reflected in clothing, so the Romanyots and the Sephardim differed in appearance. Understandably, little intermarriage took place between them. The two groups of Jews did not even speak the same language; the Romanyots spoke Greek and the Sephardim spoke Ladino, a Judeo-Spanish dialect. The Romanyots followed Ashkenazic religio-legal tradition, and many of their rabbis were trained in the academies of northern Italy. The Sephardim, of course, followed the Sephardic tradition. So views differed on *kashrut,* ritual slaughtering, marital practices, prayer, and many other laws, customs, and observances.

These differences led to tension in daily contacts between members of the two communities, and to frequent legal disputes both between individuals and among the communities themselves. Because each congregation and community was autonomous, such litigation was not easily resolved. The legal decision or general decree of one rabbi could not be enforced in another's community. Eventually Sephardic leaders simply and absolutely refused to recognize the authority of the then-aged Romanyot chief rabbi Moses Capsali or his successor R. Elijah Mizrahi. This power struggle finally ended with the death of Elijah Mizrahi in 1525, the dissolution of the *Hakham Baschi* position that R. Moses Capsali first held, and Sephardic control of Constantinople.[20]

Uprooted Nobleman in Constantinople

R. David ben Judah Messer Leon was among the most distinguished immigrants in Constantinople. In Italy he had been a member of the aristocracy by virtue of his father's titles, his ties to the banking families of Norsa and da Pisa, and his ordination. His pedigree and his scholarship made him a natural candidate for leadership among Italian Jews.

R. David exhibited an aristocratic self-perception by referring to himself as "a nobleman among the nobles of this land" *(azil me-aziley ha-arez).* However, in Constantinople R. David's claim to nobility was not self-evident. Spanish families boasted ties to Spanish and Ottoman courts and could trace their lineage not only to famous fathers but to the biblical House of David itself. And, as discussed in Chapter One above, Sephardic scholars had little regard for Ashkenazic rabbinic ordination at all.[21]

To make matters worse, R. David apparently arrived in Constantinople without money. Meager information about his sources of income is found in *Magen David,* which he wrote in response to a request from his old correspondent and relative R. David ben Joab of Tivoli, then a temporary resident in Venice. In the opening of this work, R. David complains about "the princes of misery" (*sarey ha-mezukah*) who "removed the shawl of tranquility" from him and increasingly persecuted him. He alludes to his "troubles" and "pains" without specifying them. Apparently the chief source of these complaints was R. David's newfound need to support himself. His medical practice was less successful than in Italy, so R. David supplemented his income by serving as a rabbi.[22]

Maimonides had attacked the Babylonian Geonim for charging fees for rabbinic services. Although an ardent supporter of Maimonides—see Chapters Four through Seven below—R. David defended this particular practice.[23] Following R. Simon ben Zemah Duran,[24] R. David noted dryly that Maimonides could afford largess in Jewish matters, since his medical practice and the Egyptian court amply supported him.[25] Unfortunately, claimed R. David, medicine alone could not support one in the Ottoman Empire, so he was forced to charge for his rabbinic activities. The Jewish public should support not only those Torah scholars and judges who held official positions, for example, heads of academies, but all who made Torah study their predominant occupation.[26] Communal support would not only free up their time for study but also guarantee respect and elevated social status.

Following the rulings of most medieval jurists, including Maimonides, R. Meir Halevi, and R. Asher ben Yehiel, R. David further asserted that rabbinic scholars should be exempt from all taxes, individual and communal, general and occasional. Most sixteenth century Sephardic scholars, following the minority opinion of Moses ben Nahman (Nahmanides) and Nissim Gerondi, ruled that Torah scholars are exempt from general taxes, but that they are obligated to pay taxes individually imposed. The application of this halakhic ruling varied from one place to another within the Ottoman Empire in accordance with local customs and changing circumstances.[27]

R. David's perceived need to defend scholarly privileges reflected his newly precarious social and economic condition. In any case, having to earn a living as a rabbi and physician prevented R. David from devoting himself entirely to scholarship, his true passion.

R. David had begun preaching in Constantinople in order to supplement his income, and apparently his sermons contained copious references to classical, non-Jewish literature. That provoked fierce opposition, for it represented an assimilation of the humanist cultural program into traditional Jewish society.[28] We do not know whether the opposition came from other non-Italian congregations in Constantinople, namely, Sephardim and Romanyots, or perhaps even from members of R. David's own congregation. The attacks succeeded in their immediate goal: R. David was forced out of his rabbinic position.[29] Left with only a smaller medical practice than he had in Italy, R. David had both the leisure and the need to supplement his income.

R. David outwardly made virtue of necessity, remarking that he was now free to "make great investigations in the Torah, in commentaries, and in philosophy, as well as to compose many verses in Hebrew and Latin in my leisure time." But his fall from grace in fact dismayed and depressed him. His difficulties were recorded for posterity in his *Shevah ha-Nashim* written in Constantinople around 1496.

The text is a commentary on Proverbs 31, popularly known as Hymn for the Woman of Valor. The work contains R. David's request for financial support from a former Jewish patroness in Italy. Before embarking on the interpretation of the biblical text itself, R. David composed a long digression (fols. 89r-109v) whose purpose was twofold: to defend his use of non-Jewish sources in the commentary to follow and to explain and provoke sympathy for his financial plight. *Shevah ha-Nashim* sheds light on the cultural clashes among the various Jewish sub-groups in Ottoman Turkey, and on R. David's need to defend the validity of the humanist component of his Judeo-Italian culture.

Shevah ha-Nashim is extant in a single manuscript (MS. Parma 1395) known to Jewish bibliographers by the late nineteenth century. Adolph Neubauer published a segment of it but mistakenly attributed it to R. David's father, R. Judah Messer Leon.[30] This erroneous attribution was perpetuated during the twentieth century, despite the accessibility of the manuscript,[31] which Moritz Steinschneider correctly credited *Shevah ha-Nashim* to R. David.

Steinschneider also placed the work in its proper literary context — the debate over the merits and demerits of women, and considered it one of the major works on the subject. That debate had appeared in Hebrew as early as 1200 C.E. in Christian Spain, and continued in various poetic forms for nearly five centuries until last heard in late seventeenth century Italy.[32] Based on the numerous Greek, Roman, and Patristic sources cited in the text, Steinschneider observed that R. David was a typical "representative of the Renaissance," and that "his culture was a typical Italian one."

Other modern historians, although mistakenly attributing *Shevah ha-Nashim* to R. David's father, used it to demonstrate the impact of the Italian Renaissance on the culture of the Italian Jewish minority. Its citations of non-Jewish sources show Renaissance Jews' high awareness of, and involvement in, the renewed interest in antiquity. (A citation implies not only that the author recognized it but that the intended audience had at least passing familiarity with it as well.) Similarly, scholars used R. David ben Judah's discussion of Petrarch's love for Laura to illustrate the newly acquired aesthetic preference of Renaissance Italian Jews. R. David's very admiration for Petrarch was cited as evidence for the impact of the Renaissance on Jewish literary conventions.[33] However, a look at the circumstances under which R. David ben Judah wrote *Shevah ha-Nashim,* as well as a study of the text itself, shows that the picture is much more complex than merely "borrowing from," or being "influenced by," the culture of the Italian Renaissance.

R. David wrote *Shevah ha-Nashim* to a particular Jewish lady in Italy to whom he had previously composed poetry, now lost, on the subject of women:

> I have quickly remembered you, my patroness among women, and wished to carry out your order which you had commanded me while I was there—to elaborate on the tales in praise of women included in the tercets I had composed, because I referred to them briefly; and I have agreed to answer your request, because, even though "many daughters have done valiantly" [Proverbs 31:29] in importance, good taste, and knowledge, "you have excelled them all" *[ibid.].* Since "you have striven with divine beings," [Genesis 32:29] He has made you a patroness; and now I shall fulfill your wish so that "you may give me your innermost blessing" [Genesis 27:19]" and I will remain alive thanks to you" [Genesis 12:13].[34]

The word for "my patroness," *sarati,* suggests that this lady was either R. David's direct benefactor or the wife of his patron. As noted above in Chapter Two, we cannot identify R. David's patrons for sure, but R. David had probably worked as a private tutor/rabbi in the home of the da Pisa family in Florence, and his patroness could well have been Laura, the wife of Samuel ben Yehiel da Pisa. (Samuel was the son of the banker Yehiel of Pisa, who died in 1490, and the brother of Isaac, who succeeded their father Yehiel as *paterfamilias*.) In any event, by answering the woman's request "to elaborate on the tales in praise of women included in the tercets" that he had previously composed, R. David would now position himself to ask her for financial support.

Jewish patronage was a familiar institution in medieval Jewry as early as the tenth century. It originated in Muslim countries and reached its zenith during the eleventh century in Muslim Spain. In fifteenth century Italy, patronage was very common among the Italian Jewish bankers, but it is unlikely that they modeled their conduct after the activities of Spanish Jews. It is more likely that Italian Jews emulated the norms and conduct of their Italian contemporaries.[35]

Accordingly, R. David seeks support a number of times throughout the text. Most explicitly he writes:

> I am not asking you to give me money for the sake of money since it is perishable and insignificant in and of itself, ... but the reason for asking you for some money sufficient for my needs is that money will enable me to dwell in your house forever, so that I will not have to pursue my livelihood. "I choose to dwell in the house of the Lord" rather than live in the company of wicked people [Ps. 84:11] and continue to earn money as most people do.[36]

This passage and others like it suggest that R. David requested his patroness either to send him money in Constantinople or perhaps to employ him again in her household in Italy. His plea reflects a view of patronage as the only viable condition for scholarly life.

So the practical purpose of *Shevah ha-Nashim*—to request financial support—determined its subject matter—the praise of women. A literary debate about the female character had already engaged (male) Jewish intellectuals in the 1490s. R. David had written previously to refute the anti-feminine poem of Abraham Sarteano titled *Sone ha-Nashim* ("The Misogynist"). Unfortunately, that earlier response to Sarteano has not survived, but two others have: one by Abigdor of Fano, the other by Benjamin de Genazzano.[37] So a traditional   genre—biblical   commentary—and   a   contemporary debate—women—provide R. David the framework and pretext for a laudatory composition, namely, an adulation of the excellent character, fine intellect, and exemplary conduct of R. David's once, and hopefully future, patroness.

R. David suggests the analogy between the biblical model and the Italian Jewish patroness in the opening paragraph.[38] The model becomes increasingly apparent as the work progresses, and toward the end David dispels any doubt concerning the identity of his true Woman of Valor. He turns the consonants of *hayil* (valor) into an acronym for *Hemdat Ya'acov Laura* (the beauty of Jacob [is] Laura) or *Hakhamah Yafah Laura* (Laura [is] wise [and] beautiful).[39] Laura is thus the name of R. David's Jewish benefactor, and Jacob is either her father or a generic term designating the Jewish people. Whether by coincidence or not, "Laura" also makes a connection to Petrarch's Laura, whom R. David considered to be a real person (she presumably lived in Avignon) and not an abstract virtue.

Shevah ha-Nashim is therefore not simply a general treatise in favor of women. Rather, it is a laudatory composition to and about a particular, actual woman, describing her as the manifestation of feminine excellence, and written with the hope and expectation of monetary reward.

Defense of the Studia Humanitatis

R. David had long cultivated a passion toward the cultural treasures of the Greco-Roman world. The language and literature of antiquity intoxicated him. He valued them not only for their own sake but also as essential elements in the intellectual development of Jewish scholars. For R. David, as for the Italian humanists, classicism entailed a new attitude toward rhetoric. They no longer perceived rhetoric as the arid study of medieval *trivium,* akin to logic and dialectic, but as a noble and creative art characterizing man at his best.[40] Similarly, the ideal of eloquence fueled R. David's interest in classical poetry and poetic theory. He cherished the aesthetic achievements of classical poets, particularly Ovid and Virgil.[41]

R. Judah Messer Leon had written the first Hebrew manual on rhetoric, *Nofet Zufim* (published in 1475-76). Like his father, R. David insisted that eloquence could arise from the harmonious union of wisdom and style, of form and content.[42] Accordingly, the study of rhetoric and poetry could not be separated from the broader pursuits of wisdom. Father and son, along with other Italian humanists, believed that the good orator must be proficient in all branches of human knowledge. In uniting wisdom and eloquence, the Renaissance man attempted to achieve the ideal of *homo universalis,* the Hebrew *hakham kolel.*

For R. David this humanist vision demanded a change in the traditional Jewish curriculum. Wisdom required rigorous training not only in rabbinics but also in the liberal arts, philosophy, and medicine (which constituted medieval Jewish rationalism). Eloquence would be achieved through the *studia humanitatis* which extolled classical oratory and poetry. So in the name of *hakham kolel* R. David called for the study of medieval rationalism and Renaissance humanism. Other Jews in Constantinople vehemently rejected this call. In *Shevah ha-Nashim* R. David defined the debate as follows:

> whether the use and study of books about nature, books of *halaẓah* known as rhetoric, books of poetry and poetic theory written by people who were not of the religion of Israel, is proper and acceptable for rabbis and scholars.[43]

We can surmise the charges of R. David's opponents from his response. First, classical literature was essentially secular; it focused on human affairs rather than on divine revelation. Its secularist nature makes it unfit for Jewish study and could distract Jews from their true spiritual objective—the knowledge of God. Second, pagan literature was potentially subversive because it was "untrue." Poetic license permitted fictitious situations, or entities, which did not correspond to reality. Such figurative language could lead the believer away from the quest for Truth, whose ultimate objective is God. Third, classical literature, whether pagan or Christian, consists of heretical views which conflict with the tenets of Judaism. To study this literature, or worse, to cite it in sermons, is therefore tantamount to heresy. In short, R. David's opponents deemed classical literature incompatible with, indeed subversive to, Jewish religious society.

To some extent this controversy was one more chapter in the ongoing conflict of "Athens and Jerusalem." In the Middle Ages the conflict had centered on the compatibility of Aristotelian philosophy, as mediated by Muslim philosophers, with Jewish faith. By the end of the twelfth century, Maimonides had ingeniously integrated Greek philosophy and Jewish religion, although his delicate synthesis continued to be challenged in subsequent generations. By the end of the fifteenth century, Jewish rationalist tradition had so absorbed Greek philosophy that it had become far less subversive, and even palatable. By R. David's day, however, no such absorption had yet occurred of the poetry, oratory, geography, history, and letters of classical antiquity, all introduced to Jews through Renaissance humanism. These subjects, if not philosophy, still seemed to threaten Jewish traditional values, at least in Constantinople if not in Italy.

As a result of all this, R. David had to justify his use of classical sources before he could laud his patroness. He marshaled various arguments. First, he attacked his opponents *ad personam,* charging that the real cause of their hostility was an envy of his superior oratorical skills.[44] They were ignorant of the rules of rhetoric developed by Aristotle, Cicero, and Quintilian, and dismissed rhetoric as unworthy of serious study to mask that ignorance. They were reluctant to acquire the knowledge of rhetoric, like their predecessors who refused to study philosophy for fear of encountering the heretical views of Aristotle.[45]

R. David dismisses this reluctance since neither Greek philosophy nor classical rhetoric and poetry pose any real danger to Jewish religiosity:

> Those who despise a certain wisdom do so out of weakness of their intellect which is incapable of encompassing all wisdoms; they do not admit their own deficiency, but, instead, ascribe it to the [disputed] wisdom and say that one need not study it since it is utterly valueless."[46]

R. David's argument was ingenious. He not only attacked his opponents' credibility but he shifted the battle to a more convenient terrain. He purported to share their ideal of scholarly perfection but accused them of interpreting their own ideal too narrowly. His conception was broader and hence better. R. David, and not his opponents (whom he labeled "rabbanites"), was the true *hakham kolel,*[47] because the true *hakham kolel* is not the rabbi confined to rabbinic scholarship alone but the well-rounded scholar, proficient in the rabbinic tradition, the liberal arts, philosophy, medicine, and the humanities.

R. David thus defends *studia humanitatis,* and in particular rhetoric and poetry, in the context of his general defense of secular studies. Erudition in these disciplines does not deter the believer from his ultimate goal—the knowledge of God—but qualifies him to attain that goal. Only the wise man who masters all branches of human knowledge in addition to rabbinic tradition can achieve human perfection, which in turn prepares him for the attainment of religious perfection. Secular studies are thus subordinate to a religious goal; they are not an end in themselves but a means to an end whose essence is religious. Hence, secular studies including the humanities are not subversive to Jewish religious values, but conducive to the actualization of religious life.

R. David laments the limited interest in secular studies, which he blames for a general spiritual decline among the Jews.[48] He also blames the contemporary spiritual malaise upon the exile from the Land of Israel and the constant wandering brought on by persecutions and economic instability.[49] Not by coincidence does that reasoning return R. David to his purpose in writing: to seek financial support which would free him for study and contemplation.

R. David borrowed his second argument for *studia humanitatis* from the arsenal that medieval Jewish philosophers used to defend Aristotle. Human wisdom cannot in principle be subversive, because the Torah itself, the revelation of divine wisdom, contains in seminal form all branches of human knowledge. Torah is thus the supreme blueprint of all knowledge,[50] and no genuine conflict between the divine Torah and any scholarly discipline, including rhetoric and poetry, is possible. Further, as Judah Messer Leon had proved in *Nofet Zufim,* only he who knows rhetoric and poetry recognizes that they were best executed in the divine Torah.[51]

R. David concedes, however, that the sequence of study is critical. A Jew should first master the Torah as interpreted by rabbinic tradition before proceeding to secular disciplines. A fear of God is thereby instilled in the student so that no human wisdom can undermine his divine commitment.[52] R. David thus shows sensitivity to the tension between Jewish traditional learning and secular studies, but believed that tension to be resolvable.

So far R. David has defended the concededly suspect content of the humanities as not subversive, but subordinate to and supportive of Jewish religiosity. He next disputes that the humanities contain any substantive content at all. These disciplines do not teach a particular doctrine, rather only a technique of eloquent speech. As such they merely embellish rabbinic content, and make it more palatable to the audience.[53] Accordingly, rhetoric and poetry are particularly useful for "scholars, preachers, and leaders."

R. David thus combines two prevailing conceptions of rhetoric, one as the art of ornamentation, the other as the art of communication and persuasion. He recommends that Jewish preachers be versed in rhetorical art to enhance their effectiveness as teachers of the divine Torah. They can use classical rhetoric and poetry in Jewish homilies to further their teaching of the divine. A rabbi can best apply eloquence to communal purposes.

Interestingly, R. David finds support for this non-content-oriented view of classical rhetoric and poetry in the writings of the Church Fathers, particularly St. Augustine's *De Doctrina Christiana (The Christian Doctrine)* and Lactantius' *Divinae Institutiones (Divine Institutes)*. The Italian humanists early in the fifteenth century took the same course when faced with the same dilemma, namely, how a Christian believer could study pagan writings. As Christian thinkers, the Italian humanists followed the Church Fathers of late antiquity, who were challenged by the popularity of pagan rhetoric and Ciceronian theories even as late as the fourth century. The nascent Church's critical agenda was to provide a Christian framework for a society embedded in a pagan culture. Rhetoric and pagan culture in general were perceived to divert the believer from spiritual to earthly ends, from the Word of God to the word of man. Christian apologists thus heatedly debated the fate of rhetoric, an integral part of Greco-Roman culture.[54]

R. David had studied the writings of the early Church Fathers, which enjoyed new favor in Renaissance Italy. He found their predicament very similar to his own in Constantinople. Both responded to the perception of pagan literature as a threat to religion. R. David primarily followed Augustine's solution of adopting pagan rhetoric as a tool in the ministry.[55] Most Christian apologists were reluctant to acknowledge publicly the worth of Roman cultural heritage, even while they exploited it. Augustine, by contrast, elevated rhetoric to a necessary study in order for the Christian believer to understand the ways God expresses Himself. The art of rhetoric was thus added to the means of interpreting the divine word. Augustine valued the study of rhetoric as much as the study of Scripture itself, and opposed those who would deprive the Church of this useful tool in the work of winning souls. R. David also found in Lactantius an apologist who recognized the Christian preachers's dilemma. He paraphrased a section of *Divine Institutes* advising the preacher to use rhetorical devices to ornament "the naked Christian truth" and to make it more acceptable to pagan listeners.[56]

R. David then buttresses his arguments for the legitimacy of the humanities within Jewish tradition with examples of biblical and rabbinic figures known to be versed in them. The most notable Biblical example is King Solomon, who R. David claims encompassed all wisdoms and thus actualized the Renaissance ideal of *hakham kolel*.[57] King Solomon allegedly knew physics, astronomy, astrology, rhetoric, poetry, and music.[58] Likewise, R. David claims that Judah the Patriarch, the redactor of the Mishnah, was well versed not only in "the Torah, which is the true Kabbalah," but also in philosophy and medicine.[59] The Tannaim and Amoraim in general espoused scholarly versatility and encouraged the study of physics, astronomy, logic, and dialectic, as much as they appreciated rhetoric, poetry, and music. Hillel the Elder, Judah bar 'Ilay and Samuel bar Nahmani enjoyed the beauty of singing and dancing (in other words, the merits of music), and Yohanan ben Zakkai was an accomplished poet and orator.[60]

R. David emphasizes that even the Palestinian Talmud sanctions the study of rhetoric, by forbidding preaching in public "unless one is an accomplished poet, well versed in poetics, and has a quick and lucid tongue." Even the scholars of the Palestinian Talmud were not ignorant of secular studies; they were steeped in the knowledge of medicine and had a special appreciation for rhetoric.[61] R. David recounts the aggadah about the Roman procurator favoring R. Joshua ben Levi for his superb oratorical skills. In short, both Torah and rabbinic sources endorse secular studies, including rhetoric, poetry, and music, so R. David's opponents in Constantinople cannot validly reject them in the name of tradition.

Having legitimated the study of classical literature per se within Jewish religion, R. David turns to rebut the second charge: that its content is not factually correct. Poets and orators mention "things which are not [yet] real but have the potential of becoming real, since they are not [logically] impossible."[62] In other words, even if poets and orators depict images which the senses have not observed, they do not violate the laws of reality, since they do restrict themselves to the logically possible. R. David distinguishes the naturally impossible (e.g., the parting of the Red Sea) from the logically impossible (e.g., squaring a circle). The naturally impossible was permitted. For example, Ovid's *Metamorphoses* repeatedly speaks of the "transformation of one body into another,"[63] which medievals believed to be logically possible. R. David cites *Metamorphoses* as an illustration of poetic figurative expression.[64]

Ironically, R. David justifies the logical coherence of poetic metamorphosis by noting its similarity to the Kabbalist doctrine of metempsychosis. The "Kabbalists ... believe in transmigration of souls from human beings to animals according to the [principle] of punishing sinful acts."[65] If Kabbalah and pagan poetry share such an important principle, why should the study of pagan poetry be forbidden? This astonishing comment shows the eagerness of a Jewish thinker to harmonize very different intellectual traditions. It might also explain in part the tendency of Renaissance Italian thinkers to integrate pagan religious mysteries and Kabbalah.[66]

R. David asserts alternatively that poetry does not purport to represent reality accurately but rather to embellish it. To study what exists, one needs to study not rhetoric and poetry but physics and metaphysics. "Poetry is fictitious in and of itself, but it gives pleasure in its style and meter."[67] R. David clearly enjoyed the aesthetic beauty of classical poetry and did not see how it could impinge upon his religious loyalty. For this Italian rabbi, the joy of the beauty of words was quite natural. Other Italian rabbis also expressed their fascination with the beautiful, whether in music, dancing, or painting. Jews in Renaissance Italy reveled in the creativity of their contemporaries. This refined aesthetic sensitivity necessarily involved Jews in their surrounding culture, which the more insular Constantinople Jews rejected.

The third charge against R. David's use of literary sources was that they exposed their reader to heretical views. To rebut it, R. David argues that a Jew may read books by non-Jews for two reasons. First, one must become acquainted with their false opinions in order to reject them. By exposing their false nature, the Jewish reader strengthens his convictions in the superiority of his own religion. Second, one may read non-Jewish authors for the useful information found in their books or for the beauty of their writing.[68] In short, reading a non-Jewish text does not necessitate adopting heretical views, and may help demonstrate Judaism's superiority. The Christian Church Fathers (e.g., Lactantius, Jerome, and Augustine) pose no danger to the Jewish reader, since they themselves publicly acknowledged the superiority of Moses' divine revelation. R. David's treatment of Patristic views of Judaism is thus both partial and inaccurate. Employing their arguments against paganism, he claims that reading the Church Fathers poses no doctrinal danger to Jewish believers.

To conclude his defense of classical literature, R. David asserts that the ancient pagan and Christian authors, as much as their rabbinic counterparts, cherished the pursuit of wisdom. He cites a long list of classical authors who either advocated in their writings, or embodied in their lives, the perpetual quest for wisdom. With no clear organizing principle, R. David quotes Aristotle, Seneca, Cicero, Hermes Trismegistus, Jerome, Macrobius, Valerius Maximus, Plutarch, Boethius, Pliny the Elder, Lactantius, and Quintilian—all in support of the ideal of *hakham kolel.*[69]

So as a rabbi who followed Ashkenazi halakhah, R. David felt totally at liberty to enjoy the literary treasures of the classical world. He held ancient authors in great esteem and regarded their writings as instructive, albeit not authoritative. He read these texts critically and used them selectively whenever they could corroborate the truth of Judaism, and especially to teach eloquence. He did not view them as subversive to his Jewish religiosity or as undermining his firm conviction in the superiority of the Chosen People. Yet Renaissance humanism never took root in Constantinople Jewish society, so R. David's cultural orientation remained discordant and cost him his job.

The Ideal Woman

His extended apologium complete, R. David ben Judah Messer Leon turns to the ostensible subject matter of his treatise—the praise of women. His treatment of female excellence further discloses his involvement in Renaissance humanism. He asserts that all illustrations of exemplary women, whether in Greek and Roman mythology, Petrarch's poetry, or the Bible, are references to real, historical figures. This concretization contrasts with an allegorization common among both Jews and non-Jews during the Middle Ages. It and R. David's attendant willingness to consider human activities in their mundane context mark him as a Renaissance humanist.

R. David's treatment of Greek and Roman women (fol. 115r-115v) was hardly original to Renaissance Italy. He alludes in passing to three subjects of Boccaccio's *De Claris Mulieribus,* an anthology of 108 tales of famous ancient women, written between 1355 and 1359.[70] R. David then incorporates an extensive passage from *De Claris Mulieribus* about a fourth woman. Although R. David does not credit his source, a textual comparison leaves no room for doubt.[71] Nor was Boccaccio original; he collected his material from such available classical sources as Josephus Flavius, Saint Justin, Lactantius, Livy, Ovid, Pliny the Elder, Tacitus and Valerius

Maximus.[72] R. David had studied these authors in detail, so he might have borrowed from them even without Boccaccio's help. However, the very popularity of *De Claris Mulieribus* may have prompted R. David to address the subject of women in the first place.

Although Boccaccio wrote *De Claris Mulieribus* for a conventional medieval purpose, namely, to teach, his attitude toward the ancient world departed from convention. He attempted not merely to compile facts about old literary figures but instead to show that ancient myths, previously misinterpreted, contain much universal truth in their sentiments, ideals, and beliefs. At least by implication, that attempt placed classical myth on a par with Holy Writ and let pagan wisdom challenge Catholic teachings. Nonetheless, Boccaccio begat a literary movement. *De Claris Mulieribus* was immensely popular throughout the fifteenth century, and various minor Italian humanists wrote imitative anthologies of ancient women.[73] Accordingly, the debate about women that preoccupied fifteenth century Jewish intellectuals merely reflects the popularity that Boccaccio inspired among the Italian literati.

R. David's borrowing from Boccaccio is significant to our understanding of Renaissance Jewish humanism for two reasons. First, it shows that R. David's intended reader, an Italian Jewish woman, must have been conversant in classical mythology; otherwise the references would have made no sense to her. Second, R. David's (and presumably his patroness's) familiarity with Boccaccio's work is representative of a general interest among Italian Jews in biographies.[74] Like other Italian humanists, Jews and non-Jews alike, R. David avidly read the biographies of Plutarch and Pliny the Younger.[75] In fact, the rekindling of such interest in Renaissance Italy generally led Jewish authors to adopt this genre, writing about either biblical figures or near contemporaries. For example, Yohanan Alemanno composed a biography of King Solomon in his *Shir ha-Ma'alot li-Shelomo* (The Song of Solomon's Ascents), and Baruch Uzziel Forti (Hazketto) wrote a biography of Isaac Abravanel. Although R. David did not write a biography per se, his interest in ancient lives was undeniable. He discussed anecdotes about Plato, Pythagoras, Demosthenes, and Appolonius which he probably found in classical biographies.[76]

Petrarch's biography *De Viris Illustribus* probably inspired R. David's interest in classical figures. R. David memorized Petrarch's poetry. His unreserved admiration for Petrarch dominates *Shevah ha-Nashim*. There he praises Petrarch's poetry as the best ever written and imitates Petrarch's style in his own poems.[77] He quotes the first lines of several of Petrarch's sonnets,[78] and cites by name the *De Vita Solitaria* and the *De Remediis Utriusque Fortunae*.[79] Finally, R. David disputes the common interpretation that Petrarch's beloved Laura was an allegory of the virtues modesty, submissiveness, love, and charity, or the abstract entity poetry.[80] He argues instead that Laura was a real, earthly woman whom Petrarch met at a given time and place, namely, on 6 March 1327 in Avignon. If Petrarch's ideal classical Laura was real and not allegorical, then, understandably, so was R. David's ideal Jewish Laura.

In the last section of *Shevah ha-Nashim* (fols. 115r-fols. 121v), R. David finally discusses the Bible. He begins by rejecting earlier philosophic commentaries of Proverbs—particularly Joseph ibn Caspi's—which approach the biblical text as metaphysical teachings couched in allegorical language.[81] Instead, R. David insists on reading the Hymn for the Woman of Valor literally, as a practical guide for proper conduct, which he considers to be the intended purpose of Proverbs generally. In other words, R. David's commentary on Proverbs is itself a treatise in moral philosophy, as befitting a Renaissance humanist. By denying the allegorical meaning of the biblical text, R. David can depict the ideal woman in concrete terms. He shifts the discourse from the heavenly sphere to the earthly domain.

According to R. David's reading of the hymn, the ideal woman combines good character, rational conduct, acute business skills, and a passion for learning. Her major concerns are her husband and family, all of whom she manages with superb organizational skills. She provides for their needs without waste or indulgence.[82] She is a hardworking, diligent, and thrifty manager who strives for self-sufficiency.[83] She weaves her household's clothing (as the literal meaning of the biblical text indicates) and sells the surplus in the market (R. David's expansion of the biblical description). She invests the proceeds of her sales in real estate,[84] thus guaranteeing an acceptable standard of living for her family and freeing her husband to devote his time to learning.[85] (We recall R. David's original purpose in writing *Shevah ha-Nashim*.) Although her family is the focus of her concern, it does not consume all her interest. She generously provides for the needs of others, and her philanthropy is without guilt or resentment.[86] In accordance with her good character, she is always loyal, cheerful, and supportive to her husband, regardless of external circumstances. She derives her own pleasure from the well-being of her family and from her own intellectual growth. She is well versed in Torah and secular studies,[87] and educates her children to a life of Torah and good deeds.

It is hard to determine just how much this female ideal resembles the real Laura to whom R. David dedicated the composition. The description could conceivably have fit any female member of the small oligarchy within the Italian Jewish community.[88] Clearly R. David was motivated to aggrandize his portrayal because he was writing to ask for money. What is crucial, however, is not the accuracy of this portrayal; rather it is R. David's shift of the discourse from the metaphysical to the physical, from the domain of eternal truths to the realm of human activity. This shift was fostered by Renaissance historiography, and it marks R. David as a Renaissance humanist. His ability to consider the human dimension of past exempla distinguishes him from previous medieval commentators. This by no means indicates that R. David articulated a full-fledged philosophy of history. Although R. David continued to interpret Jewish history within the traditional thesis of divine activity, he could view Proverbs as a treatise in moral philosophy.

To conclude, an examination of R. David ben Judah Messer Leon's *Shevah ha-Nashim* demonstrates that there were Italian Jewish humanists during the fifteenth and sixteenth centuries. Renaissance Jewish humanism as exemplified by R. David ben Judah Messer Leon does not mean a new philosophy of Man, or a radically new world view. Nor does it stand for individualism, secularism or enlightenment, because these concepts are simply inapplicable to that period. Instead, Jewish humanism means a new assessment of the humanities as necessary studies for the attainment of religious perfection. The humanities were not to be studied as a substitute for either medieval rationalism or rabbinic Judaism but as an enrichment of Jewish curriculum. The humanities, especially rhetoric and poetry, were viewed as a tool for the proper training of the rabbinic scholar expected to assume leadership within the Jewish community.

To generalize from R. David's experience, Renaissance Jewish humanism was a distinct Italian phenomenon which could exist only within the Appenine peninsula. In Italy, and there only, Jewish intellectuals such as Judah Messer Leon and his son R. David blended a unique syncretism of Ashkenazic legalism, Maimonidean rationalism, medieval scholasticism and Renaissance humanism. This amalgam of seemingly contradictory trends was challenged when Italian Jews exported it to their new homes in the Ottoman Empire. R. David was among the few known Italian intellectuals who rose to defend the legitimacy of their culture. This defense provides us a glimpse of both the communal disputes among Ottoman Jews and the culture of Italian Jews.

We have no information about the results of R. David's plea for support, or even whether *Shevah ha-Nashim* ever reached its intended recipient. We do know, however, that shortly after R. David wrote it, Romanyot leaders in Constantinople asked him to support R. Moses Capsali—a story told in the next chapter. A few years later (about 1504) R. David appears in Salonika as the *Marbiz Torah* of the Calabrian congregation.[89] It was in Salonika that Menahem ben Joseph Ottolenghi copied *Shevah ha-Nashim*, thereby preserving this text for posterity and enabling us to gain insight into the colorful life of Jewish immigrants in the Ottoman Empire.[90] R. David's later life and works further indicate the growing dominance of Sephardic culture and R. David's frustration at his own inability to curb it. Despite R. David's protestation, Jews living outside Italy could not sustain the decidedly Italian component of R. David's heritage, namely, the humanist *paideia*.

4

Communal Tensions

Inter-communal tensions frequently erupted into open controversies as Ottoman Jewry struggled to consolidate its collective identity. R. David ben Judah became involved in three such controversies, in addition to the loss of his Constantinople pulpit discussed in the preceding chapter. They provide us with a glimpse into the political, legal, and cultural concerns of Ottoman Jewry at the turn of the sixteenth century.

Supporting the Romanyot Leader

In 1497 the leaders of the Sephardic congregation first publicly challenged the authority of the chief Romanyot rabbi in Constantinople, the aged Moses Capsali.[1] The precipitating cause was R. Capsali's ruling concerning the *suddar,* a Sephardic overcoat brought from Spain. R. Capsali assembled the rabbis and judges of the Sephardic congregations in town and decreed that the overcoat should not be worn at all. He reasoned that it should not be worn on Shabbat because wearing it constituted carrying of articles forbidden on Shabbat, and that it should not be worn in general as it violated the prohibition on imitating non-Jews.

The Sephardic rabbis, then relative newcomers to Constantinople, did not challenge R. Capsali at the assembly itself but later found it difficult to enforce his decree among their congregants. They then continued to pay at least public lip service to R. Capsali's jurisdiction over them, and to his rabbinic competence, but they did attack the decree itself. They argued that the garment did not violate the Sabbath because it was decorative only and not worn for any practical purpose, and that it no more imitated non-Jewish attire than other clothing worn by the Romanyots.

The Romanyots then asked R. David to support R. Capsali, among others, which raises several interesting questions. If Constantinople congregations were essentially autonomous, what impact would an opinion by an Italian rabbi have in a dispute between Romanyots and Sephardim? What authority did R. David possess while still so young, particularly in support of an elder such as Capsali? Since R. David's stand on humanism had already cost him his own pulpit, why would R. Capsali seek help from one whose own status was tarnished? Unfortunately, the few extant sources of our knowledge about this controversy provide no clear answers.

At first reluctant to get involved, R. David finally issued a lengthy legal opinion in defense of the decree. That raises more questions. Why did R. David get involved at all in an issue that did not concern him personally or even Italian Jews generally? Why did he side with R. Capsali, whom any astute politician could see to be losing power to the Sephardic immigrants? Finally, why did R. David write a more vehement opinion than even the Romanyot Rabbi Elijah Mizrahi (whose comments are found in the margins of R. David's response)? Again we can only speculate about the answers.

Curiously, R. David's father had fallen into a similar controversy many years earlier in Italy, over the *cappa,* an outer garment worn as a mark of distinction by physicians who had obtained doctoral degrees.[2] R. Judah Messer Leon wore the *cappa* and faced accusations of imitating non-Jews. He was supported in his defense by Joseph Colon, the French halakhist. The similarity apparently ends, for although the father wore and defended the *cappa,* the son did not wear a *suddar* and did attack its use.

The real issue under seige, however, was the same in both cases: not the wearing of an exotic garment, but rabbinic authority itself. R. Capsali's attitude toward Ottoman Jewry resembled R. Judah Messer Leon's earlier aspirations to be recognized as the leader of Italian Jewry. R. David may have supported R. Capsali on this specific issue out of general respect and approval of central rabbinic authority. Further, R. David's Ashkenazic legal orientation made him a natural ally of the Romanyot scholars against the Sephardim, and his responsum expresses animosity toward the Sephardim and an attempt to dissociate himself from them.[3] R. David considered Sephardic Jews ill-trained in halakhah and prone to religious laxity in general, and throughout his life in the Ottoman Empire, R. David exhibited marked hostility toward them. R. David's conduct in this and future controversies supports non-Sephardic rabbinic authority, exemplified in the Ashkenazic institution of rabbinic ordination.

In any event, R. David issued a threefold defense of R. Capsali's ban of the *suddar*. First, even the Sephardic rabbis conceded that Capsali was the chief rabbi of Constantinople; as such his decrees should be honored per se and not depend on anyone else's agreement or disagreement with his halakhic analysis. Second, Capsali was halakhically correct concerning the *suddar* in particular, for which R. David cites many talmudic precedents. Third, the rule of conflict resolution that local custom prevails should apply in this conflict to uphold a Romanyot practice (actually the absence of a practice) over that of newcomers.[4]

R. David's support for R. Capsali proved to be politically short-sighted. The Romanyot leader's death a short time later helped undermine the status of the Constantinople Chief Rabbinate as well as Romanyot political power in general, and Sephardic influence in the Ottoman capital grew steadily.

It is unclear how long R. David remained in Constantinople; our last dated information about him is from 1498.[5] By 1504 we find him in Salonika, the *Marbiz Torah* of the Calabrian congregation. Other contemporary sources lament the low status of scholars in Constantinople as well, which might have led R. David to leave. R. Elijah Mizrahi, for example, complains about the general public's total neglect of scholarship and preference for material gain over Torah study (a not uncommon complaint in our own day):[6]

> Torah and its scholars were spurned, and the fools and illiterates who have never seen the light of Torah felt that their stupidity and lacking were perfections and the perfections of others were stupidity.[7]

At one point Romanyot scholars even went on strike, during which they stopped teaching Torah publicly. Some, R. David among them, left to pursue scholarly opportunity elsewhere.

Marbiz Torah in Salonika

No town in the Ottoman Empire of the early sixteenth century, except Safed in the Land of Israel, could offer a better intellectual climate than Salonika. Its Jewish community had grown remarkably after the expulsion from Spain in 1492. Romanyot Jews had flourished in Salonika under Byzantine rule,[8] but Sultan Mehmet II, as noted above, had deported them in 1454-1460 to help rebuild Constantinople. Immigrants from Spain, Portugal, Sicily, Italy, Provençe, Germany, and North Africa replaced the Romanyots in a stream that continued throughout the sixteenth century, particularly after the Lisbon Massacre of 1506,[9] and the coming of the Inquisition to Portugal in 1536.[10] Among the newcomers to Salonika were many Marranos who publicly reembraced Judaism. By mid-century Salonika held some twenty thousand Jews, a majority of its entire population.

Commerce attracted Jews to Salonika. Its location in northern Greece, at the intersection of land and sea routes, made Salonika an international trade and transshipment center for such items as wool, textiles, glasswares, precious stones, and leather.[11] The Jewish immigrants could benefit from already-established business contacts among Jews (many of whom were Marranos) in France, Flanders, Egypt, North Africa, and Italy. Some of the wealthy aristocratic Sephardic families, for example, the Abravanels, the Benvenistes, and the ibn Yaishs settled in Salonika and rebuilt their businesses in international trade. Many others were engaged in silver and gold mining and in crafts, primarily related to the wool industry and to jewelry. In short, Salonika enjoyed an economic boom during the sixteenth century, and Jews were its major beneficiaries.

Unlike their counterparts in Constantinople, the newcomers to Salonika did not have to contend with a well-established local Romanyot presence. Consequently, they were free to develop their institutions without regard to any strong local precedent. They nonetheless organized themselves into congregations similar to those in Constantinople: autonomous units, divided by country of members' origin, conducting their legal, social, and cultural affairs with little intervention either from the Ottoman government or from other Jewish congregations.[12] And as in Constantinople, congregations suffered frequent divisions; their number more than doubled by the end of the sixteenth century, reaching more than two dozen.

On the one hand these frequent divisions resulted in great variety of lifestyle, but on the other hand they made the administration of public affairs very difficult. During the sixteenth century, Salonikan Jewry had to develop a supercommunal government to address communal affairs that crossed congregational lines. A small representative group of rabbinic scholars from various congregations acted as a regulatory body for the various congregations in regard to assessment and payment of governmental taxes, communal education, and a variety of religious matters.[13]

Economic prosperity in Salonika increased cultural activity. Salonika boasted unprecedented intellectual creativity in a variety of disciplines: biblical exegesis, halakhah, homiletics, poetry, philosophy, science, and Kabbalah. Hacker cites the following factors to explain this creative surge.[14] First, the Sephardic immigrants introduced the printing press to Salonika (as they did in Constantinople). Jews were of course already literate; the Hebrew press disseminated knowledge to broad segments of the Jewish community who eagerly awaited printed editions of works by contemporary and past authors. Second, private and public libraries were established in which manuscripts and printed editions were assembled for the first time under one roof, giving scholars and students easier access to the entire gamut of rabbinic and medieval literature. Third, wealthy Jewish families were highly interested in education. They supported educational institutions and individuals, they financed the printing of books and collection of manuscripts, and they regarded study per se as a worthy life-long pursuit. They thereby created a very hospitable atmosphere for learning, reminiscent of their forefathers' experience in Spain and Portugal before the expulsion.

Fourth, Jewish education was democratized. It was transformed from an activity reserved for the wealthy few to a popular enterprise open to rich and poor alike. While the wealthy continued to instruct their own children privately, they also funded public education for the less affluent. The language of instruction was not Hebrew but Ladino, the Judeo-Spanish dialect that was the vernacular among Salonikan Jews. Difficult subjects such as philosophy and law were codified and systematized to facilitate teaching. Thousands of Jewish children received their training in Salonika's Talmud Torah, one of the earliest public schools in Europe.

While the masses of younger students were taught in the Talmud Torah school, rabbinic study at the highest levels was concentrated at the academies, or yeshivot. Each yeshivah held only ten or so regular adult students. Most yeshivot were founded through endowments from private donors who supported their members for life, and many congregations supported more than one yeshivah. Members taught Torah and Talmud and arbitrated litigation in the Jewish court adjunct to the yeshivah. Then, as now, private donors exerted control over the yeshivah's internal affairs, including the selection of its scholars.

We have a firsthand description of the Sephardic academies in Salonika and the brilliant scholarly competition which occurred within them.[15] The Sephardic scholars brought with them to Salonika an elaborate method of Talmud study, developed in the years prior to the expulsion from Spain, through which students became active innovators of halakhah while engaged in the give and take of talmudic dialectic. Sephardic talmudic dialectic *(hilluq)* differed from the Ashkenazic *pilpul* in that it developed under the impact of philosophic argumentation.[16] Sephardic halakhah flourished in the sixteenth century in Salonika and throughout the Ottoman Empire.

There were many disputes between the Sephardim and Ashkenazim over various legal and religious practices. Still, in Salonika more than in Constantinople, we find collaboration and cross-fertilization between Sephardim and Ashkenazim, perhaps because they were all newcomers and thus no single group was established when the others arrived. The Sephardim even came to recognize the Ashkenazic practice of rabbinic ordination, and the Ashkenazic method of *pilpul* made its impact on Sephardic methods of talmudic learning. Ashkenazic scholars taught in Sephardic academies and vice versa.[17] This cultural and ethnic diversity of Salonikan Jewry gradually faded as the Sephardim became dominant.

A long list of distinguished Sephardic scholars made sixteenth century Salonika a vibrant, creative center of Jewish learning whose influence extended throughout the Ottoman Empire. Among the most noted were R. Samuel Franco, R. Joseph Taitazak, R. Joseph Fasi, R. Jacob ibn Habib, R. David ibn Yahya, R. Moses Cordovero, his brother-in-law, R. Shlomo Alkabez, R. Isaac Caro, and his nephew, R. Joseph Caro. Lesser known were R. Meir 'Arama, R. Shlomo Halevi, R. Moses Almosnino, R. Samuel Ozida and R. Joseph Taitazak's students, R. Isaac Aderbi and R. Isaac Aroyo. These scholars and many others brought with them the rich rationalist tradition of medieval Spain and Provençe. Liberal arts and philosophy flourished. Many rabbinic scholars studied logic, grammar, mathematics, geometry, astronomy, medicine, physics, and metaphysics, and the lay intelligentsia followed with interest works published in these disciplines.

Contrary to a widely held belief, the cultural orientation of the Sephardim in Salonika was decidedly rationalist rather than Kabbalistic; Kabbalah was only a secondary program of study.[18] Yet some Sephardic scholars did question the limits of philosophy and its legitimacy within Jewish traditional society as part of their reflection about the expulsion from Spain. This in turn would lead to renewal of the Maimonidean Controversy during the first decade of the sixteenth century, to be discussed below.

R. David's move to Salonika was well advised. His own philosophic training created a commonality of interest with the Sephardim, despite his earlier leanings to the Ashkenazic tradition noted in Chapter Two above. He became the *Marbiẓ Torah* (literally, teacher of Torah) in the Sephardic congregation founded by immigrants from Calabria in 1497, succeeding R. Jacob ibn Habib, who retired.[19] Many in the congregation had come to Calabria only after their expulsion from Sicily in 1493. R. David soon earned a reputation as a penetrating talmudic scholar who excelled in *pilpul*, as well as a great philosopher, theologian, and biblical exegete. R. David Hacohen of Corfu, a contemporary, called R. David "the comprehensive scholar, the great man, a bright light, whose name is known in the city gates, and who treats all subjects: Bible, Mishna and Gemara."[20] Another contemporary, R. Elijah Mizrahi, also called R. David "the comprehensive scholar," and cites his "sharp *pilpul* and broad Talmudic erudition."[21]

In Salonika, about 1508, R. David wrote an important work still extant: *'Ein ha-Qore,* a commentary on Moses Maimonides' *The Guide of the Perplexed,* to be discussed below.[22] With R. David's outstanding erudition in the classics, Christian scholasticism, and the entire medieval Judeo-Muslim philosophic tradition, *'Ein ha-Qore* became a virtual encyclopedia to intellectual writers of his day. He freely cites non-Jewish sources for support: Plato, Aristotle, Aristotle's Hellenistic commentators—Alexander of Aphrodisias and Themestius, Galen, Ptolemy, John Philoponus—the Kalam school of Muslim theologians, Alfarabi, ibn Sina, ibn Rushd, ibn Bajja, ibn Tufayl, Saint Thomas, and Duns Scotus. He also cites virtually every significant Jewish philosopher, among them Saadia Gaon, David Almuqamaz, Judah Halevi, Abraham ibn 'Ezra, Solomon ibn Gabirol, Samuel ibn Tibbon, Yedaya Bedersi, Isaac Albalag, Joseph ibn Caspi, Moses Narboni, Profiat Duran, Nissim Gerondi, Hasdai Crescas, Joseph Albo, Zerahya Halevi, Joseph ibn Shem Tov, Abraham Shalom, Abraham Bibago, Isaac 'Arama, and Isaac Abravanel.[23]

'Ein ha-Qore contains references to a host of R. David's other

writings which are lost, such as refutations of Gersonides,[24] Hasdai Crescas,[25] and Joseph Albo,[26] all concerning Maimonides. R. David also refers to now lost treatises in order to clarify specific philosophic questions—for example, a refutation of Aristotle's view of the eternity of the world.[27] In *Mikhtam le-David (Inscription to David)* he discussed the question of the conjunction between the human intellect and God,[28] and in *Nefesh David (The Soul of David)* he discussed the cosmological issues raised by Averroës' *De Substantia Orbis (On the Substance of the Heavenly Sphere; Maamar be-'Ezem ha-Galgal).*[29] R. David refers to a work concerning conjunction of the human intellect with God,[30] apparently based on his commentary to Averroës' *Epistle on the Possibility of Conjunction (Iggeret Efsharut ha-Devequt),* itself a work highly debated among Jewish and Christian philosophers in fifteenth century Italy.[31] R. David also composed either commentaries or glosses on the writings of Abraham ibn 'Ezra[32] and Moses Narboni,[33] two authors he held in great esteem. None of these treatises is extant today. They are known only by name through references in *'Ein ha-Qore.* It is reasonable to conclude that R. David wrote these works in Salonika, but we have no direct evidence of that.

References to these works in *'Ein ha-Qore,* and the broad knowledge of fifteenth century Sephardic philosophers demonstrated in *'Ein ha-Qore,* make clear that R. David's encounter with Sephardic scholars in Salonika stimulated his philosophic activity, and testify to the great cultural impact of the Sephardic immigrants both in Salonika generally and upon R. David in particular. As noted above, the Romanyots had already been deported to Constantinople when the Sephardic immigrants reached Salonika, so the Sephardim became entrenched in Salonika quicker than in Constantinople. R. David felt the need to immerse himself in Sephardic rationalist tradition to defend one of the pillars of his own Italian heritage, namely, Moses Maimonides. R. David's literary activity in Salonika thus was predominantly scholastic. If he wrote other compositions in the mode of Renaissance humanism, they are not extant today. R. David was especially impressed with the works of R. Abraham Bibago and R. Isaac Arama, his older contemporaries from Spain, and R. David's extant writings attest to their marked influence on him.[34]

The Maimonidean Controversy Renewed

Sephardic scholars in the Ottoman Empire pondered the meaning of the expulsion from Spain. Rabbinic Jews have traditionally

responded to catastrophe by subjecting their own conduct and culture
to close scrutiny. They blamed their own imperfect religious observance as the ultimate cause of their suffering; by deviating from the
prescribed path, Jews brought upon themselves the wrath of God who
punished them through persecution and expulsions. In the medieval
Hispano-Jewish community such self-reflection necessarily involved
rethinking the connection between rabbinic Judaism and philosophy,
which was the hallmark of Sephardic culture. Even though Sephardic
Jews cultivated philosophy for several centuries, the study of philosophy was not taken for granted. Internal turmoil or external pressures
would periodically lead Sephardic Jews to ponder the legitimacy of
philosophy in Jewish traditional society.

Moses Maimonides was the very symbol of philosophic pursuit
in medieval Jewish society. From the thirteenth century onward,
whenever Sephardic Jews reflected on the status of philosophy they
debated the legacy of Maimonides. The need to examine the status
of philosophy arose whenever Jews from Mediterranean communities, where philosophy was cultivated, encountered Jews from North
European communities, where philosophy made little impact on Jewish culture, and whenever Hispano-Jewish society experienced a
major catastrophe. Thus the so-called Maimonidean Controversy
errupted repeatedly from the thirteenth to the mid-sixteenth
centuries.[35]

Narrowly perceived, the debate raged over the correct interpretation of Maimonides—that is, what he really meant to say, especially
concerning his harmonization of Greek philosophy and Jewish Law.
Maimonides's supporters regarded him not only as the most profound Jewish thinker since the first Moses but also as the man who
rationally proved the verity of Judaism, thereby elevating it to a
higher intellectual plateau. Maimonides' opponents perceived his
philosophic teachings as a heretical departure from biblical and talmudic tradition and therefore subversive to Judaism as a religious
community. More broadly the debate concerned the status of philosophy and science within traditional Jewish culture, with each subsequent participant attributing to Maimonides his own conclusions. In
this broad sense the Maimonidean Controversy was the ideological
context for articulating Jewish identity, the meaning of Judaism, the
content of Jewish education, and attitudes toward non-Jewish culture. Each time, the peculiar circumstances and players produced
local variations on these constant themes in Jewish intellectual history, which indeed will continue to be debated as long as there are

Jews. A detailed survey of the Maimonidean Controversy goes beyond the scope of this study, but some comments on the renewal of the controversy in the fifteenth century are in order.

The Maimonidean Controversy flared anew after the traumatic events of 1391.[36] Spanish Jewry was then unexpectedly beset by riots that soon turned into massacres of entire Jewish communities throughout Castile and Aragon. Many Jews were forcibly led to the baptismal font; others converted voluntarily, some hoping to return later to their mother religion; and many others fled the country. Anti-Jewish legislation then intensified. Under the leadership of the itinerant preacher Vincent Ferrer, Christian preachers pressured Jews to convert. Mass apostasy of Jews took place. As a result, a new social class emerged in Spain, the *conversos,* leaving the still-professing Jews to contend with a myriad of legal, economic, political, and spiritual problems.[37] The traumatic events of 1391 in Spain shook the foundations of Sephardic Jewry as well as its rationalist tradition.

Spanish Jews soon faced the next crisis: a staged disputation in Tortosa with Christian polemicists in 1413-1414.[38] Christianity, particularly the scholasticism of the apostates Jeronimo de Santa Fe and Pablo de Santa Maria, emerged triumphant, while Judaism, including Maimonidean philosophy, seemed helpless and hopeless.[39] Jewish intellectuals were left to ask how this result could have occurred. According to traditional Jewish theodicy, it could not have been a manifestation of God's providential care to his people Israel, and must have been punishment for Jewish transgressions and religious disobedience. But who was to blame? None other than Maimonides, who had destroyed Jewry's bond with God by introducing "foreign wisdom," Aristotelianism. These accusations against Maimonidean philosophy as the catalyst for the moral and spiritual bankruptcy of Spanish Jewry came both from rabbinic orators who had had limited exposure to philosophic literature (such as R. Shlomo Al'ami)[40] and from scholars who were themselves products of Maimonidean synthesis of Athens and Jerusalem, such as R. Shem ibn Shem Tov[41] and R. Hasdai Crescas.

R. Hasdai Crescas was a highly trained philosopher and as such as thoroughly acquainted with scholastic literature of the thirteenth and fourteenth centuries. He fought on both flanks to rejuvenate Spanish Jewry after 1391. He first wrote *Bittul Iqqarey ha-Noẓrim (The Refutation of Christian Dogmas),* in which he employed scholastic reasoning with unprecedented brilliance to destroy the logical validity of Catholicism, and hence to minimize its attraction for Jews.[42]

Crescas then launched the most systematic refutation of Maimonideanism to date, hoping to replace Maimonideanism with his own articulation of a Jewish world view not based on Aristotle, and hence more authentically Jewish. Probably influenced by the internal critique of William of Ockham and his followers on Aristotle, Crescas became the first Jewish philosopher who attempted to discredit the logical validity of Aristotelian physics and metaphysics in order to undermine Maimonides.[43] Simultaneously, Crescas exposed the allegedly subversive nature of Maimonides' Platonic political philosophy, challenging in particular Maimonides' theory of knowledge and its implication to the belief in personal immortality.[44] Crescas' philosophic work *Or Adonai (Light of the Lord)*, completed in 1490, is a most original critique of both Maimonideanism and its philosophic underpinning, Aristotelianism. However, Crescas never completed his intended replacement of Maimonides' *Mishneh Torah* — to be entitled *Ner Mizvah* (Lamp of Commandment).[45]

Crescas went beyond criticism of Maimonideanism to offer his own comprehensive alternative. He called for liberation of religion from the clutches of reason, and he substituted the emotional value of reciprocal love between God and man for Maimonides' contemplative intellectualism.[46] Crescas thereby compelled Jewish philosophers to choose between two philosophies of Judaism.

Crescas refuted Aristotle's physics, but he failed to set forth an alternative. He wrote too early. Had he lived in the seventeenth century, his theoretical refutation of Aristotle's theory of natural places could have been supported by Galileo's experiments. But in the early fifteenth century, Aristotelianism was too deeply entrenched in Jewish world view and education, and Crescas failed to dislodge it. So although Crescas had some success, most fifteenth century Sephardic philosophers — including R. Abraham Shalom, R. Abraham Bibago, R. Isaac 'Aramah, R. Joseph ibn Shem Tov, R. Shem Tov ben Joseph, and others — were not ready to accept his refutation of Aristotelianism or of Maimonideanism.[47]

By the fifteenth century even Sephardic scholars no longer clung to the "heroic image" of Maimonides, but for Jewish intellectuals who wished to continue philosophic and scientific activity yet remain observant, there was no other system but Maimonideanism.[48] Kabbalah began to emerge as a potential alternative to philosophy; but it would become a viable substitute for Maimonidean philosophy only after the expulsion from Spain.[49] By the 1480s Kabbalah developed a particularly negative attitude toward philosophy, even viewing it as a demonic force.[50] Some Jewish intellectuals who defended Maimonides, such as R. Abraham Shalom and R. Abraham Bibago, still warmly regarded Kabbalah as an authentic part of ancient revealed tradition. They even incorporated some Kabbalistic terminology and concepts into the core of the Aristotelian outlook.[51]

The expulsion from Spain triggered the renewal of the Maimonidean Controversy among Sephardic exiles. Allegedly, the very cultivation of philosophy (culled primarily from non-Jewish texts) led Jewish philosophers to be lax about their religious observance, leading finally to their apostasy. The expulsion was thus a punishment of Jewish failure to uphold the faith. A prime example was R. Joseph Ya'abetz, a Spanish refugee who engaged in polemics against philosophy in Italy during the mid-1490s.[52] More important was the systematic critique of Isaac Abravanel in his *Commentary on "The Guide of the Perplexed," 'Ateret Zekenim (The Crown of Elders)*, and *Rosh Amanah (Principles of Faith)*.[53] Though Abravanel himself was well versed in philosophy, he attempted to replace Maimonideanism with an eclectic system integrating the views of Judah Halevi, Kabbalah, Nahmanides, and Renaissance Platonism. Another vocal critic of Maimonides in the Ottoman Empire (he lived in Thyrea) was the young Sephardic exile R. Meir ibn Gabbai, who composed his *Tola'at Ya'acov (The Worm of Jacob)* in 1507. Ibn Gabbai opposed Maimonides' rational interpretation of the commandments, as well as his claim that physics and metaphysics constitute the esoteric dimensions of the divine law identical with the *Ma'aseh Bereshit* and *Ma'aseh Merkabah* of the Talmud.[54] Ibn Gabbai was a Kabbalist, and his critique of Maimonideanism reflects the negative perception of philosophy among some Sephardic Kabbalists as well as the rise of Kabbalah as a potential substitute for Maimonideanism.[55]

R. David ben Judah Messer Leon entered the renewed Maimonidean Controversy in about 1506 after R. David's student, R. Meir ibn Verga, began to criticize Maimonides.[56] Although we do not know the precise content of ibn Verga's critique of Maimonides, we know that R. David ben Judah rebuked him for daring to speak against Maimonides. A few years later, in Valona, R. David would excommunicate Meir ibn Verga for his critique of Maimonides.[57] In Italy R. David was trained as a philosopher and held Maimonides in great esteem for transforming Judaism into an intellectual religion. He was particularly irritated when scholars who lacked Maimonides' intellectual and halakhic stature ignored Maimonides' lasting contribution and spoke lightly of him. In about 1508, to set the record straight and thus to end the criticism of Maimonides, R. David ben Judah composed *'Ein ha-Qore*, his own commentary on Maimonides' *Guide*.

In Defense of Maimonides

Like most Jewish philosophers, R. David wrote a commentary on *The Guide* not only to defend Maimonides but also to articulate his own position on major philosophic issues of his day. Nonetheless *'Ein ha-Qore* does not follow the sequence of *The Guide*'s chapters. Instead, it is thematic, lacking apparent structure, and loosely organized around several of the major preoccupations of Maimonides' interpreters. It is full of digressions, repetitions, and associative transitions. In fact, the text seems to reflect R. David's actual lectures on *The Guide of the Perplexed*—almost a set of class notes.

R. Judah Messer Leon had raised his son David with an awe of Maimonides, and with typical medieval "understatement" R. David refers to Maimonides, *inter alia*, as "a hero of his generation," "the light of the world, who enlightened the eyes of Israel," "king of wisdom," and "protector and shield."[58] R. David expressed particular annoyance with

> the recent interpreters who raised nonsensical objections to Maimonides and did not understand his roots and premises. They did not even bother to read this book carefully, thinking it is like any other book, although Maimonides declared in his introduction that he speaks only to those who study philosophy and understand philosophical premises.[59]

R. David then declares that he "could no longer tolerate those people who wished to elevate themselves by embracing the Master" —although one could accuse R. David of the same fault. He sought to show them that "Moses [Maimonides] was truthful and that his teachings were true."[60]

One of "those people" was Isaac Abravanel, who as noted above in this chapter was Maimonides' strongest critic in R. David's time. But R. David may have let personal jealousy contribute to academic conflict. Abravanel had published *Rosh Amanah* in Naples in 1494, while R. David was still there. As noted in Chapter Two above, R. David had already resented Abravanel's close ties to the Aragonese rulers of Naples. In Salonika, too, R. David had to contend with the immense political and intellectual influence of the Abravanel family.

Don Isaac's son, Samuel, and other members of the extended House of Abravanel, enjoyed economic prosperity and political power which R. David envied and resented.[61]

So with typical ardor R. David undertook to restore Maimonides and, tangentially or not, to restore himself as well. *'Ein ha-Qore* begins:

> Why should we hurt Moses [Maimonides] because of "the many of the peoples of the land professed themselves Jews" [Esther 8:17] such that as a reward of his effort any Hebrew man who did not understand even three measures of wisdom could rise and cry in great voice: "Jews, what do you have in common with Egyptian wisdom, 'to drink the waters of the Shihor' [Jer. 2:18] 'from the spring unearthed by the princes' [Num. 21:18] among our people. And 'Moses approached the dark cloud where God was' [Exod. 20:21], 'cradled in darkness, cloud and fog'" [Deut. 4:11; Job, 38:9].

> "Listen to my words" [Job 13:17] "and you will enjoy the fat of the land" [Isa. 55:2] because Moses [Maimonides] "went up to the mountain of God" [Exod. 19:3] in his fundamentals and his thorough demonstrations; for this was his main intention.

Despite strong words both supporting Maimonides and attacking the critics, R. David nonetheless maintains a critical distance from Maimonides himself. R. David is careful to distinguish between his views and Maimonides',[62] and R. David concedes that some criticisms bear weight:

> Therefore I chose the middle road between those scholars, as you have seen in this harmonization. First I will relate the view of the Master and substantiate them with his own proofs. Afterwards I will express my own opinion according to what appears to me the way of Torah. But I will respond to the proofs of the Master with respect and politeness, not in curses and abuses as did other people, God forbid.

> And why should I do all this? For the honor of the Master; I want to expound at length on his fundamentals and explain his views so that the core of this speculative work will be available to you and [embedded] in your memory in general. It is appropriate to every philosophic scholar to desire [to study] this work.[63]

R. David never regarded philosophy as an alternative to the rabbinic tradition. He acknowledged that excessive preoccupation with philosophy at the expense of Torah and Talmud could be harmful, and espoused limiting philosophy to those who already have intellectual maturity and thorough training in the rabbinic disciplines.[64] R. David therefore endorsed the Rashba's ban on the study of philosophy before age 25,[65] which R. David found consistent with Maimonides' own view.[66]

R. David begins his defense of Maimonides with a defense of philosophy itself. According to R. David, the purpose of Maimonides' lifetime activity was "to elevate our Torah from the level of anecdotes to the perfection of wisdom."[67] To do so, Maimonides "established the cornerstones of our religion by means of philosophic investigation showing that the fundamentals of our religion agree with philosophy."[68] By demonstrating that Judaism is "a true, intellectual and speculative wisdom," Maimonides raised the Jewish religion to a higher intellectual plateau. R. David welcomed this intellectualization as beneficial to Judaism and the Jews. One illustration of Maimonides' everlasting contribution to Judaism is that Christian scholars recognize and honor him, second only to Averroës among non-Christian philosophers.[69]

Despite Christian appreciation of him, Maimonides in fact attacked Christianity and the Kalam school of Islam. He accused them of wrongly substituting human imagination *(dimyon)* for knowledge and truth, because human imagination is the source of error in religion and misinterpretation of sacred writings.[70] R. David repeats this attack. Himself familiar with Christian scholasticism, R. David acknowledged "recent Christian scholastics, purporting to be philosophers, who labored to reconcile Christianity with philosophy." Such harmonization is nonetheless impossible, because Christianity and philosophy "are two opposites."[71] R. David then accuses the Islamic Kalam theologians of simply copying the earlier Christian Church Fathers. According to Kalam theologians, if we can imagine something, that thing necessarily exists; R. David claims that that proposition is so antithetical to philosophical demonstration that its very inclusion within Kalam thought proves that Kalam cannot properly rationalize religion.

R. David maintains that Maimonides, in contrast, adopted the intellectualization of religion proposed by two other Muslim philosophers in particular:

> Maimonides envied what Avicenna and Alghazali did for their religion, and borrowed "the shrines of their carved images"

[Ezra 8:12], their premises and their allusions, applying them to our religion.[72]

Maimonides eliminated all traces of human imagination from the Jewish religion and "aligned it with truth and philosophic speculation."[73] Maimonides thereby honored Judaism as they had honored Islam, and proved the verity of Judaism over Muslim theology of the Kalam school as well as over Christianity. (Maimonides' negative comparison of Jesus to Moses shows that Maimonides considered Judaism superior to Christianity.)[74]

R. David found in Maimonides the reconciliation that R. David sought for himself: in concluding that intellectualized religion is superior to religion based on authority alone, Maimonides properly followed rabbinic authority; yet Maimonides also recognized that philosophy is no substitute for religion and that the study of philosophy must begin only upon a firm grounding in the rabbinic tradition:

> It is not proper to accept religious fundamentals solely on the grounds of authoritative tradition. Rather, it is preferable that after one receives the fundamentals of religion on the basis of authority, one studies the demonstrative sciences and clarify the fundamentals of religion in accordance with philosophy.[75]

R. David thus asserts that Maimonides perfected the Jewish religion by showing it to be in accord with philosophy. However, R. David recognizes that this defense gives an opening to the common attack that Maimonides subordinated Judaism to Greek philosophy. So R. David sets out to prove that Maimonides upheld the superiority of Judaism over Greek, particularly Aristotelian, philosophy. Here R. David walks a fine intellectual line: Judaism is different from, and intellectually superior to, Greek philosophy, but Judaism is absolutely true because it is divinely revealed. To walk that line R. David resorts to Aristotle's distinction between "demonstrative knowledge" and "dialectic."[76]

Aristotle borrowed the concept of "dialectic" from his teacher, Plato, but he understood it differently. Whereas for Plato "dialectic" was "the method of working up to an ultimate or unified knowledge by a critique of special fields," for Aristotle dialectical reasoning "reasons from generally accepted opinions *(endoxa)*."[77] Thus Aristotle distinguished between sciences which are based on accepted opinions (e.g., ethics and politics) and sciences which proceed necessarily from true premises, thus resulting in philosophic demonstrations (logic, mathematics, physics, and metaphysics). Aristotle clearly regarded demonstrative knowledge as qualitatively superior to dialectical reasoning.

R. David, however, changes Aristotle's original intent by distinguishing between "demonstrable propositions" *(derushim shemeqablim mofet)* and "undemonstrable propositions" *(derushim she-ein mi-tiv'am leqabel mofet)*. According to R. David, natural, human intellectual reason may, through discursive reasoning, attain truths only about things which are prone to demonstration. Yet there are truths which human reason cannot demonstrate, and which can become known only through divine revelation. Furthermore, R. David claims that the undemonstrable truths are superior to demonstrable truths, because the former come directly from God whereas the latter are reasoned by man. R. David was not the first to remold Aristotle in this manner; he borrowed this particular interpretation from Thomas Aquinas.[78] R. David nonetheless attributes this interpretation to both Aristotle and Maimonides:

> The Torah according to Maimonides is speculative wisdom; this is its majesty and glory. This statement does not contradict Aristotle, because he already admitted that there are true propositions which cannot be demonstrated. The greatest among them concerns ultimate felicity.[79]

If Aristotle acknowledged that there are truths which cannot be demonstrated by human reason, so could Maimonides claim that certain teachings of the Torah cannot be demonstrated.

R. David interprets Maimonides to claim that all teachings of Judaism are philosophically true, but that human reason can demonstrate only some truths without divine assistance—for example, the existence of God, God's unity and incorporeality, and that prophecy exists. Other truths are undemonstrable, such as that God created the world *ex nihilo,* that God knows particulars, that God extends providential care, and that the human soul can unite with God. These truths require divine revelation (through prophecy) so that man can know them:

> [Divine] knowledge, providence, and conjunction with God are true propositions which accord with philosophy; they all originate from one source and they are true propositions which cannot be demonstrated by human reason even according to the premises of the philosophers.[80]

R. David thereby credits Maimonides with using Aristotle's own proofs to uphold the supremacy of divinely revealed Torah over Aristotelian philosophy as the repository of demonstrable and undemonstrable truths.

R. David next turns to the literary style of Maimonides' *The Guide of the Perplexed*. It is well known that Maimonides wrote for the many and for the few. While his halakhic works—especially the *Mishneh Torah* and the *Commentary on the Mishnah*—address Jewish society at large, *The Guide of the Perplexed* was written specifically for Jewish intellectuals confused by the apparently irreconcilable differences between the rabbinic tradition and the scientific disciplines. *The Guide* is written in the form of personal correspondence to a beloved student, Joseph ben Judah ibn Sham'un of Ceuta. Maimonides extracts the esoteric truths of divine revelation and shows their compatibility with philosophic truths. A rabbinic injunction existed against divulging the esoteric meaning of Torah in public, lest the masses misunderstand it. Maimonides heeded that injunction not only by resorting to the form of personal (and ostensibly private) correspondence, but also by obfuscating what he wrote. *The Guide* is full of intentional contradictions within an intricate structure.[81]

Maimonides' esoteric style of writing reflected his belief that the Torah itself was an esoteric text. The Torah which Moses communicated to the People of Israel has two dimensions: its exoteric content *(nigleh)* consists of narratives and laws understandable by all people; its esoteric content *(nistar)* consists of philosophical truths known only to the intellectually perfect men. Maimonides, however, identified the esoteric contents of the Torah—*Ma'aseh Bereshit* and *Ma'aseh Merkabah*—with Aristotelian physics and metaphysics, respectively.[82] Thus he rationalized Judaism by claiming that its inner core teaches the same truths as does philosophy.

Maimonides' writing style permitted every subsequent commentator to express his own views in the guise of finding the "true" interpretation of Maimonides.[83] Along with A. Motzkin, I believe that Maimonides deliberately obscured his positions to create this very occurrence, namely, an ongoing process of interpretation.[84] The process of interpreting Maimonides itself permitted, and continues to this day to permit, halakhic Jews to integrate Judaism and the sciences by debating Maimonides' own harmonization.[85] This view is not cynical; rather it recognizes Maimonides' true educational genius and everlasting contribution.[86]

According to R. David ben Judah, Maimonides' contradictions

are not irreconcilable and do not expose mistakes of logic or limitations of knowledge. To the contrary, blessed with a superior intellect, the Master was never mistaken in his philosophic understanding![87] Such praise, of course, conflicts with R. David's own self-professed critical distance, which shows how difficult the defense of Maimonides really was during the fifteenth century. R. David defended Maimonides first and foremost as a symbol of the synthesis between Judaism and philosophy, although R. David's own synthesis differed from that of Maimonides.[88]

R. David resolves *The Guide*'s apparent contradictions as follows. First, Maimonides did not have access to certain doctrines and texts, and so cannot be personally attacked for not knowing them. For example, Maimonides conceded that Averroës' works were unavailable, and that Maimonides' knowledge of Aristotelian philosophy came from Avicenna and Alghazali,[89] so Maimonides' conclusions should be judged only against their understanding of Avicenna. R. David makes this response against Moses Narboni's criticism of Maimonides, which R. David claims was the source of Isaac Abravanel's criticism as well, for Narboni judges Maimonides against Averroës.[90]

Second, R. David rejects as irrelevant any Kabbalistic criticism of Maimonides: "Kabbalah and philosophy proceed from diametrically opposed premises, even though in some cases their teachings accord with one another."[91] So one may not properly object to philosophy in general, much less to Maimonides in particular, from the perspective of Kabbalah. R. David nonetheless does not dismiss Kabbalah lightly; rather, he "attempted to reconcile them as much as possible, ever since he investigated both sciences in his youth." Among the Kabbalists who criticized Maimonides, R. David cites R. Shem Tov ibn Shem Tov (perhaps the most radical) and Nahmanides (perhaps the most moderate).

Third, R. David rejects the apology that Maimonides wrote with intentional ambiguity in order to convey one message to the philosophically initiated and a completely distinct message to the uneducated masses. That theory was first suggested by Maimonides' immediate follower and translator, R. Samuel ibn Tibbon, in the beginning of the thirteenth century, and was adopted by Maimonides' followers and critics alike during the fourteenth century.[92] In contrast R. David asserts the existence of an integral unity throughout the entire Maimonidean corpus: Maimonides conveyed one and the same message not only in *The Guide of the Perplexed* itself but also throughout his halakhic works, namely, the verity of Judaism as an intellectual religion.

R. David reminds us that Maimonides' message can be deciphered it we follow Maimonides' instructions in *The Guide*'s introduction:

> Maimonides warned the reader to read his words closely (because they did not come at random) and to consider all his chapters and resolve his contradictions, showing them to be deliberate contradictions.[93]

Maimonides' "deliberate contradictions" include dispersing a given teaching throughout the work so as to obscure its meaning. "Maimonides did not complete one secret in one place, but dispersed it in several places." However, Maimonides was so careful in his choice of words and order of presentation that "there was never a scholar who arranged things according to their proper order as did Maimonides."[94] Maimonides' interpreter must therefore glean information from various chapters and remain alert to the widely scattered hints and clues. With close attention as well to the tripartite division of the book, the order of chapters, and the choice of words, the underlying message emerges and the seeming contradictions vanish. Maimonides is redeemed from his opponents' attacks.

The Guide of the Perplexed is divided into three parts which, R. David claims, conform to Maimonides' distinction between demonstrable and undemonstrable truths. The first part contains Maimonides' explanation of the truth of Scripture by showing "the false nature of Kalam interpretation of biblical verses, and coordinating Scripture with Truth and philosophic speculation."[95] Readers may thus rid themselves of misunderstandings before proceeding to discuss philosophic truths. The second part contains religious truths that Maimonides proves to be philosophically demonstrable truths as well—for example, "the existence of God, the unity of God and His incorporeality."[96] In the third part, Maimonides "combined Torah and wisdom and discussed those religious fundamentals which cannot be demonstrated by human reason [only by divine revelation], such as divine knowledge, His providential care, and the ultimate felicity."[97]

This classification makes Maimonides' discussion of prophecy and creation particularly problematic, and the tension between Maimonides and R. David is most evident there. Discussions of both prophecy and creation appear in the second part of the *Guide,* so they should be classified as demonstrable truths. Yet Maimonides clearly states that human reason cannot prove or disprove creation, and that this belief therefore relies on the authority of revelation. R. David has no real solution. He responds only that "creation is among those speculative truths which cannot be demonstrated even though they are true." R. David is just as unclear on prophecy. On the one hand he claims that Maimonides understood prophecy to be an entirely natural phenomenon, and hence philosophically demonstrable. On the other hand, R. David enumerates prophecy among the class of "undemonstrable truths."

R. David analyzes chapters, sentences, and even words in *The Guide* by dissecting them into component parts so as to prove an underlying unity, a method that reflects R. David's Tosafist mindset and textual approach. The Tosafists analyzed the Talmud by reconciling apparent contradictions, variants, and redundancies in order to prove its underlying integrity and unity. Indeed R. David refers to his explication of *The Guide* as *pilpul*, the term by which the Tosafist method is known to this day, and asserts that Maimonides' critics' incompetence in that method led to their baseless charges.[98]

Whether R. David's interpretation of Maimonides is correct or not is not crucial here. Ultimately any interpretation depends upon the intellectual preferences of the commentator, leaving the Maimonidean enigma intact. What is important is the image of Maimonides that emerges from R. David's interpretation. Maimonides is not the radical who replaced Jewish revealed law and tradition with pagan logic and, implicitly, pagan culture, but the conservative who actually defended Judaism against that Aristotelian philosophy by turning it against itself, and who defended Judaism over other purportedly revealed religions as well. R. David's Maimonides elevated Judaism to a higher intellectual plane—thus closer to God—by showing that Judaism is Truth yet still recognizing that human reason, unaided by divine revelation, cannot demonstrate the entire Truth. Having portrayed Maimonides as the supreme defender of the faith, R. David ben Judah Messer Leon thus delivers the ultimate *ad hominem* counterattack: those who criticize Maimonides undermine Judaism itself.

R. David's campaign to defend Maimonides further increased R. David's fame, which now extended beyond Salonika to other Jewish communities. He received both inquiries on religio-legal issues and offers of employment. An Italian congregation in Valona pursued David ben Judah Messer Leon to serve as their rabbi, a position he finally accepted in 1510.[99]

Rabbinic Authority in Valona

Valona (*Avilona* in the Hebrew sources; now Vlore in Albania) lay on the main land route between Raguza (now Dubrovnik) and the hinterlands of the Ottoman Empire. It was an active trade post between Venice and the Balkans. Valona was a convenient refuge for Jews from Spain and Sicily after the expulsions in 1492-93, and accepted many. By the turn of the sixteenth century, Valona contained three major Jewish groups: many Italians, mostly from the province of Apulia; some Sephardim from Catalonia, Castile, and Portugal; and a few Romanyots.[100]

The Apulians invited R. David to serve as the chief rabbi of the entire Jewish community in Valona for the substantial annual salary of seventy florins.[101] R. David did not accept immediately. He first went to nearby Corfu in response to an earlier written request—we do not know if he had a rabbinic position there—and from Corfu went to Valona.[102] In 1510, after addressing each of the four local congregations, Apulian, Romanyot, Catalan, and Portuguese, R. David was formally appointed as a chief rabbi of Valona.

R. David enjoyed a very good first year. He writes that he preached each Sabbath in all four synagogues,[103] and even succeeded in uniting the Catalans and Portuguese into a unified Sephardic congregation.[104] Interestingly, the Ashkenazic legal code *Arba'a Turim* by R. Jacob ben Asher served as a unifying factor. Every day after the morning prayer R. David would teach the *Tur* in accordance to the Ashkenazic method of *pilpul*. His Sephardic congregants "had never heard such legal reasoning in Spain" and were "very happy about it."[105] R. David's authority was accepted and his intellectual powers greatly praised.

R. David's initial contract was for one year, and R. David intended thereafter to return to Corfu. He was particularly concerned about political instability in the Balkans as a result of the wars of succession among the heirs of Ottoman Sultan Bayezid.[106] The Apulians, however, implored R. David to stay and invited him to serve their congregation exclusively for the same annual salary he had received as a chief rabbi of the entire city. R. David reluctantly accepted the offer, citing as his main reason the disruption of maritime transportation in the Adriatic, probably a reference to the ongoing tension between the Ottomans and the Venetians.[107] (Sultan Selim I came to power in 1512, and the internal Ottoman strife subsided.)

Controversy arose during R. David's second year in Valona. Portuguese Jews walked back out of the unified Iberian congregation to reconstitute their own; Castilians and Catalonians remained behind. R. David was asked to intervene. He issued a comprehensive legal opinion concerning the propriety of excommunication as a sanction for congregational secession, in which he set forth in detail the facts, his decision (he was against it), and his reasoning. That opinion survives, and S. Bernfeld published it under the title of *Kevod Hakhamim* nearly a century ago.[108] The controversy itself has attracted considerable scholarly attention because R. David's opinion is one of the first published texts documenting an historically significant occurrence: internal conflict in an immigrant Jewish community of the Ottoman Empire. It was one of many among the various Jewish groups, each trying to maintain its own culture.

R. David's opinion also sheds light on the man: his personal history, his public conduct, and the community he served.[109] According to R. David's account, the united Sephardic congregation met in the private home of R. Abraham Zarfati until the Portuguese seceded and built a new synagogue near R. David's home. The united congregations' bylaws provided that the sanction for secession was excommunication (from all Jewry). Although then employed by the Apulian congregation alone, R. David still enjoyed public recognition as the *de facto* chief rabbi of Valona. He maintained good relations with the Protuguese but considered the Castilians conceited. So when the Castilians approached R. David to help them preserve the congregational union, he declined to intervene.[110]

A wealthy and well-educated Portuguese physician named Don Solomon Krisanti then rose to act. Krisanti had settled in Valona and befriended R. David. After recovering from an illness, Krisanti decided to express his gratitude to God by bringing the feuding parties together on the evening of Yom Kippur—the holiest day of the year—hoping that the conciliatory spirit of the Day of Repentance would soften all warring hearts. The Qol Nidre prayer, chanted only on Yom Kippur eve, sought forgiveness for all transgressions of the prior year and annulment of any penalty for them.[111]

Krisanti suggested that, during Qol Nidre, Rabbi R. David ben Judah Messer Leon officiate over an annulment of the Sephardic congregation's excommunication of the Portuguese, thereby resolving the matter by law. R. David agreed to try. He sent messengers to the Sephardic congregation, then meeting at R. Abraham Zarfati's house.[112] Their leaders rejected the proposal, claiming that this grave issue was inappropriate for resolution on Yom Kippur of all days, and rejected as well Krisanti's offer to arbitrate the dispute after Yom Kippur.[113]

Krisanti turned again to R. David, this time asking R. David to exercise his personal authority, as the most respected rabbi-scholar in Valona, to impose a unilateral resolution.[114] R. David preferred instead to call two other scholars, the cantors of the Catalans and the Apulians, so to convene a formal rabbinic court of three.[115] The court listened to Krisanti's case *ex parte*, but R. David wisely refused to rule before giving the other side another opportunity to participate. He therefore summoned the Castilians to appear. Twice messengers were sent, and twice they returned alone. R. David was now outraged at this direct challenge to his own personal authority.[116] He annulled the Castilians' ban in their absence.

R. David's decision provoked a written response of further defiance, composed by Meir ibn Verga (who was apparently among the leaders of the Castilian congregation) and supported by the congregation's president, R. Abraham Collier, and another lay leader, Abraham Harvon.[117] Meir ibn Verga had been a student of R. David ben Judah in Salonika, but little love was lost between the two. As indicated above they had already clashed in Valona over Maimonides. According to R. David, Meir ibn Verga had "dared to preach against the honorable Master without understanding even the surface of his teachings, let alone the foundations of his profound wisdom."[118] That had affronted not only the memory of Maimonides, but also R. David himself, since R. David "was known to uphold the views of the Master." So R. David had publicly rebuked Meir and even attempted to excommunicate him.[119] Only the support of Samuel Abravanel, the wealthy patron who had considerable political influence in Valona, had saved Meir ibn Verga from R. David's wrath.

Ibn Verga's second challenge to R. David's authority in the same city was too much. R. David summoned Meir ibn Verga to R. David's synagogue for a public apology. Meir ibn Verga refused to go. By now the controversy had probably disrupted much of the day of Yom Kippur, and in any event the Castilian leaders had now had enough. They dragged ibn Verga to appear before R. David. There ibn Verga — whether out of expedience or sincerity we do not know — expressed regret for his conduct and apologized for his wrong-doing.[120] Abraham Collier did likewise, and so was the controversy resolved.

R. David was not particularly annoyed by ibn Verga's disagreement on the religio-legal issue then before the court, namely, the propriety of excommunication as a sanction for congregational secession. Rather, R. David was enraged by ibn Verga's contempt for the court itself. Ibn Verga had challenged R. David's personal authority. Ibn Verga had doubtless looked at R. David as a peer whose jurisdiction was limited and lay elsewhere — the rabbi of a separate, parallel congregation. (In fact R. David's decision on the merits of the case actually supported that theory. It limited the authority of a congregation to impose sanctions on those who no longer considered themselves members, thus implying, at least, a limitation on the personal jurisdiction of their leaders as well.) So ibn Verga responded to R. David in kind — that is, ibn Verga received a written message and he sent a written message back.

So in *Kevod Hakhamim*, before discussing the merits of his decision at all, R. David went to great lengths to justify his very jurisdiction to act. In contrast to ibn Verga, R. David saw himself as a superior whose authority to decide, and, by implication, whose jurisdiction to enforce his decisions, extended at least to the boundaries of Valona. R. David did not base that power upon the will of the people; his contract to be chief rabbi of Valona had expired and he now was employed by the Apulian congregation alone. Nor did R. David base it upon the coincidence that ibn Verga had been his student — although R. David wrote that that added insult to injury.[121] Rather, R. David founded his personal authority and jurisdiction upon an institution: rabbinic ordination.

A brief history of the institution of the rabbinate appears above in Chapter One. As noted there, the rabbinate was the subject of strong debate even in R. David's day. Among other things, it reflected a split between Ashkenazim and Sephardim. R. Judah Messer Leon had taken the view that rabbinic ordination per se grants political authority wherever the ordained rabbi may find himself. R. David inherited his father's position, and further considered his own credentials beyond reproach since he was ordained at the age of eighteen upon the signatures of twenty-two ordained rabbis.[122] So R. David claimed that the Sephardim demeaned the title "rabbi" by invoking it too freely upon those with insufficient education, scholarship, and personal observance. His words reveal a sense of intellectual and moral superiority:

> The title of rabbi given for Torah and Talmud is one more fitting that the title of rabbi given for affairs of state; for in Spain they were accustomed to give the title to one who was appointed

by the king to be over the Jews, even though he may not have
been expert in teaching and in the laws, and not careful in his
observance and his fear of sin — like that famous rabbi of Castile
whose testifies to his beginning. A more appropriate title [than
rabbi] would be *nagid,* which is used in Egypt for this sort of
position.[123]

R. David's last comment was well directed. The government-
appointed rabbis in Castile and Aragon were primarily administrators, or liaisons between the state and the Jewish communities, as
opposed to being judges *(dayyanim).* R. David referred derogatorily
to R. Abraham Senior, the leader of Castilian Jewry who converted
to Christianity in order to avoid expulsion from Spain. In sharp contrast, asserted R. David, ordained rabbis like him were true scholars
and upholders of the ancient traditions. Their ordinations were no
less valid than ordinations in ancient Israel.[124] In fact, unordained
scholars should not even be allowed to teach![125] Contemporary scholars in the diaspora act on the premise that they are the agents of the
scholars in the Land of Israel (for example, the admission of converts
by a rabbinic court). The Tosafists had justified their authority in the
same way.[126] The ordaining rabbi has personal authority and transfers
that authority to the ordinee.

The centerpiece of his defense R. David copies almost verbatim
from a legal decision of the French rabbi Joseph Colon. However,
Colon had included that section almost as an afterthought, and had
actually reached the exact opposite conclusion concerning rabbinic
authority. By intention or not, R. David took R. Colon's words completely out of context.[127]

While in Valona, R. David himself ordained at least three scholars, two of them from Corfu.[128] The writ of ordination of the third
scholar, Shlomo ben Perez Bonfoy, recently published by R. Bonfil,
attests to the requirements.[129] R. David praised the ordinee for his
erudition in Torah, mastery of *pilpul,* pleasant character, teaching
ability, good memory, knowledge of the secular sciences, and proficiency in Kabbalah. Clearly R. David's ordinee had to integrate outstanding learning, good character, and rhetorical skills.[130]

R. David Hacohen (Radakh), the Romanyot rabbi of Corfu,
strongly supported R. David's concept of rabbinic ordination in general and his conduct in the controversy in Valona in particular.[131]
Radakh defended Ashkenazic rabbinic ordination as especially necessary at a time when so many unworthy people were using the title of

rabbi. He contrasted the truly learned, Torah-true rabbis (such as himself and R. David) to the Sephardim who abused the title, spending their time exclusively in secular studies and lacking in their religious observance. Radakh also defended contemporary ordination as the legitimate successor to ordination in the Land of Israel. He claimed that outside the Land of Israel, rabbinic ordination not only authorized the recipient to adjudicate *diney qenasot* (cases that carry the penalty of fines) but also evidenced his level of knowledge sufficient to teach halakhah. Radakh also supported R. David concerning the close relationship between teacher and student: the student may not teach without the teacher's permission.[132]

Despite R. David ben Judah, R. David ha-Kohen, and others, rabbinic ordination would soon decline. Apparently neither Radakh nor R. David were familiar with the views of the Sephardic talmudic scholar R. Isaac ben Sheshet. His discussion of rabbinic ordination was published in 1546 with the rest of his responsa, after R. David's death.[133] Those views were especially relevant then because just eight years earlier, R. Jacob Berab attempted to renew the ordination of rabbis in the Land of Israel, prompting a heated controversy with R. Levi ben Hayyim.[134] Berab's attempt to renew Palestinian ordination fizzled out after a handful of ordinations, including that of Joseph Caro, later to gain fame as the author of *Shulhan 'Arukh*. By the late sixteenth century R. Isaac ben Sheshet's view prevailed. The status of ordination gradually declined, although the Ashkenazim of the Ottoman Empire continued to practice it.[135]

The controversy in Valona ended with the authority of R. David intact but wounded. We do not know when R. David left Valona nor where he went. With S. Rosanes we may surmise that R. David returned to Salonika where he composed his last work, *Tehillah le-David*.[136] The last three chapters of this book focus not on R. David's life but on his thought.

5

Hakham Kolel: A Comprehensive Scholar

The Conflict of Reason and Faith

In his own day R. David ben Judah Messer Leon was famous as a *hakham kolel*, a scholar who excelled in both rabbinic and secular studies. As noted in Chapter Two above, this type of Jewish scholarship flourished in Renaissance Italy, undoubtedly under the impact of the Renaissance ideal *homo universalis*. Jewish scholars in Spain and Provençe also shared this ideal even though they differed as to the particular make-up of the curriculum necessary to attain this ideal. R. David mastered a broad range of disciplines within both the scholastic and the humanist curricula. He regarded the attainment of intellectual perfection as a prerequisite to ultimate human felicity which he equated with the immortality of the individual soul.

R. David began with premises inherited from Greek philosophy: man is the rational animal; in order to be truly human, man must perfect the intellectual faculty by acquiring knowledge. Knowledge is by definition abstract, theoretical, and general. Human reason discovers universal truths through philosophic inquiry. With medieval philosophers R. David viewed philosophic truths as eternal: they apply to all times, places, people, and circumstances. Philosophic truths are also objective: they are indifferent to the subjective identity of the person who pronounces them. Philosophic knowledge, in short, transcends all particularist circumstances, whether religious beliefs, social conventions, personal emotions, or collective aspirations.

Despite this philosophy R. David ben Judah was a professing Jew whose self-perception, moral standards, daily conduct, and existential concerns were all molded by rabbinic Judaism. A rabbi, *Marbiz Torah*, and *Dayyan*, R. David meticulously observed halakhah and upheld the particularist beliefs of Judaism. How could a thinking, observant Jew be a *homo universalis*? How could a rabbi who accepted on faith the particularist claims of Judaism also endorse the universalist claims of philosophy? The apparent contradictions continue. The Renaissance ideal of all-inclusive knowledge had led R. David to cultivate both the scholastic program (logic, natural philosophy, metaphysics, medicine, and theology) and the humanist program (grammar, rhetoric, poetry, history, and moral philosophy). How could R. David embrace both scholastic philosophy and humanism? On top of all this, R. David was a serious student of Kabbalah. How could he validate two different metahalakhic systems for interpreting divine revelation — namely, philosophy and Kabbalah — and how could he harmonize them?

The answers lie in R. David's synthesis of reason and faith, or philosophy and religion. There too lies the key to R. David's *weltanschauung* and his place in Jewish intellectual history. Fully cognizant of the conflict of philosophic knowledge and religious beliefs, R. David maintained that this conflict could be resolved so that a rabbinic Jew could pursue the knowledge of all things without compromising his allegiance to Judaism.

This chapter explains that resolution, namely, R. David's synthesis of reason and faith. It is not surprising that R. David ben Judah Messer Leon founded his synthesis of reason and faith upon the thought of Maimonides. It is surprising, at least to most modern readers, that R. David also relied heavily upon Thomas Aquinas.

The Meaning of Emunah

Scholars have long disagreed, at times sharply, over what Maimonides, and to a lesser extent Aquinas, really meant concerning the so-called conflict of reason and faith. Much disagreement masks a confusion that arises from different meanings of the Hebrew word for 'faith' itself: *emunah*. The changes in meaning of that word reflect the very development of the conflict, and neither the conflict itself nor R. David's resolution can really be understood without understanding the meanings of the operational terms.

Hebrew does not distinguish between 'belief' (a particular article of faith accepted on authoritative tradition) and 'faith' (a general affirmation of religious beliefs, which a philosopher can do only through systematic speculation). *Emunah* denotes both,[1] and as shown below, its meaning shifted from the Rabbinic period to the Middle Ages. Arabic, by contrast, does make that distinction: *iman* denotes a particular article of faith, and *i'tiqad* denotes affirmation of religious beliefs as a result of systematic speculation. Maimonides wrote in Arabic but failed to use these two terms consistently.[2] In the twelfth century, when the works of Maimonides and others were translated from Arabic into Hebrew, both words appeared as *emunah* and its cognates. One result was an endless series of semantic debates among Maimonides' later interpreters.

Aristotle first made the distinction that is crucial to our understanding of R. David's thought: "belief in" and "belief that."[3] The first refers to the mental disposition, attitude, and conduct of the believer. The second refers to the cognitive content of certain beliefs, or articles of faith, which the believer holds. Accordingly, belief *in* God means loyalty to God, trust that God will answer the believer's prayers, or willingness to subordinate oneself to the divine will. Belief *that* God exists, by contrast, means acceptance that the proposition "God exists" is true—that is, that it corresponds to extramental reality.

In rabbinic Judaism, as M. Kellner has convincingly argued, "faith" meant belief *in* God—for example, trust that God will provide for the needs of the believer and the People of Israel, hope that God will not forsake Israel, even though she has sinned, or observance of the will of God as it is expressed in Torah.[4] Rabbinic Judaism thus did not define Jewish faith in terms of dogmas, propositions whose affirmation makes one Jewish and whose denial makes a Jew a heretic. Further, since rabbinic Judaism equated faith in God *(emunah)* with loyalty to God's Law and interpreted that law through authoritative tradition *(qabbalah*, which itself later changed meaning to denote Jewish mysticism), *qabbalah* and *emunah* were often used interchangeably.[5] To the rabbis, then, *emunah* meant a cluster of beliefs, practices, and moral standards—in short, a comprehensive way of life.

In the Middle Ages Greek philosophy, Islam, and Karaism all challenged rabbinic Judaism. In response, the defenders of the rabbinic tradition, beginning with Saadia Gaon, attempted to show that the propositional content of rabbinic Judaism accords with truths discovered by the human intellect. They converted articles of faith into doctrines that one can firmly believe through speculation,[6] and began to discuss the Jewish faith not as "belief in" but as "belief that." *Emunah* no longer stood for mere loyalty to God through observance of the Law but signified a set of propositions about God and His relationship to the universe and to Israel. This shift marks the rise of those whom we call Jewish philosophers.

Medieval Jewish philosophers had a problem. Rabbinic Judaism is not a credal religion but a normative tradition. Though Judaism consisted of many beliefs, it emphasized not dogma but practice. Where does one begin the search for essential yet philosophically demonstrable propositions? The philosophers turned to the origin of Judaism, divine revelation, and showed how it is entirely rational. They then focused on the phenomenon of prophecy as the core of the rationalization of Judaism, and finally they interpreted the revealed Law accordingly.

Underlying this rationalization of Judaism was Aristotle's distinction between the intelligible world of universals and the perceivable realm of particulars. Following Plato, Aristotle maintained that only that which is universal is knowable, whereas particulars remain beyond the grasp of the intellect. The senses may perceive particulars, but the intellect cannot know them. Knowledge of intelligible universals can be organized in a theoretical system (i.e., science), and different sciences can be distinguished from each other according to their proper object. The practical sciences (ethics, politics, and economics) organize knowledge about things subject to change, while speculative sciences (logic, mathematics, physics, and metaphysics) concern immaterial things, not subject to change.[7] Only the speculative sciences constitute true scientific knowledge. Scientific knowledge is the result of syllogizing, that is, of thinking out from true premises to correct conclusions.

Aristotle accepted Plato's distinction between opinion *(doxa)* and knowledge *(episteme)*. But he parted from Plato in maintaining that it is possible to hold correct opinions, or true beliefs, on the basis of external authority (either social convention or authoritative tradition). No single person can hold both true belief and knowledge about the same object, but one can hold true belief and another knowledge in regard to the same object. Aristotle called the true belief based on conventions and traditional teachings "dialectic," thus changing the meaning Plato had given to this word. Whereas for Plato "dialectic" was the highest method of scientific inquiry leading to discovery of universal truths, for Aristotle "dialectic" contrasted with scientific knowledge of demonstration.

Medieval scholasticism felt the need to define the proper relationship between Greek philosophy and revealed religion. Religious philosophers—first Muslim, then Jewish, and finally Christian—developed comprehensive syntheses of human reason and divine revelation. Aristotle's view was adopted by the Muslim philosopher Alfarabi, and through him exerted enormous influence on medieval Jewish philosophy.[8] As indicated above, Maimonides and Aquinas shaped R. David's views; their views bear discussion.

Maimonides and Aquinas: Two Medieval Syntheses

Following Alfarabi, Maimonides discussed the difference between belief and knowledge in the context of Aristotelian epistemology. Maimonides identified belief, including religious belief, with opinion. In *The Guide* I:50 he defined belief *(i'tiqad)* as follows:

Belief is not the notion that is uttered, but the notion that is represented in the soul when it has been averred of it that it is in fact just as it has been represented.

Maimonides thus distinguishes between external utterance and internal conceptualization. Merely to utter a certain proposition does not entail believing it. To "believe that p" means that two conditions are present: (1) the believer has a mental representation of p and (2) the believer holds that p is true (i.e., that p corresponds to extramental reality). Only when both conditions exist does one "believe that p:"

Belief is the affirmation that what has been represented is outside the mind just as it has been represented in the mind.

S. Rosenberg has shown that Maimonides' definition of belief can be interpreted in two ways. One, called "objective," highlights the correspondence between belief and extramental reality. To "believe that p" is equivalent to thinking that p is true, namely, that the belief (or mental representation) corresponds to extramental reality. The other, called "subjective," emphasizes the element of internal conviction in the act of believing regardless of the correspondence between the content of the belief and extramental reality. It is sufficient that one accepts "that *p*" to establish that he "believes that *p*." Some beliefs may correspond to extramental reality and thus be provable as "true," while others need not.[9]

Maimonides followed Aristotle and Alfarabi in contrasting true opinion, known on the basis of accepted tradition (*qabbalah* or *taqlid*, corresponding to Aristotle's "dialectic"), with knowledge attained through rational demonstration (*mofet* or *burhan*). Tradition and demonstrable knowledge teach the same truth in different manners to two different individuals or groups.

To prove that divine revelation is entirely rational, Maimonides turned to prophecy. He followed Alfarabi to assert that prophecy is a form of human cognition explicable by the same epistemological theory that applies to other cognitive acts, a natural phenomenon which occurs as the highest stage of human knowledge.[10] The summit of human knowledge amounts to a quasi-mystical union between the individual human intellect and the semidivine Active Intellect, the last of the Intelligences that emanate from God. As A. Altman has explained, Maimonides' epistemology was tied to a concept of the universe in which

> ...total reality, including God, [is] a continuum in which the flow of emanations from God through the hierarchy of intelligences reaches down to the Active Intelligence as the immediate fountainhead of the activity and forms of the sublunar world. This entire system is a system of free-flowing grace as it were, and does not require special acts of divine grace for special occasions.[11]

The flow of divine emanation (*shefa'*) constitutes divine providence. In the physical world providence is manifested in the bestowal of forms upon matter, and in intellectual activity it results in the reception of prophecy by an intellectually perfect individual. Accordingly, the prophet is one who has attained intellectual perfection so that his intellect is united with the Active Intellect.[12] Through this union the prophet receives divine emanation comprised of knowledge of universal truths.

Moses, of course, was Israel's greatest prophet. Only he saw God face to face. Moses was thus the most intellectually perfect human being; his prophetic experience was least materially bound, and most free of any admixture of imagination and other bodily functions. He held the highest knowledge possible for man, and he attained it in a manner superior to philosophic inquiry. However, Maimonides admitted that the superiority of Moses cannot be demonstrated philosophically, and accordingly pronounced that superiority to be an article of faith.[13] Having obtained the knowledge of what exists in the most sublime manner possible for a human being, Moses then communicated this sublime truth to the People of Israel through the written Torah in a figurative language accessible to all. The Torah (Moses' prophecy) is therefore twofold: its particular narrative and figurative language clothe universal, albeit esoteric, philosophical truths.

Maimonides thus reconciled reason and faith through the uniqueness of Mosaic prophecy. Jewish faith is rational; it consists of knowledge that can be attained through teachings of Scripture, which the multitude accepts on authority, as well as through philosophy, which only the intellectual few can apprehend. Because Mosaic prophecy is perfect, no genuine conflict can exist between the two paths. Whatever can be known through revelation can also be known through human reason.[14]

While Maimonides accepted correct opinion as rational, he clearly considered it to be epistemically inferior to philosophic demonstration. The unlearned multitude, along with women and children, accept correct opinion on the external authority of tradition. Mere affirmation of revealed teachings on the basis of authoritative tradition characterizes vulgar religious observance. Intellectual elite, by contrast, attain true knowledge, the universal truths of the faith, by means of philosophic speculation.[15] They are the ideal believers.

Although the ultimate goal of human life is the intellectual contemplation of God, Maimonides fully respected the difficulties of philosophy. In *The Guide* I:35 he listed five factors that distract from devotion to it: subtlety of the subject matter, lack of mental aptitude, length of required study, lack of moral perfection, and excessive preoccupation with bodily pleasure. Because philosophic demonstration is so difficult, the truth must be revealed to man in a manner accessible to all. Religion based on external authority of divine revelation thus inculcates in the multitude correct opinions about God and His relation to the universe and the Jewish People.[16]

Maimonides boldly parted from rabbinic Judaism by introducing creed—articles of faith that the masses could not independently conclude rationally because they lacked the time or ability to engage in philosophic speculation. Since *emunah* now meant not just belief in, or loyalty to, God but belief "that *p*," the masses needed propositions. Such a list has both normative and salvific value. Affirmation of creed determines who is a Jew today—whether a convert to Judaism or a convert away—and "who will have a portion in the world to come."

Maimonides thus employed his stature as a jurist to promulgate the very essence of the Jewish faith: the Thirteen Principles.[17] Their interpretation remains the subject of controversy.[18] Did Maimonides consider all of them rationally demonstrable, or only some? If others were not, then their classification is essential to an understanding of Maimonides, who left room for many interpretations by intentionally obfuscating his views. The Thirteen Principles are discussed more fully in the next chapter. In any event, Maimonides did consider them either fully reducible to rational demonstration or at least a means to the end of attaining demonstrable knowledge. Either way the ultimate goal of human life is the knowledge of God. Philosophy is the high road to God trodden by the "solitary few," and dogmatic religion is the low road of the multitude.

During the thirteenth and fourteenth centuries, Jewish philosophers in Christian Spain and Provençe interpreted Maimonides as a strict rationalist. Under the influence of the Muslim philosopher Averroës, they reduced faith to knowledge by emphasizing the existence of one philosophic truth which can be approached in different manners in accordance with the intellectual competence of the individual.[19] The unlearned multitude reach truth solely through the figurative language of Scripture; theologians, those who begin with a set of axiomatic religious principles to attempt a rational exposition of religious belief, reach truth by proving dialectically that it does not negate reason; and philosophers reach the truth through rational demonstration. The last path is the best path for the ideal religious man. True faith was the knowledge of philosophic truth.

The Jewish rationalists were optimists concerning the human ability to cognize truth with certainty. Their mental efforts concentrated on the attainment of intellectual perfection through philosophy. Although religiously observant, they were only marginally interested in halakhah or in dogma. In Aristotelian philosophy, *praxis*—practical knowledge, which for Jews is halakhah—is always inferior to *theoria*. Similarly, defining the faith in discrete principles is unimportant to someone seeking universal truths, particularly when any principle can be reduced to philosophically demonstrable knowledge.

This rationalist assimilation of faith into knowledge explains why we find little discussion of faith at all in the writings of thirteenth and fourteenth century Jewish philosophers and why most of them rarely discuss Maimonides' Thirteen Principles. Philosophy and religion converged into one science—"the divine science" (i.e., metaphysics). Theology was not a distinct discipline at all, but submerged within metaphysics.[20]

The post-Maimonidean rationalists focused instead on prophecy—to them a natural phenomenon which occurs when an individual attains intellectual perfection. The propositional content of prophecy is therefore identical with scientific knowledge. Gersonides articulated this position most radically when he asserted that divine revelation made known not only the true conclusions of scientific syllogism but also the syllogistic procedure itself; that is, the Torah reveals both the truth and the method of attaining truth.[21] The religious philosopher has only to study the Torah and expose its philosophic content to recognize that whatever can be known through divine revelation can also be known through human reason.

The Maimonidean synthesis of reason and faith emerged out of the Judeo-Muslim cultural matrix. Judaism and Islam are both prophetic religions focusing on revealed Law as interpreted by authoritative, normative tradition (*halakhah; shari'a*). In both cases the religion-as-tradition was reconciled with philosophy through a rationalization of the Law, and in both cases that rationalization was achieved through the source of the Law, prophecy.[22] During the thirteenth and fourteenth centuries, Jewish philosophers perpetuated this Judeo-Muslim reconciliation even though they now lived under Christian rule. Some of these Jewish scholars were instrumental in transmitting the knowledge of Greek philosophy to the Latin West by collaborating with Christian scholars on the translation of Aristotle and his Muslim interpreters into Latin. This dissemination first confronted Christian scholars with the same problems which Muslims and Jews had already discussed a few centuries earlier. Scholasticism was the response of the Christian world to the conflict between Greek philosophy and the Christian faith.[23]

Unlike Judaism and to a lesser extent Islam, Christianity, especially medieval Catholicism, emphasizes the importance of creed. The Christian believer must affirm certain articles of faith. In Christianity the conflict of reason and faith therefore centered not on the phenomenon of prophecy but on the demonstrability of creed and the epistemology of belief. By the late twelfth century, the Western

Church, under the Pope, had gained sufficient political power to enforce the authoritative definition of the creed. Nevertheless, the consolidation of urban culture by then brought about a constant search for new forms of religious expression which often conflicted with ecclesiastical orthodoxy. As a result, from the second half of the twelfth century throughout the thirteenth century, the Church battled against diverse and potentially heretical positions including those expounded by philosophers in the newly established universities.[24]

Aristotelianism posed one danger to Christian orthodoxy, namely, philosophic heresy. Ecclesiastical authorities therefore declared a ban on teaching Aristotle in 1205, 1210, and 1231 at the various burgeoning universities. Their efforts failed.[25] The study of Aristotle in European universities spread throughout the second half of the thirteenth century and changed the curriculum, method of teaching, and interpretation of Christian creed.

Saint Thomas Aquinas (1225-1274) reflects the conservative response of the Church to the challenge of Aristotle. Aquinas had read The Guide of the Perplexed in its Latin translation, prepared in a collaboration among Jewish scholars and Dominican friars, and was intimately familiar with Maimonides' harmonization of philosophy and religion.[26] Maimonidean formulations, concepts, and insights deeply influenced him. Nevertheless, Aquinas responded differently to the challenge of Aristotle.[27] Aquinas was confident that Aristotle could be shaped to fit Christian perspectives and purposes, and that he, Aquinas, could create and supply the metaphysical teachings to accomplish that transformation.

Aquinas' synthesis of reason and faith greatly influenced Jewish philosophers first in Italy and later in Spain. R. David ben Judah Messer Leon was among those Jewish thinkers who were familiar with Aquinas' writings and influenced by his harmonization of reason and faith. Though R. David remained loyal to Maimonides, he also adopted and adapted the Thomistic synthesis of reason and faith to the case of Judaism. The result was a fusion of elements taken from both Maimonides and Aquinas. To understand David's position we need to explain Aquinas' synthesis of reason and faith.

Aquinas maintained that Aristotle should be adopted and adapted not to christianize the pagan thinker, rather because some of his theories were valid and true. Within the realm of human reason, the teachings of Aristotle should prevail to the extent that they can be proven to be true.[28] When Aristotle asserts conclusions incompatible with Christian doctrines, the proper procedure for a Christian philosopher is not simply to discard them but to examine whether they follow validly from true premises; it will, of course, be shown that they do not. So unlike Maimonides, who reduced faith to reason, Aquinas asserted that a qualitative difference exists between faith and knowledge with faith supreme.

Aquinas first distinguished among opinion, belief, and knowledge.[29] Belief is an intermediary type of cognition above opinion and below knowledge.[29] Belief is like knowledge in that if *a* believes "that *p*," then *a* accepts "that *p*" and does not accept "*not-p*." But unlike knowledge, belief involves the will. The believer not only holds a certain belief (i.e., conceptualizes a certain proposition) but also voluntarily accepts it, or assents to it. In belief, the will moves the intellect to accept the content of certain propositions. In general, we will something because we want to have it. Acceptance of a certain belief, then, is not an end in itself, but serves a higher end. Human beings ultimately desire happiness, so they hold certain beliefs because those beliefs somehow serve the ultimate end of human life, to be happy. T. Potts summarized Aquinas' position on this point as follows: "*a* believes that *p* if and only if *a* accepts that *p* because he wishes that *q*, where accepting that *p* is a necessary means to *q*."[30]

Aquinas then conceived of faith as a special case of belief. The proper object of faith is God, the First Truth. Because God is the ultimate object of faith, faith differs from other beliefs on several accounts. First, in belief the ground for our assent is a natural end (happiness in this world), whereas in faith the ground for our assent is a supernatural end (eternal life). Second, since the end of faith is a supernatural desire, we need God's assistance in desiring it. Faith, then, is a divine gift by which man believes supernaturally both that there is such a thing as eternal life and that it consists in the knowledge of God. Third, since the propositions of faith come from God (i.e., are revealed), they are necessarily true. In sum, "Believing supernaturally that *p* entails that God has revealed that *p*, and this in turn entails *p*."[31] Aquinas states in *Summa Theologiae* II-II, q. 6, art. 2:

> Two things are requisite for faith. First [is] that the things which are of faith should be proposed to man ... The second thing ... is the assent of the believer to things which are proposed to him ... To believe does indeed depend on the will of the believer; but man's will needs to be prepared by God with grace, in order that he may be raised to things which are above nature.

Aquinas thus teaches that "God is the object of faith, which assents to propositions concerning God under the formal aspect of their being revealed by God."[32] The knowledge of God is also the ultimate objective of philosophy. Aquinas maintains that it is theoretically possible for the philosopher to work out a system without recourse for divine revelation.[33] The metaphysician can attain knowledge about God as the First Cause and about God's relation to the universe. However, the philosopher arrives at the knowledge of God only through knowledge of material things created by God. In the process of philosophic inquiry, the philosopher abstracts the knowledge of universals from his sense-perception of material things. By means of deductive reasoning, the philosopher arrives at conclusions about the existence of God, God's attributes, and God's relation to the universe. To the extent that the philosopher can disclose the relationship of material things on one transcendent being — God — philosophy consists of a discourse about God. The philosopher can know that God exists, that God is one, incorporeal, perfect intellect. This knowledge about God constitutes natural theology, or metaphysics.[34]

Aquinas agreed with Maimonides that philosophy is for the very few. Most people are not naturally suited for intellectual activity, and they avoid it because philosophy requires long training and abstinence from bodily pursuits. But Aquinas went beyond Maimonides to emphasize the uncertainty of the philosophic procedure itself:

> The investigation of the human reason for the most part has falsity present within it, and this is due partly to the weakness of our intellect in judgment, and partly to the admixture of images. The result that many, remaining ignorant of the power of demonstration, would hold in doubt those things which had been most truly demonstrated.[35]

Further, philosophy does not provide the knowledge of God required for man's salvation. Philosophy at best leads to knowledge about God's existence. This knowledge is not salvific—at best it can secure happiness in this world. Only the knowledge of God's essence has salvific merit, namely, it leads to the attainment of eternal life. Had philosophy been the only path to God, immortality would have been impossible. Hence, it became morally necessary for God to reveal Himself to man for the sake of human salvation (i.e., to attain the supernatural end of eternal bliss):

It was necessary for the salvation of man that certain truths which exceed human reason should be made known to him by divine revelation. Even as regards those truths about God which reason can investigate, it was necessary that man be taught by a divine revelation.[36]

Aquinas then introduced the formal and qualitative distinction between theology and philosophy as two scholarly disciplines, each with its own premises and its own method of inquiry. Dogmatic theology (or *sacra doctrina*) is the science which explicates divine revelation; philosophy is the fruit of human reasoning. Theology and philosophy represent two qualitatively different ways of knowing God, and theology is supreme. Whereas theology begins with revelation from God, human reason begins with the sense-perception of the created, material world and culminates with knowledge about God. Whereas theology consists of infallible propositions with certitude, philosophy is prone to errors, deception, and sophistry. Whereas theology makes known salvific knowledge, thus securing the supernatural end of human life, philosophy at best secures the natural end of human life—happiness in this world. By distinguishing theology and philosophy, Aquinas could assert the supremacy of faith over natural human reason.[37]

Some revealed truths are nonetheless rationally demonstrable without special divine help:

Since, therefore, there exists a twofold truth concerning the divine being, one which the inquiry of the reason can reach, the other which surpasses the whole ability of the human reason, it is fitting that both of these truths be proposed to man divinely for belief.[38]

The existence of God, His unity, incorporeality, and perfection, for example, constitute truths which can be known both through revelation and through human reason. They are thus "preambles of faith," namely, they prepare the believer for those truths which depend upon faith alone. Human reason cannot independently demonstrate the essential articles of faith; these are the various doctrines of dogmatic Christian theology, including the Trinity, Transsubstantiation, Incarnation, and Virgin Birth.

Aquinas then distinguishes natural human happiness from salvation. Ultimate felicity for man is not that intellectual perfection attainable on earth which Aristotle called happiness *(eudaimonia)*; rather it is a supernatural vision of God's essence, attainable only in afterlife.[39] Further, man cannot be saved by reason alone, nor by faith alone. Only an "influx of divine goodness" by which man can recognize God's essence secures the bliss of eternal life. The divine essence is an intelligible form. In order that the created human intellect be able to see the divine essence, "it is necessary for the created intellect to be elevated for this purpose by a more sublime disposition." The revelation from God is the "influx of divine light" which "makes the intellect actually powerful enough to understand."[40] When the intellect is moved by the will to assent to the propositions of revelation, man receives the divine light. Thus, revelation completes and perfects human reason, facilitating life eternal.

Aquinas' conception of prophecy reflects the notion that revelation is supernatural because it comes from God. Altmann has shown Aquinas' debt to Maimonides on several accounts.[41] In essence, Aquinas incorporated Maimonides' naturalist conception of prophecy into a supernaturalist framework. Aquinas distinguished between 'natural' and 'divine' prophecy. In lieu of Maimonides' emanationist picture of the universe, Aquinas sharply differentiated between the natural realm of the created world and the supernatural domain of divine grace. The ontological gap between the natural and the supernatural realms is bridged by the conception of God as the act of existing. Things exist because they are created by God. Creatures participate in God's Being *(esse)* so that the created universe existentially depends on God.[42] The ontological gap is bridged through voluntary divine grace which perfects nature. In accordance with this ontology, Aquinas proposed a different epistemology in which the human cognition is no longer a result of an interaction between a transcendent Separate Intellect and the human intellect.[43] In Aquinas' system, the Active Intellect of which Aristotle spoke is an internal function, and the highest stage of human knowledge is no longer a mystical union with the Active Intellect but rather a direct illumination from God. Aquinas thus proposed a supernatural conception of prophecy as direct divine illumination upon the intellect of the recipient; that is, prophecy is a gift from God.

Revelation perfects and completes human reason because it comes from God. The verity of the propositions revealed by God depends not on the intellectual excellence of the founder of the religion—Moses, in Maimonides' view—but on its supernatural origin—God. The teachings of the Faith are true because they come from God (because they are revealed). Through revelation God makes known "the knowledge by which God is known to Himself alone and is revealed to others." By definition, this knowledge is qualitatively superior to natural human reason, which knows God through created things.[44] As created beings, humans can reason only because God implanted in them the ability to reason. The truths discovered by human reason cannot genuinely conflict with divine revelation; the former are fragmentary and incomplete, the latter reflect the infinite divine wisdom. To the extent that human reasoning yields true knowledge, this truth participates in the infinite truth of God.[45] Conversely, while human reason cannot alone discover the undemonstrable truths of faith, reason can still clarify and elucidate them after their revelation.

Accordingly, the dogmatic theologian begins with the sacred teachings of revelation and expounds on them by means of natural theology. His task is to explain revealed truths. Philosophy can remove obstacles to faith by facilitating that explanation. So does sacred doctrine *(sacra doctrina)* perfect and complete the imperfect and uncertain natural human reason.

Aquinas' influence on Jewish philosophy began in his Italian homeland even prior to his death. Several Jewish scholars, mainly in Naples and Rome, were actively engaged in transmitting Judeo-Arabic philosophy to the Latin West. Jacob Anatoly, Moses of Salerno, Hillel ben Samuel, 'Immanuel of Rome, and Judah of Rome had working relations with Scholastic masters, and through them gained knowledge of Scholastic literature and intellectual controversies.[46] J. Sermoneta has shown that Hillel ben Samuel, at the end of the thirteenth century, and Judah of Rome, in the first half of the fourteenth century, launched "the Thomistic school" of Jewish philosophy.[47] At times Jewish Thomistic scholars mentioned Aquinas by name as an authority, while at other times they incorporated his writing or his views without attribution.

Italian Jewish philosophers were staunch defenders of Maimonides. They spent their lives disseminating his teachings and popularizing his works. They wrote commentaries on *The Guide* and summaries of his ethical writings. They applied his hermeneutic principles to biblical exegesis. Some were also personally involved in the Maimonidean controversy which erupted in Italy during the 1280s and 1290s and resulted in a ban on the study of philosophy by people under twenty-five years old.[48]

Their allegiance to Maimonides firm, why and how did Italian

Jewish philosophers account Aquinas? By the late thirteenth century they recognized that the radical rationalist interpretation of Maimonides poses serious problems to Jewish orthodoxy. They therefore saw the need to reinterpret Maimonides' synthesis of reason and faith. Here Aquinas helped, for his view, dechristologized, was significantly more palatable to religious orthodoxy. Hence thinkers like Hillel ben Samuel and Judah of Rome incorporated individual Thomistic teachings into their generally Maimonidean philosophy.[49] They did not embark on comprehensive reconciliation of the two but, in the typically eclectic style of the Middle Ages, permitted them to coexist side by side.

As noted earlier, the fourteenth century closed with disaster in Spain in 1391. The systematic assault of Christianity upon Jews and Judaism, the physical destruction of Spanish Jewry, and the mass apostasy of Jews brought about a crisis of faith. Maimonidean rationalism was severely shattered. Philosophy as a discipline, the conduct of Jewish philosophers, and the Maimonides synthesis of reason and revelation were all accused of being subversive to traditional Jewish society. Moreover, the success of Christian polemics in the public debate at Tortosa in 1413-1414 appeared to destroy the claims of Jewish rationalism. Armed with a new weapon, scholastic argumentation, Christianity emerged as the rational religion, while rabbinic Judaism, and especially the Talmud, were exposed as riddled with inconsistencies, absurdities, and simplistic beliefs. The sheer volume of conversions, albeit under duress, substantiated the Christian claims for spiritual superiority. Continued contacts between professing Jews and *conversos* raised new questions such as, Who is a Jew? What constitutes the Jewish Faith? Who will have "a portion in the world to come"? What is the proper road to immortality? The conflict between reason and faith erupted anew.

By the second half of the fifteenth century, the highly polemical encounter with Christianity brought Jewish scholars into closer contact with Aquinas' teachings, both through oral public and private debates and directly through the literature itself. Only then was Aquinas' full impact felt.[50] In Spain, Provençe, and Italy, they continued to write within the parameters articulated by Maimonides, but they reinterpreted his position according to their post-Thomistic harmonization of reason and faith. Through Aquinas they could protect the rabbinic tradition against the philosophic reductionism of the radical Jewish rationalists yet still defend the rationality of Judaism against Christianity.[51] H. Davidson called the stance of fifteenth century Jewish scholarship "conservative" in comparison that of the thirteenth and fourteenth centuries.[52] This label is apt, but another befits this new scholarship even more: "theological."

M. Kellner correctly noted that, in contrast to their predecessors, fifteenth century Jewish scholars were primarily theologians who utilized their knowledge of philosophy to support Judaism's polemical claims.[53] This characterization applies to R. Simon ben Zemah Duran, R. Joseph Albo, R. Joseph ibn Shem Tob, R. Abraham Shalom, R. Abraham Bibago, R. Isaac 'Arama, and Don Isaac Abravanel, all of whom adopted the Thomistic distinction between philosophy and theology, and only then recognized theology as a discipline distinct from, and even superior to, philosophy. They reflected the Thomistic synthesis of reason and faith, and devoted much writing to the analysis of faith both as "belief in" and as "belief that." They emphasized the subjectivity of faith—the believer's personal commitment to God and to authoritative, traditional teachings—and made the definition of Jewish dogma a central issue. They discussed Maimonides' Thirteen Principles at length, often substituting their own lists (as did Duran, Crescas, Albo, and 'Arama) or opposing dogmatism altogether (as did Abravanel). They attempted to prove the superiority of Judaism by asserting that prophecy is higher in quality than demonstrative knowledge, and that prophetic revelations are superrational truths which can be understood only through faith in authoritative tradition.[54]

The fifteenth century thus witnessed a reconsideration of reason and faith, a redefinition of Judaism, and renewed attempts to juxtapose Judaism with both scientific knowledge and Christianity. Philosophy declined and theology arose, born of a profound historical change that Christianity wrought—the destruction of Spanish Jewry—and nurtured by a profound discipline that Christianity wrought as well—Scholasticism.

Faith Perfects Reason

R. David ben Judah Messer Leon was deeply interested in defining the relationship between "the path of tradition and faith" *(derekh ha-qabbalah ve-ha-emunah)* and "the path of inquiry" *(derekh ha-haqirah)*. He used *emunah* to mean both "belief that" and "belief in," and *qabbalah* to refer to the propositions of the authoritative tradition. He asserted the supremacy of faith over human reason (i.e., "inquiry" over philosophy) and used his erudition in philosophy to substantiate the claims of Judaism. He followed Maimonides and medieval rationalism to hold that Judaism is rational and teaches nothing which negates human reason, but he also borrowed from Aquinas' discussion of Christianity to consider Judaism a normative, received tradition; reason makes faith easier, but faith ultimately depends upon human free will, and faith, not reason, is necessary in order to achieve eternal life. R. David thus exemplifies the emergence of Jewish theology as a distinct discipline in the fifteenth century.

R. David includes an extensive discussion of reason and faith in *Magen David*, in which he owes a great debt to Abraham Bibago's *Derekh Emunah*. R. David copied long sections of *Derekh Emunah* verbatim and paraphrased others. He never credited Bibago by name, only as "that scholar," and occasionally did not even bother to change Bibago's first person into the third.[55] R. David adopted Bibago's understanding of *emunah* as follows:

> When I speculated about the meaning of *emunah* to the best of my ability, and sought to define it, I realized that since *emunah* is obtained through received paths *[derakhim mequbalim]* and arrived at from accepted premises [as I had explained] above, it is appropriate to define it in comparison to theoretical conclusions known through philosophical inquiry *[haqirah]*. Accordingly, the definition of *emunah* is a type of knowing habit *[qinyan sikhli]* formed on the basis of received premises *[haqdamot mequbalot]*. The import of this definition is that *emunah* is something which the soul acquires, hence "habit" is the species which consists of two genera: moral habits and knowledge.
>
> When I said "knowing" I recognized the difference between *emunah* and moral habits, so that "knowledge" is closer to the nature of *emunah*. When I said "knowing" I wanted to distinguish *emunah* from things which are [logically] impossible, so that one cannot even conceive them, let alone learn any truth from them. And when I said "accepted premises" I wanted to distinguish between *emunah* and philosophic inquiry. Philosophic inquiry is based on either *a priori* premises *[haqdamot rishonot]* or true premises *[haqdamot zodqot]*, whereas *emunah* is based on premises received from a prophet or an elder reputable man in both speculation and deed.[56]

R. David thus begins with Maimonides' distinction between

reason and received tradition. The "path of faith" consists of received teachings interpreted by authoritative tradition, and the "path of inquiry" consists of conclusions arrived at from systematic human reasoning. Both paths are rooted in undeniable premises: faith in the prophetic experience of a reputable individual and philosophy on propositions whose truth is either self-evident or verifiable (i.e., corresponding to extramental reality). But R. David then follows Aquinas and Bibago to claim that the received tradition *(qabbalah)* is epistemically superior to philosophic inquiry because it comes from God. The supernatural and superrational path of tradition and faith is superior to the natural and rational path of philosophic inquiry.

The philosophic path begins with sense perception of material objects from which the philosopher *(hoqer)* abstracts intelligible universals inherent in particulars. The philosopher then formulates propositions *(derushim)* about what exists. From true premises *(haqdamot)*, the philosopher deduces by means of syllogism *(heqesh)* propositions about things which one cannot perceive. Ultimately, the philosopher deduces the existence of incorporeal things *(ha-devarim ha-bilti muhashim)* from the perception of material things *(ha-devarim ha-muhashim)*. Philosophic inquiry proceeds from the ontologically inferior to the superior *(mi-le-matah le-ma'alah)*, from the effect to the cause *(mi-ha-'alul el ha-'illah)*, from the temporally posterior to the anterior *(me-ha-meuhar el ha-muqdam)*.[57] It culminates in knowledge about the existence of a First Cause, God, and the manner by which all things proceed from God (i.e., God's attributes). This knowledge about God, however, is inherently imperfect because it originates in perception of material things; that is, it is "tainted" with corporeality. Further, its content is difficult to comprehend, it requires prolonged training, it is prone to mistakes and controversies, and only rarely does it yield true knowledge with certainty.

The path of "tradition and faith," on the other hand, proceeds from God: from the cause to the effect, from the ontologically prior to the posterior, from the universal to the particular. The propositions attained through this path (i.e., through revelation), are necessarily true, certain, and devoid of error. Infallible, divine truths, however, do not conflict with the teachings of human reason; rather they exceed the range of human knowledge and the limit of natural human reason. Faith is thus superrational; it manifests the highest degree of rationality — Divine Wisdom.

"Inquiry" depends by definition upon logic. The philosopher

cannot choose to ignore or reject the true conclusions of an investigation. By beginning from true premises and correctly applying the rules of logic, one necessarily arrives at correct conclusions. The human will plays no role in the philosophic procedure itself or in the acceptance of philosophic conclusions. Faith, by contrast, is voluntary; it depends upon the believer's affirmative act. In order to reach this conclusion, R. David again combines teachings of both Maimonides and Aquinas. He agrees with Maimonides that faith initially depends upon a certain mental impression:

> And the Master wrote that belief is not something which is uttered by the mouth, but that which is conceptualized by the intellect; and he labeled as "stupid people" those holding to beliefs to which, in their representation, they do not attach any meaning ... It appears that according to Maimonides' view, a believer is one who conceptualizes the truth in his mind.[58]

However, "numerous people known as wise men *(hakhamim)* are not good believers at all, but in fact heretics who misinterpret the Torah." Belief then designates a certain cognitive act divorced from the verification of its content. "The specific meaning of belief *[emunah]* is that it arises in the soul of the believer, whether it is true or false." Though R. David agrees with Maimonides that faith requires a certain mental representation, he followed Aquinas in saying that faith requires the assent of the will to accept the true belief. R. David asserts that

> ...the believer must first conceptualize the belief in his mind, but in addition, he has to desire and love this belief so much so that he will be ready to give his life and his possessions for the sake of this belief. When the mind conceptualizes something it yields knowledge, but the assent of the intellectual will *[razon sikhli]* yields love which is a necessary condition of faith. Accordingly, a believer is someone who conceptualizes faith and loves it strongly as we said above.[59]

R. David echoed Aquinas in asserting that when "the intellectual will conjoins with the mental representation and with willingness to love God forever, then that person is called believer."[60]

Accordingly, faith differs from reason in requiring not only will but love and self-sacrifice as well. The believer's love of God is based on the principle of *imitatio Dei*. As a benevolent creator, God loves his creatures. Divine love is manifested in God's providential care of particulars. According to R. David,

> ...what brings the believer to love God is the contemplation of God's love to us. God's love to us consists of two aspects: first that He [and not any of His agents] loves us [directly], which necessitates that we should worship Him directly and not through intermediaries, and [second] that we should worship Him and not anything else, as much as He governs us and nothing but us.[61]

The emphasis on the reciprocal love between God and the Jewish believer was another polemical response to Christianity. Though divine love extends to all creation, God's love for the Chosen People is special. The People of Israel collectively, and each individually, are the object of God's love. In return, Israel as a people, and each and every Jew, should reciprocate divine love by imitating it—that is, by a total commitment to God. Thus, human love of God becomes the willingness to commit oneself totally to the teachings of the Faith even to the point of self-sacrifice. This association of faith and self-sacrifice evokes the traditional Jewish notion of Sanctification of the Name *(qiddush ha-shem)* as the mark of Jewish loyalty to God.

In R. David's day, loyalty to Judaism was very difficult. R. David not only suffered on account of that loyalty but also witnessed the failure of many to keep the Faith. The Christian notion of faith as divine grace appealed to R. David, perhaps because he was fully cognizant of the objective difficulties of professing Judaism in the face of mounting Christian persecution:

> Faith is like a ray of divine grace *[hesed elohi]* shining upon the believer, as Scripture says *the path of faith I have chosen* [Psalms 119:30], etc., that it to say, the path through which one arrives at faith is my choice, which is the proper way for the true Faith.[62]

Faith ultimately differs from reason in that only faith can bring eternal life. R. David first concludes logically that reason alone cannot bring eternal life because too few could thereby be saved:

> Because of the obstacles which limit natural human reason, it would have been impossible for most people to attain human

perfection [i.e., immortality]. If human perfection could be attained only by "one from a city and two from a family" [Jer. 3:14] while others would have perished forever, the divine creation of human species would have been in vain. Therefore divine providence had to find a way by which to perfect the human species, or at least, its best portion—the People of Israel.[63]

Further, reason cannot even remain an alternate path to salvation because salvation is granted as a means of divine retribution (i.e., reward and punishment); one can be rewarded only for what one freely chooses and not for something which he knows necessarily.

Accordingly, those who voluntarily affirm the authoritative tradition receive divine grace. By stressing the voluntary dimension of faith, R. David made it clear that even though Judaism can be interpreted rationally, the ultimate mark of the Jewish believer is willingness to commit oneself to God and to Judaism. The one who knows what philosophy teaches about God, but who is not totally committed to the Faith, will fail to attain eternal life.

If reason is so inferior to faith, what use is it at all? R. David accepted the fundamental premise of the philosophic tradition, namely, that man is rational. In order to attain human perfection (i.e., intellectual perfection), man must actualize the rational faculty which is only potential at birth.[64] He must study philosophy. Intellectual perfection elevates man above corporeal existence: it spiritualizes man, thereby facilitating man's attainment of the ultimate felicity, the knowledge of God.[65] Thus R. David followed Maimonides to view the study of philosophy as a religious obligation, but followed Aquinas to distinguish between the natural end of human life—happiness *(hazlahah)* and its supernatural end—life after death *(hishaarut).*[66] Reason can secure the natural end of human life in this world, and reason can make particular truths of the authoritative tradition easier to accept, but only faith that comes from God can lead man to eternal life:

Divine providence realized the need to bestow *[le-hashpi'a]* faith, which is a true knowledge without demonstrative proof and without labor and effort, upon the chosen People of Israel. Through faith the Jew is perfected because God bestows true propositions upon the intellect of each individual without falsehood and without deception, but by means of tradition *[qabbalah]* and prophecy *[nevuah]* which are superior to philosophic inquiry in regard to difficulty of comprehension, effort and error.[67]

R. David's treatment of two subjects, prophecy and the Torah, demonstrates his claim that faith perfects reason. As God's communication, revelation consists of infallible truths which comprise the Jewish authoritative tradition/religion/faith. The Torah, both Written and Oral, is the verbal manifestation of divine revelation, and prophecy is the vehicle for its delivery to humankind. As discussed more fully in the next chapter, R. David's analysis of revelation blends Maimonides, Aquinas, and Judah Halevi.

R. David followed Aquinas in distinguishing between "divine prophecy" *(nevuah elohit)* and "natural prophecy" *(nevuah tiv'it)*.[68] What the Torah calls "prophecy" *(nevuah)* is divine prophecy, an unmediated gift through which God directly illuminates the intellect of the prophet and bestows upon him God's own knowledge of reality. God selects an individual or group to receive the divine gift. Certain material conditions are prerequisite to revelation — for example, intellectual perfection — but God can provide them supernaturally if they are not naturally present. God thus provides both the content of revelation and the conditions for its reception.[69] At Sinai, for instance, God miraculously transformed all the People of Israel into the level of prophets ready to receive His revelation.[70]

Natural prophecy, on the other hand, is not a revelation from God, but the summit of philosophic inquiry, namely, knowledge of God and the supernal world as deduced through the finest inquiry. Natural prophecy is identical to what Aquinas called "natural theology."[71] R. David also called it "philosophic prophecy" *(nevuah mehqarit)*. Knowledge thus obtained equates with metaphysics, the knowledge of being as being, which, as noted above, is prone to mistakes and uncertainty and cannot secure personal immortality.

Some conclusions follow from the distinction between divine and natural prophecy. Human reason can teach revealed truths only to the extent that they are also demonstrable. Other divinely revealed truths by definition surpass the capacity of natural human reason. Since prophecy comes from God, prophets as a class are superior to philosophers, just as "the path of faith and tradition" is superior to "the path of philosophical inquiry."

Maimonides believed prophecy to result from intellectual perfection. Although R. David believed prophecy to derive instead from

God, his treatment of Moses, Israel's first and greatest prophet, again shows his loyalty to Maimonides. First, R. David adhered to the Maimonidean picture of the universe and epistemology.[72] Like other fifteenth century theologians, R. David still viewed the world as a hierarchy of three realms: the supernal world of God and the Separate Intelligences, the heavenly realm of the nine spheres and their stars, and the physical, sublunar world of particulars. Accordingly, R. David still maintained that the physical world is governed by the Active Intellect (the last of the ten Intelligences) and that human cognition is due to the contact between the human intellect and the transcendent Active Intellect. Within this picture of the universe, R. David interpreted Mosaic prophecy in the epistemological categories of the Maimonidean tradition but modified it to fit his new realization that God, and not the Active Intellect, is the direct author of revelation, and that prophecy is qualitatively different from philosophic knowledge.

R. David agreed with Maimonides that Moses alone was both "the master of the wise men" (i.e., the intellectually perfect philosopher who attained the highest level of philosophic perfection accessible to man) and "the master of the prophets." Within the philosophical theory of prophecy as a union between the human intellect and the transcendent Active Intellect, R. David differentiated between prophetic knowledge *(hamshakhah)* and philosophic knowledge *(haqirah)*. Moses attained knowledge as a prophet which not even he could apprehend as a philosopher.

Hamshakhah literally means "drawing downward".[73] R. David employs the term to denote the divine efflux which Moses drew downward when he received a revelation from God. The term connotes attainment of divine spirituality by means of mystical union with God. When R. David attempts to explain it rationally, he resorts to the cognitive language developed within medieval Aristotelianism. *Hamshakhah* is a non-discursive, non-propositional, unmediated, clear, and self-evident experience. The experience is so intense that the individual feels it sensually, although there is nothing corporeal about it. The structure of reality as a whole becomes so unusually clear and objective that the prophet can actually visualize it. *Hamshakhah* best fits what William James called the "noetic quality" of mystical experience;[74] it produces an insight into the very structure of reality.

To clarify the meaning of *hamshakhah* R. David refers to *Hayy ibn Yaqzan*, the twelfth century philosophic novel of ibn Tufayl, a

Muslim.[75] R. David lauded *Hayy ibn Yaqzan* as the best explanation of the ability of the human intellect to unite with the incorporeal entity as the Separate Intelligence. Nonetheless R. David intentionally miscited the book in order to make his point. In the original text, the protagonist, Hayy ibn Yaqzan, began with the perception of sensible, existent objects, and, after a long and arduous reflection upon them, attained an intuition of the divine essence. Real entities became clear to him in a single pattern so continuous, clear, immediate, and intense that it resembled a sensual vision, even though it was devoid of materiality. This vision was non-discursive, non-logical, non-propositional, and quasi-mystical. Through it, Hayy uplifted himself from the piecemeal knowledge of objects to a total picture of the entire universe.[76] Hayy was saved from the total annihilation in God characteristic of Sufi mystical experiences. He attained this sublime experience only through systematic philosophical reflection, and without divine revelation. For the Muslim philosopher ibn Tufayl, therefore, prophecy is but a translation of philosophical truths into a metaphoric language so that they will be accessible to all humans; prophecy is clearly inferior to philosophy.

R. David, however, ascribed Hayy's intuition not to philosophic inquiry but to prophetic experiences. In particular, the perfect prophet, Moses, received divine revelation in the state of *hamshakhah*:

> The highest cognition, which is superior to philosophic inquiry, is the true *hamshakhah*, explained in the treatise *Hayy ibn Yaqzan*, already mentioned above. This cognition is akin to the manner by which the Separate Intelligence (*ha-sekhel ha-nifrad*) cognizes itself. This cognition proceeds from the [ontologically] superior to the inferior. It is so intense that the individual can actually visualize in the state of *hamshakhah* what he has previously comprehended through reasoning and sensual perception. This is due to the intensity of such cognition. Therefore the prophet is called a visionary *[roeh]* ... because in his *hamshakhah* he can actually see what he has earlier apprehended in his intellect. This is similar to the blind man whose eyes opened up, and who could see what he has previously apprehended only in his mind. Know that.[77]

R. David also makes an etymological connection between *Moshe* (Moses) and *hamshakhah*. He quotes the Biblical passage that explains the derivation of "Moses" through the verb *limshot*, "to draw" — they share a common three letter root, namely, *mem, shin,* and a hollow third letter *heh* — and adds to it a comparison in meaning to *hamshakhah,* the root of which, *mem, shin, caf,* differs only in the third letter:

> Moses Our Rabbi, may he rest in peace, attained the highest level of the philosophical inquiry, since he was the master of wisdom. Likewise he attained the highest level of *hamshakhah.* And his name indicated who he was; he was called Moses *[Moshe]* "because from the water I have drawn him *[meshitihu]*" [Exod. 2:10] signifying that he would always draw and draw downward *[moshe u-moshekh]* the supernal things.[78]

Philosophic inquiry thus brings one to "human philosophic perfection" *(shelemut enoshi filosofi),* which is conditional to the attainment of "prophetic perfection" *(shelemut nevuit).* R. David employs the metaphor of the ladder of ascension, by then commonplace in medieval philosophical literature, to describe the progression from philosophy to prophecy.[79] The study of philosophy leads up the ladder toward the knowledge of God and culminates in the mastery of metaphysics. At that point the perfect philosopher, chosen by God, receives a direct revelation from God without any intermediaries. Because of divine grace, the perfect natural prophet becomes the recipient of divine prophecy: the prophet receives divine efflux which he then draws downward, back to the material world. Thus does faith perfect reason and reason ease the burden of faith.

Because the Torah (both Written and Oral) came from God, it is incorporeal, eternal, and true. The Torah is identical with Divine Wisdom, the knowledge by which God is known to Himself.[80] Because man is by nature corporeal, the spiritual teachings of the Torah had to be clothed in figurative language so as to make them accessible to man. The Torah then has both an exoteric dimension *(nigleh)* and an esoteric dimension *(nistar).* Exoterically, the Torah consists of a narrative, fables, similes, and metaphors; only esoterically it is identical with the divine wisdom. The Torah can be understood exoterically by all people, but esoterically it can be known only through faith. Man attains salvation (i.e., eternal life) through faith in the Torah as God's revelation.

R. David followed Aquinas in dividing the truths of divine revelation into two groups: those that are demonstrable *(devarim sh-mi-*

tiv'am le-qabel mofet), that are provable by human reason without special assistance from God; and those that are undemonstrable *(devarim she-'ein mi-tiv'am le-qabbel mofet)*, that human reason alone cannot discover.[81] As to the first group, "the Torah is equally faith and reason." The believer is encouraged to know them through reason in addition to affirming them on faith, even though faith teaches them with greater clarity and certitude. Undemonstrable truths, on the other hand, can be known only through revelation and must be accepted by faith in authoritative tradition. As to them, "the Torah is more faith than reason."[82] They include both dogmas of Judaism and practical commandments of the Law.

As noted above, Aquinas states that the undemonstrable truths of revelation are not, strictly speaking, the Christian Faith but only "the preambles to faith." That Christian Faith (i.e., *sacra doctrina*) comprises infallible truths which exceed human reason. R. David, on the other hand, includes the demonstrable teachings of revelation as an integral part of the Faith, but, he emphatically adds, "true felicity is not to be had from demonstrable propositions but only from propositions known through faith."[83]

In *Tehillah le-David* R. David expands the true propositions of faith into six categories. The first comprises demonstrable truths, and the last five are subsets of undemonstrable truths:[84]

1. *Demonstrable beliefs (emunot moftiyot)*. The philosopher can know them through inquiry, and the believer can accept them on faith. There is no difference between "what the wise man obtains through demonstration and what the believer receives through tradition — for example, concerning God's existence, His unity, and incorporeality. The believer should still study philosophy to gain a more refined conception of God and to see that these doctrines do manifest total accord between tradition and inquiry.

2. *Legislated beliefs (emunot mehuqaqot)*. These are particular, practical commandments which human reason fails to discover. "Who can conceptualize in the mind that *Zizit, Sukah* and *Lulav* bring about closeness *(qirvah)* and conjunction *(devequt)* with the First Being?" Unlike the rationalist philosophers who demoted the practical commandments to the level of ethics and social order necessary for the attainment of intellectual perfection, R. David thus places them in a category of revealed truths which exceed human reason. As an immediate political consequence, R. David thereby elevated halakhah above philosophy, placing himself to the right of Maimonides.

3. *Beliefs which demonstration can neither prove nor disprove.* Creation is an example. Following Maimonides, R. David argues that human reason cannot prove that the universe was created either out of nothing or out of some existing matter. Acceptance of creation out of nothing relies on the authority of revelation. R. David places that belief as the cardinal dogma of Judaism, and from it derives three others: that the Torah is from Heaven, that God is the author of miracles, and that angels exist.

4. *Beliefs concerning time.* One example is eating unleavened bread in the month of Nisan. This category comprises practical commandments that specify the details of religious performance as interpreted by the rabbinic tradition. Unaided human reason cannot uncover the details of observance.

5. *Beliefs concerning miracles (emunot nissiyot).* These are beliefs "that God can change nature, and that His power extends to all things which are naturally impossible." Miracles recorded in Scripture are examples. R. David distinguishes between that which is naturally impossible and that which is logically impossible. As Creator, God can intervene in nature and change its order, so the belief in miracles is not itself irrational as long as it does not negate the rules of logic. God cannot do what is logically impossible, because faith perfects reason and does not contradict it. Judaism does not include "beliefs which contradict *a priori* truths *(muskalot rishonot)* because they teach things which are logically impossible." The Torah does not include any irrational beliefs either exoterically *(al derekh ha-pirsum)* or esoterically *(al-derekh ha-emet).* The very rationality of the Torah excludes any belief concerning the logically impossible.

6. *Beliefs that appear to contradict human reason.* For example, God wondered about Sarah's laugh, and the serpent spoke with Eve. These beliefs, claims R. David, arise from the figurative language of Scripture, intended to make revelation accessible to all people. "We have to interpret these verses so that they will agree with reason."

In sum, R. David ben Judah Messer Leon's position concerning the conflict between reason and faith can be labeled "moderate fideism."[85] Faith is supreme (fideism), but that faith perfects reason rather than negating it, and reason facilitates the attainment of faith. Faith is not irrational but superrational. That R. David insisted on the rationality of faith and attempted to harmonize the two realms marks him as an heir to medieval patterns. That he acknowledged the intrinsic limitations of natural human reason shows his departure from the strict rationalism of his Jewish predecessors in the thirteenth and fourteenth centuries. R. David turned to theology in response to contemporary historical realities.

Response to Contemporary Challenges

R. David's synthesis of reason and faith resolves the apparent conflicts noted at the beginning of this chapter, such as: In what sense was R. David a Jewish Renaissance man? How could a halakhic Jew be a Renaissance *homo universalis*? How could a rabbinic scholar be well versed in both medieval scholasticism and Renaissance humanism? How could a talmudic Jew accept two distinct metahalakhic programs, philosophy and Kabbalah, as legitimate interpretations of divine revelation?

For R. David ben Judah Messer Leon, faith perfects reason; theology perfects philosophy. R. David patterned his synthesis of reason and faith on the Thomistic model, which enabled him rationalize his loyalty to Judaism without shunning interaction with the non-Jewish Renaissance culture all around him. Concomitantly, by virtue of this claim, he integrated the different visions of Jewish spirituality held by Talmudists, philosophers, and Kabbalists.[86]

The syncretist fusion of halakhah, philosophy, humanism, and Kabbalah was uniquely characteristic of Jewish culture in Renaissance Italy. It is found nowhere else. Only in Renaissance Italy did rabbinic Jews steeped in Ashkenazic halakhah also cultivate the sciences; only in Italy did Jewish scholars embellish the medieval scholastic curriculum to include the newly discovered body of the *studia humanitatis*; only in Italy did Jewish scholars well-versed in the sciences attempt to harmonize philosophy and Kabbalah.

Undoubtedly R. David's reconciliation of reason and faith served polemical and apologetic needs from within and from without. From within, R. David thereby served to curb radical rationalism while justifying the study of philosophy against its Talmudist or Kabbalist opponents. Conversely the theory helped him justify the study of Kabbalah in the face of those who considered it a non-rabbinic mode of thought and those who denied its Jewishness.

From without loomed the menace of Christianity. Though fifteenth century Italian Jewry enjoyed some measure of stability and even material wealth, the status of Jews as an infidel minority remained as precarious as ever. The age-old animosity toward Jews did not vanish, and in fact increased in certain segments of Italian society. Neither did the pressure for the conversion of Jews diminish. Rather, it led to a hostile papal policy by the mid-sixteenth century.[87] Harassment of Jews, missionizing, and attacks on rabbinic Judaism were daily realities in R. David's life. His own expulsion from Naples only underscored the vulnerability of Jewish life in Christendom.

R. David intended his synthesis of faith and reason to defend rabbinic Judaism against the attacks of Christianity. One common Christian argument was that rabbinic Judaism—especially the Talmud and the Midrashim—consisted of irrational, nonsensical, and absurd teachings.[88] Against this claim R. David highlights the rationality of Judaism. Along with prior Jewish philosophers, R. David insisted that Judaism is a rational religion because it does not teach anything which is logically impossible. The claim that the Jewish Faith consists of demonstrable truths entailed that the Faith itself (and not only the preambles of Faith) is rational, contrary to Christian allegations. Moreover, it can even be shown that none of the teachings which admittedly exceed human reason is logically impossible. Unlike Christianity, which teaches the Trinity of God, Judaism holds that "two contradictory statements cannot refer to the same objects simultaneously." And unlike the Christian doctrine of Virgin Birth, Judaism holds that "a corporeal thing cannot come out of another corporeal thing without disruption."[89] In R. David's view, the rationality of Judaism is one sign for its superiority over Christianity.

Another argument that figured prominently in Christian polemics was that Judaism represented the corporeal interpretation of divine revelation due to the carnal nature of the Jews. R. David refutes the claim that rabbinic Judaism is legalism devoid of spirituality by highlighting the spirituality of the Torah. Moses and the entire public at Sinai received a spiritual revelation from God. The Torah, and hence the Jewish Faith as a whole, is eternal; it cannot be abrogated or superseded. Because the Torah comes from God, its propositions are necessarily true and salvific. Only adherence to the Faith as interpreted by the revealed tradition may lead one to salvation.[90] The upshot of this argument is that Judaism (and not Christianity) is the true spiritual religion; Judaism promises both material and spiritual rewards. Allegiance to the Jewish Faith guarantees perfection in this world and eternal life in the world to come. Christian missionizing is thus proven futile.

Christianity, however, was not only a menace to Jews but also a lure. In Renaissance Italy Christianity was the religion of an unusually creative society boasting innovation and progress in all aspects of human life, from art to architecture through science and technology to literature and thought. A Jew could no longer justify allegiance to the Faith by condescension to a surrounding culture alleged to be inferior to his own.[91] Renaissance creativity increased the attractiveness of Christianity and the temptation to convert. True, individual professing Jews could take part in Renaissance society as moneylenders, printers of books, physicians, or teachers, thereby boasting Jewish contributions to Renaissance achievements; but the Jews as a group were barred from participating in Renaissance culture. How to join in and benefit from Renaissance culture without compromising the allegiance to Judaism was indeed a formidable challenge.

Renaissance humanism further complicated the tenuous relationship between Judaism and Christianity. Renaissance humanists exhibited unusual respect for Hebrew and Hebraic culture. As noted earlier, the humanists considered ancient Judaism an integral part of perennial philosophy originating in a primordial revelation.[92] Hence they cultivated working relations with individual scholars and, for a while, fostered an atmosphere of relative tolerance and mutual respect. Yet the humanist theory of a universal truth in which all ancient religions and philosophical schools participate was a decidedly Christian theory. The humanists maintained that Christianity was the ultimate perfection of ancient wisdom, so that ancient Judaism was valid only to the extent that it taught the mysteries of Christianity. Furthermore, the humanists claimed that only Kabbalah—the mystical tradition of Judaism—is intrinsically valid whereas the Talmud and its cognate literature reflect the external and carnal interpretation of the spiritual truth.[93]

Thus, although humanism inspired a relative measure of tolerance toward contemporary Jews and a genuine interest in Hebraic culture, Renaissance humanism also contributed to the traditional Christian bifurcation between the inner, spiritual meaning of revelation, of which Christianity is the ultimate perfection, and the external, carnal, legalistic Judaism of the Talmud. A professing Jew could not fully participate in Renaissance humanism without converting to Christianity. It is no surprise that the humanists attracted Jewish apostates and, in several cases, directly influenced their conversion.

R. David could not ignore the creativity of the Italian Renaissance and did not wish to be excluded from it. As noted in Chapter Two above, R. David adopted humanist educational programs and literary conventions to Judaism and patterned his own prose and poetry in accordance with humanist literary standards. The humanist search for the universal truth underlying diverse modes of thought led R. David to master all known scholarly disciplines and literary traditions. Like the humanists, R. David attempted to reconcile the various positions into a coherent whole resulting in syncretism.[94] But R. David could not remain a professing Jew and fully endorse the humanist theory of one universal truth. He had to articulate a Jewish version of this theory. The Thomistic theory on the relation of reason and faith enabled R. David to resolve the dilemma.

The Thomistic emphasis on the limitations of natural human knowledge freed R. David to cultivate a broad range of scholarly disciplines, thereby responding positively to the cultural wealth of the Italian Renaissance. Jewish participation in Renaissance culture could be rationalized if the advancements of the society are relegated to the realm of natural human knowledge. Indeed, how could human knowledge undermine Judaism if the former is declared imperfect and incomplete from the outset? Whether human knowledge is pronounced by a pagan, a Christian, or a Muslim, by a schoolman or a humanist, by a contemporary or an ancient sage, in principle it could not conflict with infinite revealed wisdom. Ultimately, all branches of human knowledge and all human theories represent a partial truth to be completed and perfected by divine revelation. Each of them is true only to the extent that it participates in the infinite Wisdom of God as revealed in the Torah. Thus, by asserting that revelation and human reason form a hierarchy of knowledge in which revelation is supreme, R. David took the venom out of the bite of the secular sciences and legitimated Jewish involvement in Renaissance culture. Jews could engage in the study of all sciences and all literary traditions as long as they subordinated them to the revealed faith. Relegating all human knowledge to the realm of nature was another way of highlighting the spiritual superiority of Judaism.

R. David articulated a Jewish version of the Renaissance search for universal truth. The primordial revelation from which all truth springs is the Sinaitic revelation to the People of Israel. That revelation has a twofold nature: an inner, esoteric, and spiritual dimension; and an outer, exoteric or material dimension. The two are inextricably intertwined; one cannot be affirmed without the other. The inner and the outer dimensions of divine revelation constitute one whole—the received tradition, or in Hebrew, *qabbalah*. Thereby R. David rejects the humanist attempt to validate Kabbalah (i.e., the theosophy) as the spiritual dimension of Judaism at the expense of talmudic Judaism. The theosophic doctrines of Kabbalah which the humanists highly esteemed are but one element within the rabbinic tradition which interprets divine revelation. Kabbalah is valid not because it teaches the spiritual truths of Christianity, but because it is an authentic rabbinic tradition interpreting Sinaitic revelation.

As a Jewish scholar who pursued all-inclusive knowledge, R. David could not ignore the spread of Kabbalah in Italy, especially when the humanists appropriated it to Christianity. He insisted on the Jewishness of Kabbalah as an authentic rabbinic tradition, taking *Sefer ha-Zohar* at its word to be a Midrash by the Tanna R. Shimon bar Yohai.[95] For R. David, medieval Kabbalah (i.e., the theosophic doctrines of the Spanish school) was a speculative knowledge, something like philosophical lore, which interprets divine revelation. Kabbalah was one strand within Jewish theology, the discipline which interprets divine revelation.

R. David asserted the common perception in Renaissance Italy that mastering Kabbalah would spiritualize the knower and enable him to enjoy the divine efflux. Typical to Renaissance syncretism, it became necessary to show that Kabbalah accords with other bodies of speculative knowledge which inquire into the mysteries of God and His relation to the universe. If Kabbalah is an authentically Jewish, speculative knowledge, it has to be compatible with other Jewish, speculative sciences taught by the Jewish theologians. Therefore, R. David was among the first Jewish scholars to reconcile Kabbalah and Jewish theology. Since theology can be interpreted by means of human reason, so can Kabbalah. R. David then employed philosophical categories to explain the meaning of Kabbalistic doctrines. Such "philosophization" of Kabbalah was rather common in Renaissance Italy, but it did not find favor in the eyes of Iberian Kabbalists who regarded Kabbalah as an esoteric knowledge intended for theurgic purposes.[96]

R. David's cultivation of philosophy, theology and Kabbalah was an expression of his pursuit of all-embracing knowledge of things human and divine. R. David considered the study of philosophy a religious obligation. Philosophy actualized the human rational potential and prepared man for the understanding of revealed truths. The study of philosophy "eliminates corrupt opinions, silly notions and many heretical views which destroy the foundation of the Torah."[98] Philosophy further perfects the human intellect and facilitates the knowledge of God, the ultimate goal of human life. Thus, in contrast to some Kabbalists or Talmudists who viewed the study of philosophy negatively, R. David praised it for its religious benefits. He went further to argue that the revealed tradition itself sanctions the cultivation of wisdom. Since revelation consists of demonstrable truths that can be known as well by human reason, reason and revelation overlap to some extent. Therefore, the study of the sciences is permissible from the point of view of religion.

The cultivation of philosophy could become subversive to Judaism only when philosophy is mistakenly considered an end in itself. R. David therefore opposed Jewish rationalists who reduced revelation to scientific knowledge and who diminished the importance of the practical commandments. Instead, he highlighted the supremacy of theology over philosophy and insisted that theology consisted of demonstrable and undemonstrable teachings. The latter include the dogmas of Judaism and the practical commandments. Eternal life, R. David taught, could be attained not through philosophy but through affirmation of the undemonstrable truths of divine revelation. Only when the believer affirms the dogmas of Judaism and submits himself to the commandments of the Law (both practical and rational) can he enjoy eternal life.

Through this view, R. David could be the halakhist who is totally concerned with minute observance of the Law, the loyal believer who affirms the belief of the Jewish faith, and still the scholar who cultivates all branches of human knowledge. In this sense, R. David ben Judah Messer Leon was a Jewish version of the Renaissance ideal *homo universalis.*

6

A Jewish Dogmatist

In medieval culture, theology was "the queen of the sciences." Medieval intellectuals, among them R. David ben Judah Messer Leon, regarded theology the most abstract and intellectually demanding science, requiring prior mastery of all other branches of human knowledge. Only a scholar who has actualized his intellectual potential may begin to study theology at all, and only the most accomplished theologian may presume to articulate Jewish dogmas.[1] It is not surprising that toward the end of his life, R. David devoted his literary efforts to theology. Indeed, his last work, *Tehillah le-David*, is a summary of Jewish theology of an encyclopedic scope typical among Sephardic scholars of the postexpulsion era.[2] Like his Sephardic coreligionists in the Ottoman Empire, R. David sensed that he stood at the end of an epoch and viewed his own task as consolidating existing knowledge.

In structure and style, in ideas and concepts, *Tehillah le-David* also attests to the impact of Aquinas' *Summa Theologiae*. Many chapters are arranged in direct imitation of the *questiones* of the *Summa*. R. David organized *Tehillah le-David* according to the scholastic method: first, stating the question under consideration; second, outlining arguments and counterarguments; then proposing his own position; and finally, responding to the objections. R. David's contemporaries, such as the Sephardim R. Joseph Taitazak and R. Abraham Bibago, and the Italian 'Obadia Sforno, also incorporated the scholastic method and relied on Aquinas.[3]

Theology is rooted in dogmas. A dogma is a principle that a person must believe in order to be considered an adherent of a given religion. Dogmas, or creeds, "serve as an admission test for converts and as a loyalty oath for the faithful."[4] As noted in the previous chapter, rabbinic Judaism defined itself as a religion of observance or practice rather than creed. Not until the Middle Ages, in response to the challenge of Greek philosophy, Muslim and Christian theologies, and Karaism, did rabbinic thinkers articulate the dogmas of Judaism.[5] Indeed, R. David's preoccupation with the dogmas of Judaism puts him squarely within the medieval philosophic tradition in Judaism.

Medieval Jewish Dogmatism

Moses Maimonides was the first Jewish thinker to articulate the dogmas of Judaism. He set forth thirteen "foundations of the Torah" *(yesodot ha-Torah)* in which every person must believe in order to be considered a Jew and to have "a portion in the world to come." They were necessary, but not sufficient, for salvation; observance of the practical commandments was also needed. The Thirteen Principles are discussed in greater detail below.

Maimonides sparked a twofold debate: first, what, if any, are the Jewish dogmas (i.e., those principles without which a person, no matter how saintly his actions, should not be considered a Jew nor attain salvation as a Jew)? Second, which dogmas must be accepted entirely on faith, and which may be logically derived from other dogmas? The debate began soon after Maimonides' death and was a major theme in the Maimonidean Controversy of the thirteenth century. It died down in the fourteenth century, when post-Maimonidean rationalism prevailed, and flared up in the fifteenth century as the concept of faith gained importance. The debate virtually ended with R. David ben Judah Messer Leon, who considered the issue of Jewish dogmas to be of utmost importance. R. David devoted two thirds of his *Tehillah le-David* to dogmas, in which he first reviewed the debate itself, then defended Maimonides' Thirteen Principles, and finally formulated his own list.

Discussion of dogmas presents the same semantic problem as discussion of faith. Three distinct concepts are relevant, but different

writers used different words to identify them — in addition to disa-
greeing over which concepts fell into which categories. First, any
principle deemed essential to adherence to a religion will be called a
dogma, as noted above. Second, some dogmas were considered to be
incapable of rational proof and thus capable of acceptance on faith
alone; they will be called *axioms*. Third, other dogmas were deemed
rationally provable from the foundation of axioms; they will be called
theorems.

Maimonides not only called dogmas "foundations of the Torah"
but also employed two Arabic terms interchangeably: *qa'ida* and *aṣl*.
While each of the "foundations" is introduced with the word *qa'ida*,
Maimonides referred to the group as a whole by either term.[6] Maimonides did not clearly distinguish between axioms and theorems
and intentionally obscured his view concerning the demonstrability
of the Thirteen Principles. Later scholars most commonly referred to
Maimonides' dogmas in Hebrew as "principles" *('iqqarim)* but disagreed over their meaning. By the fifteenth century, Jewish scholars
introduced   "foundations"   *(yesodot)*,   "cornerstones"   *(pinot)*,   and
"pillars" *('amudim)*. Some used these terms to distinguish clearly
between theorems and axioms, but others, especially toward the end
of the century, were more haphazard.

Despite their semantic inconsistencies, however, all writers
within the Maimonidean tradition agreed that Judaism has dogmas.
In order to understand R. David's conception of Jewish dogmas, we
need to situate his views in the context of medieval Jewish
dogmatism.

Jewish dogmatism was a by-product of medieval Jewish rationalism, and the history of Jewish dogmatism was coterminous with
the history of the rationalist tradition. Rabbanite Jews began to
define Judaism in terms of dogmas in order to defend their tradition.
The rise of rationalism among Muslim thinkers brought with it the
consolidation of Muslim theology and a sharper articulation of Muslim creed. Within the Jewish community, Karaite thinkers, challenging the validity of rabbinic tradition, were the first to insist that Judaism has beliefs obligatory upon all. The Karaites went further to
articulate the dogmas of Judaism and to explain their status vis-a-vis
human reason.[7]

Writing in defense against Karaism, Saadia Gaon was the first
rabbanite scholar who attempted to prove the rationality of the Jewish tradition. Interpreting the rabbinic tradition in the light of reason,
Saadia introduced a distinction between "rational" and "practical"

commandments, claiming that the former are universal truths which human reason can discover, whereas the latter can be known only through revelation.[8] However, Saadia held that even the practical commandments are compatible with the truths of reason. The notion of "rational commandments" was the first step toward creed formulation in rabbinic Judaism.

Though Saadia Gaon did not articulate the dogmas of Judaism, he did argue that the fundamental teachings of rabbinic Judaism (e.g., creation, the unity of God, the rational character of the Law, freedom of the will, and future life) can be demonstrated by rational speculation. That Saadia discussed these beliefs and not others suggests that he considered them more central to Judaism. Even so, Saadia did not define these beliefs as obligatory to all Jews so that their denial entails heresy. Nor did Saadia explain why these beliefs are more fundamental than others. Saadia was interested merely in proving rationally that the teachings of rabbinic Judaism are not contrary to human reason.

The Jewish philosophers of the eleventh century, such as Bahya ibn Pakuda, perpetuated the distinction between the rational and practical dimensions of the Law. Writing under the sway of Muslim Neoplatonism with its strong mystical overtones, Bahya contributed to the spiritualization of Judaism. He highlighted the supremacy of internal, spiritual worship over external, practical observance. Bahya insisted that the knowledge and love of God are the ultimate ends of Jewish religious worship.[9] While Bahya defined what Jews should know about God and emphasized the importance of internal religious life, he did not define a Jew as a person who holds a particular notion of God. Bahya's major intention was to internalize religious worship as a means of securing the faith against perfunctory observance.

In the second half of the twelfth century, Maimonides consolidated the intellectualization of Judaism by legislating the rational commandments of Judaism. Maimonides introduced dogmas in his *Commentary on the Mishnah*, Tractate Sanhedrin, Chapter Ten, and later included several dogmas in his *Book of Knowledge* in his *Mishneh Torah*.

Maimonides did not choose that particular passage of the Mishnah by coincidence. As widely noted, that is the only place in rabbinic literature in which salvation is linked to the acceptance of particular beliefs. Mishnah Sanhedrin Chapter Ten concerns capital punishment. It teaches that even one whom a court condemns to death can have a "portion in the world to come," in contrast to one "who says there is no resurrection, [one who says] that the Torah is not from heaven, and the *epikoros*." Maimonides utilized this text to develop a full-fledged conception of Jewish dogmas whose affirmation is necessary for eternal life.

Maimonides' Thirteen Principles are as follows:

1. that God exists;
2. that God is one;
3. that God is incorporeal;
4. that God is ontically prior to the world;
5. that God alone may be worshiped;
6. that certain people are prophets;
7. that the prophecy of Moses was unique;
8. that the Torah came from Heaven;
9. that the Torah was precisely transcribed from God by Moses and cannot be changed;
10. that God knows all that men do;
11. that God rewards those who observe the commandments and punishes the transgressors;
12. that the Messiah will come;
13. that the dead will be resurrected.

Scholars disagree over what motivated Maimonides to articulate the Thirteen Principles at all and thereby to define a Jew as a person who accepts certain dogmas.[10] One view regards widespread persecution and Marranism under the fanatical regime of the Almohades as the cause. Since Jews, and perhaps even Maimonides himself, were forced to adopt Islam outwardly, it was necessary to define the minimal beliefs whose affirmation in the heart is sufficient to be considered a Jew. The very fact that Almohades' fanaticism manifested itself, among other things, in affirmation of creeds (beyond the initial declaration of faith required for all Muslims) necessitated a Jewish credal response. A second view highlights the tension between Maimonides' philosophic posture and his halakhic activities. According to this view, Maimonides formulated the dogmas for pedagogical purposes: to inculcate the masses (who lack philosophic competence and training) with the main tenets of Judaism. A third view asserts that Maimonides formulated dogmas in order to ensure proper worship. Proper worship requires holding correct beliefs about the object of Jewish worship (God), the reasons for worship (Torah), and the purpose for worship (salvation).

The influence of Maimonides' formulation of dogmas was particularly remarkable because, unlike papal Christianity, for example, Judaism did not have a political mechanism to enforce beliefs. This was particularly true in the Middle Ages when world Jewry was highly fragmented and decentralized. Although in theory one could be excommunicated, that punishment did not work in practice and merely resulted in incessant controversies and internal division, as different communities and individuals would accept or reject the excommunication.

Nevertheless, Maimonides was regarded as the utmost halakhic authority in Sephardic Jewry, and that regard facilitated the dissemination of the Thirteen Principles as the definitive tenets of Judaism. This is not to say that the Thirteen Principles went unopposed. Some of Maimonides' opponents, such as the Provençal Talmudist Rabbi Abraham ben David (Rabad), rejected Maimonides' claim that all Jews must believe in the incorporeality of God or else be branded heretic.[11] Others, such as Nahmanides, opposed Maimonides' specific formulation of beliefs about God and suggested other beliefs instead: creation, omniscience, providence.[12] Still others, like R. Meir Abulafia (Ramah), were concerned about the potential negative impact that Maimonides' principles would bring to Jewish religious observance.[13]

As noted above, dogmatism was one of the main themes of the Maimonidean Controversy during the thirteenth century. The fourteenth century was quieter. By then the loyal Maimonists who accepted Maimonides' Thirteen Principles as authoritative found little need to go beyond them.[14] To the rationalists who radicalized the intellectualization of Judaism as a philosophic religion, dogmas were either unimportant or, at best, secondary. If dogmas are rationally demonstrable, they are assimilated into philosophy. And if dogmas are not demonstrable, then they are mere pedagogic devices helping the masses to worship properly. In either case, the result was the same: the dogmas of Judaism were not in the forefront of Jewish philosophic speculation.

In the fifteenth century, dogmas again became a major concern of Jewish theologians.[15] In fact, practically every Sephardic scholar trained in the rationalist tradition discussed them. Four factors account for this. First, the Church began an assault on Judaism, which we call Christian triumphalism. In public and private debates, Jewish theologians were pressed to define articles of the Jewish faith and explain why they refused to accept Christianity. Maimonides' twelfth principle—the belief in the Messiah—was the focal point of the debate. Christian polemicists argued that the belief in the Messiah was central to Judaism and that Jews misinterpreted their own sacred texts to deny Jesus. The Jews, in turn, attempted to minimize the importance of the Messianic belief and to prove that the Messiah is yet to come.[16]

Second, Jews adopted Christian modes of thought. By the fifteenth century, Iberian Jewry completed the transformation from the cultural orbit of Islam to that of Christendom. Further, anti-Christian polemical treatises written during the fifteenth century are ample evidence of growing Jewish knowledge of Christian theology.[17] As shown in the previous chapter, Jewish scholars were influenced by scholasticism to adopt a new conception of theology as the science of divine revelation. Qua science, theology must have its proper subject matter, theorems, and axioms—that is, its dogmas.[18]

Third, Iberian Jewry engaged in mass conversions. On the one hand, those who remained loyal to Judaism had to justify to themselves the merits of Judaism. To do so they had to clarify the propositional content of the Jewish faith resulting in the articulation of Jewish dogmas. On the other hand, that many *conversos* continued a secret allegiance to Judaism transformed their Judaism from a matter or practice to one of belief. Crypto-Judaism could survive precisely because Judaism became a matter of creed accompanied by very few symbolic acts. Continued contacts between Jews and Christians, and the assumption that conversos were sinning Jews, further implied that Judaism is a religion of creed. Accordingly, the cardinal beliefs of Judaism had to be defined for the sake of professing Jews and *conversos* alike, and, directly or indirectly, the apostasy and Marranism strongly encouraged a credal definition of Judaism.[19]

Finally, fifteenth century Jewish scholars had to define the dogmas of Judaism in order to clarify the proper relationship between reason and faith. As noted above, Maimonides was a symbol of the synthesis of reason and faith; events at the turn of the fifteenth century prompted a reevaluation of that synthesis, which thus entailed reconsideration of the focus of Maimonides' concept of dogmas, namely, the Thirteen Principles. Was Maimonides correct in selecting any beliefs as "the Foundation of the Torah?" Why did Maimonides select these particular beliefs? In what sense are they fundamental to Judaism? Why did Maimonides exclude others that appear more important? Why did Maimonides fix the number of cardinal beliefs at thirteen? Do the Thirteen Principles fall under any logical classification, thereby suggesting that other principles are the foundations of Judaism? By analyzing the structure and content of Maimonides' list, Jewish theologians formulated their own Jewish dogmas.

The intense discussion of Jewish dogmas in the fifteenth century yielded various definitions of Jewish "catechism."[20] One could be considered a Jew according to one definition and a heretic according to another. We should keep in mind, however, that dogmatism was essentially an academic issue with but limited political or practical import. Although in theory one could be excommunicated for heretical views, Jewish communities were too localized and fragmented to make excommunication effective. Therefore, the historical significance of Jewish dogmatism lies not in the battle against heresy but rather in the clarification of what Judaism means for its adherents. One's understanding of the cardinal beliefs of Judaism reflects one's interpretation of Judaism.

The debate on the dogmas of Judaism received new impetus after the expulsion from Spain in 1492. Iberian exiles discussed dogmas in their spiritual grappling with the trauma of their expulsion. Don Isaac Abravanel, the most illustrious scholar among the Spanish exiles, devoted an entire work, *Rosh Amanah*, to a detailed analysis of Maimonides' Thirteen Principles.[21] He reviewed the entire debate concerning dogmas from Maimonides forward. He addressed Crescas and Albo by name and reflected as well the contributions of Bibago, Shalom, and 'Arama, the major contributors to the discussion of Jewish dogmas. *Rosh Amanah* is thus the most systematic account of the fifteenth century debate on Jewish dogmas.

Rosh Amanah is ostensibly a defense of Maimonides' Thirteen Principles, but it is a qualified defense. Abravanel supported the need for dogmas. With Maimonides, Abravanel regarded affirmation of doctrine as a necessary condition of inclusion in the People of Israel and for salvation, and as grounds for deeming a nonaffirmant as a heretic. However, Abravanel opposed the notion that Judaism has only thirteen dogmas. Abravanel asserted instead that each and every teaching of the Torah is a necessary dogma which every believer must affirm in order to be saved:

> There is no need to lay down principles for the Torah of God which ought to be believed by every Israelite in order to merit life in the world to come as Maimonides and those who follow him wrote, for the entire Torah, and every single verse, word and letter it is a principle and root which ought to be believed.[22]

Abravanel's rigid fundamentalism, or orthodoxy, reflects the influence of Kabbalah in two ways.[23] First, like the Kabbalists, Abravanel denied the assumption that the science of the Torah is like any other science, with its own axioms and theorems. Second, the Kabbalists also objected to the dogmatic enterprise on the ground that the Torah is a unity which does not allow internal division between primary and secondary teachings. Each and every teaching in the Torah, indeed each word and even each letter, has a religious significance; each directs the believer to a specific locus in the Godhead. Like the Kabbalists, Abravanel believed that acceptance of the Torah as a whole is necessary for human salvation. So while paying lip service to Maimonides that Judaism has dogmas, Abravanel rejected the dogmas proposed by Crescas, Albo, and those who followed them, and opposed the view that Judaism has axioms without which the entire faith would collapse.

Abravanel did recognize one sense in which some beliefs are more important than others: teaching. As a renowned courtier in three royal courts (Portugal, Aragon, and Naples) and an immensely learned scholar, Abravanel was no less an elitist than Maimonides. They both recognized the need to inculcate correct beliefs in the unlearned multitudes. So Abravanel defended Maimonides' principles as heuristic devices for the education of the masses,[24] and for that purpose alone concedes that a Jew must believe one concept in particular: creation.

> Were I to choose principles to posit for the divine Torah I would lay down one, the creation of the world. It is the root and foundation around which the divine Torah, its cornerstones, and its beliefs revolve and include the creation at the beginning, the narrative about the patriarchs, and the miracles and wonders which cannot be believed without belief in creation. The belief in Creation facilitates the belief in miracles which is necessary for the belief in the Torah. So, too, with belief in punishment according to [one's observance of] the commandments, none of which can one perfectly believe without believing in the volitional creation of the world.[25]

Abravanel thus holds that creation, the cardinal dogma, facilitates belief in miracles. Messianic redemption is the most important miracle, especially in the period of unusual tribulation and suffering in which Abravanel lived. To console his people and strengthen the belief in coming redemption, Abravanel posited the belief in creation as the prime dogma of Judaism. So did Abravanel continue the dominant trend in fifteenth century Jewish dogmatism.

As noted above, R. David ben Judah Messer Leon was intimately familiar with *Rosh Amanah* and Abravanel's other writings, and whether from academic displeasure, personal animosity, or both, sharply rejected Abravanel's criticism of Maimonides generally. It is not surprising that R. David disagreed with Abravanel on dogmas. *Tehillah le-David* is in part a response to Abravanel's critique of Maimonidean dogmatism.

The Science of Jewish Theology

R. David ben Judah Messer Leon maintained that Judaism has dogmas. He began with the premise that theology is the science of divine revelation and that the Pentateuch is a revealed text. Thus he defines Jewish theology as the science of the divine Torah *(hokhmah toriyyit)*. The science of the Torah has structure like any other science, such as medicine or geometry, and it is the task of the Jewish theologian to articulate that structure: a subject matter *(nose)*: axioms *(yesodot)*: and theorems *('iqqarim)* that derive logically from *yesodot*. Modern writers reserve the word *dogma* for theology, and occasionally for political science, but R. David expressly equated the "dogmas" of the Torah with "theorems" and "axioms" of the other sciences.

R. David next addresses the counterargument that the Torah, as divine revelation, is qualitatively different and therefore structurally different from all other bodies of knowledge. In response, he concedes that "the divine Torah does have a special subject matter *[nose]* by which is can be distinguished from all other sciences,"[26] but — begging the question — he asserts that this special subject matter encompasses its various *derushim* or theorems, which presuppose certain *shorashim* (literally, roots) or axioms.

The second argument against dogmatism is that the Torah is a unity which defies any differentiation into primary and secondary teachings.[27] R. David responds that internal divisions do not necessarily jeopardize unity; following Aristotle, he raises the universe itself as an example. The universe as a whole is a unity, yet reasoned examination shows that the universe has a three-tiered structure: a first principle (God) which is the foundation of all existents, intermediaries through which God's will is known (the Separate Intelligences and the celestial spheres and a receptive element (the sublunar world).[28]

R. David borrowed from a well-known Midrash (Bereshit

Rabbah, 1, 5) to draw the parallel between the Torah and the universe. The revealed Torah (i.e., Scripture) is a created entity, the exoteric expression of the spiritual, esoteric Torah. That spiritual Torah is Divine Wisdom, and God consulted Divine Wisdom when He created the universe. The spiritual, esoteric Torah is thus the blueprint of existence as such *(ha-Torah demut ha-nimza bi-khlalo)*, and the structure of the revealed Torah must therefore correspond to the structure of the actual universe.[29] Like the universe, the revealed Torah may have internal divisions without compromising its unity. Accordingly, the revealed Torah has "roots" (*shorashim*; i.e., first principles) and "branches" (*'anafim*; i.e., derivative teachings). The "roots" and the "branches" correspond to the "principles" *('iqqarim)* and "foundations" *(yesodot)*, respectively.

The third argument against dogmatism is that the teachings of the Torah are too diverse and complex to fit any single structure. Here R. David borrows Joseph Albo's defense:[30] First, even the narrative portions set forth principles. The stories of the Tower of Babel and of Sodom and Gomorrah, for example, teach

> ...that there is one being whose existence is necessary; that there is no other being but the Necessary Existent; and that He provides, rewards and punishes."[31]

Second, direct commandments also teach specific principles; for example, Exod. 20:2 teaches that God exists, and Exod. 20:4 teaches the creation of the world. Finally, the Torah itself cites specific punishments to anyone who denies certain principles, namely, the existence of God or the creation of the universe.

The fourth argument against dogmatism is that the rabbinic tradition does not single out certain beliefs to be more important than any others. In response, R. David cites Mishnah Sanhedrin Ten, for which Maimonides created the Thirteen Principles, and several talmudic passages as proof texts that the Torah recognizes certain beliefs as principles. R. David cites Maimonides' own warning to steer away from "corrupt opinions" as proof that the Torah insists on true beliefs as its central principles.

Having defended the study of Torah as a science at all, R. David then addresses the question, What is the subject matter of Jewish theology? R. David cites three views prevalent among his contemporaries: first, the "commandments and the warnings;" second, "man as a free agent;" and third, God. Typical to his tendency to harmonize wherever possible, R. David states that all three represent different aspects *(behinot)* of the subject matter of the Torah. These three aspects are common to any science, namely, (*a*) the object to which the science pertains (in this case, man), (*b*) the specific content which that science teaches (the commandments and warnings), and (*c*) the end or objective (God). By comparison, the science of medicine pertains to the human body, teaches particular lessons, and has the objective of good health.[32]

R. David's threefold exposition was not coincidental. In *Sefer ha-'Iqqarim*, R. Joseph Albo had addressed a common Christian polemic against the Torah as a science, namely, that a true science must be categorized within the fourfold classification of Aristotelian causality, but that the Torah cannot be so classified.[33] Aristotle distinguished between four types of causes which bring a thing into existence: material, formal, efficient, and final. The material cause is that out of which a thing is composed; the formal cause is the way the material is organized; the efficient cause is the maker of the thing; and the final cause is the end or goal toward which the thing is moving or working. This analysis is tied with Aristotle's twofold analysis of form and matter. Form combines the efficient and final causes with the formal cause, leaving the material cause as matter.

R. David refutes the Christian polemic by positing the three aspects of the science of the Torah and then adapting the four aspects of Aristotelian causality to them, as follows: man is like the material cause; the commandments are the efficient or formal causes; and the knowledge of God is the final cause.[34]

The Defense of Maimonides' Thirteen Principles

R. David followed those Iberian scholars who regarded Maimonides as the foremost halakhic and spiritual authority in medieval Judaism and the Thirteen Principles as the authoritative tenets of the Jewish faith. R. David therefore expressly defended the Thirteen Principles against fifteen objections or doubts *(sefeqot)*. Abravanel had already recited most of these *sefeqot* in *Rosh Amanah*, so Jewish theologians in the early sixteenth century appear to have hotly debated such issues.[35] Although occasionally inconsistent, R. David's defense of the Thirteen Principles presents a generally coherent view of the dogmas of Judaism.

The first two *sefeqot* concern the Thirteen Principles generally:

Safeq 1: Why the number thirteen? Some have suggested that the

Thirteen Principles correspond to the thirteen attributes of God or to the thirteen hermeneutical principles of the Torah.[36] R. David rejected both suggestions, and instead based the Thirteen Principles on four primary beliefs: the existence of God; the resurrection of the dead; that the Torah is from heaven; and that the Torah is incorporeal. Further, Maimonides chose these four beliefs specifically to correspond with Aristotelian causality:

> You should know that Rabbi Moses was compelled by reason to assert that each existent — be it natural or artificial, corporeal or incorporeal — must have four causes ... efficient, final, formal [and] material, so must the Torah have four causes.[37]

Maimonides then applied the metaphysical rule of causality to the Torah. The language of the Mishnah taught Maimonides the four "general causes" (sibbot kolelot) for the Thirteen Principles and thus for the entire Torah:

> Afterwards Maimonides learned from the Mishnah, Chapter Helek that the efficient cause of the Torah is God Blessed Be He, that the final cause is resurrection after death, that the formal cause [of the Torah] is its revelation from heaven, and that its material cause [homrah] is the divine things.[38]

R. David returns to the passage of the Mishnah from which Maimonides derived the Thirteen Principles: The epikoros suggests Aristotle's efficient cause, because, by despising the received tradition, the epikoros ridicules those scholars who demonstrate the existence of God as an efficient cause of all existents as well as the giver of the Torah; one who rejects resurrection denies the final cause; and one who rejects the divinity of the Torah denies both the material and the formal cause.

R. David then classifies Maimonides' Thirteen Principles as follows:

1. *God: The efficient cause of the Torah.* Principles 1-5: God exists; He is one; He is eternal *aparte ante*; He is incorporeal; and He is the only thing worthy of worship.
2. *Resurrection: The final cause of the Torah.* Principles 10-13: God knows particulars; God rewards and punishes; the Messiah will come; the dead will be resurrected.

3. *Torah from Heaven: The formal cause of the Torah.* Principles 6-8: prophecy exists; Mosaic prophecy was unique; and the Torah is from Heaven.
4. *The Divine Nature of the Torah: The material cause of the Torah.* Principle 9: the Torah is eternal and cannot be changed or abrogated.

R. David's classification is but an expansion of Duran's initial tripartite division of the principles into three subgroups: God, Torah from Heaven, and reward and punishment. Albo also accepted this division and considered these three categories to be the three axioms of all divine laws. In essence, R. David adopts their view that these three beliefs are more general so that other principles fall under them. R. David separated out the ninth principle (which Duran included in his second subgroup of Torah from heaven) as a separate belief which teaches the material cause of the Torah.

Safeq 2: Why are commandments included among the Thirteen Principles? Crescas raised this second doubt, but R. David refutes Crescas without mentioning him by name.[39] R. David first summarizes Crescas as follows: (1) Principles are axioms; by definition they are logically prior to commandments; therefore, the list of principles should not include commandments. (2) A commandment presupposes the existence of a commander; since Exod. 20:2 commands Israel to believe in God, how could Maimonides list the existence of God as the first principle? (3) In the *Book of Knowledge,* Maimonides listed the existence of God and the unity of God as two commandments; if so, they must be posterior to the principles. But in his *Commentary on the Mishnah* he listed them as principles. It appears that Maimonides contradicted himself. (4) Commandments require a free agent who either observes them or does not. The principles are theorems; as such they have logical necessity which involves no free choice. For all these reasons the dogmas of Judaism should not include commandments.[40]

In response R. David agrees with Crescas and Crescas' followers that there is a difference between commandments and principles; that principles are logically prior to commandments; and that as theorems, principles do not involve choice. However, R. David denies that Maimonides was inconsistent. Maimonides did not confuse principles and commandments, because he talked about the existence of God and His oneness from two different perspectives *(behinot)*.

R. David interprets Maimonides to have differentiated between "the path of reason" and "the path of received tradition." The belief in the existence and the unity of God are rationally demonstrable. Reason can demonstrate that "there is one Necessary Being *(nimza mehuyav ha-meziut)* who is absolutely simple."[41] (For medieval philosophers, the oneness of God was predicated upon incorporeality, (or total simplicity). From the perspective of reason, God is the cause *(sibah)* and foundation *(yesod)* of all existents, including the revealed Torah. Since reason can discover the existence of God and His oneness, the first two principles cannot be considered commandments. However, it is the tradition which teaches that "the Supreme Being *(ha-nimza ha-'elyon)* voluntarily chose to select one nation which would accept Him as King and believe that there is one Being superior to all others."[42] From this perspective, the existence and unity of God are commandments, which require the participation of will for their affirmation. Hence, *Mishneh Torah* listed them as commandments.

Sefeqot 3-6 concern the first part of Maimonides' Thirteen Principles and God. R. David discusses specific questions raised over the centuries against both Maimonides' choice of specific beliefs about God and Maimonides' abstract conception of God.

Safeq 3: Are Unity and Incorporeality Necessary Principles? In other words, are principles 2 (unity of God) and 4 (incorporeality of God) necessary? R. David replies yes, because they ensure the perfection of the soul in this world and in the world to come. The Torah prescribes practical commandments which bring about the sanctification of the Jewish believer through perfection of the body — for example, the prohibitions on certain foods and sexual acts. Concomitantly, the Torah also reveals true beliefs necessary in order to perfect the soul. Perfection of the soul entails incorporeality and unity because the human soul then unites with the incorporeal forms, the Separate Intelligences, thereby becoming eternal. Since incorporeality and unity are the very nature of eternal life, God must be incorporeal and singular (i.e., without equals) as well. Maimonides recognized that "the Torah is divine because it instructs its adherents to be like God in this world and to unite with the spiritual substances in the world to come." Hence Maimonides listed the unity and incorporeality of God as the Foundations of the Torah.

Safeq 4: Is God in fact incorporeal at all? In the late twelfth century, the Provençal halakhist Rabbi Abraham ben R. David (Rabad) in his *Glosses (Hasagot)* on Maimonides' *Mishneh Torah*, raised the following *safeq*, which figured prominently in the debates during the twelfth century:[43] Scripture commonly refers to God in corporeal language (for example, "He walked through the Garden" [Gen. 3:8], which literally appears to conflict with Maimonides' Fourth Principle, but there is nothing in the Jewish tradition itself which teaches the incorporeality of God or the inadmissibility of literal interpretation.

R. David agreed with Rabad that one who errs on the basis of the literal interpretation of Scripture should not be considered a heretic; rather, a heretic is someone who willfully rejects the tradition "because his evil inclination overcomes him and his evil deeds tempt him to deny truth and miracles."[44] But R. David supports the inclusion of incorporeality as a principle; he cites Exod. 20:4, "You shall not make for yourself a graven image[,]" and interprets it as commanding the incorporeality of God.

Safeq 5: Why is "God is eternal" a Principle but not "God is living," "wise," "omnipotent," or "willing?"[45] God's eternality is the Third Principle. R. David defends Maimonides' choice of this particular attribute, and not others, by saying that Maimonides listed only those attributes of God which correspond to the Torah itself. The ontic priority of God corresponds to the ontic priority of the spiritual Torah.

> Maimonides listed as Principles only things which accord with the virtues *[segulot]* of the Torah. One of the characteristics of the divine Torah is that it is an eternal wisdom *[hokhmah qeduma]* by which God created the world. About the eternal Torah [the Rabbis] said that the Torah preceeded the world two thousand years and that God looked at it when He created the world. And because the Torah is eternal *[qeduma]*, Maimonides listed the attribute eternal *[qadmon]* as one of the Principles of the Torah.[46]

Safeq 6: Is not the obligation to worship God redundant?[47] Maimonides' Fifth Principle—that God alone must be worshiped—was attacked as redundant because it logically follows from the commandment to pray to God. R. David correctly suggests that this question is a variation on a broader question, namely, Can the Principles of the Torah include particular commandments? However, the Fifth Principle is not a commandment. Rather, it directs the believer to another attribute of God—omnipotence. Worship is due to God alone because only He is truly omnipotent. R. David refers to the biblical account of King Ahazya who was punished because he sent messengers to consult with the Canaanite god, Ba'al Zebub (2 Kings 1:1-6). R. David interprets Ahazya's conduct as a mistrust in God's omnipotence, for which the king was punished.

Sefeqot 7-12 concern the Torah. Belief in the Torah is necessary for defining one as a Jew, so these principles are the core of Jewish dogmatism. R. David explains away what appears as omission or redundancy in Maimonides' list, which in turn reflects as much R. David's own conception of the Torah as Maimonides'.

Safeq 7: In "The Guide of the Perplexed" II:25, Maimonides said that the belief in creation is a foundation of the Torah, and that whoever denies it undermines the entire Torah. How could Maimonides not reassert that thought among the Thirteen Principles in Mishneh Torah?[48] R. David responds that the belief in creation is implicit in the Fourth Principle — that God is ontically prior to the world. The attribute *qadmon* (eternal *aparte ante*) entails that everything else is created *(mehudash)*.

Further, *The Guide* and *Mishneh Torah* address different audiences. In *The Guide* Maimonides argued "against those who believe in the eternity of the world; [therefore,] he wrote that creation is a fundamental belief without which the Torah would collapse."[49] In contrast, *The Commentary of the Mishnah* is written to people who already accept the divinity of the Torah. To them, there is no need to specify the belief in creation but only to clarify the main teachings of the Torah. As noted below, R. David held belief in creation to be the first and most important axiom of Judaism.

Safeq 8: The belief in Torah assumes free choice. In the "Mishneh Torah," Laws of Repentance, Maimonides called free choice "a great principle and a pillar of the Torah". Why did Maimonides omit it from the Thirteen Principles?[50] R. David again explains an omission by reference to the specific context of the Thirteen Principles. He agrees that the belief in Torah presupposes human, free choice. Free choice, however, concerns the receiver's acceptance of the Torah *(meqabel)*, not the giving of the Torah. Maimonides therefore properly listed the belief in human, free choice in the *Mishneh Torah*, Laws of Repentance, because repentance concerns the recipient of the Torah and repentance is predicated upon a voluntary acceptance of the Torah. In contrast, the Thirteen Principles concern only the conditions for the giving of the Torah, so free choice was not relevant.[51]

Safeq 9: The tradition (qabbalah) is the "true interpretation of the Torah." Why did Maimonides omit belief in this "true interpreta-

tion" from the Thirteen Principles?[52] Again R. David responds by finding a belief through implication. The Eighth Principle is that Torah is from Heaven. Maimonides thereby meant that

> [God gave Moses the interpretation of the Torah, and that our religious practices today such as Sukah, Zizit and Lulav were already given to Moses from the mouth of the Almighty, so that whoever denies this belief excludes himself from the people of Israel.[53]

Safeq 10: Are not the existence of prophecy (Principle 6), the uniqueness of Moses' prophecy (Principle 7), and Torah from Heaven (Principle 8) really the same principle? Belief in Torah from Heaven already presupposes the beliefs in prophecy and in the uniqueness of Mosaic prophecy. R. David defends the separate contribution of each Principle as follows: First, the existence of prophecy per se is necessary to affirm that any teaching is divine (i.e., from God). Second, there are different degrees of prophecy, and only one prophecy resulted in the giving of the Torah—hence, the need to affirm that the Torah in particular is divine. Third, since Moses was the only recipient of the Torah it was necessary to establish that no other prophet in the past or in the future could surpass Moses.[54]

Safeq 11: Is it not tautological (and therefore unnecessary) to say that the Torah is from Heaven? R. David responds that this principle really has two meanings. First, one thereby accepts the belief that God has the ability *(yekholet)* to reveal a Law and that a certain nation has the ability to receive such Law. This belief is general and axiomatic to the acceptance of the Torah. Second, one thereby accepts the particular belief that the Israelites received the Torah at Sinai in the third month after the Exodus from Egypt. This belief is not tautological with acceptance of divine revelation in general, because the revelation could have happened anywhere at any time.

Safeq 12: Is it necessary to believe (the Ninth Principle) that the Torah is eternal and can never be uprooted, not even at the Redemption? Abrogation of the Torah does not imply any deficiency in the Torah, but rather than the Torah adapts to ultimate change.[55]

R. David's response to this *safeq* reveals his view of the Torah. The Torah teaches beliefs that save mankind. The cardinal teachings of the Torah bring about (literally, direct; *madrikhim*) the immortality of the soul.[56] These teachings are eternal truths; they cannot be altered, abrogated, or superseded. The Torah also consists of directives which prepare and refine the human soul *(melatshim)*, but whose status is not equal to the eternal truths of the Torah. These are the practical commandments of the Torah. At Redemption, when the entire world will recognize God, every person will choose to affirm the essential teachings of the Torah—that is, its eternal truths—so they will remain valid. Only the practical commandments of the Law would no longer be necessary. Accordingly, when Maimonides asserts that the Torah cannot be uprooted, abrogated, or superseded, he refers to its eternal truths and not to the practical commandments.

R. David's statement is startling. In addition to conceding that the practical commandments are just means to an end, it reflects a far reaching spiritualization of Judaism and opens the door for eschatological antinomianism. In a redeemed world, the practical commandments will be unnecessary! However, R. David was not a religious revolutionary. Eschatological antinomianism exists, at least potentially, in both Maimonideanism and Kabbalah. Maimonides' exposition of the rationale of the commandments related specific commandments to the degree of intellectual perfection among the people of Israel at the time of revelation. Thus, Maimonides introduced a certain evolutionary dimension to Law which, at least implicitly, rendered certain commandments obsolete with the increase of intellectual perfection among the People of Israel. Antinomian tendencies were even more noticeable in Kabbalah, especially in those texts that speculated about cosmic cycles, such as the *Sefer ha-Temunah (Book of Configuration)* and *Tiqquney Zohar*. The authors of these texts envisioned a spiritual Torah that would differ from the revealed Torah. Concomitantly, they speculated about a different type of religious worship.[57]

The last three *sefeqot* (13-15) concern eschatology. This section of the Thirteen Principles was the most controversial, especially during the first phases of the Maimonidean Controversy. Maimonides' natural conception of the Messianic age,[58] the highly intellectualist and individualistic conception of the world to come, and his ambiguity concerning the literal interpretation of resurrection were at the core of the debate. R. David attempts to show that these principles accord with the Jewish tradition. Maimonides did not depart from the tradition; he only enriched it.

Safeq 13: Are not Reward and Punishment (Principle 11), the Coming of the Messiah (Principle 12), and Resurrection (Principle 13) redundant? In short, does not Reward and Punishment necessarily imply the other two principles?

R. David responds that each principle concerns a different type of reward *(sakhar)*. The Messiah brings bodily reward. R. David here endorses Maimonides' conception of the Messianic Age as a naturalist, nonmiraculous epoch whose essence is the perfection of the body. R. David cites as proof-text "each man sits under his vine and under his fig tree," from the eschatological passage at Mic. 4:1-4 that begins, "In the end of day it shall come to pass..."—thus signifying physical prosperity and security. R. David then cites the talmudic dictum of Rabbi Samuel: "There is no difference between this world and the Messianic age except for the subordination of kingdoms." Maimonides had used this statement to prove that the Messianic age is a natural, nonmiraculous epoch. This endorsement is the only discussion of the Messianic Age in R. David's extant writings. Only once more did R. David even mention the Messiah, whom he describes as a person of great learning, and he gives no description of life in the Messianic Age. Undoubtedly, like other followers of Maimonides, R. David muted the traditional Messianic impulse and highlighted instead the ideal of personal immortality.

Divine retribution for individual human goodness is spiritual reward: the person's soul enters the "realm of the souls" *('olam ha-neshamot)*. R. David borrowed this term from Kabbalistic literature but stripped it of Kabbalistic import. The reward of the soul is its conjunction with the spiritual substances, the Separate Intelligences, by which it attains immortality.[59] R. David's biblical prooftext is Ps. 31:20: "How abundant is thy goodness which thou hast laid up for those who fear you." The goodness stored for the individual soul is eternal contemplation of God by the soul which had attained perfection. This conception of spiritual reward is entirely personal and intellectual. It mutes the collective and miraculous aspects of traditional Jewish eschatology.

The third reward affects both body and soul: resurrection of the dead. R. David repeats Maimonides' teaching that resurrection differs from the Messianic Age. The resurrection of the dead, a miracle wrought directly by God, will take place in the remote future after the coming of the Messiah.[60]

Safeq 14: If the Messiah [Principle 12] and Resurrection [Principle 13] are part of the divine plan in any event, why is it necessary to believe them? The Messianic Age and the Resurrection of the Dead must come about if they are part of a divine plan. At the final Redemption, therefore, these principles will no longer pertain to the future but to the actualized present. It follows that Maimonides includes principles which will be abrogated upon their own fulfillment, and which, accordingly, cannot be essential to Judaism.

R. David asserts that every Jew must believe that in the future the Messiah and the Resurrection of the Dead will be an actuality. This, however, is not a reason to exclude these two beliefs from the essential dogmas of Judaism. R. David resorts to the Aristotelian understanding of potentiality and actuality in order to defend Maimonides. He tells the reader that "what is in actuality more appropriately deserves to be call principle [shoresh, literally, "root"] than what is only in potentiality before it is actualized."[61] If the objector agrees that the coming of the Messiah and the Resurrection of the Dead are possible and accept them as the principles of Judaism, he could certainly accept them as principles once they are actualized.

Safeq 15: Hillel II said that the Messiah will not come. Hillel II is credited with saying, "There shall be no Messiah for Israel, because they have already enjoyed him in the days of Hezekiah" [Babylonian Talmud, Sanhedrin 99a]. If Hillel erred, why was he not regarded a sinner and excluded from the community of Israel like Elisha ben Abuya?[62] Furthermore, it is possible to conceive of divine Torah even without the Messiah—or for that matter, without Resurrection. R. David responded by differentiating between the "necessary" and the "contingent" coming of the Messiah. The Messiah will necessarily come at the time designated to it either "in a generation which is totally righteous or one which is totally sinful." The contingent coming of the Messiah refers to the attempt to hasten the coming of the Messiah through righteous deeds. Hillel II disputed only the contingent coming: the Messiah will not be hastened by righteous deeds, because the generation of Hezekiah enjoyed them all. But Hillel II did not dispute the designated coming, and in fact advised to wait patiently for the coming.[63] R. David concludes that Maimonides included the coming of the Messiah and the Resurrection of the Dead as principles because they are the final causes of the Torah.

R. David then concludes his discussion of the Thirteen Principles. He unequivocally reasserts their authority ("One who denies even part of them denies the entire Torah"), and he finally proposes an alternative classification. Following Bibago,[64] R. David divides the Thirteen Principles into two sections: principles concerning God's attributes and principles concerning God's actions. He then divides the second set into two. The result is a fourfold division: (1) principles concerning God's attributes (1-5); (2) principles concerning divine actions as the giver of the Torah (6-9); (3) principles concerning continuous actions (10-11); and (4) principles concerning future actions (12-13).

In an eclectic manner typical of the Middle Ages, R. David per-

mits this second classification to coexist with the classification discussed above without any comment whatsoever—another indication
that by R. David's day, dogmatism was not a rigid enterprise, but
rather a search for the "path of faith."

The Axioms of Judaism

R. David defended Maimonides' Thirteen Principles as
'Iqqarim, or theorems. R. David then sets forth his own dogmas, of
which there are three, all axiomatic. He calls them *yesodot
ha-emunah* ("foundations of the faith"). They are as follows:

> First that the eternal Divine Wisdom created the world
> *ex-nihilo*; second, that God who governs His world reveals to
> the prophets the government of the People and [the path for]
> salvation; third, that sometimes God, Blessed be He, cancels
> habitual order of nature in order to make known His providen-
> tial care over all His creation [i.e., miracles].[65]

These three principles make possible the belief in the Torah and, in
turn, the science of the Torah. R. David considers denial of any of
the three to be heresy, and advises the reader to exert caution before
proceeding with the next section of *Tehillah le-David*.

R. David adopted Aquinas' position, discussed in the previous
chapter, to assert that these three "foundations of the faith" are
indeed axiomatic—that is, that they cannot be demonstrated by
human reason alone. They are true and authoritative because they
are divinely revealed. Reason, however, can explain and clarify them.
R. David's very employment of reason or philosophy to explicate
these axioms demonstrates his indebtedness to the medieval rationalist tradition and particularly to Maimonides.

Before analyzing R. David's dogmas, we might ask, Why did he
choose them in the first place? R. David chose these three axioms,
in great part, in order to solve a puzzle that Maimonides created and
that scholars still debate today. In *The Guide* II:32 Maimonides com-
menced his discussion of prophecy with a cryptic remark: "The opinions of people concerning prophecy are like the opinions of people
concerning the eternity of the world or its creation in time." On the
basis of that opening comment, the reader was instructed to relate
the three views on prophecy (i.e., "prophetology") which Maimonides
sets forth in that chapter to the three views on the origins of the world

(i.e., "cosmology") that Maimonides set forth earlier in II:13. However, Maimonides did not explain that relation, thus giving rise to what is called the "prophetology-cosmology puzzle."[66]

To understand the puzzle we must begin with the three views on the origin of the universe (cosmology) in *The Guide* II:13. They are as follows (and will be called "C-1," etc., following their order in Maimonides' text):[67]

C-1 is the opinion of "those who believe in the Law of Moses (i.e., creation *ex nihilo*). Prior to the existence of the world, God existed alone, so that no other power or principle assisted God in the creation of the world. God created the world out of complete nonexistence, through "His will and His intention," in a nontemporal act. Creation *ex nihilo* thus implies that God created the world voluntarily, without any external compulsion or internal necessity. Creation *ex nihilo* also implies that God is omnnipotent (since nothing else existed to help in creation) and that God is omniscient (since nothing else existed to understand the process or the products of creation). Omnipotence and omniscience, in turn, facilitate a belief in miracles (divine intervention that contravenes the laws of nature), including the miracle of revelation.

C-2 is ascribed to Plato. This view holds that the world came into being from "a certain matter that is eternal as the deity is eternal; and that He does not exist without it, nor does it exist without Him." According to Plato, at least as Maimonides interprets him, God created the world out of preexistent matter which is coeternal with Him; that is, the world is created in respect to form but is uncreated in respect to matter. If matter is eternal, God was not alone prior to the creation of the universe. Yet since God brought the world into existence by conferring Forms upon preexistent matter, God can be said to be the creator of the world. God then has knowledge of particulars and can change the order of the created world—that is, bring about miracles. Thus, the Platonic view is compatible with the traditional conception of divine knowledge and with the belief in miracles including divine revelation.

C-3 is the opinion of "Aristotle, his followers and the commentators of his books." The world as a whole "has never ceased to be and will never do so." All that exists can be said to be brought into existence by God, the First Cause, but "it was not produced after having been in a state of non-existence." The world as a whole "never ceased to be as it is at present and will be as it is in the future eternity." The world is eternal both *a parte ante* and *a parte post*. The world relates to God as an effect relates to a remote cause. God has no knowledge of the particulars in the world, and God is not interested in the affairs of the world. Rather, God is a mind that thinks itself and has no knowledge of things outside itself. God and nature exist as two coequal principles, almost independent of each other.

Maimonides' own position on cosmology, and in turn on miracles, is notoriously difficult to interpret. Exoterically at least, Maimonides upheld a "theology of creationism"[68] according to which God created the world *ex nihilo*. Maimonides upheld the authority of the traditional view in which God is the author of nature and, as such, has the ability to contravene the laws of nature. Maimonides conceded, however, that there is no "decisive demonstration" for the belief in creation *ex nihilo*: it is an axiom, not a theorem. Despite that, the arguments in favor of it are rationally more compelling than the Aristotelian position. Maimonides also rejected Plato's view as philosophically erroneous, even though he admitted that it is compatible with the Scriptural account on prophecy.

Interpreting Maimonides on cosmology becomes even more difficult once we follow Maimonides' direction to relate those views to the three views on prophecy listed in *The Guide* II:32.[69] The prophetology opinions are as follows:

P-1 is the opinion "of the multitude," according to which God "chooses whom He wishes from among men, turns him into a prophet, and sends him with a mission." Accordingly, God is the immediate author of prophecy. Prophecy requires no special preconditions and is directly brought about as a miraculous event by God's will.

P-2 is the opinion of the "philosophers" who "affirm that prophecy is a certain perfection in the nature of man." Prophecy can occur only in an individual who possesses the natural disposition for it and only when that individual actually attains moral and intellectual perfection. Prophecy is entirely a natural phenomenon; it does not come from God directly, but represents a perfection of a natural disposition that occurs automatically when certain prerequisites are present. God is only its remote cause.

P-3 is "the opinion of our Law and the foundation of our doctrine." Maimonides states that this view is

> ...identical with the philosophic opinion except in one thing. For we believe that it may happen that one who is fit for prophecy and prepared for it should not become a prophet, namely on account of the divine will.

This view thus combines elements of both the first and the second positions. Prophecy is a natural phenomenon, but God may at times intervene and prevent its occurrence even when the necessary prerequisites are present.

Scholars have disagreed over what Maimonides himself thought about prophecy ever since Maimonides wrote. Maimonides presented the third position as the "opinion of our law," which implies that Maimonides subscribed to it. But this view seems to conflict with Maimonides' statement that creation *ex nihilo* is also the Torah view. As noted above, a God that can create *ex nihilo* can also bring about prophecy whenever and through whomever He wishes, regardless of any prior knowledge or intellect that the designated prophet may have. Yet Maimonides ascribed that view of prophecy to the unenlightened "multitudes" from which Maimonides assiduously and repeatedly disassociated himself. This was the prophetology-cosmology puzzle: Which view of cosmology is consistent with which view of prophetology; and what is the legitimate Jewish view?

R. David solves the puzzle by matching the two sets as follows: The belief that God created the world *ex nihilo* corresponds to the belief that God is the immediate cause of prophecy; that it, C-1 goes with P-1. Plato's view that God created the world from preexistent matter corresponds to the view that prophecy is a natural phenomenon in the sense that it requires presence of certain perfections, but that God may prevent its occurrence if He so wishes; that is, C-2 goes with P-3. Finally, Aristotle's view that the world is eternal corresponds to the philosophers' view of prophecy as a totally natural phenomenon; that is, C-3 goes with P-2.[70] Other sixteenth century theologians, for example Mordecai Yaffe, shared this solution. The modern scholar L. Kaplan advocates this interpretation.[71]

What do this puzzle and R. David's solution have to do with the axioms of Judaism? To R. David the first pairing represents the traditional view of Judaism, the three axioms of which are (*a*) that God created the world *ex nihilo* (C-1), (*b*) that God is the immediate author of prophecy (P-1), and (*c*) that God is the author of miracles (implied from C-1).[72] Asserting that these three beliefs are the axioms of Judaism is a veiled critique of Maimonides. Maimonides' puzzle obscured the beliefs of rabbinic Judaism, and gave rise to misinterpretations. To guard against heresy, the Jewish theologian should specify unambiguously the beliefs which all Jews should affirm. These three axioms are such beliefs.

The second pairing—C-2 (the world is created from preexistent matter) and P-3 (prophecy requires natural prerequisites)—is logically incorrect but nonetheless religiously acceptable. These are Plato's views. Maimonides and Halevi already recognized their compatibility with the scriptural account of creation, since the world does have a temporal beginning, and Maimonides perhaps even held this view as his esoteric position.[73] Gersonides went further to endorse this view openly.[74] R. David must, therefore, concede that this position is not heretical, but he still demeans it as unbecoming to the "true believer."[75]

R. David dismisses outright the third pairing, C-1 (the world is eternal) and P-2 (prophecy is totally natural involving no divine intervention whatsoever), as both religiously unacceptable (i.e., heretical) and philosophically incorrect (i.e., irrational). This third pairing comprises Aristotle's views. R. David ascribes them to the radical Jewish rationalists, citing only Isaac Albalag by name, and rebukes those Jews for holding them.

R. David thereby introduces his three axioms of Judaism: creation *ex nihilo*, prophecy, and miracles. They are true because they are revealed, and unaided human reason cannot demonstrate them. Nevertheless, human reason can clarify their meaning, which R. David then proceeds to do. He tries to show that these principles, albeit axioms of traditional Judaism, are fully consonant with philosophic knowledge. In so doing, R. David reveals that his interpretation of these axioms is anything but simplistic or literal.

Creation Ex-Nihilo

R. David sets forth the first axiom as follows:

> The first true belief of our holy Torah is the belief in the creation of the world, that is to say, that the world is created absolutely *[be-muhlat]*.[77]

R. David follows the dominant fifteenth century trend in recognizing the primacy of creation *ex nihilo* and in regarding that belief to be logically prior to the belief in the Torah.[78] Only an agent who created the world could perform miracles and could reveal Himself to the People of His choice. The belief in creation is thus the heart of a theism—that is, the conception of a personal, voluntary, omnipotent, omniscient, and benevolent God who provides for the needs of His creatures.

In accordance with the scholastic style, R. David first recites arguments supporting the position with which he disagrees, namely, that the world is eternal. These arguments were examined first by Maimonides and reconsidered later by Gersonides and Crescas, and R. David does not expand on those examinations.

The arguments are as follows. First, to show that the world is eternal it is enough to show that certain existents are eternal. Aristotelian physics teaches that prime matter, motion, time, and the celestial spheres are all eternal: therefore, the world in its totality must be eternal. Second, everything which comes into existence is generated from something else. Every change presumes the existence of a substratum in which change takes place. This is true about the world as a whole. Even if one says that the world is generated (i.e., created), one must presume the existence of a substratum in which this change takes place. This substratum, at least, must be eternal. Therefore, one can say that the world is eternal. Third, if one assumes that a benevolent creator brought the world into existence, one has to explain why He created at a particular point in time rather than another. The only explanation is that some internal or external factors prevented God from creating the world at another time. This in turn implies that God is not eternally benevolent. But this conclusion is false; therefore, the premise is false. God is eternally benevolent so that His goodness implies perpetual creation. In sum, the world perpetually emanates from God.[79]

R. David then cites two arguments against the eternity of the world, both of which Maimonides raised and fifteenth century Maimonideans frequently cited. First, any attempt to deduce the origin of the world from the physical conditions which obtain in the present world are invalid, because these conditions did not prevail before the world came into being. No analogy can be drawn between the nature of the existing physical world and conditions at creation. Second, if one assumes that the world is eternal then one invalidates the notion of causality: cause and effect will be coextensive, which is patently false. Hence, the world must be created. The belief in creation thus establishes two important beliefs about God: His omnipotence and His eternity.[80]

R. David next cites four arguments in favor of creation which Saadia Gaon had introduced five centuries earlier.[81] First, if one assumes that the world is eternal, it follows that the celestial spheres are moved by an infinite force. But since the celestial spheres themselves are corporeal bodies, they must be finite, unable to sustain an infinite force. So the world cannot be eternal. Second, things come into being on account of certain remote or approximate causes. If the world is eternal, there must be an infinite series of causes. That is impossible, so the world cannot be eternal. Third, if the world is eternal then time must be eternal or infinite as well. If so, segments of time are also infinite. But since the past is smaller than the future, we reach the absurd conclusion that one infinite segment is smaller than another, which is false. Hence the world cannot be eternal. Finally, if the world is eternal then every motion is composed of two forces: an infinite force (on account of the eternal motion of the world) and a finite force (the force which brings this particular motion into existence). But if each mover is composed of these two forces, we end up with an infinite series of movers, which is impossible.

Why does R. David go through this exercise? To satisfy himself that even pure philosophy cannot support the belief that the world is eternal.[82] Thus, belief in creation does not negate the precepts of human reason. Moreover, that Scriptures teach creation is for R. David the ultimate proof of its verity, so R. David turns to religious proofs *(reayot)*.[83] These proofs can be persuasive only to the person who already accepts the authority of the Torah as supreme and divinely revealed. However, these proofs are not devoid of rationality; rather, they provide a comparison between the Scriptures and accepted scientific knowledge. Needless to say, whenever a discrepancy arises, the authority of Scriptures prevails.

The first proof of creation is based on the nature of light. Gen. 1:3 states: "And God said let there be light; and there was light." According to some Neoplatonic philosophers (R. David mentions only Solomon ibn Gabirol),[84] the very nature of light supports the belief in creation. These philosophers distinguished between two types of light: "sensible light" *(or muhash)* and "spiritual light" *(or ruhani)*. All forms of corporeal things can be reduced to sensible light. Since forms determine the nature of things, sensible light can be said to be the cause of corporeal existents. In comparison, God is spiritual light, and He can be said to be "the beginning of all existents" *(hathalat ha-nimẓaim kulam)*, namely, of the world in its totality.

The second proof of creation derives from the celestial spheres. Gen. 1:6 states that "God made the firmament," and that He fixed in it the heavenly bodies, the sun, the moon, and the stars. The account of creation in the Bible conforms with our scientific knowledge of the celestial spheres. The heavens exhibit order *(siddur)* which can only be ascribed to the work of an intelligent, voluntary agent *(po'el sikhli be-razon)*. Rabbinic literature also attests to the orderliness of the created world. R. David adduces a talmudic Midrash about Abraham, who reportedly recognized the existence of God the Creator from his awareness of orderliness in creation.[85] The design of the world attests to the existence of designer (i.e., God) and, in turn, to the fact that the world was created.

The third proof is based on omnipotence. In Gen. 1:9 God said, "Let the water gather into one place." This account contrasts with our scientific knowledge. According to the Aristotelian picture of the universe, water surrounds the earth. From this discrepancy between Scripture and science R. David infers the existence of an omnipotent God who created the universe: Gen. 1:9 attests that "divine omnipotence and providence is extended to existents in order to preserve and maintain them."[86] The rest of the biblical account of creation further supports the notion that God provides for the needs of His creatures.

The fourth proof is based on the nature of will. Gen. 1:14 teaches that God fixed lights in the firmament. Science (in R. David's day) taught that the celestial spheres are by nature in constant motion, whereas the sun, the moon and the stars are by nature at rest. If one assumes that the world came to be in an eternal, necessary process, one cannot explain this peculiar fact. R. David maintains that this phenomenon can be explained only if we assume that "God voluntarily fixed [the stars] wherever He wished, because such things follow the will of the agent and not the nature of the recipient."[87] Certain natural phenomena, then, attest to the existence of a voluntary agent who brought the world into existence by will and intention.

The fifth proof is based on Gen. 1:20, "Let the water bring forth swarms of living creatures." Water is a simple, natural element which does not possess the ability to produce life. Only voluntary, divine involvement can explain this peculiar phenomenon. For R. David, the verse teaches that God can create "from absolute nothingness" and that He requires no material preparedness. The universe as a whole came into being from nonexistence.

Finally, the very nature of human beings attests to the existence of a creator. Human beings comprise three "diverse natures" *(teva'im mithalfim)*: intellect, appetites, and bodily functions. Each of these natures corresponds to a distinct realm of reality (literally, world, *'olam*). Only an intelligent and omnipotent Creator could compose such a creature that represents all levels of existence. That such a creator exists suggests, in turn, that the world was created.

Accordingly, R. David writes, sacred tradition teaches, and philosophy supports, the creation of the world. That proves the first half of the first axiom, which is not only that God created the world but that He did so *ex nihilo*. In regard to the second half, R. David is aware that the creation account in Genesis does not explicitly say that the world was created *ex nihilo*. In fact, some biblical commentators (e.g., Gersonides) claimed that the word "beginning" *(bereshit)* indicates the existence of a "material beginning," namely, preexistent matter. Likewise they claim that the word *created (bara)* does not mean that God "brought something into existence from absolute nothingness," but rather that God fixed and shaped something which was already in existence.

R. David therefore concedes that creation *ex nihilo* is not based on Scripture directly but on the "received tradition" *(ha-qabbalah ha-mesurah).*[88] According to that authoritative interpretation, "beginning" does not indicate an existing material cause but rather the first point in time. Creation is the "beginning of future." Likewise, the word *created* does not stand for having shaped an already existing matter but for having brought something into existence which involves some distinctness.

In accordance with Aristotelian philosophy, R. David teaches that all existents are comprised of matter and form. The Bible uses the term *created* in three ways, all of which involve some peculiarity *(zarut)* in regard to matter and form. The first way concerns the coming-into-being of the universe at large, when matter was completely nonexistent. The omnipotent agent brought matter into existence and shaped it according to His will. Second, *created* is used in regard to creatures in whom there appears to be a discrepancy between their particular matter and their particular form, as in the case of the sea monsters. Third, *created* is applied to the coming-to-be of a creature composed of two substances: corporeal body and incorporeal soul. Man is such a creature. All three cases exceed the power of nature, and can be explained only on the premise of divine activity. Thus, *created* does not signify having shaped an already existing matter, but having brought into existence things which could not have existed otherwise.[89]

A close examination suggests that R. David's view of creation *ex nihilo* differs from the literal meaning of this traditional belief— creation of the world from absolute nothingness at a temporal beginning—and, in fact, reflects both the Platonic and the Aristotelian views which R. David ostensibly rejected as religiously unacceptable. The following definition of creation *ex nihilo* suggests the philosophic approach to creation:

The true tradition *[qabbalah]* compels the community of Israel to believe that the First Cause existed alone without any thing else, neither a participating principle *[shutaf]* nor an affect *[mesovav]* ... The First Cause possesses ultimate power and has the ability to bring into existence something from nothing *[yesh me-ayin]*. In His wisdom, God has shaped *[tiqqen]* that something and from it created the most perfect universe possible.[90]

R. David thus views creation as a two-phase process: the first phase was indeed the creation of something out of absolute nothingness, and the second phase involved shaping an already existing "something" into a specific thing. In other passages R. David terms the first phase of creation as *universal creation (beriah kelalit)*, and the second phase, *particular creation (beriah peratit)*. God first brought into being the "universe in its totality" *(havayah kelalit)*. God then shaped the universe into the diversified reality of multiple existents, each according to its specific nature.

From absolute nonexistence God brought into existence the universe at large, or "nature" *(teva')*. God created nature according to His Wisdom by arranging it as a hierarchy of remote and approximate efficient causes *(sibbot rehoqot; sibbot qerovot)*. The natural world therefore exhibits order, stability, and purposefulness. By operating through these efficient causes, God brought into existence individual particulars, each according to its "specific nature" *(teva' perati)*.[91] The creation of particulars is not, strictly speaking, creation *ex nihilo*, but rather creation of something out of something *(yesh mi-yesh)*.

This interpretation of creation is close to Plato's. Both teach that particulars were created out of an existing something rather than out of nothing. R. David's "something" is Plato's Prime Matter, except that R. David's God created that Prime Matter, and Plato's God was coexistent with Prime Matter. R. David found this difference at the heart of Judaism, and hence asserted creation *ex nihilo* as Judaism's first axiom.

R. David goes on to apply this two-phase interpretation of creation to the biblical account. Medieval commentators already noted the inconsistency between the creation in Genesis 1, ascribed to the Elohist author, and creation in Genesis 2, ascribed to the Yahwist author. They resolved the discrepancy by pointing to the qualitative difference in the two divine names, each representing a certain aspect of divine activity. R. David connects the difference between the two names with the difference between the two phases of the creative process: YHWH is the proper name of God. It indicates the divine essence. As noted in the next chapter, the divine essence is identified with the act of being. Since the essence of God is to be, only God can confer existence on nonexistence. And because only God can bring something into existence from absolute nothingness, YHWH signifies divine omnipotence, and YHWH created the world in its totality. Elohim, by contrast, refers to divine justice. Working through the hierarchy of efficient cause, God shaped existents each according to its specific nature. The creation of particulars in the world is ascribed to the divine name Elohim.

This interpretation faces a textual difficulty: Genesis 1 does not mention YHWH, although R. David's analysis referred to a verse from this chapter. R. David resolves the difficulty by saying that YHWH is the implied subject of the verb *created* in the opening verse of Genesis.[92]

R. David not only distinguished these two phases of creation, he also went on to identify the first phase, "universal creation," with emanation. The coming-into-being of the universe in its totality was not an instantaneous act *(pe'ulah)* but rather an emanation *(azilut)*. He specifically says that "the total reality" *(ha-havaya ha-kelalit)* was brought into existence from absolute non-existence and is called "emanation and overflow" *(azilut ve-hashpa'ah)*.[93] Emanation is not an involuntary, necessary process but rather a purposeful, voluntary activity of God. God willed the world and brought it into existence:

> That prior to the creation of the world God was alone and in His Wisdom and Omnipotence he began to emanate *[hithil le-hashpi'a]* the reality of something other than Himself; and this reality that emanated from Him is called "something" *[davar]* ... and this existent *[nimza]* corresponds to the creator.[94]

The identification of creation and emanation becomes most evident when R. David reinterprets the Midrash "prior to creation of the world, God Blessed Be He was alone," by adding to the statement "and existents emanated from Him without material cause." R. David thus appears to hold that the world emanated from the divine essence.

In this context we can understand R. David's reference to Kabbalistic interpretation of creation.[95] R. David incorporated Kabbalistic cosmological doctrines which correlate the structure of the universe to the internal dynamics of the Godhead. Kabbalah teaches that God created the world according to His own internal dynamic represented in the ten powers known as *Sefirot*. As discussed in the next chapter, R. David identifies the *Sefirot* with the divine perfections that exist in God united with His essence. He had no problem incorporating Kabbalistic cosmology into his own philosophical exposition of the belief in creation. In both theories God created the world from his own essence.

R. David then adopted the common Kabbalistic cosmology which links the various parts of the universe to the internal structure of the *Sefirot* as follows. The first three *Sefirot (Keter, Hokhman, Binah)* indicate "the perfection of the first existent." The following two *Sefirot (Hesed* and *Gevurah)* indicate that "the world was created in loving kindness" and that God "governs His world in power." The lower two *Sefirot (Nezah* and *Hod)* correspond to the realm of the Separate Intelligences and the realm of the celestial spheres, respectively. The next *Sefirah (Yesod)*, which symbolizes male sexuality, corresponds to the sublunar world of "procreation and multiplication." And at last comes *Malkhut*, the female aspect of God which "governs and sustains the entire world." Because the world was created according to the example of the *Sefirot*, observance of the world yields knowledge of the internal structure of the Godhead.

The theory that the world emanated from the essence of God minimizes the ontological gap between God and the world. It implies that somehow the world existed in God prior to its coming into being at creation. Indeed, R. David specifically teaches that "the essence of God Blessed Be He is the paradigm *[defus]* of all existents; in Him they are conceived and elaborated in the most perfect way possible."[96] God is the utmost perfection of all existents; in God all things exist ideally prior to their coming into being in the extradeical world.

This theory was quite popular among Jewish thinkers of R. David's generation. It was advocated by, among others, R. Abraham Bibago, R. Abraham Shalom, R. Joseph Taitazak, R. Isaac Aderbi and R. Shlomo Alkabez.[97] The philosophically oriented thinkers among them used the theory to explain how God knows particulars simply by knowing Himself; those more inclined toward Kabbalah employed the theory to explain Kabbalistic doctrine of *Sefirot*. The theory has a clear Neoplatonic tinge to it, but it was articulated first by the Muslim Aristotelian philosopher Averroës,[98] and, through him, it influenced later Jewish philosophers. Regardless of the origin of the theory, the idea that God is "the paradigm of the world" changes the meaning of creation *ex nihilo*. Creation is not an instan-

taneous act by a totally transcendent God but the process by which
the world emanated from the divine essence.

R. David realized that his idea of emanation was open to the
same objections he had raised earlier against the philosophers' theory
of emanation. If creation *ex nihilo* is identical with emanation from
the essence of God, does it mean that the world proceeded from God
necessarily? R. David already rejected the Aristotelian position on
the grounds that it teaches that the world proceeds from God necessarily. This position is not compatible with the Jewish traditional
belief that the world was created by will and intention. To protect
the traditional Jewish position, R. David employs the philosophic
analysis of "necessary" and "possible."

Beginning with Avicenna, Aristotelian philosophers distinguished between necessary-possible per se *(mi-zad 'azmo)* and
necessary-possible *ab alio (mi-zad sibato)*. Applying this to the origin
of the world, R. David states that the world as a whole is both possible per se *(efshari mi-zad 'azmo)* and possible *ab alio (efshari mi-zad
sibato)*.[99] Since God is the cause of the world, the world is possible
per se; the world is not its own cause. And because emanation is a
voluntary process, the world is also possible *ab alio*. God willed the
best possible world. R. David finds support that the world is possible
per se in the opening verse of Genesis:

> When Scripture says "In the beginning God created" it means
> that there is an Efficient Cause *[sibba po'elet]* whose power and
> duration are infinite. He is called *Elohim*, that is to say, He pos-
> sesses all powers *[kohot]* because He is the Necessary Existent
> *[mehuyav ha-meziut]* in itself. And because of his [infinite]
> power He has the ability to emanate *[le-hamshikh]* existents
> which are contingent in themselves without material cause
> *[sibbah homrit]*.[100]

A Midrash by R. Abahu teaches that the world is possible *ab
alio*: "God created worlds and destroyed them." According to R.
David, "'and He destroyed them' means that God conceived *[ziyyer]*
all existents that could possibly be and did not like some of them."[101]
R. David concludes that God willed the best possible world, and it
is this world which He brought into existence.

In sum, the first axiom of Judaism teaches that God created the
world as a whole out of absolute nothingness. The world emanated
from God's essence as a result of a purposeful, voluntary activity in

which God willed the best possible world. The world preexisted in God ideally, and creation confers secondary existence on that ideal, but the very details of this process exceed the limitation of natural human reason.

Prophecy

R. David's second and third axioms follow creation *ex nihilo*. If God created the world, God could reveal His will to the prophets of Israel, and God could perform miracles. But if prophecy and miracles logically follow from creation *ex nihilo*, then why does R. David raise them to the level of axioms at all? Are they not simply theorems derivable from a single axiom, no higher in R. David's scheme than Maimonides' other ten principles?

R. David's choice and treatment of his second axiom, prophecy, shows his ambivalence toward Maimonides. On the one hand, R. David defends the Thirteen Principles—which include both prophecy per se and the uniqueness of Moses' prophecy—and employs Maimonides' reasoned, philosophical analysis of the prophetic phenomenon. On the other hand, R. David concludes through this analysis that the view of prophecy which Maimonides denigrated by ascribing it to the "multitudes" (P-1) is correct, and that Maimonides' preferred views that prophecy is totally natural involving no divine intervention (P-2), or a natural phenomenon that God can still prevent (P-3), are wrong. Indeed, R. David calls them "foreign teachings" *(devarim zarim)* that negate both Scripture and rabbinic tradition, and accuses Maimonides of too readily compromising tradition in order to accommodate philosophy.[102]

R. David's second axiom is as follows: God will reveal His will to whomever He wishes, regardless of the recipient's preparation; God initiates both the prophetic message and the way it is experienced; and everyone present at Sinai underwent a prophetic experience. He postulates this axiom to defend the "multitudes'" view (i.e., the rabbinic tradition) as legitimate Jewish belief. R. David satisfies himself that, although derivable, it is nonetheless an axiom, by acknowledging the capacity of philosophy to aid in explaining even that which must ultimately be taken on faith.

R. David's tactic is to concede Maimonides' point but then to limit it. He first distinguishes between "philosophic prophecy" and "divine prophecy," and then equates "philosophic prophecy" with Maimonides' view of all prophecy.[103] As explained in the previous chapter, philosophic prophecy represents the highest stage of human natural knowledge, the summit of philosophic activity: a natural phenomenon in which an individual endowed with the proper mental disposition, who has already reached moral and intellectual achievement, attains the highest form of human knowledge.

In philosophic prophecy the human intellect unites or conjoins with the Active Intellect, the last of the Ten Intelligences, so the prophet gains knowledge of reality in the most abstract and sublime manner possible for human reason. The Active Intellect is considered the "immediate cause" *(sibba qerovah)* of prophecy. The cognitive content of philosophic prophecy is knowledge which is within the range of natural human reason. Following Alfarabi, his teacher, Maimonides adopted the Platonic conception that the wise man is the just ruler, and that laws based on knowledge are the most perfect laws.[104]

R. David agrees that the "philosophic prophet" is called "divine man" because he "promulgates *[mesadder]* true laws and statutes to the community *[ummah]* within which he lives."[105] R. David then asserts that "philosophic prophecy" is not strictly prophecy—at least, not as far as Jewish dogma is concerned:

> God Himself bestows upon man knowledge of the forms of existents *[zurot ha-nimzaot]* and other matters necessary for the perfection of the soul after its separation from the body.[106]

By asserting that God is the immediate cause of prophecy, R. David rejects Maimonides' position, which Gersonides rigorously defended, that prophecy comes from the Active Intellect.

A prophecy which comes from God is the result of an intentional act of a personal, all-knowing, and all-powerful God. Unlike philosophic prophecy, divine prophecy is not automatic upon the attainment of perfection; rather it occurs when God as a voluntary agent chooses to communicate His divine will to an individual or group. Such prophecies, therefore, require "specific divine assistance" *('ezer elohi perati).*

Although he asserts that God is the efficient and immediate cause of all prophecies, R. David also asserts that God may communicate His will through intermediaries. The intermediary may itself be a Separate Intelligence, such as the Active Intellect, which produces "intellectual prophecy" with content similar to that of philosophic prophecy. The Active Intellect functions only as a medium *(keli)* for the communication of the divine efflux, and is not the author. The intermediary may also take corporeal form created by God for a specific time and place, in which case prophecy may involve visions and sounds.

R. David differs from Maimonides on the origin of the corporeal dimension of prophecy. Maimonides may be interpreted to say that the prophetic imagination is the source of the visions and sounds reported in biblical prophecies.[107] R. David rejects this notion and claims that the human imagination is merely a passive receptacle of "individuated" forms. The prophet does not fabricate the sensual aspects of his prophecy but receives them directly from God.

> God, blessed be He, confers a particularized form for each time, place and person. The corporeal aspect of prophecy is not the product of the [prophet's] imagination *[dimyon]*; rather, the imagination is [merely] the receiving faculty. God, blessed be He, bestows this particularized form.[108]

R. David then breaks with Maimonides in interpreting the revelation at Sinai, once again using philosophical analysis to return to the traditional belief. Maimonides departed from a literal reading of Scripture to assert that at Sinai "only those who were fit for it achieved the rank of prophecy and even those in various degrees." Moreover, in *The Guide* II:33, Maimonides taught that "not everything that reached Moses also reached all Israel."

S. Klein-Braslavy has shown that Maimonides then offered three different interpretations of Sinaitic revelation.[109] According to the first, Moses alone heard articulated speech, so that he alone understood the content of the divine revelation, which he later communicated to the Israelites below. They did not hear the precise words of the commandments, but only "one great voice" created by God. This interpretation sharply distinguishes between what happened to Moses and what happened to everyone else at Sinai.

Maimonides was aware that this interpretation flatly contradicts a rabbinic statement (*Babylonian Talmud*, Makkot 24a) that everyone at Sinai received the first two commandments from "the mouth of the Force." So Maimonides suggested a second interpretation: the first two commandments consist of philosophic truths—"the existence of the Deity and his being One"—which humans can know through philosophic analysis. That, and not specific divine revelation, is how the Israelites gained knowledge of them. The other eight commandments still require direct divine revelation because "they belong to the class of generally accepted opinions and those adopted in virtue of tradition."

Maimonides then offered a third interpretation which integrated the first two: "All Israel only heard in that gathering one voice only one single time — the voice through which Moses and all Israel apprehended 'I' and 'Thou shall not,' which Commandments Moses caused them to hear again as spoken in his own speech with an articulation of the letters that were heard" (*The Guide*, II:33).

R. David accepts the assertion that Moses' prophecy was qualitatively different from others' at Sinai, but, in accordance with the rabbinic tradition and a more literal reading of Scripture, R. David rejects the thought that Moses received revelation alone. The very public nature of the event at Sinai was the main test of its authenticity, and therefore the authenticity of the entire Jewish tradition.[110]

Maimonides' Seventh Principle clearly asserts that the uniqueness of Mosaic prophecy lies in the transcendence of human corporeality:

> No material hindrance stood in [Moses'] way, and no defect whether great or small mingled himself with him. The imaginative and sensual powers of his soul were stripped from him. His appetitive faculty was stilled and there remained pure intellect ... His exaltedness reached beyond the sphere of humanity, so that he attained to the angelic rank and became included in the order of angels.

Transcending the limitations of human corporeality enabled the prophet Moses to comprehend metaphysical truths in the most direct, incorporeal, and comprehensive manner. Moses nonetheless managed to remain a human being. As K. Bland summarized Maimonides on Moses, "the Mosaic phenomenon emerges *sui generis*: Moses was neither altogether human nor totally divine. Because of his relative incorporeality, his apprehension of metaphysical truth surpassed the limited knowledge accessible to the greatest prophets and philosopher/scientists alike."[111]

As with the Thirteen Principles in general, R. David first endorses Maimonides' list of four unique aspects of Moses, and then stakes out a different position. The four are as follows: (1) Moses received his prophecy directly from God without any intermediaries or material hindrances; (2) Moses could prophesy at all times without a need for special preparation; (3) Moses could prophesy while being

fully awake; and (4) Moses did not suffer any emotional derange-
ment, fear, or sorrow.[112]

According to R. David, Moses received a supernatural gift from
God which R. David designates as "the Holy Spirit" *(Ruah ha-Qodesh)*:

> You should know that Moses our Master, may peace be on him,
> from the very day that he received prophetic overflow at the
> Burning Bush, was enclosed *[nitlabesh]* in the Holy Spirit *[ruah
> ha-Qodesh]* which was created *[nithadesh]* in his soul and never
> departed from him for the rest of his life.[113]

Once Moses was enclosed in the Holy Spirit, his entire psychic consti-
tution changed. Moses received an additional psychic faculty *(nefesh
yeterah)* which transformed his soul to the rank of angels. R. David
states: "A human soul cloaked *[melubeshet]* in the Holy Spirit has an
additional soul *[nefesh yeterah]* which empowers it."[114] The presence
of the Holy Spirit explains why Moses could receive direct revelation
from God while he was fully awake, at all times, without any involvement of the imagination, without fear and without moral derange-
ment. That presence also explains how Moses could live for forty
days and forty nights without food and sleep, as the Jewish tradition
teaches. It explains how Moses could transcend his human corpceal-
ity and receive an unmediated revelation from God.

So, unlike Maimonides' Moses of philosophic prophecy, R.
David's Moses of divine prophecy attained perfection not through
his own natural talents or efforts but through a divine gift—the Holy
Spirit. Moses was thereby transformed into a different level of existence: his body was like the "matter of the celestial spheres" and his
soul reached the rank of the Separate Intelligences. Moses was a spir-
itualized human being. That ontological difference between Moses
and all other human beings determined the uniqueness of Mosaic
prophecy. It cannot be repeated or superseded. Because Moses was
sui generis, the Torah which he received from God is also unique; it
cannot be abrogated or superseded.

It is thus not by coincidence that both Maimonides and R.
David emphasize the uniqueness of Moses. Rather, they sought to
prove the unity of the Torah in the debates against Christianity.

R. David concludes his discussion of this second axiom by stating that revelation was a miracle to the ordinary Israelite at Sinai.
God transformed all people present to the rank of prophets so that
they can all receive His revelation:

We have to believe that in the unique event great and awesome
miracles were performed ... God, blessed be He, miraculously
prepared the Israelites so that they all receive the rank of prophecy, each according to his ability. And that manner was not [log-
ically] impossible, but it was a miracle which does not conflict
with logical reasoning.[115]

All people present at Sinai heard all Ten Commandments. All but
Moses experienced unbearable fear and trembling after the first two,
so God had Moses create another, human-sounding voice through
which He communicated the last eight. All Ten Commandments were
thus a direct revelation, although God employed created forms to
communicate His Will. The people at Sinai never again prophesied.
Moses performed other miracles to secure his people's continued
faith in divine revelation. Those miracles lasted only a short time,
and then nature returned to its regulated order.

Miracles

R. David's third axiom is that miracles exist, that God is the author
of miracles, and that biblical miracles were true. Like the second
axiom, it is derivable from the first axiom, creation; as the author of
nature, God can intervene in nature and change natural order. Nonetheless, R. David presents this principle as one of three axioms for
immediate religio-political purposes: to defend against Christianity
on the one hand and against philosophic reductionism on the other.

R. David attacks four views of miracles as misinterpretation. First
is the belief, held by "some in our nation, presumed to be wise, who
pronounce and preach in the streets of our city that the impossible does
not have a stable nature and that nothing is absolutely impossible."[116]
R. David distinguishes between two types of impossibility: natural
impossibility (impossible *ab alio; nimna' mi-zad sibato*) and logical
impossibility (impossible per se; *nimna' mi-zad 'azmo*). R. David places
miracles in the first category, the naturally impossible, and asserts that
even God cannot bring about what is logically impossible:

God can perform things which are impossible *ab alio* and in no
time transform a tree into a lion, as he changed a rod into a
serpent. Because the divine agent is omnipotent, He requires no
preparedness in the substratum *[nose]* and no specific length of
time ... But things which are impossible per se because they
were so made by God, God cannot change.[117]

Such limitation on divine omnipotence does not ascribe an imperfection to God; rather it protects God's perfection. God is a wise, all-knowing agent. All His actions reflect wisdom, so to act against wisdom would imply self-contradiction. Therefore, to say that God cannot square the circle, or make the part greater than the whole, is to ascribe perfection to God.

This distinction permits R. David to attack Christianity as follows: Christianity is based on the belief that God can do the logically impossible, and that nothing is absolutely impossible—for example, Incarnation and Transubstantiation. But since Judaism holds that God cannot do that which is logically impossible, Jews refuse to accept the divinity of Jesus. R. David adds almost parenthetically that Jews are therefore persecuted "throughout the provinces of Spain and Naples."

R. David's second attack is against the philosophers, and he mentions Gersonides by name. They deny that God Himself is the author of miracles, because He is not involved in the affairs of the world, and accordingly they ascribe any extraordinary events in nature to the Active Intellect.[118] R. David rejects this view on religious and rational grounds. The Active Intellect cannot be the author of miracles because it would then be superior to God. More importantly, there are three preconditions for the efficient cause of miracles: (*a*) the efficient cause must know both universals and particulars; (*b*) the efficient cause must be more powerful than nature; and (*c*) the efficient cause must know the particular benefit to be derived from the miracle. Only God can fulfill all three conditions. Finally, the Scripture itself ascribes miracles directly to God.[119]

R. David next attacks the view, which he again ascribes to Gersonides, that limits natural miracles to the sublunar realm; that realm is subject to the laws of generation and corruption, but the translunar world, comprised of the celestial spheres and the Separate Intelligences, is not.[120] R. David cites Scripture to prove that God can effect miracles in both worlds: for example, Josh. 10:12 ("And the sun stood still, and the moon stayed," etc.) and 2 Kings 20:9-11 ("And Isaiah the prophet cried to the Lord; and he brought the shadow back ten steps by which the sun has declined on the dial of Ahaz").[121]

R. David makes his fourth and final attack against the most radical philosophical position: that the very concept of nature precludes the miraculous. According to this view, nature is by definition stable and permanent, and a miracle (at least in the sense of an extraordinary event contrary to nature) is a logical impossibility. Citing Maimonides' *Epistle on Resurrection* for support, R. David responds that nature is not fixed or rigid but only a highly regular system: *ha-teva' hu meodi ve-lo temidi.* Miracles, being temporary deviations from the natural order, are therefore possible.[122] After a miraculous event, nature returns to its highly regular course which God designed.

R. David accomplishes three goals by citing Maimonides. First, R. David of course raises his own standing by identifying himself with Maimonides. Second, some philosophers had claimed that Maimonides did not believe in miracles. R. David defends Maimonides against that interpretation, thus shading Maimonides toward traditionalism or religion and away from philosophy or logic. Third, by harmonizing the belief in miracles with the dictates of reason, R. David advances his own theology that philosophy is consistent with, but subordinate to, religion.

R. David classifies miracles in two steps. His first division is between "patent miracles" *(nissim geluyim)* and "latent miracles" *(nissim nistarim).* Patent miracles are those extraordinary events which patently violate the regularity of nature. R. David ascribes them directly to God. All biblical miracles belong to this category. But the very permanence, stability, and regularity of nature is itself a sort of miracle, reflecting the continual care of God to His creation. These are "latent miracles," the reward of God for Israel's obedience. They are not the result of mechanical laws, but rather of divine activity which works through a created system of remote and approximate causes.[123]

R. David borrowed this classification from Nahmanides and credited him by name.[124] In fact, in *'Ein ha-Qore*, his commentary on Maimonides' *Guide*, R. David claims that Nahmanides borrowed this distinction from Maimonides.[125] R. David may or may not be right; scholars still dispute Maimonides' view of miracles. But the claim itself shows R. David's general intent to present Maimonides in the best possible light as a traditionalist thinker.

R. David then subdivides patent miracles into three groups:[126]

1. "Miracles outside the natural order" *(nissim huẓ me-ha-teva')*; that is, a natural agent could reach the same result, but not instantaneously. R. David cites Moses' changing of a rod into a serpent as an example, which accorded with medieval science if not with our own. For R. David, a change from one material substance to another is within the very realm of nature. Hence, R. David could

say that in principle a natural agent could affect such change, although it would take an extremely long time.

2. "Miracles above the natural order" *(nissim le-ma'alah me-ha-teva')* — that is, changes in the order of nature that a natural agent could not accomplish in any event. An example of this is Joshua's halting the course of the sun and the moon in Gibeon (Josh. 10:12).

3. "Miracles contrary to nature" *(nissim hefkhiyim la-teva')* — that is, changes in the very substance of the natural thing. R. David cites as example the parting of the Red Sea in Exodus, in which, to the medieval scientist, water turned into air.

Scripture, of course, ascribes many miracles to prophets, and not directly to God. R. David therefore needs to explain the relationship between the prophet (the natural agent) and God (the principal, or cause, of miracles). First, R. David claims that performance of miracles is not a *sine qua non* of prophecy; in other words, a prophet does not have to perform miracles in order to be a prophet.

We might wonder how this question arose at all, because prophecy, at least in the sense of delivery of divine revelation, appears distinct from miracles, changes in the natural order. The question was debated at length in medieval philosophy among Muslims, Jews, and Christians, because, according to Christian Scripture, Jesus performed miracles. He correctly notes that Muslim philosophers did not consider performance of miracles a necessary characteristic of prophets; rather, they thought that political leadership marks individuals as prophets. It is Christian thinkers who highlighted the miraculous activities of prophets.[127] If miracles are the distinguishing mark of prophets, then one could argue that Jesus was a prophet. So R. David sought to deny that claim.

Second, a prophet must first attain intellectual perfection before he can perform miracles. (As noted above, a person need not attain that perfection in order to prophesy.) R. David supports this position with a cryptic remark by Abraham ibn 'Ezra in *Commentary on the Pentateuch*: "When the part knows the whole and conjoins with the whole, the part can create in the whole miracles and signs."[128] R. David interprets this to mean:

When the individual human intellect comprehends the nature of existents which is "the whole" *[ha-kol]*, [the human intellect] conjoins with "the whole" which is the Separate Intelligence and creates *[mehadesh]* in the sublunar world signs and wonders.

And prophets differ from each other in the degree of their knowledge of existents.[129]

As A. Ravitsky has shown, the notion that the intellectually perfect human soul may act on nature originated in the writings of Avicenna on the basis of classical Neoplatonic motifs.[130] The Neoplatonic thinker Abraham ibn 'Ezra and the Aristotelian thinker Abraham ibn Daud incorporated Avicenna's view into Jewish philosophy, where it developed over the next three centuries. In the fourteenth century it gained new popularity among Iberian thinkers who were interested in magic and astrology, such as Samuel ibn Zarza and Samuel ibn Motot. These thinkers wrote commentaries to ibn Ezra's *Commentary on the Pentateuch* and attempted to relate the Maimonidean concept of prophecy to this one. Another attempt was to relate ibn 'Ezra's position to Averroës' conception which holds that when the soul of the prophet is in conjunction with the Active Intellect, the prophet can act on the created order. R. David ben Judah seems to continue this trend of thought which, we should note, contrasts with Aquinas' claim that only God can work miracles. R. David's claim in the above paragraph suggests that association of prophetic miracles with knowledge of creation need not deny the belief in creation *ex nihilo,* as Ravitzky claims.[131] In the Renaissance the emphasis on the miraculous capacity of the prophet found new favor among thinkers interested in manipulation of nature through magic.

The return to the Neoplatonic tradition comports with the intellectual trends of R. David's day. However, R. David severely limits the miraculous ability of prophets by claiming that knowledge alone is not sufficient to perform miracles. Rather, prophets perform miracles only by receiving "specific divine assistance" *('ezer elohi perati)*; that is, prophets perform miracles only when God interferes in nature and bestows upon them additional powers. Moses received the greatest direct assistance from God, and hence his miracles were greater than those of other prophets.[132]

Even with knowledge, prophets have the following limitations: (*a*) they cannot effect any change in the Deity itself; (*b*) they may cancel a commandment of the Torah only temporarily; and (*c*) they perform miracles primarily to proclaim divine omnipotence and continual providential care. R. David thereby asserts that prophets are only conduits. God causes miracles, although God works through an intermediary agent, namely, the prophet.

So are the three axioms of Judaism — creation *ex nihilo,* prophecy, and miracles—intrinsically interwoven. Prophecy and miracles are logically derivable from creation *ex nihilo*. But it is not enough to assert creation *ex nihilo* as the sole dogma of Judaism, for Jews could still misinterpret all three. These dogmas thus have two important functions: First, they assure the belief in the Torah as divinely revealed; and second, they establish the belief in a personal God who is omnipotent, omniscient, voluntary and benevolent. Although they ultimately depend upon faith, all three dogmas are compatible with the dictates of human reason.

7

A Systematic Theologian

Rabbinic Theism, Philosophy, and Kabbalah

God is per se the subject of theology. R. David's literary activity culminated in a systematic exposition of the concept of God in the last section of *Tehillah le-David*. The work was written in Salonika in the 1530s, but R. David died before he finished it. R. David has written about God twice before, in *Magen David* and in his commentary of Maimonides, *Ein ha-Qore*.[1] This time he wrote in scholastic style, presenting a highly structured, logically arranged exposition.

R. David fuses three distinct intellectual traditions: rabbinic Judaism, medieval scholasticism, and Kabbalah. R. David did not espouse philosophy as a universal explanation grounded exclusively and ultimately in human reason; nor did he espouse Kabbalah as esoteric theurgy. Rather, R. David espoused theology: a systematic, reasoned exposition of propositions logically derived from axioms (i.e., dogmas) assumed to be divinely revealed. R. David was a theologian, and his God was the God of theologians.

As a professing Jew, Rabbi R. David ben Judah Messer Leon

worshiped the God of Abraham, Isaac, and Jacob. He understood the rabbinic tradition and argued that creation, prophecy, and miracles are *the* three dogmas of Judaism, specifically to protect that tradition from misinterpretation.[2] In considering theology a scientific discipline, R. David claimed that the teachings of the revealed faith were compatible with the dictates of human reason. Looked at from the opposite side, R. David asserted that reason could help explain, but could not independently demonstrate or prove, the dogmas of Judaism.

The rabbinic tradition espoused theism: "the belief in one God who is personal, worthy of adoration, separate from the world, but continuously active in it."[3] God is a Subject possessing not only mind but also will. Being fully personal, God can be conceived through images drawn from human life and can be addressed as "Thou" in prayer. This personal God is the ultimate reality. Because God is perfect, wholly good, and infinitely powerful, God alone deserves adoration (or worship). God's infinite benevolence and omnipotence manifest themselves in the very creation of the world. God created the world *ex nihilo* and continues to preserve and protect the world. As creator, God knows His creations intimately. He listens to their needs and responds to them; occasionally He intervenes in nature and history in order to benefit His creation.

In rabbinic theism, the God of Abraham, Isaac, and Jacob is the Perfect Being who has entered a covenant with Israel, the Chosen People. God revealed the Torah to Israel, and His intimate relationship with Israel is determined by Israel's observance of the Torah. When Israel is loyal to God's will, she is rewarded abundantly; when Israel transgresses the divine commands, she is punished. God judges Israel collectively and individually with justice and mercy. He rewards the righteous and punishes the sinner. The ultimate retribution would come at the end of days when all evil will cease.

R. David ben Judah Messer Leon wrote a rational, systematic, scholastic defense of rabbinic theism. Interwoven through that exposition are two contributions uniquely characteristic of Jewish writers at the turn of the sixteenth century. First, R. David adapts Thomas Aquinas' scholastic methodology to Jewish thought. Indeed, R. David's philosophical exposition of rabbinic theism closely resembles Aquinas' philosophical exposition of Christian theism. R. David cites Aquinas as an authority on divine knowledge and providence,[4] and R. David's proofs of God's existence, theory of being, and theory of divine attributes also resonate with Aquinas. Of course R. David frequently cites Jewish philosophic and religious sources; yet the manner in which he blends them — the "inner logic" of his position — is essentially Thomistic.

For example, in the third section of *Tehillah le-David*, R. David addresses the major questions of medieval scholasticism: Can God's existence be rationally proven? Is God's existence unique? How does God's existence relate to His essence? What is the essence of God? Can God's essence be known? If not, how can we talk meaningfully about God? What are the major attributes which we can predicate of God? How does God relate to the world? Does God know particulars? How does God's knowledge reconcile with human freedom? What is the nature of divine providence? R. David then responds in the scholastic style: he first reviews the opinions of his predecessors who disagreed with his own position; he then presents his own position, supporting it with both philosophical arguments and citations from texts which a believing Jew considers authoritative (the Bible, the Talmud, and the Midrash); he concludes by refuting the objections.

R. David's affinity for Thomas Aquinas should not seem strange. The very attempt to reconcile the rabbinic tradition with philosophy reflects the general conservative posture of fifteenth century Jewish thinkers, such as R. Joseph ibn Shem Tov, R. Abraham Bibago, R. Abraham Shalom, R. Isaac 'Arama, Don Isaac Abravanel. As noted in Chapter Five above, R. David and other contemporary Jewish thinkers regarded Aquinas' synthesis of reason and faith to be better than Maimonides' or Averroës'. Yet the very use of the scholastic method demonstrates an allegiance to medieval philosophy, which inevitably molded R. David's conception of God.[5] R. David's personal God of Israel was an incorporeal, simple, intellectual substance, whose essence is to exist, and whose proper activity is self-contemplation.

R. David's second contribution concerns Kabbalah, which R. David understood as an authentic rabbinic tradition. What makes R. David's employment of Kabbalah interesting is the reconciliation of Kabbalah and Aristotelian philosophy. He could incorporate Kabbalah into philosophy because he highlighted the Neoplatonic dimensions of medieval Aristotelianism. At times he quotes specific Neoplatonic sources; at others he emphasizes the Neoplatonic themes of his medieval Aristotelian sources.[6] Since Kabbalah itself presupposed Neoplatonic ontology and epistemology, the fusion of Kabbalah and philosophy was now possible.

The Zohar is the *magnum opus* of medieval Kabbalah, comprised of several strands or schools of thought.[7] Although it purports to be an ancient text by the Tanna Rabbi Simon Bar Yohai, we now know that Moses de Leon wrote it in Spain during the last quarter of the thirteenth century.[8] R. David, however, did not. He believed the Zohar to be an ancient Midrash and the works of medieval Kabbalists to be embellishments of ancient Kabbalistic doctrines.[9] R. David knew Kabbalah mostly from R. Menahem Recanati's *Commentary of the Zohar* and the *Commentary on Prayers*, and from the anonymous fourteenth century text, *Ma'arekhet ha-Elohut*.[10] These works presented a distinct conception of a God who has revealed Himself in ten dynamic powers—the *Sefirot*, (though they differed in their interpretation of the *Sefirot*, to be discussed below). Accepting Kabbalah as an authentic rabbinic tradition meant some acceptance of the *Sefirot*. R. David indeed believed that the *Sefirot* were real; they do exist in God and are identified with the essence of God.[11] But R. David believed that the revealed tradition is rationally explicable; consistent with that understanding, R. David could—indeed, had to—interpret the *Sefirot* philosophically.

Jewish scholars trained in philosophy at the turn of the sixteenth century found a rational, reconciled Kabbalah more palatable than a Kabbalah that negated Aristotelianism entirely. By attempting a philosophic interpretation of the *Sefirot*, R. David greatly contributed first to that reconciliation and ultimately to the dissemination of Kabbalah among those who rejected any reconciliation with philosophy. Several scholars among the Iberian refugees in the Ottoman Empire had a widespread knowledge of Kabbalah.[12] Perhaps for messianic purposes, Iberian Kabbalists felt a strong need to systematize the teachings of Kabbalah, even to reduce them to catechisms.[13] R. David's scholastic exposition of Kabbalah helped that process. These Kabbalists could employ R. David's exposition of Kabbalistic doctrines, yet reject his interpretations. Thus, despite both his limited knowledge of Kabbalistic lore and his own subordination of it to philosophy and rabbinic theism, R. David ben Judah helped to disseminate and to systematize Kabbalah.

This chapter presents R. David's theology in four divisions: the existence of God, the divine attributes, the divine essence, and divine knowledge and providence. These four topics generally reflect the outline of R. David's theological discussion in *Tehillah le-David*. They also encompass the major theological concerns of Jewish scholars in the late Middle Ages.

The Existence of God

R. David ben Judah Messer Leon's first dogma of Judaism is that God created the world *ex nihilo*. This dogma presupposes that God

exists; yet R. David, along with most medieval thinkers, also believed
human reason capable of proving that God exists. Reason thereby
supports faith. So in *Tehillah le-David*, Part III, Chapter 4, R. David
proves God's existence. R. David's proofs are not unique; more than
one philosopher had already proposed them.[14] What is unique is the
close resemblance of the chapter's structure, style, and vocabulary to
one source in particular: Aquinas' *Summa Theologiae*, Ia, q. 2, a. 3.[15]

A summary of that article in *Summa Theologiae* is in order.
There Aquinas proposes the proofs for the existence of God known
as the Five Ways, namely, (i) motion, (ii) efficient causality, (iii) possibility and necessity, (iv) perfection, and (v) order.[16] All of these
proofs are *a posteriori*; that is, they begin with sense perception of
corporeal things and deduce the existence of God backward from
there. They all belong to the Cosmological Argument for the existence
of God for which it is enough to prove that there exists a world of
conditioned events and objects.[17] To explore their conditions is to be
lead toward something which is unconditioned. By the same token,
to be aware of the regression of causes is to become aware that there
must be a First Cause. Without the existence of a First Cause, the
existence of the world is made unintelligible.

In scholastic style, R. David first states the question. He formulates the dispute concerning God's existence as follows:

> The ancient ones *[haqadmonim]* who did not see the light of tra-
> dition denied the existence of a First Cause from which all
> things come forth, and which serves as their beginning.[18]

Although R. David's reference to "the ancient ones" is unclear, his formulation assumes *sub silentio* that the God of Israel is the First Cause.

Continuing in scholastic style, R. David then recognizes the two
objections to God's existence that he will dispute. Aquinas recited
the same objections in *Summa Theologiae* q. 2, a. 3, in reverse order.
The first, as R. David recites them, denies the existence of a transcendent First Cause:

> [E]ffects *[pe'ulot]* are similar to reality in its totality, which is
> cyclical, [that is] it has no beginning or end; likewise ... all exist-
> ing things *[havayot]* form a circle so that no existent can be said
> to be the first one or the beginning.[19]

This objection to the existence of God admits causality in general, but denies that finite, linear series of causes which leads to a First Cause. Instead, causes and effects are circular, so that the universe is a self-contained system. Aquinas articulated this objection best: "All natural things can be reduced to one principle, which is nature." If so, there is no need to suppose that God exists in order to explain the existence of the world.

The second objection points out the existence of evil in the world, and thus denies the existence of an omnipotent benevolent agent. R. David recites it as follows:

> If a First Cause exists as the cause of all other existents, it must be infinite in all respects, especially in regard to goodness which is appropriate to such cause. It follows that there exists an infinite goodness *[tov bilti ba'al takhlit]*. Such [infinite] goodness must destroy evil which is its corrolary *[maqbilo]*, because evil is finite whereas goodness is infinite. It would mean that evil does not exist. But we witness that evil prevails. Therefore an infinite goodness does not exist.[20]

Aquinas' influence on R. David is clear when that passage is compared to Aquinas' formulation:

> It seems that God does not exist; because if one of two contraries be infinite the other would be altogether destroyed. But the name God means that He is infinite goodness. If, therefore, God existed there would be no evil discoverable; but there is evil in the world. Therefore God does not exist.

R. David then refutes the two objections. He discusses the first (denial of a first cause) at length and the second (presence of evil) only as an afterthought. To refute the first, R. David sets forth three arguments: (i) efficient causality, (ii) motion, and (iii) possibility and necessity. A fourth argument, perfection, appears throughout R. David's writings. Here are those four arguments, which represent R. David ben Judah Messer Leon's four proofs of the existence of God:

R. David's first argument, efficient causality, corresponds to Aquinas' Second Way. It is based on Aristotle's notion of causality, according to which nothing can be said to be its own cause. Everything must be brought into existence by a thing other than itself. But since an infinite series of causes is impossible in actuality, there must be a First Cause which is itself uncaused.

Maimonides articulated this argument in *The Guide* II:1. Aquinas followed Maimonides in arguing for a finite series of causes but differed in emphasizing that this series has what could be called a "vertical" hierarchy.[21] Aquinas wrote about "order" of efficient causes, in which a subordinate member in the series depends upon the causal activity of the higher member, or one more perfect in regard to existence than the member subordinate to it. Each member of the hierarchy is brought into existence because of the essence of the cause above it. Aquinas insists that such series of causes cannot go to infinity. If such a series had no first member—if it were infinite—then that series itself would not exist. But since sense-experience shows that efficient causality exists, a series of efficient causes must be finite. Its first member is God.

Aquinas' Second Way is closely related to his Fourth Way, called "the argument from perfection": Different kinds of finite things possess different perfections in diverse limited degrees. Not only are there different degrees of goodness, but there are also different degrees of being.[22] There must be one being which is the most perfect being, whose being is the cause of all beings: this is God.

R. David's argument from causality follows Aquinas more than Maimonides. In fact, R. David seems to condense Aquinas' Second and Fourth Ways into one argument:

> In Book XII of *Metaphysics* Aristotle already demonstrated that there is a first existent from which all other things derive their existence. And he explained it by the categories of causes and effects which belong to the science of metaphysics. [Therefore] all existents can be classified as either causes or effects, and they are arranged according to their perfection and imperfection *[hozeq ve-hulshah]*. Thus some causes are more perfect than others and the same [is true] about effects, such that every predicate exists in a perfect or imperfect form *[be-pahut ve-yeter]* [i.e., according to its position in the causal hierarchy]. Necessarily *[be-hekhrah]* we arrive at an existent that has this predicate [i.e., to be an efficient cause] in the utmost perfection. Like heat which is found in various degrees [in existents] but in fire is in utmost perfection, so God is the cause of the utmost perfection *[sibbah be-takhlit ha-hozeq]*.[23]

To paraphrase R. David, unaided human reason proves not only that God exists as the First Cause, but also that He is the most

Perfect Being, the Ultimate Perfection. Although R. David does not differentiate the argument from perfection and give it a name, as Aquinas does with his Fourth Way, the notion that God is the sum of all perfections is a leitmotif in R. David's writings, discussed further below.

R. David cites Isa. 12:4 for support: "Give thanks to the Lord, call upon his name; make known his deeds among the nations, proclaim that his name is exalted." R. David interprets this verse to mean that "existents *[nimẓaim]* are divided into causes and effects and that the first cause is the most perfect cause [because] it has no imperfection *[hulshah]* whatsoever; rather it is absolutely perfect and true."[24]

R. David's second argument, and thus his second major proof of the existence of God, concerns motion. Like the first, it is a refutation of the argument that God does not exist because there is no first cause. It is based on Aristotle's conception of physical motion articulated in *Physics*, Book VIII. Maimonides cited this as his first proof of God's existence. Averroës discussed it at length in *Tahafut al-Tahafut (The Incoherence of the Incoherence* or *Destruction of the Destruction)*. Aquinas elaborately cited it as his first proof of God's existence in *Summa Contra Gentiles*, apparently considering it the most persuasive.[25] Although familiar with Aquinas' extensive discussion, R. David truncated the argument.

R. David renders the argument from motion as follows:

> The scholars of physics explained this matter [i.e., the existence of God] by reference to the categories of mover and moved which belong to the science of physics. Accordingly, every natural existent is either a mover or a thing being moved, as Aristotle said in Book VIII of *Physics*. Necessarily we arrive at a first existent which is unmoved both in regard to its substance and in regard to its accidents. And this is the First Mover toward which all things yearn to return.[26]

In condensing Aquinas, R. David left implicit a necessary step, namely, the identification of God with the Unmoved Mover. The meaning of the Unmoved Mover was itself in dispute. The Muslim philosopher Avicenna claimed that a first intelligence emanates from God and moves the first sphere. Averroës, on the other hand, thought that the Unmoved Mover (i.e., God) *is* the First Intelligence, so that God Himself moves the first sphere. Averroës' Unmoved Mover is pure form, an intelligence operating not only as the source of the celestial bodies and all subordinated motions but also as the creative originator and sustaining force behind all lesser intelligences.[27]

R. David followed Averroës. R. David viewed God as the Unmoved Mover of the first sphere and attributed all motion in the world to one simple universal being — God. R. David supports that view with Isa. 12:5, "Sing praise to the Lord, for he has done gloriously," which he interprets as follows:

> God is the mover of the [first] sphere which surrounds all. And this proof from physics becomes apparent to whoever observes the sun as it rises and sets.[28]

R. David continued to present the Unmoved Mover not only as the source of all motion, but also as the source to which all existents yearn to return. This second theme originated in such early medieval, anonymous, Neoplatonic texts as *The Book of Causes* and *Theology of Aristotle*, which medieval philosophers wrongly attributed to Aristotle.[29] This particular Neoplatonic theme dominated the thought of Aquinas, and some modern scholars assert that it even explains the structure of the *Summa Theologiae* and Aquinas' Five Ways.[30] R. David again shows Aquinas' influence by repeating it.

R. David's third major proof for the existence of God, and refutation of the objection that there is no first cause, is possibility and necessity. R. David often referred to God as "the Necessary Existent" *(mehuyav ha-meẓiut)*, as did other Jewish writers of his day, such as Abraham Shalom and Abraham Bibago.[31] R. David alludes to the proof of possibility and necessity when he writes:

> ...the two sciences [metaphysics and physics] prove that there is a First Cause which is the Necessary Existent per se *[mehuyav ha-meẓiut be'aẓmo]*.[32]

To understand fully R. David's view of God as the Necessary Existent, and in turn his fourth proof of God's existence (the proof from perfection), a brief historical digression is in order.

Avicenna originated the proof from possibility and necessity.[33] He thought that Aristotle's argument for the existence of a prime mover was not conclusive proof of the existence of God, because it only established the existence of a First Intelligence, and God is not the First Intelligence. To prove that God exists, Avicenna analyzed the very concept of existence and concluded that if we examine any existing species, we find nothing in its essence to account for its existence. In itself, such an existent is only possible — that is, it can exist or not exist. Something else must confer existence upon essences in order for essences to exist. This something, says Avicenna, must be its necessitating cause. If it were not, we would have to suppose another cause, and so on, to infinity. But even an infinity of such causes would not grant existence to the possible. Hence, the existence of the possible must be necessitated by the essence of another existent. This chain of essential causes cannot go on to infinity, but must proceed from an existing essence that does not derive its existence externally. This is God, the Necessary Existent.

Avicenna thus distinguished two kinds of necessity: necessity per se (when a thing is necessary in its very nature) and necessity *ab alio* (when a thing is necessary in regard to its cause).[34] Avicenna's God is the only being who is necessary per se. The celestial spheres and the Separate Intelligences are necessary *ab alio*. Although they exist necessarily (that is, eternally), their necessity or eternity comes not from their nature but from an external source. All other existents in the sublunar world are possible in both respects: both in themselves and in regard to their cause. Thus Avicenna bridged the ontological gap between God and the sublunar world by positing the existence of the translunar world which is both possible and necessary.

Maimonides followed Avicenna in this proof. For all things except God, to exist is tantamount to being caused.[35] Therefore, existence must come from an external agent and is thus accidental to the essence. To exist also means to be actual. But everything that passes from potentiality to actuality is caused by an external agent. It follows that existence is due to some external agent, the efficient cause, and is therefore accidental to the thing itself. God is the only being whose existence is not merely actual but also necessary. Maimonides wrote:

> In the essence of this Cause nothing exists potentially, for if its essence included any possibility of existence it would not exist at all.[36]

God is the Necessary Existent whose essence and existence are one and the same. The Tetragrammaton (YHWH) and the name which God revealed to Moses (i.e., I AM WHO I AM [Exod. 3:14]) indicate God as the Necessary Existent.

Unknown to Maimonides was Averroës' critique of Avicenna.

Averroës denied that existence is a predicamental accident external to the essence of things. Averroës noted two meanings of "existence," one logical, the other ontological.[37] The logical meaning of "existence" is synonymous with "true" and applies to mental constructs. When our ideal of a thing corresponds to extramental reality, then our concept is true; when it does not so correspond, then our concept is false. Only in this sense is existence an accident external to essence. "Existence" is different in the ontological sense. In all existing things—not only in God—existence is due not to an external agent but to the very nature of that thing. Averroës concluded that existence applies to substance essentially and to the other ten Aristotelian categories secondarily. Existence is an analogical predicate. It applies to God in a most primary sense, and to everything else only in a secondary sense.

Averroës' analysis of existence led him to reject the proof from necessity and possibility. Averroës claimed that the very distinction between necessary per se and necessary *ab alio* is erroneous.[38] He argued that the Separate Intelligences, for example, cannot be both possible and necessary at the same time. Once a thing is proven necessary, it cannot be said to be possible, for whatever reason. Having rejected Avicenna's view of necessity, Averroës had to emphasize the proof from motion. Unlike Avicenna, Averroës identified the Prime Mover with the First Intelligence, thus jeopardizing the transcendence of God.[39]

Averroës' critique of Avicenna influenced the course of medieval Jewish philosophy from the thirteenth to the fifteenth centuries, including R. David's views. During the thirteenth and fourteenth centuries, Jewish philosophers followed Averroës to criticize Maimonides. R. Moses Narboni, among the most outstanding Jewish Averroists, rebuked Maimonides for not distinguishing between the two senses of "existence"[40] and for making the proof of possibility-necessity the core of the analysis of God's existence. Narboni and other Jewish philosophers in the fourteenth century followed Averroës in identifying God with the First Intelligence, which in turn affected their interpretation of the relationship between God and the world and their theories of divine attributes, divine knowledge, and providence. Fifteenth century Jewish philosophers were familiar with this critique of Maimonides, but in order to defend the Master they attempted to find a middle course between Avicenna and Averroës.

Among the Christian scholastics, Aquinas suggested such a course.[41] Like Avicenna and Maimonides, Aquinas distinguished between the essence and the existence of things. But like Averroës, Aquinas claimed that existence is not a predicamental accident but belongs essentially to existing things.[42] Aquinas' contribution was the interpretation of existence as an act. Being *(esse)* is the act of existence. The act of existence is different from the essence, yet it is not something superadded by way of accident to the essence.[43] A thing's being is described as though it followed from the principles that make up the nature or essence.

Aquinas concluded that being in creatures is neither only accidental nor only essential. Being *(esse)* is unique. In itself, being is neither diverse nor plural. But being can be diversified, or pluralized, by the different subjects that share it.[44] For example, the being of a stone is different from the being of man; that is, being a stone is certainly different from being a man. Both the stone and man share, or partake, in being. Thus, although being itself is not diverse or plural, it can be pluralized in becoming the being of this or that individual.[45]

Aquinas linked his theory of being to his interpretation of efficient causality. He asserted that when being is participated (and a given thing comes into existence), no new formal characteristic is added to the thing. Being (i.e., the act of existence) leaves a thing's formal nature entirely untouched. But how is being to be shared? Aquinas answers thus: only through efficient causality. In its highest instance, being is an efficient cause, and not the formal cause of things. How do we know this? By tracing the being of observable things to its source as we do in the proofs of God's existence. If being did not subsist in things, there could be no efficient causality and so no participation of being.

With the exception of being, all common natures are formal causes. For example, "animal," "man," or "stone" are the formal causes of individual animals, humans, or stones. In contrast, being is a common nature which is not a formal cause, but rather an efficient cause. Being can be shared only by making things be, without adding anything to their nature. When things exist, being "diversifies itself under the conditions of the here and now." The intellect does not abstract being (as it does in the case of "animal," "man," or "stone") but conceptualizes it as the first and most basic actuality of things.

Aquinas' theory of being underlies his Fourth Way, whereby he proved the existence of God from observing degrees of perfection in sensible things.[46] Some things are discovered to be more or less good, or true, or noble than other things. But things are said to be more or less *F*, for example, to the extent to which they approach something which is most *F*. Something therefore exists which is truest and best and noblest of things, and consequently most in being, for Aristotle says that the truest things are the things most in being.[47] Now whatever is the most *F* is the cause of whatever else is *F*. Therefore there is something which causes being and goodness and any perfection in all things—God.

If there are degrees of perfection then there must be a supreme perfection which serves as the cause for limited perfections in things. To exhibit a particular perfection (e.g., goodness) implies not only that there is a supreme good but also that the supreme good is the cause for the existence of limited goodness in things. Existents form a hierarchy of being in accordance with their degree of participation in the Divine Being. The Fourth Way concludes that there must be "something that is for all existents the cause of existents and goodness and every perfection whatsoever." This is God.

In God, as Avicenna rightly taught, existence is identical with essence. The essence of God is to exist. But because being is pluralized, or diversified, in existing things, all things can be said to participate in God. The various degrees to which things partake in the divine being determines their ontological status. Thus reality as a whole is an organic hierarchy of grades of being whose perfection is the Divine Being. Aquinas spoke about modes of being—that is, levels of existence commensurate with the degree of participation in the divine being. Following Maimonides, Aquinas concludes that the name I AM WHO I AM is the proper name of God, signifying the Diving Being as efficient cause of the world. The name I AM WHO I AM signifies God's essence as the act of existence.

R. David ben Judah Messer Leon was very familiar with these debates. He reviews them in *'Ein ha-Qore* and refers to them in *Magen David*.[48] In *'Ein ha-Qore*, R. David attempts to prove that Maimonides was consistent. R. David correctly notes that since Maimonides had no access to the writings of Averroës he could not have known Averroës' critique of Avicenna.[49] On the basis of Avicenna alone, R. David apologizes, Maimonides was correct to reach his conclusions. R. David himself sided with Averroës and with Aquinas, who denied that existence is an accidental predicament: "Existence in the ontological sense is identical with the essence in all existence and not only in God, blessed be He."[50] Thus, R. David states that although God's essence is identical to His existence, that identity is not to be understood as Maimonides understood it.

R. David's analysis of God's existence appears closest to that of

Aquinas; that is, R. David takes the middle course between Avicenna and Averroës. Like Aquinas, Averroës, Gersonides, and Narboni, R. David states that being is not a predicamental accident added to the essence but something that belongs to the very nature of the existing thing. And like Aquinas, R. David highlights the principle of participation: things exist because they participate in the Divine Being. The various degrees of participation in God's being result in diverse modes of existence. As much as things participate in the Divine Being, so does God (as the act of existence) exist in things in accordance with their mode of being. The various degrees of participation result in different modes of existence ordered hierarchically in the Great Chain of Being.

Here is an example of this key doctrine in R. David's writings:

> (a) God Blessed be He is the ultimate end [takhlit aharon] of all existents and the one most desired by all; that is to say, that all things [nimzaim] exist because of God, namely, that they all participate in His perfection [yeshu'aru bi-shlemuto]; they partake in His exalted nature to a certain degree as determined by their very nature. Because God Blessed be He is the First One who imparts being to all existents as Aristotle explained in Book Ten of *Metaphysics*.[51]
>
> (b) And all things participate in Truth and in Goodness according to their participation in Being. And as God Blessed be He is the absolute Necessary Existent so is He the absolute Goodness and Truth, [as it is said] "the Lord God is truth" [Jer. 10:10].[52]
>
> (c) The truth and essence of every substance corresponds to the degree to which it participates in the Divine Being [ha-heyot ha-elohi]. And His Being, His Light and His Splendor extend to all existents according to their gradations [madregotehem].[53]

These statements present God as the perfection of being and, therefore, as the perfection of all existents. They and others like them reflect the logic of Aquinas' Fourth Way, the argument from perfection. In other words, for R. David the First Cause is the Perfect Being, and to prove that the First Cause exists is to prove that a Perfect Being exists. Thus although R. David does not formally cite the argument from perfection in *Tehillah le-David* III:4, he clearly incorporated this argument in his works.

The logic of the Fourth Way becomes evident in R. David's picture of the universe. The universe forms an organic whole hierarchically ordered. Each being has its proper place in the hierarchy according to its degree of participation in the Divine Being (and interchangeably in Truth and Goodness). The doctrine of participation in the Divine Being seems to R. David to best resolve the puzzle of rabbinic theism: How can God be both outside the world and in it at the same time? As Creator who exists necessarily, God is transcendent to His creation, but as being which is participated in all existents, God is in all things. This is exactly Aquinas' position. R. David praises this view as "a wonderful thought" *('iyyun nifla)* and wonders how could it have eluded Maimonides.

The Neoplatonic bent of this doctrine is evident. It is no surprise that R. David cites as his authority Rabbi Abraham ibn Ezra, the twelfth century Jewish Neoplatonist. R. David takes a cryptic remark from ibn 'Ezra's *Commentary on the Pentateuch*—"God Blessed be He is All, and the image of all *[temunat hakol]*"[54]—and interprets it to mean "that all existents derive their existence from none else but God Blessed be He, and therefore He is all existents in the most perfect manner."[55] Because all things come from God, where they exist in the most exalted and perfect manner, things yearn to return to God, their source. This too is a Neoplatonic theme which pervades the writings of ibn 'Ezra and other Neoplatonic authors. Among the Aristotelians, Aquinas highlighted the return to God as the ultimate end of all existents. By following Aquinas' example and underscoring Neoplatonic motifs within an Aristotelian framework, R. David could then fuse Aristotelian philosophy and Kabbalah, as discussed below.

We can return now to R. David's formal exposition of the arguments for God's existence in *Tehillah le-David* III:4, which he concludes by responding to each specific objection. The first objection (denial of a finite series of causes) is wrong, because in the case of efficient causes *(sibbot po'alot)* if one denies the existence of a first cause, one denies the existence of effects as they are known in the world. The prooftext is Isa. 48:12, God's statement that "I am the first and I am last," which R. David interprets:

> There is no other cause superior to me, and "I am the last" [in the sense that] the last cause comes from me and cannot operate without the power given to it by the First Cause.[56]

In short, all existents derive their existence from God, the First Cause.

Having refuted one objection to God's existence, namely, the denial of a First Cause, R. David spends little energy on the second objection, the existence of evil in the world.

He responds simply:

> You should know that God is infinitely good and he establishes existents according to their nature; and if there is evil in the world it is necessitated by the existence of matter; but good overcomes evil.[57]

Here R. David follows Maimonides and Aquinas. Evil does not exist as an independent principle, but is only a by-product of corporeality. Since matter is necessary for the existence of the corporeal world, evil is also a necessary by-product. R. David supports this position with Hab.1:13. "Thou who art of purer eyes to behold evil," which he interprets to mean that evil never exists in isolation and is always fused with good.

So did R. David continue the medieval rational approach to the existence of God. Utilizing *a posteriori* proofs, R. David claims that human reason can demonstrate that God exists. These proofs establish that God exists necessarily, that there is a causal connection between God and the world, that God is the source of all motion in the world, and that God is the perfection of being.

Divine Attributes

Talking about God is the very core of religion. The belief in a direct encounter between God and man (i.e., revelation) justifies talking about God and engenders anthropomorphism. God has a hand and an eye; God walks, listens, and talks; God is compassionate, loving, angry, and sad. For the biblical authors, talking about God in general and anthropomorphism in particular did not raise any theoretical problems concerning divine attributes, but simply manifested the intimacy between God and man.[58] The rabbis of the Second Temple period also indulged in bold anthropomorphism and vivid descriptions of God, but showed sensitivity to the problem of divine attributes by qualifying their statements with the expression "as it were" *(kivyakhol)*.[59]

In the Middle Ages, under the impact of philosophy, Jews began to think systematically about the God-talk of their canonic sources. If God is so radically different from anything else, how can we know Him at all? If He cannot not be known in Himself, how can we talk about Him? If we talk about God, what is the meaning of that which we ascribe to God? And since we describe God in many terms do we not jeopardize God's unity? These questions and others like them comprise the so-called problem of divine attributes. The problem arose only upon reasoned reflection about the meaning of religious discourse.

R. David ben Judah Messer Leon was fully aware of the problem of divine attributes and of earlier attempts to resolve it. Maimonides' contribution was major; he influenced subsequent discussion of divine attributes not only among Jews but also among Christian scholastics, especially Aquinas.[60] R. David articulated his own view by discussing Maimonides, his followers (for example, Aquinas), and his critics (for example, Gersonides and Crescas). So a discussion of R. David's concept of divine attributes must include a short history of the subject.

Maimonides set forth his theory of divine attributes in *The Guide of the Perplexed* (I:56-60). He was deeply concerned that mistaken understandings about God destroy something in God. For example, by describing God as corporeal we introduce corporeality where it does not belong. Maimonides was concerned because he thought that predicates (i.e., attributes, words used to describe) do have some real reference to the thing predicated. Maimonides thus held a non-nominalist theory of universals.[61]

Caution in our language about God is thus crucial to avoid heresy. To distinguish proper God-talk from improper one, Maimonides — in typical fashion — analyzes and classifies. He divides all assertions about God into five categories, rejecting the first four groups and deeming only the fifth to be permissible God-talk. Here is a summary of each category and Maimonides' reason for rejecting or accepting it:[62]

i) *Definition.* As Aristotle showed, a definition includes (albeit implicitly) a reference to the "four causes," namely, material, efficient, formal, and final.[63] But as noted above in this chapter, God is the First Cause and is Himself uncaused. Therefore, He cannot be defined, and no attribute or definition should be made of Him.

ii) *Part of definition.* An attribute which constitutes a part of definition implies not only that God can be defined but also that God is composed of parts. Since God cannot be defined and God is absolutely simple, God's essence has no parts. Therefore, parts of definition should not be attributed to God.

iii) *Qualities.* Qualities are properties which are external to the essence of things — that is, accidents: for example, moral or psychological traits, natural capacities, and quantitative properties. But God has absolute unity. Accidents or qualities should not be attributed to God, because the distinction between essence and accident is not applicable to God.

iv) *Relation.* Predicates of relation present a more difficult case. Maimonides distinguished between predicates of "correlation," which involve reciprocity (for example "father of"), and predicates which posit "some relation," which are one-sided (for example, the Creator and created).[64] Maimonides emphatically denied any attributes which involve reciprocity, because God "is necessarily existent while everything else is only possibly existent."[65] The ontological gap between the Necessary Existent and all contingent things excludes any reciprocity between creatures and God. Maimonides then ruled out any attribute which implies "some relation." Only things which share the same ultimate species can have "some relation." But given the absolute difference between God and all other things, not even attributes which apply "some relation" should be ascribed to God. God has no relation to anything else, so no predicate of relation should be attributed to God.

v) *Action.* Maimonides permits only attributes of action, namely, attributes which describe the activities of the thing described. Attributes of action do not involve reference to a real element in their subjects, only the acts or deeds which stem from that essence. By observing the world, we may know God's actions and hence refer to them; but we recognize that they tell us little of God's essence, which remains beyond the scope of our knowledge.

Maimonides' insistence on the unknowability of God's essence led him to set forth his negative theology. The language most befitting of God is negation, and the true believer knows that. We should not describe what God is, only what God is not, and even the affirmative God language of the Torah and the other Jewish canonic source should be understood negatively. Maimonides lists eight specific terms (existence, life, incorporeality, firstness, power, knowledge, will, and unity) that should be interpreted negatively in relation to God. For example, to say that God exists is to mean that God is not absent, and to say that God is powerful is to mean that He is not weak.

So when ascribed to God these terms carry a totally different meaning from their meaning in ordinary discourse. They are equivocal terms.[66]

The *via negativa* removes from God any imperfection which Maimonides considered necessary for proper understanding of God. Maimonides' emphasis on the way of negation betrays his mistrust of human language. Human language is imperfect because it is based on human knowledge rooted in imperfect human existence. Human language is wholly inadequate to describe God. Hence, Maimonides holds silence alone to be appropriate to God.[67] Silence (the absence of language) indicates the limitations of human language.

Of course Maimonides was not the first to propose what is called negative theology. Plato originated it, and the pagan Neoplatonists of late antiquity Plotinus and Proclus adopted it. The Christian Neoplatonist thinker Pseudo-Areopagite adopted it also, and contributed it to the Muslim theologians of the Mu'atazilite Kalam. Both Kalam and Neoplatonism influenced Jewish thinkers before Maimonides, such as Bahya ibn Pakuda. Maimonides more rigorously applied it to Jewish religious discourse.

But in one important case — the attribute "knowing" — Maimonides deviated from strict negative theology, which influenced all future Jewish scholars including R. David. Although Maimonides claims in several places that the attribute "knowing" is purely equivocal (i.e., the attributes carry a totally different meaning when applied to God), he did suggest that there is some similarity between human intellection and divine intellection.[68] Aristotle taught that when human intellect cognizes a certain piece of knowledge, the knower, the known, and the act of knowing are one and the same. Alfarabi accepted that theory and applied it to God. Maimonides followed Alfarabi in stating:

> [God's] essence is the intellectually cognizing subject, the intellectually cognized object and the intellect as is always necessarily the case with regard to every intellect *in actu*.[69]

Maimonides then stated unequivocally that God's essence is an intellectual substance in pure actuality. That statement is difficult to reconcile with Maimonides' negative theology. That Maimonides spoke of God as an intellectual substance in pure actuality, and talked about God's essence affirmatively, was very important, for it permitted those trying to defend Maimonides' assertion from *The Guide* I:68 that Maimonides did allow some affirmative predication of God's essence.[70]

Maimonides' theory of divine attributes directly influenced Christian scholastics, most notably Albertus Magnus, Aquinas, and Duns Scotus. Either they misunderstood it[71] or they consciously adapted it to their own theological needs,[72] but in any event they were less strict about it and essentially allowed for both negative and affirmative attributes.

Thomas Aquinas, who directly influenced R. David, agreed with Maimonides that in order to approach God one has to deny Him certain characteristics.[73] God is neither this nor that. Aquinas echoed Maimonides in saying that we know what God is not, not what God is. Aquinas acknowledged that negation could occasionally result in words which appear positive. For example when we say that God is "immutable" or "infinite" or "incorporeal." But those terms, nonetheless, are negative: they deny something to God. "Immutable" denies mutability, "infinite" denies finitude, and "incorporeal" denies corporeality. In other words, mutability, corporeality, and finitude are imperfections which we remove from God. By approaching God through negation of imperfection, we know God better.

Aquinas parted from Maimonides in permitting positive attribution. First, Aquinas interpreted the attributes of action (which Maimonides permitted to be ascribed to God) as attributes of relation.[74] According to Aquinas, creation from the essence of God means that there is a real relation between creatures and God, which relation allows us to approach God from our knowledge of finite things. This is not to say that we can ascribe imperfections to God (the way of negation rules this out); but we can ascribe to God pure perfections (e.g., goodness, truth, and beauty) which exist in God in the most eminent and exalted manner as befitting the perfection of the Divine Being.[75] Because they exist in God primarily, and only secondarily in creatures, we may analogically predicate of God positive terms.

While Aquinas allowed for affirmative predication, he insisted that all knowledge is determined or conditioned by the knower's mode of being:

> For knowledge takes place according as the thing known is in the knower. But the thing known is in the knower according to the mode of the knower. Hence the knowledge of every knower is according to the mode if its own nature.[76]

That is to say, whatever we know about God befits our mode of being as finite creatures. The perfections we predicate of God will mean one thing for us and another thing for God. Put differently, the mode of being of the one ascribing the attributes (i.e., the human being) determines the mode of signification (i.e., the attribute ascribed to God). Further, what humans can know about God reflects their mode of being, and human God-talk reflects human modes of signification. Because things exist in God in a supereminent or superexcellent way, the mode of signification of affirmative terms varies when they are ascribed to God or to created things.

Jewish fourteenth century philosophers, among them Gersonides, followed Aquinas and allowed for both negative and affirmative attributes. Gersonides rejected Maimonides' claim that affirmative attributes about God's essence are pure equivocation.[77] In accordance with Averroës, Gersonides argued that some affirmative attributes are permissible because they are predicated of God primarily and of things secondarily *(bi-qedimah u-ve-ihur)*, in particular, existence, unity, intellect, life, goodness, power of will. They should be interpreted in accordance to priority and posteriority *(bi-qedimah u-ve-ihur)* — that is, analogically.

Gersonides claimed that ordinary descriptive terms need not be eliminated from our language about God. He distinguished between "subject of discourse" *(nose be-maamar)* and "existential subject" *(nose be-meẓiut)* and asserted that grammatical distinctions do not necessarily correspond to objective differences.[78] God, therefore, may be the "subject of discourse" to whom several predicates refer without introducing any real distinction in God.

Hasdai Crescas, in the early fifteenth century, dealt the Maimonidean approach its strongest blow.[79] He rejected Maimonidean discourse of God as subversive to Judaism. Crescas admitted that the essence of God is unknowable, but he argued that this essence is revealed in infinite essential attributes *(tearim 'aẓmiyim)* which are knowable.[80] As A. Altmann explains, "the latter are neither identical with God's essence nor merely accidental to it, but inseparable from it in the sense that one cannot be thought of without the other."[81] More emphatically than Gersonides, Crescas argued that there is a real relationship between creatures and God which serves as the basis of affirmative attributes analogically predicated of God.

But Crescas disagreed with Gersonides as well, rejecting Gersonides' intellectualist conception of God. Crescas instead identified God's essence with His absolute goodness.[82] Crescas might have been influenced by scholastic theology (as S. Pines suggests) or by Kabbalah (as W.Z. Harvey and E. Schweid hold).[83] According to Crescas, the essential attributes are symbols that reveal the infinite divine essence without exhausting it. They are the perfections which exist in God in a unique unity and serve as the cause of perfection in the created world.[84]

Crescas influenced later fifteenth century philosophers, although they retreated from his virulent attack on Maimonides. Crescas' own student R. Joseph Albo allowed both negative and affirmative predication, and emphasized God's infinite goodness as the unifying content of our idea of God.[85] R. Abraham Shalom, who defended Maimonides against Gersonides' and Crescas' critiques, also made ample use of their arguments.[86] Shalom endorsed Maimonides' negative theology by denying God any divine attribute interpreted as a definition, part of definition, or quality. Shalom differed from Maimonides in allowing relations to be predicated of God in some nonreciprocal way. Shalom supported interpreting affirmative language as an attribute of action, but he did allow for some predicates to be attributed of God's essence. Shalom's major point was that while we know that certain perfections exist in God, we do not know the manner of their existence.[87] Abraham Bibago, who also defended Maimonides, was more forthcoming in asserting affirmative attributes of God and interpreting them as divine perfections.[88]

R. David ben Judah Messer Leon was familiar with all the theories of divine attributes mentioned above. He reviews the debate between the "way of affirmation" (derekh ha-hiyuv) and the "way of negation" (derekh ha-shelilah), citing Maimonides as the proponent of negation. He does not name any proponent of affirmation, but the arguments he recites can be found in Gersonides' and Crescas' critiques of Maimonides.

R. David bases his theory of divine attributes on that of Thomas Aquinas, most importantly the maxim alluded to above, namely, "The knower knows according to the nature of the knower and not according to the nature of the thing known," which reflects Aquinas' distinction between mode of being and mode of signification.[89] As a loyal Aristotelian R. David asserted that all knowledge is founded in perceivable objects. He could then follow Aquinas in arguing that from our knowledge of perceivable objects we can know not only that God exists but also something about God's nature. We can prove that God exists not only as the cause of all beings but also as the most perfect being. This positive knowledge is significant in the analysis of attributes we employ in religious discourse.

R. David allows both negative and affirmative predicates of God.[90] He adopts a weaker version of negative attributes, however, than does Maimonides, asserting that the negative terms are only formally negative. They signify a positive reality, namely, God's existence as the cause of the world. Therefore, what we say about God is necessarily true of Him precisely as the cause of all perceivable things. From our knowledge of creatures, we can correctly deduce some knowledge about God, but not vice versa; in other words, we cannot deduce from God any knowledge about creatures. With negative attributes, we deny of God the imperfection and deficiency which the attribute implies in reference to our mode of existence as created beings, but we do not deny the applicability of the term to God in a manner compatible with God's mode of existence, namely, an infinite, perfect being whose essence is identical with His act of existence.

Consequently R. David allows attributes of relation and of action to be affirmatively predicated of God's essence. He follows Gersonides in analyzing those affirmative attributes as analogical terms, asserting that some divine attributes are to be interpreted not as pure equivocation but rather as attributes *bi-qedimah u-ve-ihur (secundum prius et posterius)*. R. David copied from Gersonides (without crediting his source) a passage that differentiates between the subject of discourse *(nose be-maamar)* and the existential subject *(nose bi-meẓiut)*.[91] God is the subject of discourse of the attributes predicated of Him in human language, and as such He may be said to have many attributes without destroying His unity.[92]

R. David then returns to Aquinas: In regard to what is predicated, the analogical terms signify a perfection in God, but in regard to the manner of predicating, every such predicate bears that deficiency and imperfection of the knowledge of God which we derive from perceivable things resembling God.[93] For example, when we apply the term "good" to God, the meaning is not that God is merely the cause of goodness, but rather that what we call "goodness" preexists in God according to God's mode of existence. In other words, because God is good, He diffuses goodness into things through the creative act.[94]

R. David misunderstands Crescas' view of essential attributes, identifying it with that of the Kalam theologians which R. David had already dismissed.[95] R. David rejects Crescas for introducing multiplicity to God, but in fact R. David's own position is similar to Crescas'.

R. David's theory of divine attributes reflects his position on universals (for example, goodness), which is identical with Aquinas'. The universal exists in things because it preexists in God in a manner compatible with God's mode of existence, namely complete reality.[96] We then know the universal through an act of abstraction, such that the universal exists in our mind as a concept. This position is best characterized as moderate realism.[97]

To sum up this point: R. David ben Judah Messer Leon maintains that divine attributes such as "good," "knowing," "just," and "merciful" are analogical predicates properly predicated of God's essence. They signify perfections in God, but they do not introduce multiplicity in God. The divine attributes are ontologically identical with one another and with the divine essence. However, since we derive our concepts about God's essence from its varied representations in finite things, we introduce distinctions where no real distinctions exist. Therefore, for us divine attributes are not synonymous or redundant; rather their reference is one and the same being: God's essence identical with His existence. While we know that the proposition "God exists" is true, we do not apprehend God's mode of existence. Likewise, while we know that perfections exist in God, their mode of existence eludes us as well.

The Essence of God

Aristotle distinguished between *that* a thing is (existence) and *what* it is (essence). Essence is what a thing is by its very nature, what gives it identity, and what makes it what it is. The essence of a thing is the thing in its truest sense. Aristotle identified essence with substance, which he distinguished from accidents (i.e., properties which qualify the substance).[98] Medieval Aristotelians continued to distinguish between existence and essence even though they debated the relationship between them. R. David ben Judah Messer Leon reflects the distinction between existence and essence in the very order of *Tehillah le-David*. After proving rationally that God exists and explaining the nature of human discourse about God, R. David then discusses the essence of God.

R. David's understanding of the essence of God is particularly significant because of its relation to Kabbalah. R. David analyzed the Kabbalistic doctrine of the Sefirot in *Magen David*, and identified them with the essence of God.[99] Almost three decades later, R. David discusses God's essence again, this time in *Tehillah le-David*. The two treatments are not contradictory; rather, they fit together to demonstrate R. David's understanding of the divine essence and in turn his reconciliation of Kabbalah and philosophy.

R. David begins his discussion of the essence of God in *Tehillah le-David,* again in typical scholastic fashion, by reciting two views to be discarded. According to the first, God is a corporeal substance shaped like a human body.[100] R. David ascribes it to the uneducated who lack the intellectual ability to think about God abstractly. The same people believe that the celestial spheres are divine and guide their lives by astrology. In accord with Maimonides, R. David dismisses the ascription of corporeality to God as pure idolatry. Philosophically, the notion that God is a corporeal substance is self-contradictory. Whatever is corporeal must (a) be caused by something else, (b) have parts, and (c) extend in space. If one assumes that God is a corporeal substance, then God allows for the possibility of yet another substance greater, or more powerful, than God, which negates the first premise.[101] Religiously, the Third Commandment in the Torah directly denies God corporeality. Although R. David did not mention Christianity by name, this view is unmistakably Christian, and R. David attacks Christianity by dismissing it.

According to the second erroneous view, which the Muslim theologians who rejected the Christian Trinity espoused, God is incorporeal but composed of four essential attributes *(tearim 'azmiyyim):* life, wisdom, will, and power. These attributes were regarded as "things existing in God from eternity and inseparable from Him."[102]

Maimonides attacked this view in *The Guide,* and R. David follows Maimonides: Any composition necessitates an external agent acting as a composer. The belief that God is composed of essential attributes is tantamount to saying that God is caused by something else. But this view clearly contrasts with the already proven proposition that God is the First Cause. Therefore it must be rejected. Furthermore, the Torah itself teaches the unity of God, which excludes any composition from God. Therefore, God cannot be an incorporeal substance composed of essential attributes.

R. David then sets forth the only correct conception of God, which he ascribes to "the wise men of pure reason" *(ha-hakhamim nekiye ha-da'at):* God's essence is "an eternal intellectual substance in pure actuality" *('ezem sikhli nimza be-fo'al tamid)."*[103] This idea began with Aristotle's view of God as mind in pure actuality, and is found in Maimonides' discussion of divine intellection in *The Guide* I:68. R. David analogizes to the human intellect:

> The intellect *[sekhel]* is the most praiseworthy *[nikhbad]* and perfect *[meshubah]* among sublunar existents. Therefore it is found in man who is the end of the sublunar world. And by

virtue of the intellect man governs himself, his city and his kingdom. Likewise, the First Being is the most praiseworthy and
perfect [being] who governs the world. This is why [the First
Being] must have an intellectual nature *[teva' sikhli]*: because he
governs the world in his infinite eternal wisdom *[hokhmato
ha-qeduma she-ein lo sof]*.[104]

> R. David then follows Maimonides to assert that the essence of
an intellectual substance in pure actuality must be identical with its
existence. R. David therefore defines God's essence as

> an existent which is eternal, and whose substance *['azmut]* and
essencee *[mahut]* is to exist totally and absolutely. Because what
specifically belongs to its essence is being and absolute existence
[havayah u-meziut muhlat], we cannot differentiate between
them [i.e., His existence and His essence]; therefore the wise
men taught that eternity is essential to the First Being."[105]

Thus, to exist is essential to God. Because God's essence is to exist,
He must be pure actuality *(be-fo'al tamid; be-fo'al gamur)*.

R. David agrees with Aristotle in arguing that the proper activity for intellectual substances is self-contemplation. But for R. David,
when God contemplates Himself He contemplates the ideal order of
reality which exists in Him in a supereminent and superexcellent
way.[106] Self-contemplation is causal or creative; it imparts being on
things and brings them into existence outside God. For example,

> The intelligible order which God, blessed be He, conceptualizes
in His own mind *[mezayyer be-sikhlo]* is the efficient cause of
reality.[107]

As noted above concerning creation, R. David calls God "the paradigm of all existents" *(defus ha-nimzaot kulam)*" and "an exemplar
of reality" *(dugmat ha-meziut)*."[108] R. David returns to this concept
here: "All things are sealed in His seal and engraved in His Intellect
in the most perfect manner possible."[109]

R. David (now, of course, departing from Aristotle) then identifies ideal reality with Torah: The ideal order of reality exists in God
identical with the divine essence and exists in God as the esoteric,
spiritual Torah. Citing a Midrash that God created the world by con-

sulting the preexisting Torah, R. David concludes that when God contemplates Himself, He contemplates the spiritual Torah, and thus brings into existence extradeical reality. Because the world was created when God consulted the preexistent Torah, the latter can be said to be the blueprint of the created world. Thus, there is complete correspondence between the world as we know it and the Torah. Such correspondence can be deciphered by properly decoding the revealed Torah.[110]

R. David thereby reconciles philosophy to and under religion. No real contradiction exists between approaching God on the basis of our knowledge of the sensible world (i.e., philosophically) and on the basis of Torah (i.e., religiously). Torah is only a more perfect mode of knowing God, but both teach that God "arranges *[mesadder]* all existents in their proper rung *[madregatam]* and bonds them in a wondrous, tight bonding."[111]

From the definition of God's essence as "intellectual substance in pure actuality," R. David ascribes three perfections to God: life, eternity, and omnipotence.[112] It is appropriate to talk about God as "living" precisely because He is the creator; He is the "First Cause which imparts life to all existents in the world so that they exist according to their nature." "Eternal" belongs to God because He is an intellectual substance in pure actuality, whose essence does not fall under the category of time. God is omnipotent because He created the world *ex nihilo*. As discussed earlier, however, God is Truth, so God cannot do the logically impossible.

Of all God's names, the Tetragrammaton, YHWH, most appropriately signifies God's essence, His "being and existence" *(heyot ve-yeshut)*. The Tetragrammaton has five different qualities *(segulot)*:[113] First, it "explains the essence of God, blessed be He, and differentiates Him from all other existents, more than any other name we ascribe to God." Second, its various permutations (e.g., EHYH, and YH) do not change its meaning. Third, all other divine names (e.g., EL and SHADAY) are derived from it. Fourth, the sacrificial cult is directed to YHWH alone and not to other names. Fifth, the way the name is written indicates God's essence, whereas the way it is read ("Adonai") indicates the manner in which all existents emanate from Him. "YHWH" thus

> ...signifies God in regard to His existence, namely that He is unique and eternal; [it signifies] His essence, namely that He is a supernal intellectual substance; and [it signifies] His benevo-

lence and emanative activity, because it is His nature to emanate existents.[114]

R. David's discussion of the essence of God in *Tehillah le-David* appears at first glance to ignore his discussion earlier in *Magen David*, where he identified the essence of God with the Kabbalistic doctrine of Sefirot and interpreted the meaning of this doctrine by means of philosophical categories. Closer examination proves that appearance false. *Tehillah le-David* presumes an understanding of *Sefirot* precisely as outlined in *Magen David*; that is, the *Sefirot* are the divine perfections which exist in God in a supereminent way united with His essence. To understand R. David's view of the essence of God, and in turn of the *Sefirot*, some background on this Kabbalistic doctrine is in order.

Medieval Kabbalah distinguished itself from other intellectual trends in medieval Judaism through theosophy, namely, a doctrine concerning the very nature of God. The Kabbalists claimed to know not only that a personal God exists but also who He is. They delved into the very mystery of the divine personality, the divine Self. Kabbalists ascribed their intimate knowledge of God's personal identity either to direct mystical experience or to esoteric knowledge revealed to Moses at Sinai and transmitted orally.[115] For the Kabbalists, the divine Self was comprised of ten dynamic powers, ten vibrant, living realities, called *Sefirot*.[116] The God of the Kabbalists is a unity within plurality.

Kabbalists thereby rejected both the rabbinic injunction against speculation about the nature of God and the philosophic insistence on the unknowability of God's essence. But as late as the thirteenth century, Kabbalists followed halakhah, and some were among the most influential communal leaders of Iberian Jewry.[117] Most were also versed in Jewish philosophy of either the Neoplatonic or the Aristotelian schools. They tried to juggle three conflicting problems: the intimate knowledge of God, which is the very essence of Kabbalistic knowledge; the rabbinical reticence to open the mystery of God at all; and the philosophic emphasis on the transcendence of God.

As a result, the God of the Kabbalists is simultaneously concealed and revealed; transcendent and immanent; personal and impersonal—a paradoxical concept based on a distinction between the *Ein Sof* (literally, "Without End") and the *Sefirot*. The *Ein Sof*, or the Infinite, is the transcendent, unknowable God who remains beyond the reach of man, even in mystical experiences.[118] The *Sefirot*, in contrast, are the revealed aspect of God; they are the target of religious worship and mystical intent.

Though medieval Kabbalists argued about the precise ontological status of the Sefirot, they all agreed that the personal God of Israel reveals Himself in a unity of those ten dynamic powers. Each *Sefirah* has a proper name, a distinct character, and typical behavior.[119] Each *Sefirah* constantly interacts with the other *Sefirot*, so that each affects all others. The Godhead is a dynamic reality pulsating with life. For the Kabbalists, divine unity is not a matter of incorporeality and simplicity as the philosophers claimed; it is, rather, an equilibrium among the ten dynamic *Sefirot*.

The doctrine of *Sefirot* is inextricably linked to the Kabbalist conception of language, which radically departs from the philosophic view that any human language is inadequate to describe or even to conceive God. Kabbalists emphasized the power of Hebrew. It is not a conventional, human language at all, but literally *the* divine language, the language by which God revealed Himself at Sinai.[120] Hebrew letters are themselves divine substances, for their different combinations formed the very words of revelation. Hebrew words thus do not possess only lexical meaning (that is, their reference in daily human use); they also possess a divine meaning, which is a reference to something in the world of *Sefirot*.[121]

Mastery of the symbolic meaning of revealed Hebrew is thus the key to the Kabbalistic knowledge of God, and Kabbalistic theosophy evolved as an exegesis of Hebrew rabbinic texts. Within a century after its emergence, Kabbalah developed a consistent and systematized interpretation of rabbinic Hebrew; modern scholars call this decoding "symbolism."[122] Through highly creative hermeneutics, Kabbalists developed their own "dictionaries" of the Hebrew language.[123] In Kabbalistic parlance, individual words, literary motifs, theological concepts, biblical personalities, and even the commandments are systematically linked to specific *Sefirot*, which are then described in detail reaching mythic proportions. Because this, the mythologization of rabbinic concepts, was carried on through exegesis of canonic texts, Kabbalah appeared as a traditional force in Judaism.[124]

Kabbalah adopted the Neoplatonic principle of emanation to describe both how the *Sefirot* came forth from the *Ein Sof* and how the extradeical world came into existence. Kabbalists conceived of the universe as an organic whole that, following the Neoplatonic concept of gradations, was hierarchically ordered according to the degree of participation in the world of the *Sefirot*; however, they disagreed over the precise ontological status of the *Sefirot*. The majority identified the *Sefirot* with the essence of God (the doctrine of *'azmut*); a minority viewed them as "instruments" or "vessels" that emanated from God and were akin to the Separate Intelligences (the doctrine of *kelim*); another minority viewed the *Sefirot* as modes of Divine immanence.[125]

Even though Kabbalistic theosophy wrestled with philosophical questions and even employed philosophical vocabulary, Kabbalah was not simply a metaphysical system. Idel showed that Kabbalistic theosophy had an experiential dimension as well. Kabbalists actually lived in the presence of a God as revealed in the *Sefirot* and aligned every deed, thought, and emotion with them. In fact, every act of a Kabbalist in this world was presumed to have a direct effect on the Godhead. At best the Kabbalist can restore the harmonic balance within the *Sefirot*, which, in turn, increases divine effluence *(shefa')* in the world. But the Kabbalist who fails, errs, or transgresses actually increases evil and imperfection in the world. In short, Kabbalistic theosophy had a clear theurgy and a magical purpose; by mastering it, the Kabbalist exerts an influence on both this world and God Himself.[126]

R. David ben Judah Messer Leon brought two factors to bear on Kabbalah. The first was the uniquely Italian understanding of Kabbalah that R. David first learned. Idel showed that Kabbalah was perceived in Italy as an ancient wisdom, the mastery of which spiritualizes the knower and facilitates closeness, even union, with God. Until the *Zohar* was printed (1558-59), Kabbalah was studied primarily through Recanati's writings and the anonymous *Ma'arekhet*. The theurgic dimension of Kabbalah was muted, and instead Kabbalah was perceived as a philosophico-mystical lore whose mastery yields increase of spirituality to the practitioner.[127] Explanations of the *Sefirot* reconciled Kabbalah to philosophy. Recanati asserted that the *Sefirot* are "instruments" or "vessels" *(kelim)* for divine activity; they are closely attached to God but still ontologically distinct from God. According to the *Ma'arekhet*, the *Sefirot* "are the Godhead"; that is, they are identical with the essence of God *('azmut)*. Since the essence of God is simple unity, the differentiation in the *Sefirot* arises only "from the perspective of recipients."[128]

The second factor was R. David's own philosophic orientation. He sided with the *Ma'arekhet* against Recanati. David went on to define the *Sefirot* within a philosophical analysis of divine attributes, explaining their ontological status as divine perfections identical with the essence of God. He thereby accepted the *Sefirot* but neutralized their mythical and theurgic dimensions.

In particular, R. David identifies attributes of action, analogically predicated of God's essence, with the *Sefirot*. This reduction of the Kabbalistic to the philosophic is found at the beginning of R. David's defense of *'azmut*, which follows a reference to Plato that Averroës made in *Tahafut al-Tafafut*.[129] R. David first praises Plato as a man of virtue "who was called divine not in vain" and whose opinions are the opinions of the "true received tradition."[130] R. David continues:

> In regard to Ideas one should realize what we have already said, that He, blessed be He, encompasses all. And therefore He is said to be the Lord of hosts, since He is the Lord of hosts above and below (i.e., the hosts of the entire world). And 'judgment,' 'justice,' and 'mercy' are in God, because He is their cause, and they proceed from Him. And He is one with them, as we have explained. Now I shall prove that the *Sefirot* are the essence of God from the words of the sages and from the words of the greatest Kabbalists in the wonderful *Sefer ha-Zohar*.[131]

This passage explicitly identifies the divine attributes, signifying perfections in God, with the *Sefirot*.

More importantly, R. David thereby interprets *Sefirot* in *Magen David* with the same logic he later used in interpreting the divine attributes in *Tehillah le-David*. He distinguishes between their mode of signification *('erekh el ha-meqabbelim)* and their mode of existence *('erekh el ha-meziut)*. The mode of signification of the *Sefirot* is analogy, formed in our religious discourse, the reference of which is God's infinite, perfect reality. R. David illustrates by another analogy: we can speak of different faculties and names of the soul, although in reality there is but one substance with different activities. So, too, can we speak of God's different *Sefirot*, although there is but one God:[132]

> For the *Sefirot* are united in the essence of the Creator, blessed be He, and the multiplicity and diversity signifies *[sic]* the diverse activities which proceed from the unity of the Creator, not that there is within Him diversity.[133]

This statement is important to modern scholarship because it led to the mistaken characterization of R. David ben Judah Messer Leon as a nominalist. Cordovero copied it verbatim, took it out of context, and erroneously understood it to mean that the *Sefirot* are only names employed to refer to God's activity in the world, and so have no separate existence. On the basis of Cordovero's portrayal, a modern scholar, Joseph Ben Shlomo, mischaracterized R. David's position as nominalism.[134] In context, however, R. David's statement refers only to the mode of signification of the *Sefirot* in human discourse, which R. David explicitly distinguished from their mode of existence.

R. David dispels any doubt about that philosophic distinction in his interpretation of a *Zohar (Idra Zuta)* passage asserting that the *Sefirot* are the essence of God, which R. David condenses as follows: *"de'atiqa qeddisha hu meforash ve-eino meforash, hu metuqqan ve-eino metuqqan."*[135] R. David first rejects a literal interpretation as self-contradictory and consequently unacceptable. He then equates *meforash* with *mefursam* and interprets the first part as saying that God is known through the knowledge of His activity in the world, but His essence is now known. R. David then ties *metuqqan* to *qiyyum* (existence) and interprets the second part thusly: God is the cause of all existence, so we realize that God exists through his activities; however, we do not thereby comprehend God's mode of existence. R. David not only makes the *Zohar* intelligible by reducing its terms to philosophic concepts, he also implies that the *Zohar* is limited in its understanding of the mode of existence of the *Sefirot*.

To explain the mode of existence of the *Sefirot*, R. David follows a long medieval tradition from Neoplatonism to Christian and Islamic philosophy which asserts the existence of ideas in the divine mind.[136] As stated above, R. David identifies such ideas with both divine perfections and the *Sefirot*. He credits Plato, but he departs from the original Platonic sense of Ideas; elsewhere he adopts Aristotle's critique of such Ideas and rejects Plato's assertion that Ideas exist outside any intellect.[137] In fact, R. David employs Aquinas' theory of divine ideas: they are both exemplars (i.e., principle of making) and the objects of God's knowledge (i.e., principle of knowledge).[138] R. David also used Averroës' discussion of perfected forms in God.[139]

R. David resorts to a stock vehicle in medieval thought, the analogy of the architect:

...God knows the unity of the *Sefirot* in His mind, blessed be

He, because they exist in God like the rooms and the attics and all aspects of a house in the mind of the architect. They are there in an abstract and unified manner, but when he starts to build they then become pluralized and multiplied, because they exist outside, in matter, and no longer in the perfection they held in the architect's mind. Thus are the *Sefirot*, which were diversified and said to be ten when individual things became existent. All of them are included in those ten names according to the diversity of modes of being.[140]

R. David molds and uses the architect analogy not only to explain mode of existence, but also to summarize his ontology, theology, and epistemology—even to explain his concept of *Sefirot* as the essence of God. God knows His own essence (i.e., the *Sefirot*) by virtue of the identity of His essence and his act of existence. The content of God's self-knowledge is God's infinite perfection, in which all perfections exist under one unified, intelligible order. God's self-knowledge causes all other existence, and He knows the particulars of His creation through His self-knowledge. Those particulars share or participate in God's Being in various degrees, which constitute the hierarchy of beings in the world. Creation then proceeds from God's infinite perfection, through God's knowledge to the finite imperfection of each individual, created being. Human knowledge of God, by contrast, proceeds from human knowledge of perceivable things that resemble God. Through an act of abstraction, the human mind knows the individual essence of that thing, which participates at least to some degree in the divine essence. That knowledge is the basis for meaningful religious discourse about God, although in this life it is only a knowledge of God's representation in thing and not of God's essence.

The problem remains that the *Sefirot* have a finite number, ten. If they are the essence of God, then is God not limited as well? The problem would not have occurred had R. David embraced the theory of *kelim*, for an infinite being can have a finite number of instruments. R. David solves this problem by "philosophizing" the Kabbalistic concept *Ein Sof.*

R. David first equates *Ein Sof* with the philosophic First Cause, as had Joseph ibn Waqar and others before him. But R. David goes on to identify *Ein Sof* with the first *Sefirah*, *Keter* (Crown), thereby eliminating the transcendence of *Ein Sof* over the *Sefirot*. Since the *Sefirot* are now ontologically identical with the essence of God, they can be numerically infinite in existence, even though they are limited to ten in human discourse. That finite number is just their mode of signification, a necessary consequence of the finitude of human knowledge. R. David then discusses the *Sefirot* not to make manifest God's hidden life, as a true Kabbalist would have done, but rather to solve the ancient philosophic problem of "the one over the many" (i.e., the problem of universals).

Magen David contains a final example of philosophic reductionism at the conclusion of R. David's defense of the *Sefirot*,[141] where he asserts that the universe proceeds from the intelligible order in God's mind (which R. David equates with the spiritual Torah) and should ultimately return to its origin in God. To explain this ontological process (a typical Neoplatonic theme), R. David borrows the metaphor of a cycle from the Neoplatonic treatise *The Book of Causes (Liber de Causis)*, probably known to him through Aquinas' commentary or through the Hebrew translations of Judah of Rome.[142] R. David then equates the cycle with the Kabbalist concept of *teshuvah* (literally, repentance, or return).[143] In fact, R. David may have structured his entire discussion of this ontological process as a Jewish counterexample to Aquinas' discussion of the cosmic process of return to the divine source in *De Veritate*.[144]

In conclusion, R. David could assert as a philosopher that the *Sefirot* do exist and that they can be the subject of a meaningful human philosophical discourse, but only so far as it is meaningful to discuss the existence of universals in the divine mind, ontologically united with God. Having asserted that humans cannot comprehend God's essence and His act of existence, R. David could not indulge in Kabbalistic elaboration on the nature of the *Sefirot* or detailed Kabbalistic symbolism that unravels the dynamic process of divine life and assigns certain characteristics to each *Sefirah*. So R. David's writings contain few passages of Kabbalistic symbolism at all, and those few are all copied from other sources. R. David, therefore, differs even from those Kabbalists who joined him in embracing the theory of *'azmut* (i.e., *Sefirot* as the essence of God). Like Moses Narboni,[145] Joseph Albo,[146] Abraham Bibago,[147] Abraham Shalom,[148] and Isaac Abravanel,[149] R. David treated Kabbalistic doctrines within the framework of his philosophy. Abravanel, like R. David, asserted that the *Sefirot* are the essence of God, and Albo, Shalom, and Bibago identified the *Sefirot* with the Separate Intelligences.

R. David's exposition of the doctrine of *Sefirot* helped Kabbalists in the Ottoman Empire clarify the philosophic aspects of this doctrine. Meir ibn Gabbai, a militant Kabbalist, copied R.

David's defense of the *Sefirot* as the essence of God in order to attack Albo.[150] Comparison of R. David's treatment with ibn Gabbai's makes manifest their sharp differences. Ibn Gabbai regarded philosophy as the cause of Iberian Jewry's tribulations and presented the *Sefirot* as an alternative to the philosophic notion of divine attributes. He then could detail the character of each *Sefirah* and describe its interaction with other *Sefirot*. On the other hand, R. David ben Judah Messer Leon made sense of the theory of *Sefirot* within the context of divine attributes. His indebtedness to the medieval philosophic tradition remained strong.

Divine Knowledge and Providence

Divine providence is a central rabbinic doctrine according to which God not only created the world but actively governs it.[151] According to the rabbis, God's providence is manifest both in the stability and regularity of nature and in extraordinary events which interrupt the natural order (i.e., miracles). Miracles shape history. God revealed His will to his Chosen People, Israel, and rules over the affairs of nations in order to benefit Israel. God extends particular care to individual members of the Chosen People, listening to their needs and responding to their petitions. God brings harm to Israel upon occasion to teach her a lesson. God rewards and punishes both in this world and in the world to come. God knows particulars, for only an omniscient God can be truly just. God knows all His creations, from the most exalted to the most mundane, from the most public to the most private, from things past to things future. Divine foreknowledge conflicts with human freedom; the rabbis recognized that problem but cared too much about guarding human freedom to resolve it, as, for example, in Mishnah, Avot 3:25: "Everything is foreseen, but free will is granted."

Aristotle's God differed sharply. He knows only Himself and has nothing to do with the very world of which He is the First Cause.[152] So the Jewish Aristotelians who identified the God of Israel with the God of Philosophy found divine providence most problematic. Again, R. David ben Judah Messer Leon resolved that problem by reconciling his philosophic views to support rabbinic Judaism, and again some background must precede an exposition of R. David's thought.

Maimonides acknowledged that providence is both central to rabbinic theism and based upon divine knowledge of particulars. Exoterically at least, Maimonides professed the rabbinic view: "He who studies true reality equitably ought accordingly to believe that nothing is hidden in any way from Him, may He be exalted, but that, on the contrary, everything is revealed to His knowledge, which is His essence, and that it is impossible for us to know in any way this kind of apprehension."[153] But Maimonides also recognized the philosophic problem. He sets forth five logical difficulties, which H. Davidson summarizes as follows:

> (1) Since God's knowledge is unchanging, if He knew particular things, He would have to know them in the same way at all times, including the periods both before and after they exist; but there can be no knowledge of the non-existent. (2) Particular things are infinite, and there can be no knowledge of the infinite. (3) Particular things change and therefore the knowledge of them changes; but God and His knowledge are unchanging. (4) Knowledge which has several things as its objects would be plural; but God and His knowledge cannot contain any plurality. (5) Divine foreknowledge would imply that future events are determined, while religion assumes that future events are contingent and subject to human free will.[154]

Maimonides replied to all these difficulties essentially with one answer: They arise from the erroneous assumption that God's knowledge is like human knowledge. But given the fundamental dissimilarity between God and human beings, divine knowledge is qualitatively different from human knowledge. They bear each other no resemblance whatsoever. In short, God can know all, including events before their occurrence, without affecting the order of nature except when and where He wills. The attribute "knowing" must be understood as pure equivocation.[155]

But Maimonides did not resolve the problem. Elsewhere he distinguished between "general providence" and "individual providence."[156] General providence is identical with the operation of nature in the sublunar world; it is stable and provides each species the necessities for its operation. Individual providence, by contrast, is commensurate with intellectual perfection. Those who have attained intellectual perfection, namely the perfect philosophers, enjoy divine care, although Maimonides does not explain how that process works. However, in Maimonides' theory of knowledge, only the universal is intelligible, not the particular. One attains intellectual perfection only when the intellect grasps the intelligible aspect of things.[157] (How that occurs does not matter here.) By definition, intellectual perfection means that the human intellect loses its corporeality, or association with the corporeal, and becomes universal.

On this theory, when God knows intellectually perfect human beings, He knows them only in their universal aspect, not in their particularity. So while Maimonides paid lip service to the rabbinic concept that God knows particulars as particulars, Maimonides logically constructed a God whose knowledge of particulars is limited to their universal, intelligible aspect.

Gersonides, by contrast, discussed the problem of divine knowledge and providence openly and boldly. He analyzed each of Maimonides' five logical difficulties and Maimonides' solutions.[158] Gersonides rejected Maimonides' facile assertion that no similarity whatsoever exists between human and divine knowledge. Following Averroës' analysis of divine attributes, Gersonides argued that God's knowledge is different from ours because to God, "knowledge" applies primarily and in perfect sense, whereas to us it applies only secondarily and imperfectly. To Gersonides, the attribute "knowing" is not a pure equivocation but an analogical attribute.

Gersonides proposed an explanation of God's knowledge based on two major distinctions. The first is that between individuals and particulars.[159] Particulars are embodied individuals; they are material things. But some individuals are not particulars; that is, they are not material—for example, the Separate Intelligences and the heavenly spheres. Gersonides then stated that while God cannot know particulars as particulars, God may know immaterial individuals. If so, God does know the translunar world of the Separate Intelligences.[160]

Gersonides' second distinction is between knowing particulars in respect to their intelligible order and knowing them as particulars. God does not know material particulars, but this does not mean that He is ignorant of worldly affairs. Rather, all particular things have a universal aspect to them. Ultimately the universal aspect of the sublunar world as a whole is its most general order, which Gersonides identified with the Active Intellect.[161] God, then, knows the particulars of the sublunar world—but only to the extent that they participate in the general, intelligible order of reality. So Gersonides' God knows particulars in their universal, ordered aspect but does not know them in their particular, material, and contingent aspect.[162]

Gersonides' subtle distinctions were lost. He was misunderstood to have taught that God categorically does not know particulars in the sublunar world and that He knows the world only in a general, universal way. That denies divine retribution, because a God that does not know human beings as particular individuals cannot extend to them particular providential care. So during the attack on philosophy after 1391, Gersonides was branded a heretic. He allegedly bred indifference to religion (why should one worship God if He does not know particulars?), disregard for Jewish observance (why perform the commandments if God does not know what one actually does), and even hedonism (why worry about some future divine retribution if God cannot consider present human actions in His judgment?).[163]

The campaign against Gersonides' misunderstood theory of divine knowledge heated up in Italy during the second half of the fifteenth century. As noted in Chapter One above, R. Judah Messer Leon, R. David's father, tried to eradicate Gersonides' influence. R. Judah declared a ban on Gersonides' *Commentary on the Pentateuch*, forbade anybody to teach it, and even fired a teacher from his own academy for allegedly teaching Gersonides despite the ban.[164] R. Judah Messer Leon affirmed on both religious and philosophic grounds that divine knowledge of particulars is central to rabbinic Judaism.

R. David ben Judah Messer Leon, of course, knew firsthand his father's opposition to Gersonides, and likewise opposed Gersonides' alleged denial of divine knowledge of particulars. R. David denounced it as "an alien view which contradicts the plain meaning of the Torah, like [Gersonides'] other views regarding the fundamentals of the Law."[165] The Torah unambiguously teaches that "God, blessed be He, knows all the details of human activities and judges them accordingly."[166] As discussed in Chapter Six, R. David propounded prophecy and miracles as dogmas of Judaism in order to safeguard the Torah against heresy and philosophic misinterpretation; both dogmas presuppose God's knowledge of particulars as particulars and God's direct involvement in nature.

R. David addresses divine knowledge in *Tehillah le-David* III:16-18. He understandably turns to Maimonides for support, thereby defending Maimonides as one who, although cognizant of the philosophical arguments against divine knowledge of particulars, remained loyal to the Torah and therefore to that doctrine.[167] Gersonides, by contrast, had earlier found Maimonides' loyalty to the tradition philosophically unacceptable.

R. David's analysis of divine knowledge nonetheless looks more like a condensed version of Aquinas' *Summa Theologiae* Ia, q. 14, than a version of anything Maimonides wrote. Like Aquinas, R.

David first poses the question, "Is the First Cause, blessed be He, knowing and wise?" From the very definition of God as an intellectual substance in pure actuality, it follows that God is "knowing" and "wise." So the better question is whether God knows anything other than Himself.[168]

Following Aquinas' structure, R. David then recites two objections to the claim that God knows things other than Himself. First, according to Aristotelian epistemology, what is known perfects the knower.[169] So a God who knows things other than Himself would be deficient—which is impossible—because that God would be perfected by things other than Himself. Second, if God knows things other than Himself He must change with every new piece of knowledge—and, of course, God does not change. R. David responds in kind, with a counterobjection used by Maimonides and many who followed. To say that God does not know things other than Himself is to ascribe ignorance to God. But ignorance is an imperfection, and since God is perfect, we may not ascribe ignorance to Him. Therefore, God must know things other than himself.[170]

R. David thus considers knowledge of particulars a perfection rather than a deficiency.[171] It does not introduce composition or corporeality in God because God is the paradigm, or exemplar, of all things. R. David states:

> God's essence, blessed be He, is the paradigm of all existents and in Him they are conceptualized [literally, drawn; *mezuyyarim*] and elaborated *[mefutahim]* in the most perfect manner possible. When He cognizes His own essence he cognizes all existents other than Himself, since they are all conceptualized in His essence.[172]

All things preexist in God in a supereminent, or superexcellent way. Because God knows Himself, God knows in an ideal manner all things that exist in Him.

R. David claims that because God knows the intelligible order of reality, He knows things both universally and particularly. That view contrasts with Gersonides' view (as R. David understood it) that God knows things only to the extent that they participate in the intelligible order of reality. R. David bases his view on a distinction which Gersonides himself made between causal knowledge and derivative knowledge.[173] Whereas human knowledge is derivative from created things, God's knowledge is causal; it brings things into existence, although they already preexist in God in a supereminent way. Because God's knowledge is causal, He is not perfected by His knowledge of things other than Himself, and there is no composition or multiplicity when God knows things other than Himself. Although God knows particulars as particulars, His knowledge is absolutely simple.

R. David illustrates this unique knowledge through a metaphor: The artist knows his creation in utmost detail before its production.[174] In the artist's mind the creation exists as an ideal but in no less detailed form than after production. Likewise, God knows all particulars of His creation as particulars.[175]

Scriptural proof-texts for God's knowledge of particulars abound. R. David cites Hagar's remark in Gen. 16:13 — "You are El-roi" (apparently, "the Seeing God") — and interprets it as follows: "You [God] see me [because] my essence [*'azmuti*] is conceptualized [*mezuyyar*] in You; this is similar to a shape [*zurah*] reflected [*nirshemet*] in a mirror."[176] This interpretation smacks of pantheism. If God knows Hagar because her essence is in Him, then Hagar and all other particulars are but modes of God. R. David cites other biblical passages (Gen. 11:5 and 18:21) in which God explicitly knows human beings as particulars and "rewards and punishes them according to the merit of their actions."[177]

So Maimonides correctly understood "that God knows all particulars without accruing any deficiency and imperfection." And Maimonides correctly recognized the qualitative differences between divine knowledge and human knowledge: Whereas God's knowledge is causal, human knowledge is derivative; whereas God's knowledge is absolutely simple, human knowledge is composite; whereas God's knowledge encompasses the infinite, human knowledge is limited only to finite things; whereas God knows all things both universally and particularly, the human intellect can comprehend particulars only to the extent that it recognizes their universal aspect. Given the qualitative difference between God's knowledge and human knowledge, Maimonides was right to claim that "knowing" is an equivocal term *(shem meshutaf)*, and Gersonides was wrong to deny it.

R. David has trouble defending Maimonides against Gersonides because R. David himself holds that "knowing" is not purely equivocal but instead is analogical *(shem mesuppaq)*. R. David recites four of Gersonides' difficulties *(qushiyot)* and resolves them,[178] but R. David's defense is apologetic and perhaps even unfair; he states that "knowing" is predicated of god in "pure equivocation" because "God does not know in the same knowledge and thought as human knowledge, but in a more exalted manner." This was precisely Gersonides' position, yet R. David ascribes it to Maimonides to support Maimonides against Gersonides.[179]

This defense of Maimonides proves R. David's reconciliation of philosophy to religion. Like Abraham Shalom before him, R. David defended Maimonides on the question of divine knowledge because Maimonides supported rabbinic tradition. R. David concludes that, given the qualitative difference between our knowledge and divine knowledge, we will never know how God knows particulars. Thus, when given a choice between a philosophical (i.e., logical) answer and a religious (i.e., authoritative) one, R. David chose religion. After bringing all his reason to bear on the problem of divine knowledge, a gap still remained, and R. David took the "leap of faith."

After satisfying himself that divine knowledge of particulars does not negate human reason, R. David analyzes divine providence itself. *Tehillah le-David* III: 19, 20, and 21 roughly follow *Summa Theologiae* Ia, q. 22, aa. 1, 2, and 3. R. David addresses three major topics: the propriety of providence; the extension of providence to all creatures and to Israel in particular; and the relation between providence and human freedom, formulated in R. David's day as the relation between providence and astrology.

Like Aquinas, R. David begins the first topic with the question, "Is providence appropriate *[teot]* to God?[180] And in Scholastic manner R. David first recites three objections (Aquinas recited the same three), then defends the proposition (i.e., that providence is appropriate) generally on religious and philosophic grounds, and finally refutes the individual objections. The objections are as follows:

1. Providence is part of prudence, and every act of prudence involves good counsel *('ezah)* and deliberation. But such counsel cannot belong to God.
2. Providence requires both divine intellect (to have knowledge of particulars) and divine will. But God is not composite.
3. Things require providence because they are perishable *(nifsadim).* But God is eternal, so how can He extend providence to things which perish?

A religious response is not difficult, because R. David's religion caused him to defend providence in the first place. He begins by citing the Midrash: "God provides for the entire world, from the horns of the wild ox to the eggs of lice."[181] R. David then cites a long list of Scriptural verses which ascribe to God deliberation, counsel, and will.

R. David refutes the objections philosophically by distinguishing between two types of agents *(po'alim)*: In the first category belong beings who lack intelligence and are not cognizant of their actions (i.e., most things in nature). In the second category belong intelligent beings who are cognizant of their own actions. It is further divided in two: those intelligent beings which are conscious of their activity but have no control over it, such as celestial spheres, and those intelligent beings which possess will and therefore control their activity, such as human beings. R. David then states:

> God, blessed be He, acts with wisdom, will and choice unlike natural agents who are not conscious of their activities, and unlike the celestial spheres who act under necessity. Rather, God acts in wisdom and will and has the ability to act or not to act and His actions are superior to human actions. Because [His actions] manifest wisdom and counsel we ascribe to Him counsel although it does not entail God taking counsel from another as human beings do.[182]

After citing further rabbinic and scriptural support, R. David addresses the three objections directly:

1. When we ascribe counsel to God it is only to indicate the perfection of His activity.
2. Providence does involve understanding and will to do the multiple things, but that does not introduce change or multiplicity in God, because God knows all things in a simple, unified way.
3. There is a distinction between "general providence" (i.e., "that God provides for all things according to their nature" and "individual providence" (i.e., "that God gives each thing whatever is necessary for its survival"). Thus, God extends providential care to things to the extent that they exist, not to the extent that they are perishable.

R. David's third refutation of an objection on the first topic, propriety of providence, leads him directly into the second topic, namely, the extension of providence to all creatures. R. David addresses this topic in *Tehillah le-David* III:20, stating the questions as, "Do all things fall under divine providence?"[183] The second topic's structure is basically the same as the first: recitation of three objections, religious defense of the proposition, philosophical defense, and a direct refutation of the individual objections. However, the philosophical defense of this proposition extends to a discussion of providence vis-à-vis God's Chosen People, Israel.

R. David also takes the three objections which set the stage for his discussion of the universality of providence from Aquinas. They are as follows:

1. Physics teaches that some things in the physical (i.e., sublunar) world happen by chance. But if everything is foreseen by God, nothing will happen by chance.
2. Metaphysics differentiates between contingent and necessary things. If something exists necessarily, it can require no providential care, so providence does not extent to it.
3. Some people deny that God extends providence to human mundane affairs, saying "who will know us who will see us."

As expected, religion unambiguously refutes these objections. Torah teaches that "God extends providential care to all things."

R. David's philosophical defense of the universality of providence is extensive and digresses into a discussion of God's providence toward His people Israel, a full topic in itself. R. David begins the defense, as did Aquinas in the *Summa Theologiae* and the *Summa Contra Gentiles* with the three types of providence.[184] Aquinas developed that division in order to dispute Plato's view (which Aquinas reports in the name of Gregory of Nyssa). R. David, however, cites Plato as the authority for the tripartite division itself.[185] It is as follows:

A. *Providence at creation.* The design and beauty of nature attest to the existence of providential care in the very creation of the world. Every living form not only possesses the organs necessary for its survival; it also exhibits "beauty and ornamentation."
B. *Providence that perpetuates the diversity of species.* The very fact that nature has so many species, that each has its unique nature, and that they all remain constant reflects divine providence.
C. *Providence that extends exclusively to human beings.* God created human beings as the most nearly perfect creatures. He endowed them with intelligence in order to ensure their preservation as a

species. Human beings alone fall under divine providence commensurate to their actions.

This division reflects R. David's departure from Maimonides. R. David agrees with Maimonides that the very operation of nature reflects providence, but he disagrees with him that such providence is only general. For R. David, as for Aquinas, divine preservation of nature is extended to each created being as well as to the species in general. Providence is commensurate with the mode of being of each creature. More importantly, R. David departs from Maimonides (and Gersonides) in regard to the nature of divine providence over human affairs. R. David links providence not to intellectual perfection but to moral and religious perfection. Further, individual providence is commensurate not with knowledge but with deeds. And because individual providence is tied to religious perfection, the People of Israel enjoy divine providence more than any other nation.

Like his older contemporaries Abraham Shalom, Abraham Bibago, Isaac 'Arama, and Isaac Abravanel, R. David resurrected the teachings of Judah Halevi concerning the ontological superiority of the People of Israel, the Land of Israel and the Torah.[186] The people of Israel constitute a subgroup within the human species, born with unique ability *(segulah)* to encounter God directly. They alone could experience prophecy and receive from God the perfect code of conduct—the Torah—which preserves their purity and perfection. Hence, Israel alone can be, literally, the people of God. Although to the modern reader this appears exclusivist, Halevi's teachings regained popularity in the fifteenth century to compensate for the deterioration in the real condition of the Jewish people.

The people of Israel, according to R. David, enjoy superiority in all three types of providence.[187] First, the People of Israel are created biologically superior to other human beings. R. David derives this superiority from the commandment that (Jewish) women should immerse themselves in water after birth, which suggests to R. David that their children are consecrated to God from birth, literally the Children of God.

Second, Israel receives better protection than other peoples because God has brought His People to the Holy Land, which is endowed with perfect climate and excellent physical conditions that provide all the material and spiritual needs of those who live in it. Presumably, life in the Holy Land perfects the People of Israel in body and soul. This idealized view of the Land of Israel reflects as well the impact of Kabbalah on R. David.[188] So the People of Israel enjoy longevity and better quality of life.

Third, providence commensurate with action is evident from Israel's receipt, alone among the nations of the world, of divine revelation. Because the Torah and the commandments "safeguard us against sins and bring us closer to the right path," Israel enjoys a higher degree of individual providence. The divine Torah purifies Israel in body and soul and makes this people the beneficiary of immediate providential care.[189] R. David concludes that while all creatures fall under divine providential care, Israel enjoys such care to a higher degree. In sum, God extends special providential care to the people of Israel by creating them a more perfect people, by providing them with the perfect country, and by giving them the perfect law.

R. David then returns to refute the three initial objections of this second topic, the extension of providence to all creatures:

1. Random occurrences may appear because we do not fully understand the causes. From God's omniscient perspective, however, nothing happens by chance.[190]
2. Natural providence disproves the objection that providence cannot extend to necessary things.
3. Scripture is the best refutation of those who deny God's involvement in human affairs. The plagues visited on Egypt are the best proof that "I the Lord am in the midst of the land." (Exod. 8:18).

R. David's discussion of Israel provides the transition from his second major topic, universality of providence, to his third, providence and human freedom. This topic follows a rabbinic, rather than scholastic, structure; each subtopic flows on to the next with no unifying question. However, on this topic as well R. David relied on the teachings of Aquinas.

First, Israel's special providence does not place Israel outside the natural order. God normally dispenses His providential care to Israel through created intermediaries: "God blessed be He rewards and punishes through the intermediacy of created beings."[191] Intermediaries come in various types: natural elements—for example, water in the flood, or fire and acid in the destruction of Sodom and Gomorrah; incorporeal created beings (i.e., angels), as in the deliverance of the prophet Daniel and his three friends; human beings both to punish Israel (e.g., Nebuchadnezzar) and to reward Israel (e.g., Cyrus of Persia). But God may extend his providence directly, as in the Plague of the First Born.

R. David does not see God's extension of providence through intermediaries as a deficiency; rather, it indicates God's concern and compassion for His creatures, because human beings are unable to withstand the divine glory directly. God must mediate His providence in a manner commensurate with human capacity to receive it. Furthermore, as Aquinas has shown,[192] intermediaries attest to God's grandeur and perfection: "It belongs to the dignity of the ruler to have many ministers and executors of His will." For good measure R. David then recites Midrashim showing that God governs Israel with mercy and justice.

God's direct governance of Israel and intervention into her affairs conflicts with another firmly held medieval belief: astrology, the control of human actions by astral forces. Under the influence of Neoplatonism, most Jewish philosophers (with the notable exception of Maimonides) considered astrology a scientific discipline.[193] They tried to reconcile astrology with Ptolemy's astronomy. Even the most rigorous Jewish Aristotelians (Gersonides, for example) held that the events in the sublunar world are determined by astral influence. The talmudic rabbis openly debated the conflict between astrology and divine providence (*Talmud Babli*, Shabbat 156a). R. Yohanan held that Israel does not fall under control of the planets *(ein mazal le-yisrael)*, while R. Hanina held that Israel does.

R. David refers to an earlier work he wrote, no longer extant, entitled *Sod ha-Gemul (The Secret of Retribution)*, in which he proved that "Israel has no specific astral power *[mazal]*, unlike all other nations, each of which has a special power in charge."[194] R. David attempts to reconcile the conflict between R. Yohanan and R. Hanina by saying that direct providential care is conditional. R. Yohanan was correct that Israel has no astral power in charge of her, because Israel is under the direct supervision of God. But that supervision depends upon two conditions: first, that "the Israelites [conduct themselves] truthfully and observe the Torah and preserve it"; and second, "that the Israelites live in the Holy Land where they would conjoin *[nidbaqim]* to the divine providence on account of their worship and location."[195] R. Hanina is also correct, because Israel transgresses the Torah and is therefore exiled from the Holy Land, in which events Israel falls under astral power. God can protect Israel from the disasters which come upon her under astral influence; but when Israel is bad God removes His providential care and leaves Israel to cope alone.

God is thus omniscient, omnibenevolent, and just. God rewards and punishes Israel according to her deeds, and R. David emphasizes human freedom as the foundation of divine retribution. God's fore-knowledge does not limit human freedom for two reasons: first, God intentionally created human beings with the freedom to choose, so to deny them that freedom would contradict God's own creation; and second, given the created nature of human beings, they cannot comprehend the entire structure of reality. So although ultimately every thing in the created world falls under a general order known to God, human beings are ignorant of it. Instead, human beings act because either they "derive certain pleasure and joy from acting in a certain way," or "certain good will comes from the act."[196] In any event, human beings act freely, and God does not determine their actions.

So does R. David ben Judah Messer Leon conclude his analysis of divine knowledge and providence and so does he conclude his defense of the rabbinic God.

Conclusion

R. David ben Judah Messer Leon died some time before 1536, and before completing *Tehillah le-David*.[1] The manuscript was published in Constantinople in 1576 by R. David's grandson, R. Aharon, on the printing press of R. Joseph Ya'abez. R. Aharon added an epilogue to that printing that speaks of the decline of the House of Messer Leon. R. Aharon laments the current misery and poverty of this once glorious family, and in highly stylized language, he mentions an internal feud among the family members and their total loss of wealth and political status.[2]

R. Aharon actually published *Tehillah le-David* in an attempt to restore lost family honor. The project required assembling scattered manuscripts, because the family had lost even the writings of both R. David and his father R. Judah Messer Leon. R. David's writings were dispersed among private owners, and none of R. Judah's compositions was to be found in the Ottoman Empire at all.[3]

Other works by David were cited by Sephardic Kabbalists in Salonika during the 1540s and 1550s. R. Shlomo Alkabeẓ was familiar with both *'Ein ha-Qore* and *Magen David*. In his *Shoresh Yishai*, Alkabeẓ refers to David's defense of Maimonides, praising David as "among the outstanding ones in our generation."[4] Surprisingly, however, Alkabeẓ did not know that the same person (i.e., David) wrote both *'Ein ha-Qore* and *Magen David*.[5]

Of particular interest to Alkabeẓ and other Jewish intellectuals in Salonika were the few pages of *Magen David* concerning the doctrine of *Sefirot* as the essence of God.[6] R. David took the bulk of this discussion verbatim from the letters of Isaac Mar Hayyim to Isaac of Pisa, which R. David interpreted philosophically, identifying the *Sefirot* with divine perfections. R. Moses Cordovero was also familiar with these pages of *Magen David* and correctly understood David's philosophic posture.[7] Another Sephardic Kabbalist, R. Meir ibn Gabbai, also advocated the view of *Sefirot* as the essence of God. He incorporated R. David's discussion into his own exposition of the doctrine, not knowing that Isaac Mar Hayyim was the source.[8] Alkabez and Cordovero were versed in philosophy, but their main intellectual interest was Kabbalah. It is no wonder that they were attracted in particular to David's exposition of a central Kabbalistic doctrine such as the *Sefirot*, even though David's knowledge of Kabbalah generally was rather limited.

By the second half of the sixteenth century, the intellectual climate in the Ottoman Empire began to shift toward greater interest in Kabbalah, reaching its apex by the 1570s, when the center of intellectual activity in the Ottoman Empire shifted to Safed. There Kabbalah received a new interpretation under the leadership of R. Isaac Luria. In fact, *Magen David* was mistakenly attributed to R. David ibn Zimra, Luria's teacher in Egypt, until Gershom Scholem, the modern student of Kabbalah, correctly identified the author as R. David ben Judah Messer Leon.[9] Thus, modern scholarship on Kabbalah revived the interest in R. David ben Judah Messer Leon even though Kabbalah was not R. David's exclusive mode of self expression.

What can we learn from this case study? First, R. Judah Messer Leon and his son R. David enable us to chart the impact of Renaissance humanism on Italian Jews. R. Judah Messer Leon was among the first Jewish scholars to respond to the challenge of humanism. His manual of Hebrew rhetoric, *Nofet Zufim*, shows some Jewish familiarity both with contemporary academic debates between scholastics and humanists and with the centrality of Ciceronian rhetoric in humanist education. Arguing that Renaissance rhetorical ideals were already embedded in the Hebrew Bible, R. Judah legitimized the study of classical rhetoric for Jews, thereby facilitating Jewish involvement in the rebirth of antiquity. But R. Judah Messer Leon could hardly be called a Jewish humanist, for humanism remained peripheral to his scholastic world view and literary conventions.

R. David ben Judah Messer Leon went further than his father in incorporating the *studia humanitatis* into the Jewish curriculum. He admired Roman orators, poets, and historians, and regarded the classics worthy of emulation. Similarly, R. David was informed of contemporary debates among the Italian literatti (for example, the debate about women) and shared his contemporaries' admiration for Petrarch and Boccaccio. R. David's openness to Renaissance humanism did not come at the expense of his commitment to scholasticism but in complement to it. He enlarged the scope of secular studies to encompass both humanist and scholastic curricula. Jewish scholars during the sixteenth century (e.g., 'Azaria Figo, David de Pomis, Judah Moscato, Judah del Bene) continued to fuse scholasticism and humanism.[10]

By the 1460s, Renaissance humanism shifted its emphasis from civic humanism to Neoplatonism and Hermeticism. Florence was the center of this new activity led by Marsilio Ficino and financed by Cosimo de Medici the Elder. Again, R. Judah Messer Leon and his son, R. David, give us a glimpse of the Jewish response to that evolution. R. Judah rejected the emergence of Platonism and Hermeticism among the Florentine humanists on philosophical and religious grounds. He regarded Aristotelian philosophy superior to both and was appalled by the association of humanism with magic, alchemy, and astrology. In contrast, R. David accepted Neoplatonism as a valid metaphysical system and shared the Florentine humanists' interest in music, poetry, and the occult sciences. Like them, he was interested in the attainment of spirituality as a means for cleaving to God, the ultimate goal of human life. Neoplatonism, however, did not supplant Aristotelianism in R. David's world view. He remained committed to the Aristotelian conceptual framework and incorporated into it Neoplatonic themes culled from medieval Jewish, Muslim, and Christian sources. Such procedure was possible because Jewish Aristotelianism itself was suffused with Neoplatonic themes. To harmonize the two systems he had only to highlight the Neoplatonic dimensions of his own Aristotelianism. Jewish thinkers in sixteenth century Italy would follow R. David's fusion of Aristotelianism and Neoplatonism, though the latter would overshadow the former.

The interest of Renaissance humanists in Kabbalah led to its dissemination among Jews during the second half of the fifteenth century. The humanists highlighted the conceptual affinity between Kabbalah and Platonism, viewing it as an integral part of one ancient philosophy. As far as we know, R. Judah Messer Leon was the first Jewish scholar in Italy to note the interest of Florentine humanists in Kabbalah and to warn against it. R. David, on the other hand, cultivated Kabbalah, first in secret and later openly. Not only did he not consider Kabbalah and philosophy mutually exclusive but he attempted their systematic harmonization.

R. David ben Judah Messer Leon addressed Kabbalah in a larger context. The conflict of reason and faith was the core of medieval intellectual life as the three Western monotheistic religions (Islam, Judaism, and Christianity) responded to the challenge of Greek philosophy and science. For Jews the conflict of reason and faith was not only a theoretical problem of reconciling conflicting truth claims, but a clash of civilizations as well. First in Muslim countries and later in Christian lands of the Mediterranean basin, medieval Jews cultivated philosophy and its propaedeutic sciences and subjected the rabbinic tradition itself to philosophical examination. The attempt to reconcile rabbinic Judaism and Greek philosophy constituted medieval Jewish philosophy. Philosophy was cultivated in Sephardic and Oriental Jewries; it made little inroad into Franco-German Jewry.

Ottoman Jewry after the expulsion from Spain was an ethnically and culturally diverse society comprised of immigrants from Iberia, Italy, and Germany. Clashes among the various Jewish subgroups reflected their legal, social, and cultural differences. R. David ben Judah Messer Leon encountered opposition to the very cultivation of secular studies and especially to the humanist element of his culture. His reliance on classical authors, his rhetorical style, and the emphasis on the *studia humanitatis* gave rise to charges of heresy. R. David defended himself against these charges in the name of the ideal *hakham kolel*, itself an adaptation of the Renaissance ideal *homo universalis*. R. David called for the attainment of comprehensive knowledge as a necessary condition for religious perfection. He defended the broad scope of his scholarly ideal by marshalling talmudic precedents and classifying all non-Jewish knowledge as human knowledge.

The debate about the legitimacy of philosophy in traditional Jewish society was a constant theme in medieval Jewish culture. It appeared whenever Sephardic and Ashkenazic Jews were forced to live together (the result of persecutions or expulsions) and whenever Sephardic Jewry was forced into self-examination after a major catastrophe. In Sephardic Jewry such self-reflection was linked to the legacy of Maimonides, the symbol of fusion of Greek philosophy and rabbinic Judaism in Sephardic Jewry. The debate on philosophy as a discipline, the conduct of Jewish philosophers, and the legacy of Maimonides flared after the traumatic persecutions of 1391 and once more after the expulsion from Spain.

R. David ben Judah Messer Leon was one of the last exponents of the Maimonidean tradition. He viewed Maimonides as the embodiment of an intellectualized rabbinic Judaism to which he himself adhered. More than any other scholar, Maimonides had elevated Judaism to a high intellectual plateau by demonstrating its philosophic content. Following Maimonides, R. David maintained that the true believer must be also an informed one. Religious observance devoid of knowledge and understanding is superficial, but observance accompanied by knowledge leads the believer to the attainment of eternal life. R. David, then, upheld the intellectualized Judaism of medieval Jewish philosophy, of which Maimonides was the highest symbol.

Notwithstanding his defense of Maimonides, R. David departed from Maimonides on various important issues. His views indicate the transformation of the Maimonidean tradition at the second half of the fifteenth century; they were shared by other Sephardic scholars such as R. Abraham Shalom and R. Abraham Bibago. The essence of this transformation was a growing scepticism about the capacity of natural human reason to comprehend truth without the aid of divine revelation. Along with other late fifteenth century Jewish thinkers, R. David emphasized the inherent limitations of natural human reason (i.e., reason lacks certitude and is prone to errors and disputes) and therefore denied philosophy any salvific value. Philosophy alone cannot secure the immortality of the individual soul, the ultimate goal of human life. Salvation is possible only through knowledge that comes from God as an act of divine grace (i.e., divine revelation).

R. David's ambivalent attitude toward philosophy indicates the weakening of its status, especially after the expulsion from Spain. While Sephardic and Italian Jews continued to study philosophy and comment on medieval philosophical texts, at least until the last two decades of the sixteenth century, their perception of philosophy underwent a marked change. They were increasingly sceptical about the ability of philosophy alone to lead man to eternal life, and subordinated philosophy to theology. In part, the new perception of philosophy reflects the impact of Christian scholasticism, especially that of Thomas Aquinas, on Jewish thought.

R. David ben Judah Messer Leon, among other fifteenth century Jewish scholars, found certain Thomistic positions more helpful than early Jewish rationalism. For him Aquinas was but one authority whose thought can be adopted to the extent that it is true (i.e., that it fits Jewish tradition). R. David's indebtedness to Aquinas is discernible in the distinction between philosophy and theology, the conception of theology as the science of divine revelation, the dogmas of Judaism, the arguments for God's existence, the essence of God, divine attributes, divine knowledge, and providence. Once again, R. David's syncretism is evident when he integrates Thomistic ideas into the framework of Maimonidean philosophy.

By following Thomas Aquinas on the relationship between reason and faith, R. David articulated a hierarchical relationship between human knowledge and divinely revealed knowledge, through which he could resolve the tension between Jewish and non-Jewish knowledge in a manner which affirms the primacy of the Jewish tradition. R. David's borrowing from Aquinas is one indication among many that the Renaissance saw more continuity with the Middle Ages, and marked less of a break, than previously supposed.

Prophecy is the human agency that receives divine revelation. R. David interpreted divine revelation as a voluntary divine act which bestows upon the receiving prophet suprarational knowledge. Though R. David's conception of prophecy remained within the epistemological framework articulated by Maimonides, his analysis of the prophetic activity suggests a certain interpretation of Maimonides which is indebted to Thomas Aquinas. In particular, R. David departed from Maimonides in his interpretation of Mosaic prophecy which now incorporated strong mystical overtones.

Coming from God, revealed knowledge is qualitatively superior to knowledge discovered by natural human reason on the basis of sense-data. Yet precisely because this knowledge comes from God it is necessarily infallible; and because revealed knowledge is absolutely true, it cannot genuinely contradict the precepts of natural human reason. In case of apparent contradiction, the latter must be subordinated to the former. Conversely, since revealed knowledge is necessarily true, it can be explicated by natural human reason. Theology is thus a science: the discipline which systematically interprets divine revelation through analysis and categories supplied by human reason.

Theology as the science distinct from and superior to philosophy appeared only in the fifteenth century under the impact of Christian scholasticism, primarily Aquinas. Again R. David ben Judah Messer Leon stood between two worlds. On the one hand he continued the medieval rationalist tradition that viewed Judaism as a rational religion grounded in the revelation of philosophical truths. Accordingly, the good Jewish believer must be a good philosopher who comprehends the true meaning of divine revelation. On the other hand, R. David marks the retreat from radical rationalism that occurred during the fifteenth century. He not only posed the existence of a realm of truths which transcends the ability of natural human reason but he also claimed that the believer must first assent to the teaching of the revealed tradition through faith, and only later subject these teachings to systematic, rational explication.

The insistence on the primacy of faith over reason reflects Jewish response to Christian domination and intense Jewish suffering. Jewish scholars lost the confidence of previous generations that Judaism can be proven rationally superior to other religions or intellectual pursuits. Hence, those who remained loyal to Judaism retreated to fideism and dogmatism. They asserted axiomatically that Judaism is the supreme, divinely revealed Law. Not surprisingly, Jewish fideism itself reflects an adaptation of Christian scholasticism in order to defend Judaism.

R. David's philosophical exposition of rabbinic Judaism was a defense of Judaism against internal erosion and external attacks. An intellectualized rabbinic Judaism rejects both those who view philosophy as antithetical to Judaism and those who reduce Judaism to a set of philosophical propositions. Conversely, an intellectualized rabbinic Judaism rejects the claims of Christians (or Jewish apostates) that Judaism is devoid of spirituality. For R. David, Judaism is not mere legalism but an observance of the Law informed by knowledge. The true Jewish believer is the one who integrates practical life and theoretical life exactly as Maimonides, R. David's ideal, had done.

Within this religious intellectualism we can understand R. David's philosophization of Kabbalah. R. David studied Kabbalah as an integral part of rabbinic tradition which interprets divine revelation. But precisely because he believed that revealed knowledge is compatible with philosophy, R. David subjected Kabbalah to philosophic exposition. By highlighting the Neoplatonic dimension of Jewish Aristotelianism, R. David could argue that Kabbalah (whose affinity with Neoplatonism was noted by his father) is compatible with philosophy. His own acceptance of Neoplatonism as a valid metaphysical system reflects the growing strength of Neoplatonism in fifteenth century Italy.

The sixteenth century witnessed the shift from medieval Aristotelianism to Kabbalah. The transformation from one mode of thought to another was an evolutionary, gradual process. The shift was evident first in Italy with the publication of *Sefer ha-Zohar* in the mid sixteenth century and two decades later in the Ottoman Empire with the dissemination of Lurianic Kabbalah. I suggest that the transformation from philosophy to Kabbalah was possible precisely because there was a theoretical model that accommodated both intellectual traditions as integral parts of Jewish theology. As far as Jewish curriculum is concerned, we find that the cultivation of philosophy was still strong among the Jewish intelligentsia at least until the last two decades of the sixteenth century. Kabbalah remained the interest of but a small number of scholars, usually in addition to their other intellectual pursuits. Yet the very fact that growing numbers of Jewish scholars increasingly doubted the salvific merit of philosophy paved the way to the rise of Kabbalah as the dominant mode of thought among Jewish intellectuals. With the final disintegration of Aristotelianism in the West by the seventeenth century, Kabbalah could replace medieval Jewish Aristotelianism.

R. David's philosophization of Kabbalah helped its dissemination in both Italy and the Ottoman Empire. In Italy Kabbalah would retain its philosophic tendencies throughout the sixteenth century. It was regarded as speculative knowledge conducive to the attainment of spirituality. In the Ottoman Empire the philosophization of Kabbalah would experience a different fate. On the one hand, R. David's philosophic exposition of Kabbalah was valued for its clarity, and enabled scholars to study both. But Lurianic Kabbalah in Safed brought to the fore a different conception of Kabbalah: Kabbalah as a theurgic tool that affects the Deity itself. The theurgic and mythic conception of Kabbalah prevailed by the end of the sixteenth century, with the dissemination of Lurianic Kabbalah, and doomed R. David's work to eclipse.

R. David ben Judah Messer Leon is thus an illustrative figure in Jewish intellectual history whose views can and should be studied within their intellectual and cultural contexts. In the final analysis, R. David ben Judah Messer Leon was a rabbinic Jew who reaffirmed the primacy of rabbinic Judaism. Jewish suffering led him to reaffirm as well classic Jewish covenantal theology: Israel has an eternal covenant with God that guarantees continued divine providential care and demands Israel's unreserved loyalty to God. Thus, R. David ben Judah Messer Leon exemplifies not only Jewish willingness to converse with non-Jewish cultures but also the limits of such conversation.

Notes

Abbreviations

ST   *Summa Theologiae*
TD   *Tehillah le-David*

Introduction

1. On the methodological difficulties of interpreting Jewish culture in Renaissance Italy see Hava Tirosh-Rothschild, "Jewish Culture in Renaissance Italy — A Methodological Survey," *Italia* 9 (forthcoming).

2. I concur with Bonfil's critical review of this view which has dominated modern Jewish historiography until quite recently. See Robert Bonfil, "The Historian's Perception of the Jews in the Italian Renaissance. Toward a Reappraisal," *REJ* 143 (1984): 59-82.

3. On the diversity of Jewish response to Renaissance Italy see David B. Ruderman, "The Italian Renaissance and Jewish Thought," in *Renaissance Humanism: Foundations, Forms, and Legacy,* edited by Albert Rabil Jr. (Philadelphia: University of Pennsylvania Press, 1988), vol. 1, 382-433, esp. 416.

4. See Elliot Horowitz, "The Dowering of Brides in the Ghetto of Venice: Between Tradition and Change, Ideas and Reality" (in Hebrew), *Tarbiz* 57 (1987): 347-71.

5. Such a negative attitude toward the quality of Jewish philosophy in the fifteenth century is evident in Julius Guttmann, *The Philosophies of Judaism,* translated by David W. Silverman (Philadelphia: Schocken, 1964), 275.

6. The contextual approach to intellectual history received its most lucid articulation in the works of Quentin Skinner. See Quentin Skinner, "Meaning and Understanding in the History of Ideas," *History and Theory* 8 (1969): 3-53; idem, "Hermeneutic and the Role of History," *New Literary History* 7 (1975-76): 209-32. For a critique of Skinner's contextual approach see James Tully ed., *Meaning and Context: Quentin Skinner and his Critics* (Princeton: Princeton University Press, 1988). Skinner's *The Foundations of Modern Political Thought,* 2 vols. (Cambridge: Cambridge University Press, 1978) remains one of the best examples of the contextual approach to intellectual history.

7. The discipline of intellectual history is now in disarray as it tries to cope with the impact of Post-Structuralism on the analysis of historical documents. A recent forum of American Historical Association, published in *The American Historical Review* 94 (June 1989) reflects the current methodological debates among intellectual historians. So far Jewish historians have shown little interest in the ongoing debate.

8. I thank the Montefiore Endowment Committee, and Mr. Ezra Kahn, Librarian of Jews' College, London.

Chapter One

1. For general surveys of the history of Italian Jewry during the late Middle Ages and the Renaissance see Cecil B. Roth, *The History of the Jews of Italy* (New York: Schocken, 1975), 66-328; idem, *The Jews in the Renaissance* (Philadelphia: Jewish Publication Soceity of America, 1959); Moses A. Shulvass, *The Jews in the World of the Renaissance*, translated by Elvin L. Kose (Leiden: E.J. Brill, 1973); Salo W. Baron, *A Social and Religious History of the Jews* 2d rev. ed. (New York: Columbia University Press, 1952-1980), vol. 10, 220-96 (hereafter cited as *SRH*); Attilio Milano, *Storia degli ebrei in Italia* (Turin: Giulio Einaudi, 1963), 129-61; *Encyclopaedia Judaica* (hereafter cited as *EJ*), corrected edition, edited by Cecil B. Roth (Jerusalem: Keter, 1971; New York: Macmillan, 1972), s.v. "Italy." For an extensive bibliography on Italian Jewry consult Daniel Carpi ed., *Bibliotheca Italo-Ebraica: bibliografia per la storia degli ebrei in Italia, 1964-1973* (Roma: Caracci, 1982).

2. See Umberto Cassuto, "The Destruction of Academies in Southern Italy during the Thirteenth Century (in Hebrew)," in *Memorial Volume for Asher Gulak and Samuel Klein* (Jerusalem: Hebrew University, 1942), 139-52; Joshua Starr, "The Mass Conversion of Jews in Southern Italy (1290-1293)," *Speculum* 21 (1946): 203-11. On the demographic impact of these events on Italian Jewry see Shulvass, "The Jewish Population in Renaissance Italy," *JSS* (1951): 3-24.

3. Concerning the tragic events of 1391 in the Jewish communities of Aragon and Castile see Yitzhak F. Baer, *The Jews in Christian Spain*, translated by Louis Schoffman (Philadelphia: Jewish Publication Society of America, 1961-66), vol. 2, 95-138; on the expulsions of the Jews from France see Baron, *SRH*, 11: 211-25. For the impact of these events on the make-up of Italian Jewry see Shulvass, *The Jews in the World of the Renaissance*. 4-5.

4. My reconstruction is based on Richard L. DeMolen, "The Age of the Renaissance and the Reformation," in *The Meaning of the Renaissance and Reformation*, edited by Richard L. DeMolen (Boston: Houton Mifflin Company, 1974), 1-25, esp. 4-5; Robert Lopez, "Hard Times and the Investment in Culture," in *The Renaissance: Six Essays* edited by Wallace K. Ferguson (New York: Harper Torchbooks, 1953), 29-54; Harry A. Miskimin, *The Economy of Early Renaissance Europe 1300-1460* (Cambridge: Cambridge University Press, 1975); John Day, "The Great Bullion Famine of the Fifteenth Century," *Past and Present* 79 (1978): 3-54.

5. On the evolution of Jewish and Christian attitudes toward moneylending with interest see John T. Noonan, *The Scholastic Analysis of Usury* (Cambridge Mass.: Harvard University Press, 1986); Benjamin Nelson, *The Idea of Usury: From Tribal Brotherhood to Universal Otherhood* (Princeton: Princeton University Press, 1949), 3-28; Judah Rosenthal, "Usury from a Gentile" (in Hebrew), in his *Studies and Texts in Jewish History, Literature and Religion* (Jerusalem: Rubin Mass, 1966), 253-323; Solomon Grayzel, *The Church and the Jews in the XIIIth Century*, rev. 2d ed. (New York, 1966) 41-9; Kenneth R. Stow, "Papal and Royal Attitudes Toward Jewish Moneylending in the Thirteenth Century," *AJS Review* 6 (1981): 161-84.

6. On the residential and business charters — the *condotti* — see Shulvass, *The Jews in the World of the Renaissance*, 113-33. For detailed accounts on the spread of Jewish settlements in Italy see Vittore Colorni, "The Jews in Ferrara in the Thirteenth and Fourteenth Centuries," (in Hebrew), in *Studies in Jewish Themes by Contemporary European Scholars*, edited by Menahem Zohory and Aryeh Tartakover (Tel Aviv: Tel Aviv University Press, 1969), 311-33; Umberto Cassuto, *Gli ebrei a Firenze, nell'eta del Rinascimento* (Florence, 1918), translated into Hebrew by Menahem Artom *Ha-Yehudim be-Firenze* (Jerusalem: Kiryat Sepher, 1967), 5-53; Ariel Toaff, *The Jews of Medieval Assisi 1305-1487: A Social and Economic History of a Small Jewish Community in Italy* (Florence: L.S. Olschki, 1979), 3-27; idem *Gli ebrei a Perugia* (Perugia: Fonti per la storia dell'umbria, no. 10, 1975), 11-57; idem "Jewish Banking in Central Italy in the 13th-15th Centuries," in *Jews in Italy: Studies Dedicated to the Memory of U. Cassuto on the 100th Anniversary of his Birth* (Jerusalem: Magnes Press, 1988), 109-30; Shlomo Simonsohn, *The Jews in the Duchy of Mantua* (Jerusalem: Publications of the Diaspora Research Institute, 1977), 1-21, 99-112, 196-228; Daniel Carpi, "The Jews in Padua at the Age of the Renaissance" (in Hebrew), Ph.D. diss., Hebrew University 1967, vol. 1, 3-59.

7. For a general sruvey of Jewish demography in Italy from the Middle Ages to modern times see Sergio della Pergola, "The Geography of Italian Jews: Countrywide Patterns," in *Studi sull'ebraismo italiano in memoria di Cecil Roth*, edited by Elio Toaff (Rome: Barulli, 1974), 95-128 and the extensive bibliography cited there. Most of the data in that survey comes from the eighteenth century and later. Very few demographic facts are known of the tiny Jewish settlements during the fifteenth century. Consult also Shulvass, "The Jewish Population in Renaissance Italy."

8. See Bonfil, "The Historian's Perception," 59-82.

9. See Anthony Molho, "A Note of Jewish Money Lenders in Tuscany in the Late Trecento and Early Quattrocento," in *Renaissance Studies in Honor of Hans Baron*, edited by Anthony Molho and John Tedeschi (Decalb: Northern Illinois University Press, 1971), 101-17.

10. On the evolution of the Christian charity funds in northern Italy and their impact on Jewish livelihood see Brian Pullan, *Rich and Poor in Renaissance Venice: The Social Institutions of a Catholic State* (Oxford: Basil Blackwell, 1971), 431-75.

11. For an analysis of the Italian patriciate see Gene Brucker, *Renaissance Florence* (Berkeley: University of California Press, 1969), 89-127; Lauro Martines, *The Social World of the Florentine Humanists (1390-1460)* (Princeton: Princeton University Press), 18-62.

12. Roth in particular emphasized the lavish life style of the Italian Jewish bankers. In his earlier *History of the Jews of Italy*, Roth ascribed this opulence to Italian Jews in general, but in his later work, *The Jews in the Renaissance*, Roth limited this phenomenon to a narrow class of Jewish oligarchs. Cf. Shulvass, *The Jews in the World of the Renaissance*, 241-51.

13. I follow Bonfil's reconstruction of the relationship between internal and external forces in shaping Jewish cultural history. Bonfil's position is accord with earlier views by Schirmann and Adler. See Jefim H. Schirmann, "Theatre and Music in the Jewish Ghettos in Italy (from the 16th to the 18th Centuries" (in Hebrew) *Zion* 29 (1964): 61-108; Israel Adler, "Art Music in the Italian Ghettos: The Influence of Segregation on Jewish Musical Praxis," in *Jewish Medieval and Renaissance Studies* edited by Alexander Altmann (Cambridge: Harvard University Press, 1967), 321-64.

14. See Eduard Birnbaum, *Jewish Musicians at the Court of the Mantuan Dukes (1542-1628)*, edited by Judith Cohen (Tel Aviv: Tel Aviv University, 1978), 10-11.

15. Jewish patronage was a known institution in medieval Jewry as early as the tenth century. It originated in Muslim countries and reached its zenith during the eleventh century in Muslim Spain. Most of the illustrious achievements of Jewish literature, philosophy, and science were indebted to the financial support of Jewish patrons mostly in service of Muslim administration. It is unlikely that Jewish Italian bankers in the fifteenth century modeled their conduct after the activities of their coreligionists in medieval Spain. It is much more likely that Italian Jews emulated the norms and conduct of their Italian contemporaries. On the patronage system in Renaissance Italy see David S. Chambers, *Patrons and Artists in the Italian Renaissance* (Columbia: University of South Carolina Press, 1982); Charles Hope, "Artists, Patrons and Advisers in the Italian Renaissance," in *Patronage in the Renaissance*, edited by Guy F. Lytle and Stephen Orgel (Princeton: Princeton University Press, 1982), 293-343; Lauro Martines, *Power and Imagination: City States in Renaissance Italy* (New York: Knopf, 1979), 241-76.

16. This view of Renaissance humanism is accepted by most current historians. For an extensive bibliography on Renaissance humanism see Paul O. Kristeller, *Renaissance Thought and Its Sources*, edited by Michael

Mooney (New York: Columbia University Press, 1980), 272-87; Martines, *Power and Imagination*, 339-51. For an historical survey on the various uses of the term 'humanism' see, Vito R. Giustiniani, "Homo, Humanus, and the Meaning of Humanism," *JHI* 46 (1935): 167-96.

17. Paul O. Kristeller, "The Impact of Early Italian Humanism, in *Developments in the Early Renaissance*, edited by Bernard S. Levey (Albany: State University of New York Press, 1972), 120.

18. Excerpted in Martines, *Power and Imagination*, 200.

19. See Martines, *The Social World*, 18-62; idem, "The Italian Renaissance," in *The Meaning of the Renaissance and Reformation*, 27-64.

20. William J. Bouwsma, "Changing Assumptions in Late Renaissance Culture," *Viator* 7 (1976): 423.

21. On the distinction between Scholasticism and Aristotelianism see Charles B. Schmitt, "Toward a Reassessment of Renaissance Aristotelianism, *History of Science* 11 (1973): 159-93, esp. 160-61, reprinted in his *Studies in Renaissance Philosophy and Science* (London: Variorum Reprints, 1981). On Renaissance Aristotelianism see Kristeller, *Renaissance Thought and its Sources*, 32-49.

22. See Kristeller, "Humanism and Scholasticism," in *Renaissance Thought and Its Sources*, 85-105.

23. This view was articulated first by Arthur M. Lesley in his "Hebrew Humanism in Italy: The Case of Biography," *Prooftexts* 2 (1982): 163-77. I fully endorsed Lesley's approach in my "In Defense of Jewish Humanism," *Jewish History* 3 no. 2 (1988): 32-57, selections from which are incorporated into Chapter Three below.

24. On the activity of Abraham ibn 'Ezra in Italy see Colette Sirat, *A History of Jewish Philosophy in the Middle Ages* (Cambridge: Cambridge University Press; Paris: Editions de la Maison des Sciences de L'homme, 1984), 104.

25. On Jacob Anatoli's career in Italy see Isaac Barzilay, *Between Reason and Faith: Anti-Rationalism in Italian Jewish Thought 1250-1650* (The Hague, Paris: Mouton, 1967), 28-32. On Zerahya b. Isaac b. Shealtiel see Aviezer Ravitzky, "The Thought of R. Zerahya b. Isaac b. Shealtiel Hen and the Maimonidean-Tibbonian Philosophy in the 13th Century," Ph.D. diss., Hebrew University 1977, passim.

26. The complete history of the Maimonidean Controversy is yet to be written. The renewal of the Controversy in the fifteenth century is discussed in Chapter Four below; some pertinent bibliography is provided there in n. 35.

27. For a general discussion of the secular sciences in medieval Jewish educations see Harry A. Wolfson, "The Classification of Sciences in Medieval Jewish Philosophy," in *Studies in the History of Philosophy and Religion*, edited by Isadore Twersky and George H. Williams (Cambridge: Harvard University Press, 1979), vol. 1, 493-545; Arthur Hyman, "The Liberal Arts and Jewish philosophy," in *Arts Libéraux et Philosophie au Moyen Âge* (Montreal: Institut D'Études Médiévales; Paris: Libraire Philosophique, 1969), 100-10; Joseph Sermoneta, "The Liberal Arts in the Jewish Community" (in Hebrew), in *Town and Community: Lectures Delivered at the 12th Convention of the Historical Society of Israel* (Jerusalem: Historical Society of Israel, 1978), 249-58. On the liberal arts in medieval European education see David L. Wagner ed., *The Seven Liberal Arts in the Middle Ages* (Bloomington: Indiana University Press, 1983) and the relevant bibliography cited there.

28. On Jews in Italian universities see David B. Ruderman, "The Impact of Science on Jewish Culture and Society in Venice (with Special Reference to Jewish Graduates of Padua's Medical School)," in *Gli ebrei a Venezia secoli XIV-XVIII* (Venice: Editioni Comunita, 1987), 417-48 and consult the bibliography cited in p. 439, n. 1.

29. To date the only systematic study of Hebrew poetry in Italy is Dan Pagis, *Change and Tradition in the Secular Poetry: Spain and Italy* (in Hebrew), (Jerusalem: Keter, 1976), 247-355.

30. On the poetics of Hebrew secular poetry in Spain see Dan Pagis, *Secular Poetry and Poetics of Moses ibn Ezra and His Generation* (in Hebrew) (Jerusalem: Mosad Bialik, 1970).

31. The very interest of Italian Jews in classical literature and history was long recognized; see Moses A. Shulvass, "The Knowledge of Antiquity among the Italian Jews of the Renaissance," *PAAJR* 18 (1948-49): 291-99. The precise meaning of Jewish interest in the rebirth of antiquity especially for the rise of Jewish historiography is still disputed. See Robert Bonfil, "How Golden was the Age of the Renaissance in Jewish Historiography?" in *History and Theory: Studies in the Philosophy of History; Essays in Jewish Historiography*, edited by Ada Albert-Rapaport, *Beiheft* 27 (1989): 78-102. This study supports Bonfil's view.

32. See Lesley, "Hebrew Humanism", n. 21 above.

33. On 'Azariah de Rossi see Robert Bonfil, "Some Reflections on the Place of Azariah de Rossi's *Meor Enayim* in the Cultural Milieu of Italian Renaissance Jewry," in *Jewish Thought in the Sixteenth Century*, edited by Bernard D. Cooperman (Cambridge: Harvard University Press, 1983), 23-48; Joanna Weinberg, "Azariah De Rossi and the Septuagint Traditions," *Italia* 5 (1985): 7-35.

34. See Yacob Boksenboim, *Letters of Jewish Teachers in Renaissance Italy (1555-1591)* (Tel Aviv: The Chaim Rosenberg School of Jewish Studies Tel Aviv University, 1985), and consult the bibliography in the introduction, 1-54.

35. See David B. Ruderman, "An Exemplary Sermon from the Classroom of a Jewish Teacher in Renaissance Italy," *Italia* 1 (1982): 7-38.

36. On the impact of this Ashkenazic legal code see, Robert Bonfil, *The Rabbinate in Renaissance Italy* (in Hebrew) (Jerusalem: Magnes Press, 1979), 164-5.

37. On the rise of representational communal structure in Italian Jewry see Salo W. Baron, *The Jewish Community: Its History and Structure to the American Revolution* (Westport: Greenwood Press, 1972), vol. 2, passim.

38. The following discussion on the history of rabbinic ordination is based on Jacob Katz, "Ordination and Rabbinic Authority in the Middle Ages" (in Hebrew), in his *Halakhah and Kabbalah: Studies in the History of Jewish Religion, Its Various Faces and Social Relevance* (Jerusalem: Magnes Press, 1984), 201-212. For further analysis of the Talmudic texts concerning rabbinic ordination see Lawrence A. Hoffman, "The Origins of Ordination," in *Rabbinic Authority* edited by Elliot L. Stevens (New York: Central Conference of American Rabbis, 1982), 71-94 and the secondary literature cited there.

39. Katz, "Ordination," 202; Harold I. Saperstein, "The Origin and Authority of the Rabbi," in *Rabbinic Authority*, 16.

40. The biblical prooftext for the ceremony of ordination is Num. 27:18. The precise origin of the notion of an uninterrupted chain of ordained scholars going back to Moses is not known today. See Hanokh Albek, "Ordination, Appointment and Court" (in Hebrew), *Zion* 8 (1943): 85.

41. Katz, "Ordination," 202.

42. Katz, "Ordination," 206-8.

43. On the rise of local Jewish self-government by lay leaders see Baron, *The Jewish Community* 2:69.

44. R. Judah ben Barzilay, *Sefer ha-Shetarot* (Berlin, 1899), 132-33; Katz, "Ordination," 208; Saperstein, "The Origin," 18.

45. Katz, "Ordination," 209.

46. Baer, *The Jews of Christian Spain* 1:119.

47. So far the only systematic study of the institution of *Marbiẓ Torah* is Meir Benayahu, *Marbiẓ Torah: Samkhuyotav, Tafqidav ve-Helqo*

be-Mosedot ha-Qehilah be-Sefarad, be-Togarmah u-ve-Arẓot ha-Mizrah (Jerusalem: Mosad Ha-Rav Kook, 1953); see also Bonfil, *The Rabbinate*, 94-101.

48. Mordecai Breuer, "The Ashkenazic Ordination" (in Hebrew), *Zion* 33 (1978): 18-23.

49. Katz, "Ordination," 208.

50. See n. 48 above.

51. Bonfil, *The Rabbinate*. 24-26; 27.

52. Bonfil, ibid. 33.

53. Bonfil, ibid. 44-56.

54. Katz, "Ordination," 210.

55. David ben Judah Messer Leon, *Kevod Hakhamim* edited by Simon Bernfeld (Berlin: Meqiẓe Nirdamim, 1899), 63.

56. Breuer, "The Ashkenazic Ordination," 28-33.

57. Bonfil, *The Rabbinate*, 34-37; we turn to this dispute below.

58. Bonfil, *The Rabbinate*, 34.

59. Bonfil, ibid. 35.

60. Daniel Carpi, "R. Judah Messer Leon and his Activity as a Doctor" (in Hebrew), *Michael* 1 (1972): 277-301, reprinted in *Korot* 6 (1974); abbreviated English version, "Notes on the Life of Judah Messer Leon," in *Studi sull'embraismo italiano*, 39-62.

61. Robert Bonfil, "Introduction," *Judah Messer Leon: Nofet Ẓufim on Hebrew Rhetoric* (Jerusalem: The Jewish National and University Library Press and Magnes Press, 1981), 7-53.

62. Isaac Rabinowitz, trans. and ed., *Judah Messer Leon, The Book of the Honeycomb's Flow: Sēpher Nōphet Sūphīm* (Ithaca: Cornell University Press, 1983), xv-1xx.

63. Abraham Melamed, "Rhetoric and Philosophy in Nofet Sufim by R. Judah Messer Leon" (in Hebrew), *Italia* 1 (1978): 7-39.

64. *Shevah ha-Nashim* is extant in a single manuscript, MS. Parma 1395. It is David's commentary on the last chapter of Proverbs, the so called Hymn for the Woman of Valor, and is the subject of Chapter Three below.

65. On Judah b. Yehiel's place of birth see Rabinowitz, *Honeycomb's Flow*, xix. Colorni and Carpi located Montecchio in the region of La Marche, but Rabinowitz convincingly argued that it should be identified as Montecchio Maggiore in the Vincenza province, situated between Padua and

Mantua. On Judah's date of birth see Rabinowitz, *Honeycomb's Flow*, xxi. Both Rabinowitz and Carpi deduced this approximate date of birth from Judah Messer Leon's letter to the Florentine Jewish community dated January 8, 1455. The letter was written in Ancona and in it Judah Messer Leon referred to himself as *"'ul yamim,"* (infant of days). However, both scholars agree that Judah Messer Leon could not have been younger than thirty years of age, since Italian Jews did not customarily grant a Rosh Yeshivah status to scholars any younger. The early 1420s could be accepted as a plausible time for the birth of Judah b. Yehiel.

66. Rabinowitz, *Honeycomb's Flow*, xxii. According to Rabinowitz's rendering of available information, Judah b. Yehiel twice received honorary titles from the German Emperor Frederick III: "Messer" in 1452 and his doctorate in 1469. In contrast, Bonfil conjectured that Judah b. Yehiel was actually granted a title only once, in 1469, when he received his doctorate, and that his other titles accompanied his status as a doctor. Bonfil's suggestion, although reasonable, conflicts with available data according to which Judah b. Yehiel already was known as "Messer Leon" in 1455. For the time being we will have to accept Rabinowitz's reconstruction and hope that further information will be unveiled in the future.

Whereas Judah b. Yehiel was certainly awarded the title "Messer," there is no evidence that his son David ever received it, although by the sixteenth century he was referred to as "Messer David Leon" in MS. Parma-Perreau 44, which comprises R. David's composition *'Ein ha-Qore*, and in the edition of his *Tehillah le-David* printed in Constantinople, 1576. On this basis, modern scholars (including me) have referred to R. David b. Judah as David Messer Leon. This book nonetheless reflects the limits of our knowledge by referring to him as R. David or R. David b. Judah Messer Leon.

67. On Jews in the private service of popes and other ecclesiastical authorities see Harry Friedenwald, "Jewish Physicians in Italy: Their Relation to the Papal and Italian States," *Publications of the American Jewish Historical Society* 20 (1922): 133-211; reprinted in his *The Jews and Medicine* (Baltimore: The Johns Hopkins Press, 1944), vol. 2, 551-612.

68. In fifteenth century Italy, recipients of doctorate degrees, especially physicians and judges, were elevated to the knightly rank and wore distinguishing garb. The local government provided them with a horse and a groom for the horse. See Bonfil, *The Rabbinate*, 59, n. 233.

69. See Bonfil, "Introduction," 25.

70. See Shalom Rosenberg, "Logic and Ontology in Jewish Philosophy of the Fourteenth Century" (in Hebrew), Ph.D. diss., Hebrew University 1974, vol. 1, 47-49. So far, this is the only systematic study of the unique place which Judah Messer Leon held among medieval Jewish logicians. In part, Judah Messer Leon's distinction stemmed from his indebted-

ness to Christian scholastic logicians. His *Supercommentary on Porphyry's Isagoge* was based on Walter Burleigh's *Super artem veterem expositio.* See Isaac Husik, *Judah Messer Leon's Commentary on 'Vetus Logica'* (Leiden, 1906). Cf. Moritz Steinschneider, *Die hebräische Übersetzungen des Mittelalters und die Juden als Dolmetscher* (Berlin: 1893. Reprint. Graz: Akademische Druck-U. Verlaganstalt, 1956), 76-86.

71. See Rosenberg, "Logic and Ontology," 1:14.

72. This reasoning is expressed in Judah Messer Leon's introduction to *Mikhlal Yofi.* A section from this introduction was published by Steinschneider in *MGWJ* 37 (1893): 313-14. The opening poem of the introduction was published in *Jeschurun* vol. 7, edited by Joseph I. Kobak (Bamberg, 1872), 67.

73. The first decree was published by David Frankel, *Divrey Rivot ba-She'arim* (Husiatin, 1902), 1a-1b. It was sent to the Jewish communities in the region of La Marche, Abruzzi, Apulia, Naples and Rome. We learn the destination of the first decree from the letter of Judah Messer Leon to the Jewish community in Florence published by Simha Assaf, "From the Hidden Treasures of the Library in Jerusalem" (in Hebrew), in *Minha le-David: Qovez Maamarim be-Hokhmat Yisrael ... R. David Yellin* (Jerusalem, 1935), 221-37, reprinted in *Meqorot u-Mehqarim be-Toledot Yisrael* (Jerusalem: Mosad Ha-Rav Kook, 1966), 218-29. Judah Messer Leon's decree was rejected by R. Joseph Colon. The latter's response was published in *New Responsa and Decisions of Rabbi Joseph Colon* (in Hebrew), edited by Eliyahu D. Pines, 2d. rev. ed. (Jerusalem: Makhon Or Ha-Mizrah, 1984), no. 49. The political meaning of the first decree is discussed by Bonfil, *The Rabbinate*, 165-66. The effect of Messer Leon's decree, if enforced, was to revolutionize practices of female sexual purity among Italian Jews in accordance with Ashkenazic customs. Hence, Judah Messer Leon supported his position by references to Ashkenazic codes, *Sefer ha-Terumah*, and *Arba'ah Turim* and intentionally ignored Maimonides' code. Messer Leon's reliance on the Ashkenazic codes was another cause for R. Benjamin of Montalcino's opposition.

74. Information about the second decree is also included in the letter of Judah Messer Leon to the Jewish community of Florence, cited in the above note. Judah Messer Leon objected to Gersonides' position concerning divine providence and miracles, which the Provençal philosopher articulated in his *Commentary on the Pentateuch.* Judah Messer Leon first refuted Gersonides' views in his own *Supercommentary on Aristotle's Posterior Analytics*, and then attempted to block the spread of these allegedly heretical views among the Ashkenazic communities of north-central Italy. Messer Leon referred to Gersonides as "the wise in his own eyes" and ridiculed the inability of Gersonides to distinguish between the genuine positions of Aris-

totle and Averroës' interpretation of them. See Husik, *Judah Messer Leon Commentary*, 99-108. R. David ben Judah Messer Leon wrote that this ban on Gersonides' works lasted for a long time, but the son may have exaggerated the impact of the ban in order to magnify his father's political power.

75. See Moses A. Shulvass, "The Disputes of Messer Leon and His Attempt to Exert His Authority on the Jews of Italy" (in Hebrew), *Zion*, 12 (1947): 17-23; reprinted in his *Bi-Zevat ha-Dorot* (Tel Aviv: Ha-'Ogen, 1950), 56-66; Cf. Bonfil, "Introduction," 14-16.

76. On the rabbinate as a political institution and on Judah Messer Leon's conception of rabbinic privileges see Bonfil, *The Rabbinate*, 27-66, esp. 34-37.

77. The response of R. Benjamin of Montalcino was published in Frankel, *Divrey Rivot*, 2a-4a. The dating of this letter is crucial to the reconstruction of Judah Messer Leon's biography. In two extant manuscripts the date appears as "רט"ו", i.e., [5]215 (Heb.) or 1455 (Greg.). R. Bonfil suggests that this date reflects a copyist's mistake, and should be רל"ו, so that the letter was in fact written in 1476 (Heb. [5]236). See Bonfil, "Introduction," 18. Bonfil's suggestion is plausible, but the absence of support an any other extant manuscripts necessitates caution in amending the date. I therefore regard 1455 as the date of the controversy.

78. *Divrey Rivot*, 2a: כי יש כח בידם לגמול חסדים ולשמור הבטחתם ולקיימם באמת.

79. See Bonfil, "Introduction," 18, n. 29.

80. On the use of these titles among Ashkenazic rabbis see Mordecai Breuer, "The Position of the Rabbinate in the Leadership of the German Communities in the Fifteenth Century" (in Hebrew), *Zion* 41 (1976): 48-52.

81. Bonfil, "Introduction," 8; for a different chronology see Rabinowitz, *Honeycomb's Flow*, xxii-xxvii.

82. About David b. Joab of Tivoli and his family see Cassuto, "La Famiglia di David da Tivoli," *Ill Corriere Israelitico* 45 (1906): 149-52, 261-4, 297-302.

83. On the status of foreign students at the university of Bologna see Pearl Kibre, *The Nations in the Medieval Universities* (Cambridge: Harvard University Press, 1948), 29-64.

84. On the university of Padua as a stronghold of Aristotelianism see Bruno Nardi, *Saggi sull' Aristotelisimo padovano dal secolo XIV-XVI* (Florence, 1958); John H. Randall, "The Development of Scientific Method in the School of Padua," *JHI* I (1940): 170-206, reprinted in his *Saggi e Testi* (Padua: Editrice Antenore, 1958), 15-68; idem "Paduan Aristotelianism

Reconsidered," 275-82 in *Philosophy and Humanism: Renaissance Essays in Honor of Paul Oscar Kristeller*, edited by Edward P. Mahoney (New York: Columbia University Press, 1976), 275-82.

85. The original privilegium was published by Carpi in his "Judah Messer Leon," 297-99. Although this was indeed a unique privilegium, we need not exaggerate its significance. In 1469, Emperor Frederick III granted honorific titles quite liberally as a measure of securing his political base in Italy. See Shulvass, "The Disputes," 21, n. 25.

86. Carpi, "Judah Messer Leon," 295-6, 299-300.

87. Rabinowitz conjectured that R. Judah Messer Leon facilitated Judah Minz' move to Padua. This view arises from Rabinowitz's reconstruction of Judah Messer Leon's biography, according to which he resided in Padua from 1455 to 1470. Yet both Carpi and Bonfil, with whom I concur, suggest that Judah Messer Leon came to Padua in the mid-1460s and associated himself with R. Judah Minz, who was already there. See Rabinowitz, *Honeycomb's Flow*, xxv; Carpi, "Judah Messer Leon," 289-90; Bonfil, "Introduction," 15-18.

88. The ban on Jewish settlement in Venice was instituted in 1412, but was not strictly enforced. Throughout the fifteenth century, Jewish physicians were given residence permits despite the official ban. See Cecil B. Roth, *The History of the Jews in Venice* (Philadelphia: Jewish Publication Society of America, 1959. Reprint. New York, 1975), 18-38; Bonfil, "Introduction," 9, n. 3.

89. On the ties between Judah Messer Leon with the Norsa brothers and the role of Mordecai Farissol as a copyist of Messer Leon's works see David B. Ruderman, *The World of a Renaissance Jew: The Life and Thought of Abraham ben Mordecai Farissol* (Cincinnati: Hebrew Union College, 1981), 12-13.

90. Ibid.

91. On Moses Narboni's commentary of Alghazali's *The Intention of the Philosophers*, see Rosenberg, "Logic and Ontology," passim.

92. See "Two Letters by R. Judah entitled Messer Leon," in *Jeschurun*, vol. 6, edited by Joseph I. Kobak (Bamberg, 1868), 26-32.

93. Rabinowitz, *Honeycomb's Flow*, xxix; Cf. Bonfil, "Introduction," 24.

94. Tzvetan Todorov, "The War of the Words," review of *In Defense of Rhetoric* by Brian Vickers (Oxford University Press, 1988), *The New Republic* (Jan. 1989): 36.

95. On the status of rhetoric in Renaissance Italy see Hanna H. Gray,

"Renaissance Humanism: The Pursuit of Eloquence," *JHI* 24 (1963): 497-514; Donald L. Clark, *Rhetoric and Poetry in the Renaissance* (New York: Columbia University Press, 1922; Reprint. New York: Russel and Russell, 1963), 1-75; Richard Meckeon, "The Transformation of the Liberal Arts," in *Developments in the Early Renaissance*, 158-222 and Kristeller's article in this book, referred to in n. 17 above.

96. For additional information on the significance of *Nofet Zufim* for the reconstruction of Jewish culture in Renaissance Italy see Alexander Altmann, "Ars Rhetorica as Reflected in Some Jewish Figures of the Italian Renaissance," in his *Essays in Jewish Intellectual History* (Hanover: University Press of New England, 1981), 97-118. Consult also Arthur M. Lesley, review of Isaac Rabinowitz ed. and trans., *The Book of the Honeycomb's Flow: Sēpher Nōphet Ṣuphīm, Prooftexts* 4 (1984): 312-16.

97. Melamed, "Rhetoric and Philosophy," 16.

98. For a different rationale for the publication of *Nofet Zufim* see Rabinowitz, *Honeycomb's Flow*, 1-liv. Rabinowitz suggested that the text was written at the request of R. Judah Messer Leon's students, to help prepare them for the study of medicine in Italian universities. Bonfil, on the other hand, emphasizes the internal Jewish significance of rhetoric for the attainment of leadership within the Jewish community. Even if the two interpretations are not mutually exclusive, they do present different approaches to the activities of Renaissance Jews. I have followed Bonfil's reconstruction.

99. The polemical intent of *Nofet Zufim* is evident throughout the work. A typical example is Book 1, ch. 13.

100. Gedalya Ibn Yahya, *Shalshelet ha-Kabbalah* (Jerusalem, 1962), 143. Shulvass accepted Ibn Yahya's version as factual in his "The Disputes of Judah Messer Leon," but Simonsohn already proved Ibn Yahya's accounted to be unreliable. See Simonsohn, *The Jews in the Duchy of Mantua*, 704.

101. We learn about the brief visit of Judah Messer Leon and his family in Lucca from a letter that David of Tivoli, relative and former student of the Messer Leons, sent to his son Joab, then in Florence. David of Tivoli was dissatisfied with his son's progress in Florence and instructed him to return to Lucca before the Passover holiday. The father assured his son that his studies would not suffer in Lucca, because a private tutor could surely be found after the holidays, and the son could study "The exegesis of the *Song of Songs* from the Messer Leoni, who would be reading it and expounding on it to his son." These are evidently references to Judah Messer Leon and his son David, although there is no evidence that Messer Leon's academy

also moved to Lucca. The letter is extant in MS. Firenze-Laurenziana Plut. 88/12, fol. 11r, and the relevant part was published by Cassuto, *Ha-Yehudim be-Firenze*, 342, doc. 57.

102. On the pro-Jewish policies of Ferrante I see Nicola Ferorelli, *Gli ebrei nell'Italia meridionale dall'eta romana al secolo XVIII* (1915. Reprint. Bologna: Arnoldo Forni, 1966), 85; on his struggle with the landed barons see Jacob Burckhardt, *The Civilization of the Renaissance in Italy*, translated by S.G.C. Middlemore (New York: Harper & Row, 1958), 51-52.

103. We learn about the size of Judah Messer Leon's academy from David's account, according to which "Twenty two ordained rabbis ... from France, Germany and other countries" taught there under Judah's leadership. See *KH*, 64.

104. There is no evidence to support Rabinowitz's conjecture that Judah Messer Leon fled from Naples to Monastir (then in the Ottoman Empire; now Bitula in Yugoslavia). See Isaac Rabinowitz, "A Rectification of the Date of Judah Messer Leon's Death," in *Studies in Jewish Bibliography, History, and Literature in Honor of I. Edward Kiev*, edited by Charles Berlin (New York: Ktav, 1971), 399-406; idem, *Honeycomb's Flow*, xlv.

105. For a complete list of Judah Messer Leon's works and their extant manuscripts see Bonfil, "Introduction," 22-29.

Chapter Two

1. See Carpi, "Judah Messer Leon," 301. Modern scholars question R. David's birthplace, perhaps overlooking David's opening remark in *Magen David* which notes that the letter from his relative David b. Joab of Tivoli, the pretext for writing *Magen David*, was "sent from Venice, a joyous city, the town of my birth." *MD*, fol 1r: מכתב אלהים ... השלוח מויניציאה קריה עליזה עיר מולדתי.

2. The dispute involved the Spanish and Portuguese communities in Valona (*Avilona* in the Hebrew source). It is discussed in detail in Chapter Four below.

3. *KH*, 28:

רביעית מצד היות החכם ההוא הגדול שבחכמי העיר ורב מוסמך מילדותו בהיותו בן י"ח שנה עד עתה שהגיע לזמן ההוראה.

p. 53:

ואולם ברביעי בבחינת היות זה החכם שבזוהו רב מוסמך מי"ח שנים עד עתה שהוא בן ארבעים זמן הוראה מכל רבני ישיבות נפוליש.

p. 77:

שראויים להיות נכנעים לרב מוסמ׳ מפורסם שהיה מוסמ׳ מראשי ישיבות
והיה רב יותר מעשרי׳ שנה עד שמנו שיש לו מי שנה שהוא זמן ההוראה.

4. See Solomon Rosanes, *A History of the Jews in Turkey* (in Hebrew),
vol. 1 (Tel Aviv: Dvir, 1930), 85; Umberto Cassuto, *EJ*, s.v. "David Messer
Leon;" Rabinowitz, *Honeycomb's Flow*, xxv.

5. Carpi, "Judah Messer Leon," 285, n. 51.

6. Three objections can be raised against Carpi's dating of David's
birth to 1460. First, the controversy in Valona cannot be dated earlier than
1508, since R. David's legal decision mentions Judah Minẓ as a person
already deceased and also refers to the publication of *Hagahot Maymoniyot*
(1509). Second, it is also impossible to dismiss R. David's emphatic statement that he was forty years old at the time of the controversy, cited in n.
3. Third, Carpi's reconstruction of the relationship between R. David ben
Judah Messer Leon and David of Tivoli requires correction. As Carpi correctly indicated, the two could not have been childhood friends, if David had
indeed been born in 1470-71. I suggest that since they belonged to the same
extended family, their correspondence reflects the relationship between an
old, wise, and well-established member to a young and rising star.

7. On the status of Italian private tutors see Boksenboim, *Letters of
Jewish Teachers*, 4-5; Alexander Marx, "R. Joseph of Arles in the Role of a
Teacher and Head of a Yeshivah in Siena," in *Jubilee Volume in Honor of
Levi Ginzberg*, Hebrew Section (New York: American Academy for Jewish
Research), 271-304, esp. 271-84; Shulvass, *The Jews in the World of the Renaissance*, 148-155, 168-172. Shulvass identified Jewish private teachers as
"humanists" and describes their social status in the same categories. Private
teaching was common among the wealthy Jews, reserving public education
to children of less affluent families.

8. See Moses A. Shulvass, "Torah Study among Italian Jews in the Period of the Renaissance" (in Hebrew), *Horev* 10 (1948): 105-28.

9. The difference between the Italian schools in central-southern Italy
and the Ashkenazic schools in northern Italy is well attested in the sources
of the period. Compare, for example, the description of a typical northern
school of Judah Minẓ in Padua in Simha Assaf, *Meqorot le-Toledot
ha-hinnukh be-Yisrael* (Tel Aviv: Dvir, 1925-42), vol. 2, 105 ff. with the
description of a typical southern-central school in Marx, "R. Joseph of
Arles," 284-86. For a detailed description of Ashkenazic education see
Isadore Twersky, "Jewish Education in Ashkenaz in the Middle Ages" (in
Hebrew), in his *Studies in Jewish Law and Philosophy* (New York: Ktav,
1982), Hebrew Section, 69-75.

10. Moshe Idel, "The Study Program of R. Yohanan Alemanno" (in Hebrew), *Tarbiz* 48 (1979): 303-30.

11. Idel, "Study Program," 304-5; Boksenboim, *Letters of Jewish Teachers*, 5.

12. Idel, "Study Program," 304. The scope of R. David's actual knowledge of the Talmud was far greater than Alemanno's list reflecting his further education in the Yeshivah of R. Judah Minz's in Padua. In his extant writings R. David cites as well the following tractates from the Babylonian Talmud: *Erubin, Bezah, Rosh ha-Shanah, Yoma, Ta'anit, Megillah, Mo'ed Qatan, Hagigah, Yebamot, Nedarim, Sotah, Kiddushin, Baba Qama, Makkot, Shevu'-ot, 'Edduyot, 'Abodah Zarah, Hullin, Bekhorot,* and *'Arakhin.* He also referred to the Palestinian Talmud, tractates *Shevu'ot, Kilayyim, Berakhot* and *Gittin.*

R. David also used other sources belonging to what is broadly classified as Talmudic literature: the standard Aramaic translations of the Bible, *Targum Onkelos* and *Targum Yerushalmi,* the Halakhic Midrashim, *Mekhilta, Sifra,* and *Sifre,* and the Aggadic Midrashim, *Bereshit Rabbah, Shemot Rabbah, Vayiqra Rabbah, Eikhah Rabbah, Tanhuma, Midrash Tehilim, Midrash Ruth, Avot de-Rabbi Natan,* and *Pirqey de-Rabbi Eliezer.* R. David often referred to Midrashic literature as *qabbalah* (i.e., Jewish received tradition), and called the rabbinic scholars *hakhmey ha-qabbalah* (i.e., the sages of the Jewish tradition). Similarly, he referred to the anonymous authors of Midrashic literature as *hakhmey ha-aggadah,* whose task is to interpret divine revelation.

13. See Ephraim Urbach, *The Tosaphists: Their History, Writings, and Methods* (in Hebrew) (Jerusalem: Mosad Bialik, 1980), 575-80.

R. David's Halakhic training was a combination of Italian and Ashkenazic legal traditions. His command of post-talmudic Halakhic literature ranges from Geonic literature to the legal compendia and codes by Italian, French, and Spanish Halakhic authorities. Among the Italian Halakhic works, R. David cites the *'Arukh,* the tenth century talmudic lexicon by R. Nathan ben Yehiel of Rome, and the late thirteenth century *Shiboley ha-Leqet* by R. Zedekayah ben Abraham ha-Rofe of Rome. In *Kevod Hakhamim* (*KH,* 9) R. David states that the latter "intended to preserve our rite, the Italian ritem because this scholar was from Rome," thereby documenting his allegiance to Italian legal tradition. Of the Italian *posqim,* R. David mentions R. Isaiah ben Mali di Trani the Elder, the most important thirteenth century Italian jurist, and his grandson, R. Isaiah ben Elijah di Trani the Younger. Though R. David referred to both Italian jurists with utmost respect, their impact on his legal orientation was rather limited. Both in method and in literary sources, R. David followed the German and French legal authorities whom he studied in his father's Yeshivah in Naples and at R. Judah Minz's Yeshivah in Padua.

In accordance with the Ashkenazic method, R. David studies Talmud with the Tosafot and Rashi's commentaries. In *Kevod Hakhamim* (*KH*, 10), R. David states that "my approach is always to rescue Rashi from the difficulties raised by the Tosafot as was the custom in my time in the great Yeshivot; hence I began to compose my own treatise to comment on Rashi's method." That commentary on Rashi is not extant.

The Tosafot were R. David's major tool for studying the Talmud. He refers to them either by generic term "Tosafot," or by specific reference such as Tosafot of R. Eliezer of Tousque, R. Perez, or R. Samson of Sens (*KH*, 79-80). R. David treated French and German Tosafists as one unified intellectual and literary tradition. He also cites the foloowing by name: R. Samuel ben Meir (Rashbam), R. Jacob Tam, R. Judah of Paris (Sir Leon), R. Isaac ben Samuel, R. Isaac the author of *Or Zaru'a*, R. Eliezer ben Joel Halevi (Rabyah), R. Isaac of Corbeille, R. Moses of Couci, R. Moses of Zurich, R. Meir of Rothenberg, and R. Meir ha-Cohen. At R. Judah Minz's Yeshivah R. David ben Judah studied primarily *Sefer Mizvot Gadol* by R. Moses of Couci, *Mordecai* by R. Mordecai ben Hillel, and *Hagahot Maymoniyot* by R. Meir ha-Cohen (*KH*, 79).

Of the Ashkenazic legal codes, R. Jacob ben Asher's *Arba'ah Turim*, which compiled many Sephardic traditions, played a prominent role in R. David's writings, reflecting the code's popularity in the northern Jewish community of fifteenth century Italy. His reliance on *Arba'ah Turim*, as well as his early training in the Sephardic legal codes of Alfasi and Maimonides, customary for Italian Jews, explains the interesting mixture of Ashkenazic and Sephardic Halakhic traditions in *Kevod Hakhamim*. Undoubtedly, he considered Maimonides the greatest of all the *posqim* (*KH* 79, 86-7). Interestingly, however, he claimed that only those trained in the Ashkenazic method of *pilpul* could really understand the Sephardic Maimonides. Moreover, in *Kevod Hakhamim* (*KH*, 85) R. David shows that by applying *pilpul* to the study of the *Mishneh Torah*, Maimonides' legal reasoning can be harmonized with the Tosafot.

In addition to Maimonides, R. David cites the following Sephardic authorities: R. Isaac Alfasi, R. Joseph ibn Megash, R. Meir Halevi (Ramah), R. Moses ben Nahman (Nahmanides), R. Solomon ibn Adret (Rashba), R. Nissim Gerondi (Ran), R. Simon ben Zemah Duran (Rashbaz) and R. Isaac Aboab. The disciples of R. Isaac Aboab, of whom R. Joseph Fasi was the most notable, were R. David's contemporaries in Salonika, and most likely another source of his knowledge of Sephardic legal traditions. In fact, R. David's close contact with Sephardic scholars influenced his manner of studying the Talmud. At one point in *Kevod Hakhamim* (*KH*, 129), and despite his allegiance to Ashkenazic legal method, he caught himself imitating the method employed by Ramban in his talmudic *Novellae*.

14. On Alemanno's interest in music see Idel, "The Magical and Theurgical Interpretation of Music in Jewish Texts: Renaissance to Hassidism"

(in Hebrew), *Yuval* 4 (1982): 32-63, esp. 37-42. Music was known to medieval Jews in Spain and Provençe, who regarded it as part of the quadrivium and consulted Arabic texts for their knowledge of music theory. See, Nehemyah Aloni, "The Term 'Music' in Our Literature in the Middle Ages" (in Hebrew), *Yuval* 1 (1968): 12-35; Hanokh Avenary, "The Hebrew Version of Abu L-Salt's Treatise on Music" (in Hebrew), *Yuval* 3 (1974): 7-13. Alemanno differed from the earlier medieval conception of music in his emphasis on the ability of music to affect the supernal worlds.

15. Idel, "Study Program," 304.

16. Ibid. Yohanan Alemanno does not specify which rhetorical texts should be studied in order to cultivate perfect prose style, but he clearly had in mind the Ciceronian tradition cultivated in Renaissance Italy. The extent of R. David's knowledge of Ciceronian rhetoric can be gleaned from his extant *Shevah ha-Nashim*, where he cites Cicero's *De Inventione, De Oratore, Tuscalanae Disputationes, De Officiis, De Natura Deorum,* and *De Amicitia.* Another source of Ciceronian rhetoric mentioned by R. David was Quintilian's *Institutio Oratoria* which proposed a complete system of education of the ideal orator. R. David's training in the art of rhetoric was also based on this text. The works of Abraham Farissol provide another record for the cultivation of Ciceronian rhetoric by students of Judah Messer Leon. See Ruderman, "An Exemplary Sermon," 17-27.

17. Idel, "Study Program," 304-5; Rosenberg, "Logic and Ontology," 1: 47, 109-10.

18. Idel, "Study Program," 305. On the mathematical works of R. Levi b. Gershon (Gersonides) and Abraham ibn 'Ezra see Ben Ami Zarfati, *The Mathematical Terms in Hebrew Scientific Literature of the Middle Ages* (in Hebrew) (Jerusalem, 1979), 220ff.

19. Idel, "Study Program," 305, n. 18.

20. Idel, ibid. 305-6.

21. Idel, ibid. 306. Alghazali's work is a summary of Avicenna's philosophy, written as the first phase of Alghazali's polemics against the philosophers. Despite the original intent of this work, it became a major text for the study of philosophy by Jews during the fourteenth and fifteenth centuries. This text was the subject of controversy in the Yeshivah of Judah Messer Leon, when the master dismissed a teacher for using it ostensibly to propagate heresy.

22. Idel, "Study Program," 307. The last four cited texts indicated that Alemanno, and most likely the program in Messer Leon's Yeshivah, included ethics in the curriculum. Following Aristotle, medieval Jewish philosophers considered ethics part of practical philosophy (along with politics and eco-

nomics), a preliminary subject to the study of speculative philosophy: physics and metaphysics.

23. Idel, "Program Study," 307-8.

24. Italian Jews studied Latin grammar and calligraphy with private Christian tutors. See Shulvass, *The Jews in the World of the Renaissance*, 172.

25. These Kabbalistic texts were the only ones available in Italy in the fifteenth century. The *Zohar* began to spread in Italy only during the early sixteenth century, introduced by Spanish exiles. See Moshe Idel, "Major Currents in Italian Kabbalah between 1560-1660," *Italia Judaica* 2 (1986): 243-62. For further discussion of the nature of Kabbalah in Italy see Chapter Seven below.

26. On Alemanno's peculiar mixture of Kabbalah and the occult sciences see Moshe Idel, "The Magical and Neoplatonic Interpretations in the Renaissance" in *Jewish Thought in the Sixteenth Century*, edited by Bernard D. Cooperman (Cambridge: Harvard University Press, 1983), 186-242.

27. See Idel, ibid. 190ff; Arthur M. Lesley, "'The Song of Solomon's Ascents' by Yohanan Alemanno: Love and Human Perfection according to a Jewish Colleague of Giovanni Pico della Mirandola," Ph.D. diss., University of California at Berkeley 1976, 27-50.

28. Under the influence of Ashkenazic immigration the Italian Yeshivot adopted the method of *pilpul*. See Shulvass, "Torah Study", 113. On the method of *pilpul* in the Ashkenazic Yeshivot see Mordecai Breuer, "'Aliyat ha-Pilpul ve-ha-Hiluqim be-Yeshivot Ashkenaz," in *Sefer Zikkaron le-Morenu ha-Rav Weinberg* (Jerusalem, 1970), 241-55; Hayim Dimitrowski, "'Al Derekh ha-Pilpul," in *Jubilee Volume in Honor of Salo Baron*, edited by Saul Lieberman (Jerusalem: American Academy for Jewish Research, 1975), Hebrew Section, 111-81.

29. I studied this letter in the Microfilm Institute of the Hebrew and National Library at the Hebrew University, Israel. For information on David ben Joab of Tivoli see Chapter One, n. 82.

30. MS. Firenze-Laurenziana 88/10 fol. 11v.

31. Ibid.

32. The letter was published first by Solomon Schechter, "Notes sur Messer David Leon: tirées de manuscrits," *REJ* 24 (1892): 120-21. Schechter's rendering of the original text was reissued by Husik in *Judah Messer Leon's Commentary*, 5. Rabinowitz used Schechter's text in his English translation of the letter, *Honeycomb's Flow*, xlvi-1. Schechter's flawed reading of the original manuscript affected Rabinowitz's reconstruction of Judah Messer Leon's biography. Bonfil reexamined the manuscript and published a correct version of the letter in his "Introduction," 23-4.

33. See Bonfil, "Introduction," 24.

34. See Cassuto, "La Famiglia di David da Tivoli," 263.

35. On the customary age for rabbinic ordination (40) see Bonfil, *The Rabbinate*, 41-42; Mordekhai Breuer, "The Ashkenazic Ordination" (in Hebrew), *Zion* 33 (1978): 40.

36. On the social import of rabbinic ordination in Italian Jewry see Bonfil, *The Rabbinate*, 33-37, 44-66.

37. See *KH*, 64-65.

38. See *MD*, fol. 1r:

עם היותי נער ורך בן י"ח שנה בשנת חופתי.

39. The term *hakham kolel* was already used by earlier Jewish scholars in Spain and Provençe to signify mastery of secular studies and rabbinic tradition. See, for instance, Asher Crescas' reference to Yedayah Bedersi in *Perush le-Moreh Nebukhim*, II:30. On the social import of the title as far as the family of Judah Messer Leon was concerned see Bonfil, "Introduction," 19-20. On David's self-perception as the comprehensive scholar, see Chapters Three and Five below.

40. See *KH*, 64. Perhaps the first ordination in his father's Yeshivah entitled David only to *semikhah me-haverut*, while the second ordination was *semikhah me-rabbanut*. R. David himself does not report such difference but only states that R. Judah Minz would not ordain a scholar "unless that scholar studied in his Yeshivah."

41. See Elijah Capsali, *Seder Eliyahu Zuta* edited by Meir Benyahu, Aryeh Shmeulevitz and Shlomo Simonsohn (Jerusalem: The Ben Zvi Institute of Yad Ben-Zvi and the Hebrew University; Tel Aviv: The Diaspora Research Institute Tel Aviv University), vol. 2, 246-47. The description of R. Judah Minz's Yeshivah was printed separately by Assaf, see n. 9 above, and consult Boksenboim, *Letters of Jewish Teachers*, 7-8.

42. *KH*, 63:

וזה מפני שכל זה קבלנו אנחנו האיטלייני מרבותינו הצרפתיים האשכנזים
אשר מהם תצא תורה ומפיהם אנחנו חיים.

43. *KH*, 7, 45. For information on Eleazar of Worms, *Seder Teshuvah*, see Ivan Marcus, "The Penitential Writings of the Hasidim of Ashkenaz" (in Hebrew), in *Studies in Jewish Mysticism, Philosophy, and Ethical Literature Presented to Isaiah Tishby on His Seventy-Fifth Birthday*, edited by Joseph Dan and Joseph Hacker (Jerusalem: Magnes Press, 1986), 369-84.

44. On this literature see Joseph Dan, *The Esoteric Theology of Ashkenazi Hasidism* (in Hebrew) (Jerusalem: Mosad Bialik, 1968), 9-67.

45. *MD*, fol. 1r, printed in Schechter, "Notes sur Messer David Leon," 121.

46. For a detailed description of the career of Elijah del Medigo in Italy see Jacob J. Ross ed., *Sefer Behinat Hadat of Elijah Del Medigo* (in Hebrew) (Tel Aviv: Tel Aviv University, 1984), 18-35; David Geffen, "Insights into the Life and Thought of Elijah del Medigo Based on His Published and Unpublished Works," *PAAJR* 41-42 (1973-74): 69-86.

47. For a full list of del Medigo's translations to Pico see David Geffen, "Faith and Reason in Elijah del Medigo's Behinat Hadat," Ph.D. diss., Columbia University 1970, 10; idem, "Insights," 85-86; cf. Cassuto, *Ha-Yehudim be-Firenze*, 223-4. On the contribution of Elijah del Medigo to the knowledge of Averroës' commentaries on Aristotle see Alfred Ivry, "Remnants of Jewish Averroism in the Renaissance," in *Jewish Thought in the Sixteenth Century*, 243-265.

48. The letter is excerpted in Ruderman, *The World of a Renaissance Jew*, 40, and the scholarly collaboration between Jews and Christian surrounding Pico and Ficino in Florence is described in detail in 40-43.

49. See Geffen, "Insights," 78. Cf. N. Porges, "Elie Capsali et sa Cronique da Venisa," *REJ* 78 (1924): 21-25; Milano, *Storia degli ebrei in Italia*, 619-20, 666-7; Ross, *Sefer Behinat ha-Dat*, 23.

50. Aryeh L. Motzkin, "Elia Del Medigo, Averroës, and Averroism," *Italia* 6 (1-2) (1987): 7-19. Motzkin sheds light on the controversy in Padua:

> We conclude: Del Medigo is an Averroist, or more properly, Averroian, in that he follows the teaching of Averroës. He is a follower of Averroës in that he believes with Averroës that Philosophy and Religion should be kept distinct and separate.

(P. 19). If Motzkin's interpretation is correct, then del Medigo called for the pursuit of philosophy free of religious considerations, which may well have been seen as a challenge to established religious order.

51. This interpretation connects the departure of Elijah del Medigo to the ecclesiastical opposition to Averroist teachings on the unity of the human intellect. While Averroism was strongly represented at the University of Padua by the late fifteenth century, Averroës' theory on the unity of the intellect did not pose a theological problem as it did in the thirteenth century at the University of Paris. On the Averroist school at the University of Padua see Paul O. Kristeller, "Paduan Averroism and Alexandrism in the Light of Recent Studies," in *Aristotelismo padovano e filosofia aristotelica*, Atti del XII congresso internazionale di filosopfia, IX (Florence, 1960), 147-55; John H. Randall, "Paduan Aristotelianism Reconsidered," in *Philosophy and Humanism*, 275-82. On Averroist scholars in Padua who taught the doctrine

of the unity of the intellect without arousing ecclesiastical opposition see Edward P. Mahoney, "Nicoletto Vernia and Agostino Nifo on Alexander of Aphrodisias: an Unnoticed Dispute," *RCSF* 23 (1968): 270-71; Ross, *Sefer Behinat ha-Dat*, 23.

52. The third interpretation connects del Medigo's departure with the death of his patron, Pico della Mirandola, in 1494. See his *Mazref la-Hokhmah*, 4a. But this explanation, proposed by Joseph Shlomo Delmedigo (Yashar of Candia), is also untenable, since del Medigo left prior to the death of Pico. See Ross, *Sefer Behinat ha-Dat*, 23, 66. n. 66.

53. R. David's query and R. Jacob Provenzali's response were published in Eliezer Ashkenazi ed., *Divre Hakhamim* (Metz, 1849), 63-74. Large segments of the response were published in Assaf, *Meqorot le-Toledot Ha-Hinnukh Be-Yisrael* 2: 99-102.

54. Assaf, *ibid.* 101:

> האם הנה אהובות או מרוחקות אצל הנכבדים רבותינו, עליהם השלום,
> חכמי המצות, כי נראה מעניינם שהם שונאי הפלוסופיא.

55. Assaf, *ibid.* 100:

> שאין ספק שכל חכמה מהשבע חכמות המדעיות הן משובחות ונערכות בעיני
> חכמינו ואהבו אותה אהבה גמורה.

56. Assaf, *ibid.* 101:

> אבל בעבור כי התורה נקלה בעיני בני הדור, והתלמידים שהיה ראוי
> שיעמידו הרב בכבוד אינם רוצים לתת כבוד לשום יודע בתורה או בתלמוד
> ואפילו הוא גדול כר' עקיבא, כי בעלה לבם של תלמידים טינא לאמר: הלא
> טוב לנו לשמוע מחכמי הנוצרים אשר ילמדו חכמה בדמים קלים וזה
> אומרים בעבור שחכמי הגוים ופקחי האומות יש להם פרס גדול בבית המלך
> או מתקיפי העיר אשר הם יושבים, ובעבור זה מקילים לתלמידים ואין
> שואלים להם דבר בין שיהיו גויים או יהודים, ובעבור זה היהודים
> התלמידים אינם רוצים לפזר ממון לתת לשום חכם יהודי.

57. Assaf, *ibid.*

> ויותר רע מזה כי אין משבח התורה אפילו בדברי פה: אין איש אומר כמה
> יפה מאמר זה, או אם יחדש אדם איזה דבר חכמה, (או) כמה הפליא לעשות
> פלוני בדרשה פלונית או בהוראה פלונית, אבל ירצו שיתנו להם הדברים
> בחנם, אפלו משבח דברי פה, ולא יחושו אם הרב האמתי אוכל ושותה או
> מוטל ברעב ... כל אלה הדברים הרעים והמנהגים המתעים ארעו והיו לנו
> זה כמה ימים אשר הניאו לבית החכמים לעשות קבע בתורה, כי ראו עצמם
> מתים ברעב ומוטלים כל הקרי וההזדמן.

58. A segment of the letter to David of Tivoli was published by Cassuto in his "La Famiglia di David da Tivoli," 301, doc. 8. David da Tiv-

oli then still resided in Lucca, before his final departure to Pisa. See also idem, *Ha-Yehudim be-Firenze*, 200-01. In this letter David recommended Rabbi 'Azriel, whom he met in Florence, to tutor the son of David of Tivoli. Apparently David ben Judah Messer Leon was concerned about the education of David of Tivoli's son, Joab, since David ben Judah discusses it again in another letter which he wrote from Naples. These letters are extant in MS. Firenze-Laurenziana 88/12.

59. On Florence before the rise of the Medicis see John H. Plumb, *The Italian Renaissance* (New York: American Heritage, 1961), 52-58; John R. Hale, *Florence and the Medici: the Pattern of Control* (London: Thames and Hudson, 1977), 11-42, and consult the rich bibliography in 197-98; Brucker, *Renaissance Florence*, 51-88; idem, "The Medici in the Fourteenth Century," *Speculum* 32 (1957): 1-26; Marvin B. Becker, "The Republican City-State in Florence: An Inquiry into its Origin and Survival," *Speculum* 35 (1960): 39-50.

60. See Hans Baron, *The Crisis of the Early Italian Renaissance*, rev. ed. (Princeton: Princeton University Press, 1966), 3-120. For a critique of Baron's position see Jerrold Seigel, "'Civic Humanism' or Ciceronian Rhetoric," *Past and Present* 34 (1966): 3-34.

61. See Gray, "Renaissance Humanism: The Pursuit of Eloquence," 497-514. For further bibliographical information see Chapter One, n. 16.

62. On Florence's artistic achievements and their influence on Italian culture see Brucker, *Renaissance Florence*, 213-55 and the bibliography cited in 295-97.

63. On Jewish moneylending in Florence see Cassuto, *Ha-Yehudim be-Firenze*, 29-76; Toaff, "Jewish Banking," 121-27.

64. See Roth, *The Jews in the Renaissance*, 111-136.

65. See Melamed, "Rhetoric and Philosophy," 16-18.

66. On Isaac b. Yehiel da Pisa see Cassuto, *Ha-Yehudim be-Firenze*, passim. Mourning over the death of Yehiel da Pisa was recorded for posterity in an elegy composed by Eleazar of Volterra. The poem was published by David Kaufmann, *REJ* 26 (1893): 228.

67. On these poems and their literary context see, Chapter Three below.

68. On the da Pisa family see Umberto Cassuto, "Sulla Famiglia Da Pisa," *Rivista Israelitica*, 5 (1908): 227-38; 6 (1909): 21-30, 102-13, 160-70, 223-36; David Kaufmann, "La Famille de Yehiel de Pise," *REJ* 26 (1893): 83-110, 220-39.

69. The travelogue of David Ha-Reubeni was published by Adolph Neubauer, "Sippur David Ha-Reubeni" in *Medieval Jewish Chronicles* (in Hebrew) (Oxford: Clarendon Press, 1887-95. Reprint. Jerusalem, 1967), vol. 2, 133-223. The relevant section is found in pp. 163-65.

70. See Lesley, "'The Song of Solomon's Ascents'," 5 and 269, n. 14.

71. See Carpi, "Judah Messer Leon," 295-7.

72. The line is taken from the first letter of Isaac Mar Hayyim to Isaac da Pisa published by Yael Nadav, "An Epistle of the Qabbalist Isaac Mar Hayyim Concerning the Doctrine of Supernal Lights" (in Hebrew). *Tarbiz* (1957), 458. R. Isaac Mar Hayyim wrote two epistles from Naples to Isaac ben Yehiel da Pisa in Florence, in which he expounded on Kabbalistic doctrines. The first was published by Yael Nadav and the second was published by Arthur Greenup, "A Qabbalistic Epistle," *JQR* 21 (1931): 365-75. Ephraim Gottlieb was the first to note that R. David ben Judah Messer Leon incorporated long sections from both epistles into his *Magen David* fols. 7v-11v. See his "Or 'Olam le-Elhanan Sagi Nahor," in his *Studies in the Kabbalah Literature* (in Hebrew), edited by Joseph Hacker (Tel Aviv: The Chaim Rosenberg School for Jewish Studies Tel Aviv University, 1976), 404-12. The epistles were written in 1490-91, so R. David's access to them supports my reconstruction that he resided at the da Pisa's household in Florence about 1491.

73. On the relationship between Pico della Mirandola and Yohanan Alemanno see Moshe Idel, "The Magical and Neoplatonic Interpretation," 190-98; Lesley, "'The Song of Solomon's Ascents'," 1-11; 27-50; Franz J.E. Rosenthal, "Yohanan Alemanno and Occult Sciences," in *Prismata: Naturalwissenschaft Geschichtliche Studien: Festschrift für Willy Hartner* (Wiesbadden, 1977), 349-61.

74. On the concept of universal truth in Renaissance humanism see Paul O. Kristeller, *Renaissance Thought and its Sources*, 196-210, and the notes in 311-12. The impact of Renaissance search for *prisca theologica* on Jewish thinkers is discussed in detail by Ruderman, "The Italian Renaissance and Jewish Thought," 396-404.

75. On Pico's peculiar interpretation of Kabbalah see Chaim Wirszubski, "Giovanni Pico's Companion to Kabbalistic Symbolism," in *Studies in Mysticism and Religion Presented to Gershom G. Scholem on His Seventieth Birthday by Pupils, Colleagues and Friends*, edited by Ephraim E. Urbach, R.J. Zwi Werblowsky and Chaim Wirzubskui (Jerusalem: Magnes Press, 1967), 353-62; idem, *Three Chapters in the History of Christian Kabbalah* (in Hebrew) (Jerusalem, 1975); Ruderman, *The World of a Renaissance Jew*, 400-4; Joseph L. Blau, *The Christian Interpretation of the Cabalah*

in the Renaissance (Port Washington: Kennikat, 1944. Reprint. New York: Columnbia University Press, 1965); Baron, *SRH* 13: 172ff.

76. See Aryeh Grabois, "The Hebraica Veritas and Jewish-Christian Intellectual Relations in the Twelfth Century," *Speculum* 50 (1975): 613-34.

77. Pico's discussion of Kabbalah in his "Oration on the Dignity of Man," is a typical example of the claim that Kabbalah is identical with the mysteries of the Catholic faith. See Ernest Cassirer, Paul O. Kristeller and John H. Randall eds., *The Renaissance Philosophy of Man* (Chicago: The University of Chicago Press, 1948), 223-54, esp. 249-52.

78. The literary activity of Flavius Mithridates was studied by Wirszubski. See his "Flavius Mithridates" (in Hebrew), *Israel National Academy for Sciences Proceedings* 1 (1966): 1-10; idem, "Flavius Mithridates' Christological Sermon" (in Hebrew), in *Yitzhak Baer Jubilee Volume* (Jerusalem: Israel Historical Society, 1960), 191-206; see also François Secret, "Qui etait l'orientaliste Mithridate," *REJ* 116 (1957): 96-102; idem, *Les Kabbalists chretiens de la Renaissance* (Paris, 1964). The social context of this intellectual circle is best described in Ruderman, *The World of a Renaissance Jew*, 35-56.

79. In addition to participation in oral disputations with Christian theologians, both Abraham Farissol and Elijah del Medigo defended Judaism in their writings. On Abraham Farissol's *Magen Abraham* see Ruderman, *The World of a Renaissance Jew*, 57-84. On the polemical content of Elija del Medigo's *Behinat ha-Dat* see Daniel Lasker, *Jewish Philosophical Polemics Against Christianity in the Middle Ages* (New York: Ktav, 1977), passim.

80. The polemical intent of R. David's philosophic interpretation of Kabbalah is discussed in Chapter Five below. See Hava Tirosh-Rothschild, "Sefirot as the Essence of God in the Writings of David Messer Leon," *AJS Review* 7-8 (1982-83): 409-25.

81. R. David's defense of humanist curriculum is discussed in Chapter Three below.

82. There is nothing new about the use of grammar as a tool of biblical exegesis; indeed, this is the very essence of the rationalist tradition in biblical hermeneutics. R. David ben Judah Messer Leon, however, uses grammatical analysis to justify a certain theological position. Thus, for example, he claims that the present participle verb *barukh* (literally, the blessed one) reflects the ability of human beings to derive spirituality from the supernal world. R. David's emphasis on the passive form of the verb reflects his belief that Hebrew language contains divine mysteries. This belief undoubtedly attests to the impact of Kabbalah on his thought.

83. A discussion of the classical sources that David read is found in Chapter Three below.

84. In *SH*, fol. 111r R. David praises Petrarch's *Trionfi (Triumphs)* as follows:

ולשונו הוא נכבד ומעלה מאד יותר מכל הספרים שחוברו בפואיסיה בלשון
לעז, עד שלרוב נעימותו ייטב בעיני מאד ונעשיתי בקי בו הרבה עד שכמעט
אני יודע אותו ע"פ כולו. וכל זה נעשה בעבור לאברה הנכבדת. גם עשה
בעבורה הרבה חרוזים, הנקראים שוניטים אצלם, טובים מאד, גם אני
עשיתי מהן בכאן הרבה בלשון מפואר, שאם היית שומעים היו יקרים בעיניך
מאד.

The context of this paragraph as well as the structure and purpose of *Shevah ha-Nashim* are discussed in detail in Chapter Three below.

85. R. David's musical composition entitled *Abir Ya'acov (The Mighty One of Jacob)* is cited in *SH*, fols. 95v:

והנה גם אני נתעסקתי בנערותי בשירים ובחכמת המושיקא הלא היא חכמה
מפוארה מז' החכמות וביארתי מעלתה בס' אביר יעקב בפ' הז' שם ביארתי
כל עיניניה.

Abir Ya'acov is also cited in fol. 103v.

86. The theurgic conception of music is found explicitly in *SH*, fol. 95v:

והנה בזאת [החכמה] היו כל הלויים בקיאים בה כמו שמשוררים על הדוכן
והיא נכונה מאד אל המעיינים לעזר השפע, כמו שקרה לאלישע "והיה כנגן
המנגן ותהי עליו רוח ה'" [מלכים ב, ג, 15]. ומי לנו בקי בזאת יותר מדוד
והנביא [עמוס] העיד על גדולתו בשירים כמש' [כמו שכתוב] "הפורטים ע"פ
[על פי] הנבל כדוד חשבו להם כלי שיר" [עמוס ה, 6].

The view that music is a useful means for stimulating the divine effluence was articulated in Renaissance Italy by Marsilio Ficino. See Paul O. Kristeller, "Music and Learning in the Early Italian Renaissance," in his *Renaissance Thought II: Papers on Humanism and the Arts* (New York: Harper and Row, 1965), 142-162. It is doubtful that R. David derived his conception of music directly from Ficino, but R. David's views do fit into prevailing ideas. Ficino, however, influenced Yohanan Alemanno directly, and perhaps R. David developed his theurgic conception of music from Alemanno.

See also David's further comments in *SH*, fols. 95v-96v. R. David's defense of music, among other arts, is discussed in detail in Chapter Three below.

87. On R. Yohanan Alemanno's theurgic conception of music see Idel, "The Magical and Theurgic Interpretation of Music," 37-42.

88. For a survey of Hermetic literature and concepts in Renaissance culture see John G. Burke, "Hermetism as a Renaissance World View," in *The Darker Vision of the Renaissance*, edited by Robert S. Kinsman (Los Angeles: University of California Press, 1979), 95-117; Wayne Shumaker,

The Occult Sciences in the Renaissance: A Study in Intellectual Patterns (Berkeley: University of California Press, 1972), 201-48, and the bibliography cited in 263-66.

89. Burke, "Hermetism," 99.

90. See Paul O. Kristeller, *The Philosophy of Marsilio Ficino*, translated by Virginia Conant (New York: Columbia University Press, 1943), 1-29.

91. *SH*, fol. 107r:

> Hermes Trismegistus, a great philosopher, would say that the greatest portion of what we know is the smallest portion of what we do not know.

92. See Moshe Idel, "Kabbalah and Ancient Philosophy in R. Isaac and Yehudah Abravanel" (in Hebrew), in *The Philosophy of Love of Leone Ebreo*, edited by Menahem Dorman and Zvi Levi (Haifa: Hakibbuz Hameuhad, 1985), 73-112.

93. *MD*, fol. 5v (printed in Schechter, "Notes Sur Messer David Leon," 122:

> From the above discussion it appears that Plato lived at the time of the Prophet Jeremiah, and therefore, since Plato stated that he had studied from a man called Jeremiah we have to deduce that it was Jeremiah the Prophet, as we said above.
>
> And I have found that Averroës, the profound philosopher, while praising the sages of Israel at the end of his *The Destruction of the Destruction* substantiated [the praise] by reference to the books of King Solomon. Likewise, [Averroës] praised them in another place in reference to Plato. He [i.e., Averroës] said that Plato joined one of the sages of Israel who studied theology. Plato then said:
>
> > "In the beginning I saw nothing great [about this Jewish sage], but when we reached the study of the Deity, I witnessed his conjunction with the Separate Intellects. I saw something which terrified me and my ultimate goal was to understand but a little of what this sage would say. And I knew that he had attained a position higher than the status of all human beings because he was among the prophets, hence his words are divine."
>
> It appears from this [statement] that, since Plato referred to the Jewish sage as 'prophet,' he must have lived during the time of the above mentioned prophet. You should realize the virtue of this man [Plato] who was called 'divine' not in vain, because whoever studies his books will find in them profound, awesome,

divine mysteries and all their teachings are [identical with] the teachings of the men of true Kabbalah.

94. For more information on the alleged relation between Plato and the prophet Jeremiah in the writings of these scholars see Idel, "Kabbalah and Ancient Philosophy," 77-78. The tale that Plato sat at Jeremiah's feet was invented by some Christian apologist to counter the Neoplatonic charge that Christianity had borrowed from Plato by asserting that Judaism had also. Augustine first believed this tale but later ruled it out by chronology. See Elias J. Bickerman, *The Jews in the Greek Age* (Cambridge: Harvard University Press, 1988), 13-14.

Medieval Jewish philosophers then adopted this fiction in their attempt to legitimize Jewish preoccupation with the secular sciences — in particular, philosophy. Associating Plato and Jeremiah is but another way of saying that philosophy was an indigenous Jewish knowledge which the Greeks appropriated to themselves. See Norman Roth, "The 'Theft of Philosophy' by the Greeks from the Jews," *Classical Folia* 2 (1978): 53-67.

95. On the new approach of Renaissance humanists to history see Felix Gilbert, "The Renaissance Interest in History," in *Art, Science and History in the Renaissance* edited by Charles S. Singleton (Baltimore: The Johns Hopkins University Press, 1967), 373-87.

96. *SH*, fol. 108v.

97. R. David's signature appeared in the *haskamah* to Jacob Landau's *Sefer ha-Aggur* written in 1480 and published in Naples about 1492, which suggests that R. David was a recognized rabbinic authority in Naples.

98. *MD*, fol. 96v.

99. The identity of this Laura is not known for sure. I have already suggested that Laura, the wife of Samuel da Pisa, and the mother of Nissim Yehiel da Pisa, could have been the addressee of David's laudatory composition. For further discussion see Chapter Three below.

100. *MD*, fol. 50r: כמו שהארכתי בזה במאמר מיוחד בספר מגדל דוד. Ibid. fol. 29r: ואני חברתי בזה מאמר גדול תלמודי בספרי ספר מגדל דוד. Abraham David mistakenly referred to this work as *Migdal 'Oz* in his "New Information about Caleb Apandopolo" (in Hebrew), *Kiryat Sepher* 48 (1973): 180.

101. *Mizmor le-David* is mentioned in *MD*, fol. 152r:

ראיתי להודיעך כי נמשכתי אחרי שני צנתרות הזהב ... הא" עיוני תוריי
רדפתי אותו בעין הקורא בהרים התורה ומעלתה והוספתי עליהם כהנה
וכהנה וקורא להם שמי מזמור לדוד.

Menorat ha-Zahav is cited in two of David's extant works: *PE*, fol. 241r: מצד היות התורה כוללת כל החכמות כו שביארתי בס' מנורת הזהב. Cf. *SH*, fol. 103r:

הנה אקצר כללי הדברים בכאן כי כבר הארכתי בחבורי' רבי' בס' מנורת הזהב שחברתי
זה ו' שנים. David wrote *Menorat ha-Zahav* six years before *Shevah ha-Nashim*,
while still in Italy.

102. *PE*, fol. 245r: ואני הארכתי הרבה בזה במאמ' נפלא ופשטי' נכבדי'
אף כי דעתי בפרוש הפסוק ההוא. Cf. *ibid*, fol. 264r: במאמר יקר מאמ' נחל עדנים
כמו שפרשתי בספרי ספר נחל עדנים.

103. *PE*, fol. 239r: כמו שבארתי בספ' סגולת המלכים בזאת המלאכה מקור
מענין הקל מפעלי הכפל.

104. *PE*, fol. 261r: וכמו שהוכחתי זה בספר תפארת אדם ובדרוש אחר שעשיתי
בענין התכונה. The title *Tiferet ha-Adam (The Glory of Man)* is very intriguing,
since it alludes to one of the favorite themes of the Italian Renaissance,
namely, the dignity of man; yet as discussed below in Chapter Five, R. David
had a decidedly medieval conception of man and of the ultimate end of
human life was decidedly medieval in orientation. The word *derush* in this
sentence is problematic: it could be interpreted as either "sermon" or
"treatise". The second part of the statement indicates that David composed
a short treatise on astronomy, among the liberal arts of the *quadrivium*.

105. R. David refers to his poems in praise of women in *SH*, fol. 89r:
הנה מהרה זכרתיך שרתי בנשים לקיים את מצותך שצויתני מאז הייתי שם לפי' כל
המעשים משבח הנשים שהבאתי בהלצה הג' שחברתי. "*Ha-halazah ha-gimel*" refers
to tercets as clarified in *SH*, fol. 96v:

> והנה מלת שגיון לדעתי היא כמו ההלצה הג' שעשיתי אני ונעשית אצל
> הנוצרים הרבה מהפואיטי' כי היא מג' השירים וכל טור וטור מעשר תנועות
> וכל זה רמוז במלת שגיון [תהלים ז', 1].

The tercet is a particular pattern of rhyming (*aba, bcb, cdc, ded, efe,* etc.)
commonly used in an epic poem, narrative, or polemical poem. It originated
in Provençal poetry and was adopted by Dante in his *Divine Comedy*. Jewish
poets in Italy adopted this pattern quite early. In 1415 Moses Rieti wrote
Mikdash Me'at (Lesser Temple) in the tercet form imitating Dante's master-
piece. See Pagis, *Change and Tradition*, 329-33.

106. See *SH*, fol. 95v:

> והנה גם אני נתעסקתי בנערותי בשירים ובחכמת המושיקא הלא היא חכמה
> מפוארה מז' החכמות וביארתי תועלתה בס' אביר יעקב בפ' הז' שם ביארתי
> כל עניניה.

107. See Jacob Barukh b. Judah Landau, *Sefer ha-Aggur ha-Shalem*
edited by Moshe Hershler (Jerusalem, 1970).

108. *Sefer ha-Aggur* is the first Hebrew book to carry an
approbationary writ by outstanding rabbis and scholars, a fixture of the
Hebrew book ever since. The Hebrew text of this *haskamah* with an English

translation appears in the *Jewish Encyclopedia* edited by Isidore Singer (New York, 1904), vol. 2, 27; Cf. David W. Amram, *The Makers of Hebrew Books in Italy* (Philadelphia, 1909. Reprint. London: The Holland Press, 1963), 66-8. R. Jacob Landau was a proponent of Kabbalah and incorporated in his legal decisions several Zoharic positions. See Katz, *Halakhah and Kabbalah*, 61. While R. David's support for the publication of this text is understandable, his father's is peculiar, since Judah Messer Leon attempted to curb the spread of Kabbalah.

109. For the primary sources relating the poor status of the Spanish refugees in Naples see Alexander Marx, "The Expulsion of the Jews from Spain Two New Accounts," in his *Studies in Jewish History and Booklore* (New York: The Jewish Theological Seminary, 1944), 84-87; Joseph Hacker, "Some Letters on the Expulsion from Spain" (in Hebrew), in *Studies in the History of Society Presented to Professor Jacob Katz on his Seventy-Fifth Birthday*, edited by Emanuel Etkes and Joseph Salmon (Jerusalem; Magnes Press, 1980), 64-97.

110. On the career of Don Isaac Abravanel at the Aragonese court in Naples see Ben Zion Netanyahu, *Don Isaac Abrabanel: Statesman and Philosopher* (Philadelphia: Jewish Publication Society), 62-71.

111. *'Ein ha-Qore* is extant in two manuscripts: Bodleian MS. Reggio 41, Opp. Add. 108 (= Neubauer 1263) and MS. Parma-Perreau 44. While I consulted both, the citations are taken from the Oxford manuscript.

112. Shulvass already suggested that one views this animosity in the context of the power struggle between the native Italian Jews of Naples and the growing Sephardic population after 1492. See Shulvass, *The Jews in the World of the Renaissance*, 59. A typical example of the derogatory language R. David uses against Abravanel is *EH*, fol. 57r:

אבל זה האחרון אשר הכביד עוז ותעצמות, דון יצחק אברבניל, עם היותו
באין אונים והרבה להתפאר בעצמה, ולרש אין כל, לא תאר לו ולא הדר
בשרשים הפלוסופים, ומתפאר בקטן המפרשים אשר קטנם עבה ממתניו. זה
דרכו כסל לו להשתבח במה שאין בו, כי כל מה שראיתי ממנו בפירוש זה
הספר [מורה נבוכים] הכל הבל ורעות רוח וסכלות בשרשי הרב, לחסרונו
בפלוסופיא בדרושי מעמקיה, ובפרט בפי' זה הסוד אשר רצה להעמיק
במאמ' עטרת זקנים שחבר נגד הרב.

For other such remarks about Isaac Abravanel see fols. 38r; 44v; 61r; 81r.

113. *EH*, fol. 129r.

114. A detailed description of Jewish suffering in the wake of the French invasion into Naples is given by Isaac Abravanel in his introduction to the *Commentary on Deuteronomy*, (Jerusalem: Hoẓaat Sefarim Abravanel, 1979), 3.

115. The responsum is extant in two manuscripts: MS. Montefiore 106, fols. 129v-139r; and MS. Bodleian 834, fols. 55r-66r. Schechter published parts of the texts in his "Notes Sur Messer David Leon," based on the Oxford manuscript. Assaf, apparently unaware of Schechter's earlier discussion, published the same responsum, but used the other extant manuscript. See Simha Assaf, "Responsa and Letters by R. Moses Capsali" (in Hebrew), *Sinai* 5 (1939): 485-6. Recently, Joseph Hacker printed larger sections of this responsum in his "The Jewish Community of Salonika from the Fifteenth to the Sixteenth Centuries: A Chapter in the Social History of the Jews in the Ottoman Empire and their Relations with their Authorities," Ph.D. diss., Hebrew University 1978, Appendix D. I used Hacker's rendering of the original text. In this responsum David b. Judah Messer Leon specifically mentions the difficult circumstances of his departure from Italy:

כי גנב גנבתי מחמדת לבי, ומעשה ידי בזוזי ובזוזי דבזוזי כל ספרי ומעוני
רעיוני שמו פיהם בידיהם ולקחו, ונפשי שכולה וגלמודה בתעודה גולה
וסורה.

Chapter Three

1. On the impact of the Ottoman conquest on Byzantine Jewry see Steven B. Bowman, *The Jews of Byzantium 1204-1453* (University: University of Alabama Press, 1985), 172-95.

2. See Joseph Hacker, "Ottoman Policy toward the Jews and Jewish Attitude toward the Ottomans during the Fifteenth Century," in *Christians and Jews in the Ottoman Empire: The Functioning of Plural Society*, edited by Benjamin Braude and Bernard Lewis (New York: Holmes and Meier, 1982), vol. 1, 117-26.

3. On the legal status of Romanyot Jews in Constantinople see Haim Gerber, *Economic and Social Life of the Jews in the Ottoman Empire in the 16th and 17th Centuries* (in Hebrew) (Jerusalem: The Zalman Shazar Center, 1982), 11-35, esp. 25-7; cf. Rivkah Cohen, *Constantinople-Salonica-Patras: Communal and Supra-Communal Organization of Greek Jewry under the Ottoman Rule (15th-16th Centuries)* (in Hebrew) (Tel Aviv: Tel Aviv University Press, 1984), 38-89.

4. For bibliography on the legal status of non-Muslim subjects of the Muslim state see Mark R. Cohen, "The Jews Under Islam: From the Rise of Islam to Sabbatai Zevi," in *Bibliographical Essays in Medieval Jewish Studies*, edited by Yosef H. Yerushalmi (New York: Anti-Defamation League of B'nai Brith, 1976), 169-229; Bernard Lewis, *The Jews of Islam* (Princeton: Princeton University Press, 1984), 193, n. 1.

5. Until recently scholars of Jewish history in the Ottoman Empire accepted the prevailing notion that the Jewish minority was included in the *millet* system alongside other ethnic and religious minorities. According to this view, a chief rabbi with extensive political, legal, economic and spiritual powers represented Ottoman Jewry at large toward the Muslim administration. Recently, this view has been challenged and shown to be an anachronistic interpretation of the available sources by 19th century Jewish historians. See Benjamin Braude, "Foundation Myths of the Millet System," in *Christians and Jews*, 69-88. The recent studies of Hacker further support Braude's position. See Joseph Hacker "Jewish Autonomy in the Ottoman Empire: Its Scope and Limits," in *Transition and Change in Modern Jewish History: Essays Presented in Honor of Shmuel Ettinger* (Jerusalem: The Historical Society of Israel and The Zalman Shazar Center, 1987), 349-88.

6. See Joseph Hacker, "The Institution of the Chief Rabbinate in Constantinople in the Fifteenth and Sixteenth Centuries" (in Hebrew), *Zion* 49 (1984): 225-63, and consult the extensive literature referred to in 22, n. 1, and 227, nn. 6-10.

7. Ottoman Jewry during the fifteenth and sixteenth centuries has been a subject of renewed scholarly interest in the last three decades. My short discussion of Ottoman Jewry at the turn of the sixteenth century is intended merely to provide the necessary background for the career of David ben Judah Messer Leon. For general surveys see Hayim Z. Hirschberg, "The Oriental Jewish Communities," in *Religion in the Middle East* edited by Arthur J. Arberry (Cambridge, 1969), vol. 1, 146-57; Jacob Barnai, "The Jews in the Ottoman Empire" (in Hebrew), in *History of the Jews in the Islamic Countries*, edited by Yosef Tobi, Jacob Barnai and Shalom Bar Asher (Jerusalem: The Zalman Shazar Center, 1981), 73-118; Mark A. Epstein, *The Ottoman Jewish Communities and Their Role in the Fifteenth and Sixteenth Centuries*. Islam Kundlische Unterschuungen, vol. 56 (Freiburg: K. Schwarz, 1980); Gerber, *Economic and Social Life*, 9-77; Lewis, *The Jews of Islam*, 107-44, and the notes in pp. 209-16; Aryeh Shmuelevitz, *The Jews of the Ottoman Empire in the Late Fifteenth and the Sixteenth Centuries: Administrative, Economic, Legal and Social Relations as Reflected in the Responsa* (Leiden: E.J. Brill, 1984).

8. Elijah Capsali in particular interpreted the activities of the Muslim ruler in the categories of traditional Jewish Messianism. See *Seder Eliyahu Zuta* 1: 135; and Charles Berlin, "A Sixteenth Century Hebrew Chronicle of the Ottoman Empire: the *Seder Eliyahu Zuta* of Elijah Capsali and its Message," in *Studies in Jewish Bibliography and Booklore*, 27-31, 34-8.

9. See Mark A. Epstein, "The Leadership of Ottoman Jews in Fifteenth and Sixteenth Centuries," in *Christians and Jews* 1: 105, n. 15.

10. For details on the economic activities of Sephardic immigrants in

the Ottoman Empire see Gerber, *Economic and Social Life*, 61-77; idem, "Initiative and Commerce in the Economic Activity of the Jews in the Ottoman Empire during the Sixteenth and Seventeenth Centuries" (in Hebrew) *Zion* 43 (1978): 38-67. On the textile industry in the Ottoman Empire see Shmuel Avitsur, "The Woolen Industry in Salonica" (in Hebrew), *Sefunot* 12 (= *Book of Greek Jewry* 2) (1971-1978): 147-68.

11. For bibliographical information on Hebrew printing presses in the Ottoman Empire consult the studies cited in Joseph Hacker, "The Intellectual Activity of the Jews of the Ottoman Empire during the Sixteenth and Seventeenth Centuries," in *Jewish Thought in the Seventeenth Century*, edited by Isadore Twersky and Bernard Septimus (Cambridge: Harvard University Press, 1987), 102-3, n. 13.

12. On Jewish physicians in the personal service of Ottoman rulers see Uriel Heyd, "Moses Hamon Chief Physician to Sultan Suleyman the Magnificent," *Oriens* 15 (1963): 152-70; Bernard Lewis, "The Privileges Granted by Mehmed II to His Physician," *BSOAS* 14 (1952): 551-63.

13. To date there are no systematic studies of Hispano-Jewish aristocracy in the Ottoman Empire, only studies about individuals or families. In addition to the studies mentioned in the previous notes consult Meir Benayahu, "The House of Abravanel in Saloniki," *Sefunot* 12 (= *The Book of Greek Jewry* 2) (1971-1978): 9-29; idem, "Moshe Benvenest Court Physician and Rabbi Yehudah Zarko's Poem on His Exile to Rhodes" (in Hebrew), ibid. 123-44; Epstein, "The Leadership of the Ottoman Jews," 101-26; Cecil B. Roth, *The House of Nasi: The Duke of Naxos* (Philadelphia: The Jewish Publication Society, 1930. Reprint. New York: Schocken, 1975; Mina Rosen, "The Activities of Influential Jews at the Sultan's Court in Istanbul in Favor of the Jewish Community in Jerusalem in the Seventeenth Century" (in Hebrew), *Michael* 7 (1982): 394-430.

14. On the Sephardic aristocratic self-perception see Hayim H. Ben Sasson, "The Generation of Spanish Exiles on Itself" (in Hebrew), *Zion* 26 (1961): 23-34. Ben Sasson's views were further documented and expanded by Hacker. See Joseph Hacker, "The Intellectual Activity," 106-7.

15. Hacker, "Intellectual Activity," 111-113.

16. See Uriel Heyd, "The Jewish Communities of Istanbul in the Seventeenth Century," *Oriens* 4 (1953): 294-314. Heyd was the first to note that the fragmentation of Ottoman Jewry corresponded to legal and administrative categories of the Muslim state. For a recent summary see Lewis, *The Jews of Islam*, 120-23.

17. On Jewish taxation in the Ottoman Empire see Gerber, *Economic and Social Life*, 36-60; Azriel Shohat, "Taxation and Its Administration" (in Hebrew), *Sefunot* 11 (= *The Book of Greek Jewry* 1) (1971-1978): 301-39.

18. For a detailed description of these clashes see Cohen, *Constantinople-Patras-Salonica*, 13-51.

19. On the history of the Karaite community in Byzantine Constantinople see Zvi Ankori, *Karaites in Byzantium: The Formative Years, 970-1100* (New York: Columbia University Press, 1959), 137-48. On Karaite status under Ottoman rule see Abraham Danon, "The Karaites in European Turkey," *JQR* 15 (1924-25): 285-360, esp. 298-322. On the relationship between the Karaites and the Romanyots see also Bowman, *The Jews of Byzantium*, 106-15. In *Magen David* R. David notes the peaceful coexistence between Karaites and Romanyots in Constantinople and voices his opinion that for Halakhic purposes the Karaites should not be likened to the *minim* (heretics) but rather to the *annusim* (the Marranos). R. David himself had personal contacts with the Karaite philosopher Caleb Apandopolo, to whom he sold a copy of Gersonides' *Milhamot Adonai (The Wars of the Lord)* on "Monday the 11th of Ab [5]258," (i.e., 1498). See David, "New Information" cited in Chapter Two, n. 100.

20. See Hacker, "The Institution of the Chief Rabbinate," 251-254.

21. R. David's defense of rabbinic ordination against the attacks of the Sephardic scholars is discussed below in this chapter.

22. See *MD*, fol. 96r:

מי יתן החרש יחריש הרב עם תפארת רבנותו והקפתו בתלמוד, כי להיות
גם אני נוהג מנהגם לקחת פרס אחר צרות הגרוש, צריך שאוכיח היותו בלתי
עובר בדברי התלמוד ח"ו, ובלתי טועה במאמרים המפורסמים שהביא הרב
בגודל לבב, ולשונו כאש אוכלת להכות החכמים בעברה, מפני שעזרו המזל
להיות תמיד קרוב למלכות ועשיר, ולא הוצרך ליטול פרס. לכן שאגה לו
כלביא, ירדוף ישיג ויאכל טרף, ישכיר חציו מדם החכמים העניים האביונים,
כי אשר כן לא יעשה, כי גם כי למדנו בכל החכמות וגם ברפואות, לא נחשבה
בכאן הרפואה כמו בארצות הגויים והוכרחנו להתפרנס בכבוד.

That R. David was a physician is not surprising, given that his father, Judah Messer Leon, was a highly respected physician with ties to the University of Padua. R. David probably studied medicine under his father, and perhaps even at the University of Padua, but no official record of his medical degree is extant today.

23. Shimon ben Ẓemah Duran, *Sefer Tashbeẓ* (= *Tehuvot Shimon ben Ẓemah*) (Amsterdam, 1738-41), no. 147.

24. See n. 22 above.

25. *MD*, fols. 96r-108v.

26. *MD*, fol. 97v:

דבר זה מפורש הרבה בתלמוד, שהצבור חייבים להושיב בראש לחכמיהם,
כדי לפרנסם דרך כבוד, ודבר זה מוטל על פרנסיהם ומנהיגיהם להתעסק
בעיניניהם עם הצבור, ולא יוכל אדם לחלוק בדבר זה כלל, ואפי׳ התלמידים
העוסקים בתורה כל ימיהם, אע״פ שאינם ראשי ישיבות חייבים הצבור
לפרנסם דרך כבוד.

R. David goes even further to demand tax exemption for scholars:

שהצבור חייבים לפטור אותם מכל מסים ותשחורות וארנוניות, והמחייבו
בזה עובר על התורה על הנביאים ועל הכתובים.

27. On the various approaches to the problem of tax exemption to
scholars see Israel Ta-Shema, "On the Exemption of Scholars from Taxes
during the Middle Ages" (in Hebrew), in *Studies in Rabbinic Literature, Bible
and Jewish History Dedicated to Professor Ezra Zion Melamed* (Ramat Gan,
Bar Ilan University, 1972), 312-22; Joseph Hacker, "The Payment of Djizya
by Scholars in Palestine in the Sixteenth Century" (in Hebrew), *Shalem* 4
(1978): 63-117 esp. 73-81, 88-90; Baron, *The Jewish Community* 2:276-8,
3:193-4; idem, *SRH* 12:226-7.

28. Direct references to the opposition to R. David's preaching are in
fol. 89v, where R. David discusses rabbinic opposition to the art of rhetoric:

וידעתי כי ימאנוה הרבה רבנים וחכמים מבני עמנו שירחיבו פה יאריכו לשון
ירבו ידברו עתק נגדי כחק כמנהגם לכן אחקור בכאן חקירה נכבדת
להשתיקם ולשים מחסום בפיהם.

Cf. R. David's comment in fol. 90r concerning his use of non-Jewish sources
in sermons:

כשיראו שהדורש יזכיר שם חכם נוצרי או ישמעלי יאמרו שהוא כופר וכ״ש
כשמזכרין מליץ או פואיטה ליפות העניינים ... אז יקמו עליו ... יעלילו עליו
עלילות דברים;

and another general comment in fol. 94r:

כי ברוב צרותי ומחשבותי וחסרון ממוני לא אנוח ולא אשקוט בעיון
החכמות עד שישקיף וירא ה׳ משמים וא״כ אין לאלה האנשים לדבר עתק
נגד המבקשים החכמות.

29. This reconstruction is based on the opening paragraph of the text.
SH, fol. 89v:

הנה מאז נסעתי מארץ הוללה, ובדד ישבתי מחוץ למחנה, לרעות בגנים
ללקוט שושנים, ובהיותי כי פני מעסקי העולם, עם כי נפשי שוממה, כל היום
דוה, עד דוד הגדיל, ביגונות ומחשבות משתנות, הכוני פצעוני ילידי הזמן,
הלמוני בל ידעתי, צפו על מר הצרות על ראשי, לולי ה׳ שהה לי, לחמלתו לו עלי,
ה׳ השפיע משפע חכמתו ורוח נדיבותו, ויסתורני, ויסתורני, טהרני לעשות חבורים רבים
אחר נסיעתי, ועשיתי חקירות חקירות גדולות, בין בתורה, בין בפלוסופיא, גם חרוזים
רבים בלשון עברי ובלשון נוצרי, בעתות הפנאי.

For an English translation of this passage see Rabinowitz, "A Rectification of the Date," 406. We know that R. David indeed stayed at home from his own comment concerning the next controversy in which he was involved. In the responsum he issued in support of Capsali he says:

> They implored me to hurry, following the order of the above mentioned rabbi [i.e., Moses Capsali], and pronounce my opinion against my will, since it is not my habit to intervene in communal affairs, but rather I sit at home and occupy myself with my work.

See Hacker, "The Jewish Community," Appendix D, 32; Assaf, "Responsa," 46. I believe that David was forced into seclusion and did not choose it freely.

30. Adolph Neubauer, "Petrarque a Avignon," *REJ* 10 (1885): 94-97.

31. See Shulvass, *The Jews in the World of the Renaissance*. 231; Roth, *The Jews in the Renaissance*, 312; Pagis, *Change and Tradition*, 274.

32. See Moritz Steinschneider, "Zur Frauenliteratur," *Israelitische Letterbode* 12 (1884-85): 56-62. On this literary genre in medieval Hebrew literature see also A. B. Rhine, "The Secular Poetry of Italy," *JQR* n.s. 1 (1910-11): 352-54; David Kaufmann, "Leone De Sommi Portaleone 1527-92)," *JQR* o.s. 10 (1898): 446-49; Pagis, *Change and Tradition*, 279-82; Jefim Schirmann ed., *The Comedy of Betrothal by Yehuda Sommo 1527-92* (in Hebrew), 2d. ed. (Jerusalem: Tarshish, 1965), 121-25; Sandra de Benedetti-Stow, "Due poesie bilingui inedite contro le donne de Semuel da Castiglione (1553)," *Italia* 2 (1980) 7-27; Norman Roth, "The 'Wiles of Women' Motif in the Medieval Hebrew Literature of Spain," *Hebrew Annual Review* 2 (1978): 145-65; Tova Rosen, "On Tongues Being Bound and Let Loose: Women in Medieval Hebrew Literature," *Prooftexts* 8 no. 1 (1988): 67-87; Talya Fishman, "A Medieval Parody of Misogyny: Judah ibn Shabbetai's 'Minhat Yehuda Sone ha-Nashim'," ibid. 89-111.

33. Shulvass, *The Jews in the World of the Renaissance*, 231; Roth, *The Jews in the Renaissance*, 312-14; Pagis, *Change and Tradition*, 274.

34. *SH*, fol. 1r:

הנה מהרה זכרתיך שרתי בנשים, לקיים את מצותך שצויתני, מאז הייתי שם,
לפרש כל המעשים משבח הנשים, שהבאתי בהלצה הג׳ שחברתי, כי הבתין[!]
שם בקצור. והואלתי לעשות בקשתך, כי אם רבות בנות עשו חיל בחשיבות
וטוב טעם ודעת, את עלית על כלנה, כי שרית עם אלים, לכן שרה ממך,
ועתה אמלא את שאלתך למען תברכני נפשי בגללך.

35. On patronage in Renaissance Italy see Chapter One, n. 15. On female learning and patronage in Renaissance Italy see Werner L. Gunersheimer, "Women Learning and Power: Eleonora of Aragon and the

Court of Ferrara," in *Beyond Their Sex: Learned Women of the European Past*, edited by Patricia Labalme (New York: New York University Press, 1980) 43-65; Margaret L. King, "Book-Lined Cells: Women and Humanism in the Early Italian Renaissance," ibid. 66-90; idem, "Thwarted Ambitions: Six Learned Women of the Italian Renaissance," *Soundings* 59 (1976): 280-304; Stanley Chojnacki, "Patrician Women in Early Renaissance Venice," *Studies in the Renaissance* 21 (1974): 176-204; Lauro Martines, "A Way of Looking at Women in Renaissance Florence," *JMRS* 4 no. 1 (1974): 15-28.

36. *SH*, fol. 93v:

איני שואל ממך שתתן לי ממון בעבור הממון עצמו, כי הוא דבר כלה ונפסד
מצד עצמו ... אבל הסבה, שאני שואל ממך מעט ממון ודי מחסורי, הוא מפני
שיהיה סבה, אלא תמיד יעמידני בביתך, ולא אהיה צריך לבקש טורפי, כי
בחרתי להסתופף בבית אלהי, יותר מהיות עם הרשעים בחברתם, ולבקש
להרויח ממון עמהם בדרך רוב העולם.

The yearning for tranquility and the exasperation of human worldly affairs are reiterated throughout the text, intertwined with envy of the rich who can afford to pursue a life of scholarship if they so wish. Cf. *SH*, fol. 92v:

לא הייתי חפץ בממון אלא בעבור זה הטעם, כי רואה אני שמי שאין לו
ממון, העולם נתן בלבו, והולך מרע אל רע, ועוזב העיון והתלמוד, וכל פחדי
מזה הענין פן אצטרך ללכת אנה ואנה, והוא סבה לשכחת התלמוד והחכמה.

37. The poem by Abraham Sarteano was published by Schirmann, *Mivhar ha-Shirah ha'Ivrit be-Italya* (Berlin: Schocken, 1934), 210-15. The responses by Avigdor of Fano and Benjamin de Genazzano in favor of women were published by Neubauer, "Zur Frauenliteratur," *Israelitische Letterbode* 10 (1880-81): 101-3, 104-5. The anonymous rebuttal to this defense was published by Neubauer in *Israelitische Letterbode* 11 (1882): 62-5. Finally, David b. Samuel of Rossena attempted to mediate the dispute by rebuking all participants for discussing such a delicate matter.

38. The identification of the addressee with the biblical Woman of Valor is hinted in the following phrase on fol. 89v: "יען כי נשאל דוד מאשת חיל"
"משכלת ויראת ה' and again in the same fol.: "הסכמתי לפרש הפרשה האחרונה"
"שבסוף ספר משלי שהתחלתה אשת חיל מי ימצא שנעשה על שבחי האשה המשכלת.

39. *SH*, fol. 121r: כי היא חמדת יעקב והוא נרמז במלת חיל חמדת יעקב
Cf. ibid, fol. 111v: לאברה ותזכה לבנים עוסקים בתורה ובמצוות .והנה לשמחה
ראיתי להביא שבחיה הנרמזי' בזה הפסוק לדעתי והיא אשת חיל כי היא חיל בדת
חכמה יפה לברה[!]. Unfortunately, we cannot identify this Laura with a person known to us from other historical sources. The most likely candidate is Laura the wife of Samuel ben Yehiel of Pisa and mother of Yehiel Nissim of Pisa. We should remember that Abigdor of Fano's poem in favor of women was composed for Hanna, the daughter of Yehiel ben Isaac of Pisa, and wife of

Eleazar of Voltera. If these interpretations are correct, then the two ladies who inspired the defense of women in the literary debate of 1490s were sisters-in-law, and 'Jacob' cannot refer to the husband of either; it must then refer to the people of Israel.

40. On the status of rhetoric in Renaissance Italy see Jerrold Seigel, *Rhetoric and Philosophy in Renaissance Humanism: The Union of Eloquence and Wisdom, Petrarch to Valla* (Princeton: Princeton University Press: 1968); George A. Kennedy, *Classical Rhetoric and Its Christian and Secular Traditions from Ancient to Modern Times* (Chapel Hill: The University of North Carolina Press, 1980), 195-219, and the articles cited in Chapter One, n. 94.

41. Ovid's *Ars Amatoria* is referred to in fol. 110v, and Virgil's *Eclogues* and the *Aeneid* are mentioned in fol. 113v.

42. On R. Judah Messer Leon's conception of rhetoric and its relation to other sciences see Chapter One above.

43. *SH*, fol. 89v:

אם העסק והעיון בספרי הטבע ובספרי ההלצה הנק׳ רטוריקה ובספרי
החרוזים והפואיסיה מהאנשים שלא מבני ישראל המה הוא דבר נאה
ומתקבל לרבנים ולחכמים.

44. *SH*, fol. 89v:

אין לתמוה אם רוב האנשים מבזים החכמות שאינם בקיאים בהם ... כמו
שתמצא לקצת דורשי בני עמנו, שלא הגיעו למעלת הדרש ועיניניו, הנה
כשרואין אדם אחר שדורש באופן נאות ומהודר, אז אומרי׳ שהיא מלאכת
הנערים, אבל בזמן שהם דורשים אז ישכחו אותו הדרש...
שכיון שהם מגנים דרשות האחרים הנכונים על צד הקנאה.

The specific reference to R. David's public preaching has led us to assume that he held a public office prior to his forced seclusion. In the above cited passages, it appears that R. David's preaching standards and aesthetic conventions differed from his opponents', from which we may infer that other rabbis and religious functionaries were his adversaries.

45. *SH*, fol. 91v:

אמ׳ העצל [משלי, כ״ב, 13] שמתעצל מלמוד החכמות, לפוחדו פן יסירוהו
מדרך הנכונה, לחולשת שכלו, הנה איני רוצה ללמוד פלוסופיא, כי שם אני
מוצא האר, והוא ארסטו, שכפר בחדוש העולם, ומאריך בזה בחריפות,
ולא ידע כי לו לקבל האמת ממי שאמרו, יהיה מי שיהיה, ואם יש לו יראת
ה׳, לא יפחד פן יסרהו מהיסוד האמתי.

46. *SH*, fol. 89v:

האוילים [משלי א, 7] הם המבזים לחולשת שכלם, שאינו יכול להיות מקיף

בכל החכמות, ואינם מודים שזהו לחסרונם, אלא תולין החסרון בזאת
החכמה ואומרים כי אין לחוש לאותה חכמה מפני שכלה הבל הבלים.

47. *SH*, fol. 101r:

ועתה נקרא לרבנים השונאים האיש שהוא כולל.

48. *SH*, 91v:

האמנם מניעת האנשים מלמוד החכמות הוא אצלי לב׳ סבות הא׳ מצד
עכירות השכל כי לא כל אדם זוכה לשכל זך ובהיר והוא התנאי העיקרי
בלמוד החכמות כלם ... ג״כ בזכות האויר ולכן אין לו לעמוד במקומות
העכורים שיעכרו שכלו יותר ... ולזה תמצא ששם בא״י היו רוב חכמי העיון.

The connection between intellectual cognition and geophysical conditions is
not R. David's innovation, but an adaptation of the theories of Judah Halevi.
On R. David's indebtedness to Halevi see Hava Tirosh-Rothschild, "The
Influence of Judah Halevi on the Thought of David Messer Leon" (in
Hebrew), *Proceedings of the Eighth World Congress of Jewish Studies* (Jerusa-
lem: World Union of Jewish Studies, 1982), vol. 3, 79-84.

49. *SH*, fol. 92r: וזה א׳ מהסבות שפסקה הנבואה ממנו לרוב עכירות שכלנו
בסבת הצרות המתרגשות עלינו מכל האומות בכל יום ויום ואנו עשוקים ורצוצים ואין
לאל ידנו.

50. On R. David's conception of the Torah as both Divine Wisdom
and the blueprint of creation see Chapter Eight below and Hava Tirosh-
Rothschild, "The Concept of Torah in the Works of David Messer Leon" (in
Hebrew), *JSJT* (1982): 94-117. The argument that the Torah comprises of
all knowledge (divine and human) was also advocated by David's contemporary, Abraham Farissol:

> ...and also at our wondrous station at Mt. Sinai He crowned us
> in the perfect Torah — including all the natural, speculative,
> divine, legal and political wisdom from which all the world
> drank.

Excerpted in Ruderman, *The World of a Renaissance Jew*, 76-77. On this
popular notion among medieval Jewish philosophers see Roth, "On the Theft
of Philosophy," cited Chapter Two, n. 94.

51. See Rabinowitz, *Honeycomb's Flow*, 142-46.

52. *SH*, fol. 94v: שתעשה יסוד בתורה כי אז כיון שביסודה יהיה קיים אז תוכל
לקרות בשאר החכמות.

53. *SH*, fol. 98r. Cf. *SH*, fol. 97v:

כי אחר שאני בקי בחכמת ההלצה, אני לוקח משפטי פרק וענייני תורתך
ואני מפרש אותם, ואני מפאר אותם בשפתי, ... ענייני התורה כשהן מפורשים
בלשון נאה, הם נשמעים יותר בשמחה, ומקובלות יותר, וכן ההלצה
והפואישיה צריכין הרבה לדורש מזה הצד.

54. See James J. Murphy, *Rhetoric in the Middle Ages: A History of Rhetorical Theory from St. Augustine to the Renaissance* (Berkeley: University of California Press, 1974), 57-64; Gerhard L. Ellsperman, *The Attitude of the Early Christian Latin Writers toward Pagan Literature and Learning*, Catholic University of America Patristic Studies, vol. 82 (Washington DC, 1949).

55. *SH*, fol. 105r:

והנה אגושטי' ג"כ בס' הב' מהלמוד הנוצרי וז"ל אם ימצאו דבר הפלוסו'
שיהיו מוכנים לאמונת ה' הנה לא בלבד נירא מלהביא אותם אבל ג"כ נקח
ראיה מהם על שלמות התורה.

56. *SH*, ibid.:

ולסיוע זה אנו רואים מ"ש לאטאנציו בס' הב' מהנחת האלהיות וז"ל הנה
זאת היא א' הסבות שהתורה הקדושה לא היתה נחשבת בעיני החכמי'
והמשכילי' שהם בעולם ולא נתנו בה שום אמונה מצד שאזניהם לא תשמענה
אלא המא' ההלציי בלשון מכובד ונעלה מה שאין זה בקצת הנביאים
ובתורה כי הם בלשון פשוט ונגלה ולזאת יחשבו בעיניהם כדברים קלים
שחושבים שאין דבר יותר נכבד מהערבות.

57. *SH*, fol. 94v:

שהש' תכן אותו משכל זך ובהיר וזכירה טובה ומרצון טוב ומענוה גדולה עד
שילמד מכל אדם וכל חכמה א"ז שיהיה כאילו תאמר שלומד מזה חכמה א'
ומזה אחרת ואז הוא יהיה כולל לכולן וכן עשה שלמה ולכן היה מקיף בכל
החכמות.

The view that King Solomon embodied the Renaissance ideal of *homo universalis* was elaborated most notably by Yohanan Alemanno in the introduction to his commentary on the Song of Songs. Titled *Shir ha-Ma'alot li-Shlomo, (The Song of Solomon's Ascents)* it was written between 1488 and 1492 in Florence, and might have been known to R. David, since he resided in Florence in 1490, probably at the da Pisa household where Alemanno was a scholar-in-residence. For a critical edition of Alemanno's text see Lesley, *"The Song of Solomon's Ascents',"* 109-29 English translation, 409-50 Hebrew text. Isaac Abravanel also viewed King Solomon as a Jewish embodiment of the Renaissance ideal of the "universal man." See Isaac Abravanel, *Commentary on I Kings: 3*. R. David's discussion is extremely close to the wording of Abravanel.

The influence of Alemanno on the views of R. David ben Judah is further supported by reference in *Magen David* (fol. 176r) to the theurgical practice of deriving spirituality from the supernal realms *(horadat ruhaniyyut)*. While R. David discusses this notion in reference to Judah Halevi's *Kuzari*, it is very likely that Alemanno was his immediate source. For a phenomenological analysis of this practice among Jewish mystics including Alemanno see Moshe Idel, *Kabbalah: New Perspectives* (New Haven: Yale University

Press, 1988), 166-170. On the meaning of this practice in Judah Halevi's *Kuzari* see Shlomo Pines, "On the Term 'Ruhaniyyot' and Its Origin and on Judah Halevi's Doctrine" (in Hebrew), *Tarbiz* 57 (1989): 511-540, esp. 524-30.

58. *SH*, fol. 95r:

ולכן מצינו ששלמה היה בקי בכל החכמות וידע כל טבעי העניינים הנכללים
בחכמת הטבע שנא׳ [מלכים א׳ ה׳ 13] וידבר על העצים ועל האבנים מהארז
ועד האזוב וכו׳ ר״ל שדבר על טבעי העניייני׳ והעשבי׳ וסגולותיה׳ לפי מה
שכתבו חכמי המחקר גם אפי׳ במשלי׳ שנר׳ דברים של הבל כמו שאמר
[מלכים א׳ ה׳, 21] ג׳ אלפים משל גם במלאכת השיר והפואישיה היה בקי
כמו שאמר [שם] ויהיו שיריו אלף שמדבר בחרוזים והשירים שקולים א״כ
מה איסור יש בדבר.

59. *SH*, fol. 103r; R. David interprets the Aggadah in *Babylonian Talmud, 'Abodah Zarah* 11a (also cited in *Berakhot* 57b) about Antoninus and Rabbi, "whose table never lacked radish, lettuce or cucumber either in summer or winter," to signify Rabbi's proficiency in medicine.

60. R. David composed a book on music theory, which may explain his eagerness to find talmudic precedents to the study of music. See *SH*, fol. 95v, cited in Ch. 2 n. 106.
Some evidence of David's knowledge of music is extant in *Shevah ha-Nashim* in a long discussion of vocal techniques (fol. 95v-96r). In Renaissance Italy the gulf between musical theory and practice was narrowed as theorists, composers, performers, connoisseurs, critics, and public experienced intimate contacts. See Edward E. Lowinsky, "Music of the Renaissance as Viewed by Renaissance Musicians," in *The Renaissance Image of Man and the World*, edited by Bernard O'Kelly (Columbus: Ohio University Press, 1966), 29-177. It appears that this involvement in music did not find favor in the eyes of R. David's opponents in Constantinople. R. David finds support for rabbinic interest in music in the talmudic description of the Water-Drawing Festival (*Babylonian Talmud, Sukkah* 53a, 53b). See *SH*, fol. 103r. R. David's portrayal of Yohanan ben Zakkai is based on *Babylonian Talmud, Sukkah* 28a, where the Tanna is said not

> ...to leave [unstudied] Scripture, Mishnah, Gemara, Halakhah, Aggada, details of Torah, details of the Scribes, inferences a minori ad majorum, analogies, calenderical computations, gematriot, the speech of ministering angels, the speech of spirits and the speech of palm trees, parables and fox fables, great matters and small matters.

David interprets "speech" *(sihah)* to mean rhetorical expression and asserts from it that Yohanan ben Zakkai is said to have been versed in rhetoric and poetry.

61. R. David expresses special joy for finding support for the study of rhetoric and poetry in the Palestinian Talmud. To him, this was the most conclusive proof for the legitimacy of these disciplines. Could we infer from this that his opponents came from Ashkenazic circles who viewed the Palestinian Talmud as more stringent? See *SH*, fol. 104r:

ואני כ"כ שמחתי בו [במאמר מירושלמי] בעת שמצאתיו יותר ממוצאי שלל
רב כי בזה המא' מאין ס[פק] אוכל להסיר מעלי כל תלונות שונאי ההלצה
והפואיסי'.

62. *SH*, fol. 98v; cf. Aristotle, *Rhetoric* I, 1, 1355a; II, 19, 1391b.

63. *SH*, fol. 99r.

64. Ovid's *Metamorphoses* was one of the most popular texts in fifteenth century Italy. By the 1490s new commentaries were written to it. For example, Raffaelo Regio, the professor of rhetoric in Padua, published his commentary in 1493 in Venice. A new literary genre of Ovidian commentaries developed subsequently. Interestingly, the text is cited by another sixteenth century Jewish scholar in the Ottoman Empire, R. Solomon le-Bet Halevi, in his *Lehem Shlomo*. R. Solomon notes a similarity between Midrash Genesis Rabbah and Ovid's *Metamorphoses* which he explains by citing the writings of Plato as a common source for both. See Hacker, "The Intellectual Activity," 125.

65. *SH*, fol. 99r:

שכל ענייני הס' ההוא [ספר ההשתנות] הן מאלו ההמצאות עם שזה
ההשתנות והגלגול אין כ"כ רחוק כי גם המקובלים יאמינו גלגול הנפשות
מאדם לב"ח לפי עונש העוונות.

On the doctrine of metempsychosis in the Kabbalah see, Gershom Scholem, *Von der Mystischen Gestalt der Gottheit* (Zurich: Rhein Verlag, 1962), 203-5; idem, *Kabbalah* (Jerusalem: Keter, 1974), 344-50; idem, *Elements of the Kabbalah and Its Symbolism* (in Hebrew), translated by Joseph Ben Shlomo (Jerusalem: Mosad Bialik), 308-80. For a discussion of other contemporary attempts to use the theory of metempsychosis to legitimize Jewish interest in non-Jewish literature see Idel, "Kabbalah and Ancient Philosophy," 86.

66. See Idel, "The Magical and Neoplatonic Interpretations," cited above; Jean Seznec, *The Survival of the Pagan Gods: The Mythological Tradition and Its Place in Renaissance Humanism and Art*, translated by Barbara F. Sessions, 2d. ed. (Princeton: Princeton University Press, 1972), 84-181; Daniel P. Walker, *Spiritual and Demonic Magic from Ficino to Campanella* (London: The Warburg Institute, 1958).

67. *SH*, fol. 100v:

שהשיחה נאמרת על הדבור שאין בו תועלת מצד עצמו, אבל נותן תענוג
לשומע, לא שיהיה דבור אמתי, ובעבור היות הפואשי׳ רובה כוזבת מצד
עצמה כמו שאמרנו, אבל נותנת תענוג מצד הלשון והשיר.

68. *SH*, fol. 104r:

כי הקריאה והעסק באותם הספרי׳ אשר יהיה בב׳ פנים, אם שיקרא כדי
לדעת דעותיהם הנפס׳, שלא היו מאמי׳ בדת, וכדי שנוכל להכחישם,
וההעמידה על הפסד הסברות במושג דעתם הוא הבל, כמ״ש אבוחמד
בתחלת ס׳ הכוונות, או שיעסוק בהם מפני שאמרו דברי׳ מדיניי׳ טובי׳ וכמה
לשונו׳ במדות נכבדות, כדי שנוכל להוכיח לבני עמנו שהם עם סגולה
בדבריהם הטובי׳, או שיעסוק בהם כדי לקחת איזה תועלת רב או מעט, אם
בלשון הנכבד אם במשלי׳ וחידות.

69. *SH*, fols. 105r-109r.

70. See Guido A. Guarino ed. and trans., *Concerning Famous Women by Giovanni Boccaccio* (New Brunswick: Rutgers University Press, 1974).

71. Compare the story of Thamyris (queen of Scythia) as retold by David in *SH*, fol. 115r, with Boccaccio's *Concerning Famous Women*, 104-6. This is the most elaborate example that shows R. David's indebtedness to Boccaccio. R. David mentioned other famous women in passing — for example, Camila (queen of the Volscians), Panthesilea (queen of the Amazons), and the Roman lady Paulina, assuming that his reader had a familiarity with this literature. R. David could have known the story of Paulina not only from Boccaccio's anthology, but also from the *Josippon*. See David Flusser ed., *Sefer Josippon* (Jerusalem, 1978-81), vol. 1, 267-71.

72. A complete list of the classical sources utilized by Boccaccio is provided in Guarino, *Concerning Famous Women*, 253-57.

73. See Conor Fahy, "Three Early Renaissance Treatises on Women," *Italian Studies* 2 (1956): 30-55; Constance Jordan, "Feminism and the Humanists: The Case of Sir Thomas Elyot's *Defense of Good Women*," in *Rewriting the Renaissance: The Discourses of Sexual Difference in Early Modern Europe*, edited by Margaret W. Ferguson, Maureen Quilligan, Nancy J. Vickers (Chicago: University of Chicago Press, 1986), 242-45.

75. See Lesley, "Hebrew Humanism in Italy," 163-67.

75. *SH*, fols. 108r, 108v.

76. *SH*, ibid.

77. *SH*, fol. 111r:

לכן אביא בכאן הלצה החשובה שהבתי[!] ראשונה בהלצתי בספורי
המליצים, והיא לאברה הנכבדת, והנה האוהב אותה שהנחתי שם היה

פרנסישקו פיטראקא, הפואיטא הגדול, שלרוב חשיבותה ונועם מדותיה כמו
שנסםר עשה ס׳ א׳ בעדה, וחלק אותו לו׳ חלקים, ... ולשונו הוא נכבד ומעלה
מאד, יותר מכל הספרי׳ שחוברו בפואיסיה בלשון לעז, עד שלרוב נעימותו
ייטב בעיני מאד, ונעשיתי בקי בו הרבה, עד שכמעט אני יודע אותו ע״פ כולו,
וכ״ז נעשה בעבור לאברה הנכבדת. גם עשה בעבורה הרבה חרוזי׳ הנק׳
שוניטי׳ אצלם, טובים מאד, גם אני עשיתי מהן בכאן הרבה בלשון מפואר
ומהודר, שאם היית שומעם היו יקרים בעיניך מאד.

David's praise is reserved to Petrarch's *Trionfi (Triumphs)*, written in Italian.
See Ernest H. Wilkins ed. and trans., *The Triumphs of Petrarch* (Chicago: Chicago University Press, 1962).

78. *SH*, fol. 111v.

79. Petrarch's *De Vita Solitaria* (referred to as *Sefer Haye ha-'Iyyun*)
and *De Remediis Utriusque Fortunae* (referred to as *Sefer Tiqqun
ha-Mazzalot*) are cited in *SH*, fol. 111v.

80. Consult *SH*, fols. 111r-111v. A typical statement is expressed in
the following paragraph:

ולכ״א מפרשי ס׳ הפטריאק׳, שהאהובה לא היתה מאד ארצית, אלא קצתם
יאמרו שהאהובה היתה החסידות, וקצתם יאמרו ההכנעה, וקצתם א׳
החכמה, וקצתם אמ׳ הפואישי׳, זהו דעת שאר המפ׳ בזה המקום, והנה אנכי
יען כתבתי בהלצה ההיא, וזאת האהובה היתה לאברה, אצטרך בהכרח
לקיים דעתי, ולכן ארחיב בכל דרכיו הפטריאק׳ שהם בזכרוני, ואוכיח ממך
דבריו בהכרח, שזאת האהובה היתה אשה ארצית, ואח״כ אוכיח שהיתה
לאברה ואודיעך איך היתה אהבתה עמו.

81. *SH*, fols. 109v-110r:

כמה נבהלתי מן כספי שפ׳ כל הפסו׳ ממשלי מעניני ההגיון וכאלה הסברו׳
הזרות תמצא למפרשי׳ וכל ראייתם של אלו המפרשים ס׳ משלי בדרך נסתר
אינה אלא בעבור מלת משלה מורה על משל א״כ יש בו ענין נסתר שהוא
הנמשל האמיתי.

David's novel approach to Proverbs stands in stark relief to the commentaries of his Italian predecessors Jacob Anatoli and the cousins 'Immanuel of
Rome and Judah of Rome. These late medieval philosophers followed the
footsteps of Samuel ibn Tibbon in interpreting Proverbs as an allegory of
metaphysical truths. See Aviezer Ravitzki, "On the Sources of the Commentary to Proverbs by 'Immanuel of Rome" (in Hebrew), *Kiryat Sepher* 56
(1981): 6-39.

82. *SH*, fol. 115v.

83. *SH*, fol. 116r.

84. *SH*, fol. 116v.

85. *SH*, fol. 117v.

86. *SH*, fol. 117r.

87. *SH*, fol. 118r.

88. R. David's idealization of female conduct is not totally divorced from reality if we assume that the lifestyle of Jewish patrician families was basically similar to that of the Italian patriciate. I see no reason to assume otherwise. This lifestyle does not entail "female emancipation" as Roth assumed, but rather an adaptation to harsh circumstances of living in small, isolated households. See Bonfil, "The Historians' Perception," 74-5. In daily manners, social mores, and aesthetic sensibilities the Jews in Renaissance Italy were probably undistinguishable from their neighbors. For a recent attempt to utilize a laudation to a concrete woman in the reconstruction of medieval Jewish family history see Kenneth R. Stow, "The Jewish Family in the Rhineland in the High Middle Ages: Form and Function," *The American Historical Review* 92 (1987): 1085-1110; and for an attempt to reconstruct the reality of Jewish women in Rome during the sixteenth century see Kenneth R. Stow and Sandra De Benedetti-Stow, "Donne ebree a Roma nell'-eta del ghetto: affett, dipendenze, autonomia," *RMI* 52 terza serie (1986): 64-115.

89. On this congregation and David's activity as *Marbiẓ Torah* see Abraham S. Amarillio, "The Great Talmud Torah of Salonika" (in Hebrew), *Sefunot* 13 (1979): 279.

90. The colophon to MS. Parma 1395 reads as follows:

תם ונשלם ש"ל [שבח לאל] ב"ע [בורא עולם] העתקתי אותו במצות הנבון
ומאד נעלה בן בנו של קדושים ר' מנחם בכמהר"ר [בן כבוד מורנו הרב ר']
יוסף אוטלינג' פה שלוניקי ותשלם המלכה[!] יום א' ב לחדש שבט א"ך טוב
לפ"ק.

Chapter Four

1. The dispute is known to us from the responsum that R. David ben Judah Messer Leon wrote in defense of R. Moses Capsali. For information about the extant manuscripts of R. David's legal opinion see Chapter Two, n. 115.

2. On this controversy see Pines, *New Responsa and Decisions*, 25-26; Shulvass, "The Disputes of Messer Leon," 17-18.

3. See Hacker, "Jewish Community," Appendix D, 32:

לכן אמרתי מה לי ולהם ולמנהגותיהם אם תחת ספרד יעלה הדס, אם תחת
נעצוץ יעלה ברוש, ואני מבית יעקב מעם לועז ובית יהודה לקדשו.

4. Ibid., "Jewish Community," Appendix D, 33:

ראשונה כי הגזירה קיימת מטעם היותו רב על כל אלה הקהלות וזה אף כי
מצד הדין היה מותר. שנית, מצד הדין בעצמו יש פנים לאסור. שלישית, מצד
שאלו החכמים מהגרוש הם חדשים במקום הזה ונותנים עליהם חומרי
המקום שהלכו בו.

5. R. David's contacts with the Karaite scholar Caleb Apandopolo in 1498 in Constantinople attest to this date. See David, "New Information" cited Chapter Three, n. 19.

6. See Hacker, "The Intellectual Activity," 97-101.

7. Excerpted in Hacker, "Intellectual Activity," 97.

8. See Hacker, "The Jewish Community," 92-8, 161-6. 221-2; cf. Joseph Nehama, *Histoire des Israelites de Salonique* (Paris-Salonique: Libraire Molho, 1935-36), vol. 2; Morris S. Goodblatt, *Jewish Life in Turkey in the XVIth Century as Reflected in the Legal Writings of Samuel de Medina* (New York: Jewish Theological Seminary, 1952), 8-23.

9. For a reconstruction of this event and its impact on Jewish history see Yosef H. Yerushalmi, *The Lisbon Massacre of 1506 and the Royal Image in the Shevet Yehudah* (Cincinnati: Hebrew Union College, 1976).

10. On the establishment of the Spanish Inquisition in Portugal see Baron, *SRH* 13:44-61.

11. See Barnai, "The Jews of the Ottoman Empire," 99; cf. Cohen, *Constantinople-Salonica-Patras*, 90-96.

12. Hacker, "Jewish Community," 221-75.

13. Hacker, ibid., 249-260.

14. Hacker, "The Intellectual Activity," 102-10.

15. For a detailed description of the Sephardic Yeshivot in the Ottoman Empire see Hayim Bentov, "Methods of Study of Talmud in the Yeshivot of Salonica and Turkey after the Expulsion from Spain" (in Hebrew), *Sefunot* 13 (1979): 39-102.

16. See Hayim A. Dimitrowosky, "The Academy of R. Jacob Berab in Safed" (in Hebrew), *Sefunot* 7 (1973): 41-102; Katz, "Halakhah and Kabbalah as Competing Study Subjects," in his *Halakhah and Kabbalah*, 89; Daniel Boyarin, "Studies in the Talmudic Commentaries of the Spanish Exiles" (in Hebrew), *Sefunot* 17 (= n.s. Book 2) (1983): 165-84.

17. Bentov, "Methods of Study," pp. 46-7.

18. Hacker, "The Intellectual Activity," 116-23.

19. See Amarillio, "The Great Talmud Torah," 279; David Pipano,

"The Dynasty of Salonika's Rabbis" (in Hebrew), in his *Hagor Ha-Efod* (Sofia, 1925), 3b.

20. R. David ben Hayyim Hacohen (Radakh), *Responsa*, no. 22:

בהיותו נדרש אל עם קורא בשמי ק"ק אבילונא ובראשם החכם הכולל גברא
רבא בוצינא דנהורא אשר נודע שמו בשערים ידו בכך במקרא במשנה ובגמ'
הן כי עיני לא ראתהו וידיעתו וגדולתו שמעה אזני ותבן לה הוא החכם
הכולל כמה"ר דוד בן הגאון החסיד ר"מ ור"ג כמה"ר יאודה ז"ל.

21. R. Elijah Mizrahi, *Responsa*, no. 47:

והם שלחו אלי קונטריס הוראת החכם הכולל אשר בו הראה עוצם פלפולו
והפלגת בקיאותו בתלמוד מוהר"ר דוד בן הרב הגדול כמוהר"ר יהודה זכרו
לברכה.

22. On 1508 as the year of composition see Gottlieb, "Or Olam," 415.

23. For precise citations of these authors in R. David's extant writings see Hava Tirosh-Rothschild, "The Philosophy of R. David ben Judah Messer Leon," Ph.D. diss., Hebrew University 1978, 43-51.

24. *EH*, fol. 131v:

אחרי שהשלמתי התלונה הרבה אשר עלי מהחכמים הנז' אשר כלם חגרו
שקם עלי וכלי מלחמתם כנגד הרב הגדול מה שלא עשו כן נגד מלחמות יי'
לרלב"ג, אשר בו ודאי לכם עם השם, שהיה ראוי להשרף מרוב כפירותיו
בכל הפנות התוריות ובפרט מה שדבר בפרסום ובעזות מצח וגלה פנים
בתורה שלא כהלכה, שכפר בחדוש העולם, ובנסים, ובידיעה הפרטית, כמו
שיודע מי שרגיל בספרו הנז' ואפי' בפלוסופיא טעה ... ויש לי בזה ספר מיוחד
נגדו אפי' בחכמה.

R. David's approbrium against Gersonides should be taken with a grain of salt. On the one hand it reflects the campaign his father launched against Gersonides charging him with heresy. On the other hand we should recall that David in fact owned a copy of Gersonides' *Milhamot Adonai* even though he calls for its burning.

25. *EH*, fol. 86r: כמו שנראה מפורסם מספר אור יי' לך חסדאי' שחשב
להחשיך החכמה ולא ידע מקומה ונמשך אחר המדברים שהרחיק הרב מגבולו ... שחברתי
מאמר נגדו. R. David dismisses Crescas' views in *Or Adonai* as "things one need not waste time discussing, because they are groundless and patently wrong" (*EH*, fol. 113v). In fact, R. David did not fully understand Crescas' original attack on both Aristotle and Maimonides. He dismissed Crescas' discussion offhand precisely because it undermined the very foundation of medieval Aristotelianism which R. David still held dear. Nevertheless, there are times when R. David's own position is not so far from Crescas'.

26. *EH*, fol. 131v: וכמו בעל העיקרים שאותו חסר בשרשים במוחלט כמו
שחברתי ספר נגדו. According to R. David, Albo's critique of Maimonides

amounted to a renewal of the Kalam school in Jewish thought because of
Albo's inadequate training. It appears that R. David opposed Albo on dogmatic grounds. Albo challenged Maimonides' Thirteen Principles and, following Crescas, proposed a different list of Jewish dogmas. R. David
defended the validity of Maimonides' Thirteen Principles, even though he
too reduced the list to four cardinal dogmas to be discussed in Chapter Six
below.

27. *EH*, fol. 11v: אבל דעת הרב לשלול ראיות ארסטו בקדמות, וכבר הארכתי
אני בזה מאמר.

28, *EH*, fol. 110r: כי כבר פירשתיו באורך בספר מכתם לדוד

29. *EH*, fol. 38v: והיא חקירה גדולה כבר ביארתיה באורך בספר הנעים
ספר נפש דוד.

30. *EH*, fol. 101r: ואני לא תקוה ממני שאעמיק כאן בשרשים ובמלות
החכמה, כי יש עמוקות בזה ובמאמרי בדבקות הארכתי, אלא בדברים מבוררים יותר
אבאר הענין. Cf. *EH*, fol. 116v; fol. 217r.

31. Moses Narboni translated Averroës' epistle into Hebrew and commented on it. See Kalman P. Bland ed. and trans., *The Epistle on the Possibility of Conjunction with the Active Intellect with the Commentary of Moses
Narboni* (New York: The Jewish Theological Seminary, 1982). In the fifteenth century, R. Joseph ibn Shem Tov wrote two commentaries to this
epistle; the short one was published by Shaul Regev, in *JSJT* 2 (1982): 38-93.
R. David was apparently familiar with the commentaries of both Narboni
and ibn Shem Tov. On R. David's attitude toward Narboni see n. 33 below.
The writings of R. Joseph ibn Shem Tov exerted important influence on R.
David's views. He cites by name ibn Shem Tov's *Kevod Elohim* in *MD* fol.
39r, from which R. David copied long sections either in agreement or not.
R. David also knew ibn Shem Tov's *Supercommentary on "Averroës Com-
mentary to Alexander's 'On the Intellect'"* as well as his *Commentary on
Guide I:68.* In *'Ein ha-Qore* he made extensive use of these two texts in his
interpretation of Maimonidean epistemology.

32. *EH*, fol. 66r: ועם שאני הארכתי בפי' ר' עזרא בכתוב ההוא ובחלופיהם שהם
עמוקים מאד בפלפול גדול כדרכי בלשונות ר' עזרא בזולת זה המקום. It is interesting
to note that R. David considered Abraham ibn 'Ezra a philosopher who followed the metaphysics of Avicenna and hence succeeded in properly integrating religion and philosophy. See *EH*, fol. 240r:

ואני עוד רגיל בשאני מספר דעת ב"ס לכבוד ר' עזרא אהובי, שהיה מדעתו להיות ראש
מפרשי התורה בדרך הפשט, להעלותו בזה האופן בשרשי החכמות האלהיות.

R. David's high esteem for ibn 'Ezra is indicative of the growing popularity
of ibn 'Ezra among Sephardic philosophers from the second half of the fourteenth century onward. This so-called renaissance of ibn 'Ezra deserves fur-

ther research. In addition to the *Commentary on the Pentateuch*, R. David cites ibn 'Ezra's *Sefer ha-Moladot* (*EH*, fol. 12r), his *Commentary on Psalms* (*EH*, fol. 63r), and *Sefer ha-Shem* (*MD*, fol. 2v). R. David mistakenly ascribes *Sefer ha-'Azamim* (*MD*, fol. 163v) to Ibn 'Ezra, as was customary in the Middle Ages. The last two works preserved important astrological and magical information utilized by Renaissance Jewish scholars, primarily Yohanan Alemanno. Both texts were printed in *Kitve Abraham ibn 'Ezra*.

33. *EH*, fol. 37r: וזה מופת חותך אצל שרשי ב"ס אע"פ שלדעת ב"ר יש להשיב בזה בשרשים חזקים אין זה מקומו, כבר ביארתים בהרחבה בלקוטי על פי' הכוונות ועל פי' המורה.

That R. David composed supercommentaries to Narboni's commentary on Alghzali's *The Intention of the Philosophers* and on Maimonides' *The Guide of the Perplexed* indicates the important impact Narboni exerted on R. David's thought. Indeed, R. David considered Moses Narboni second in importance to Maimonides. See, for example, *EH*, fol. 31v, where R. David praises Narboni's philosophical competence: כי כבר ידעת עומק דברי זה הנרבוני שהיה בתכלית העומק בחקירות הפילוסופיות ובלשון קצר מאד. Nevertheless, R. David does not consider Narboni an original philosopher. He flatly states that "all of Narboni's views are the words of Averroës" (*EH*, fol. 53r), an observation proven true by modern research as well. See Alfred Ivry, "Moses of Narbonne's 'Treatise on the Perfection of the Soul': A Methodological and Conceptual Analysis," *JQR* (1966): 271-97. Further, R. David argues that Narboni's faithfulness to Averroës caused him to criticize Maimonides unfairly.

34. R. David refers to Abraham Bibago as *"ha-filosof ha-shorshi"* (literally, "the fundamental philosopher"), namely, one knowledgeable in the fundamentals of philosophy. R. David praises Bibago's respectful attitude toward Maimonides and his awareness for the religious virtues of philosophy. R. David specifically states that he followed Bibago. See *EH*, fol. 131r:

ובאמת עלינו לשבח הפלוסוף השרשי אברהם ביבאגי כי בכל פרושיו וספריו שראיתי וגם בדרך אמונה כבד הרב בכל המקומות והחזיק שרשיו, שהתורה זה על עומק עיונו בפלוסופיא והכרת מעלת החכמה אשר אחריו נמשכתי בחקירתי זו, שהוא המציא המצאות רבות עיוניות בדקות התורה ובכתובים ובמאמרי חז"ל.

In *Magen David* R. David incorporated long sections of Abraham Bibago's *Derekh Emunah*. Compare *MD* fols. 30r-32r with *Derekh Emunah* (hereafter *DE*), 49a-b; *MD* fol. 144v and *DE*, 53b; *MD* fol. 145r and *DE*, 73b-746; *MD* fols. 146r-147r and *DE*, 72b; *MD* fol. 147r and *DE*, 58b; *MD* fol. 148v and *DE*, 67b; *MD*, fols. 150r151v and *DE*, 59a. It is very difficult to distinguish between the views of R. David and those of Abraham Bibago. That Bibago was both a trained Averroist philosopher and a defender of Maimonides, while also affirming the superiority of Jewish faith, explains R. David's high regard for him.

R. David cites 'Arama's *Aqedat Yizhaq* in *EH*, fol. 131r. According to R. David, 'Arama's major competence was ethics rather than metaphysics. Therefore, R. David did not think Arama was competent to comment on Maimonides. Yet on various points we find R. David's position remarkably close to 'Arama's.

35. A full history of the Maimonidean Controversy is yet to be written. To date the Maimonidean Controversy of the thirteenth century received most of the attention but we still lack critical editions and analysis of the pertinent texts. In the meantime the reader may consult the following studies: *Encyclopaedia Judaica* s.v. "Maimonidean Controversy"; Daniel J. Silver, *Maimonidean Criticism and Maimonidean Controversy 1180-1240* (Leiden: E.J. Brill, 1965); Bernard Septimus, *Hispano-Jewish Culture in Transition: The Career and Controversies of Ramah* (Cambridge: Harvard University Press, 1982); idem, "Piety and Power in Thirteenth Century Catalonia, in *Studies in Medieval Jewish History and Literature*, edited by I. Twersky (Cambridge: Harvard University Press, 1979), vol. 1, 197-230; Jeremy Cohen, *The Friars and the Jews: The Evolution of Medieval Anti-Judaism* (Ithaca: Cornell University Press, 1982), 52-60; and the bibliography cited there; Sirat, *A History of Jewish Philosophy*, 222-28; Joseph Schatzmiller, "Between Aba Mari and the Rashba — The Negotiations Preceding the Ban in Barcelona" (in Hebrew), *Studies in the History of the People of Israel and the Land of Israel* 3 (1975): 121-37; Abraham Halkin, "The Ban on the Study of Philosophy" (in Hebrew), *P'raqim: Year Book of the Schocken Institute for Jewish Research*, edited by E.S. Rosenthal (Jerusalem, 1967-1968), vol. 1, 35-55.

36. For a description of these events and their aftermath see Baer, *The Jews in Christian Spain*, 2:95-174.

37. The complex relationship between the *conversos* and professing Jews in fifteenth century Spain cannot be discussed here in any detail. For a general survey see Baer, ibid. 244-99; Ben Zion Netanyahu, *The Marranos of Spain from the Late XIVth to the Early XVIth Centuries According to Contemporary Hebrew Sources* (New York: American Academy for Jewish Research, 1966) and the review by Gerson D. Cohen, *JSS* 29 (1967): 178-84. For the methodological problems facing the historian of Marranism see Yosef H. Yerushalmi, *From Spanish Court to Italian Ghetto, Isaac Cardoso: A Study in Seventeenth Century Marranism and Jewish Apologetics* (Seattle: University of Washington Press, 1971), 21-31.

38. Baer, *The Jews in Christian Spain*, 2:174-243.

39. My interpretation of the meaning of the Tortosa Disputation concurs with Cohen's as opposed to Baer's.

40. R. Shlomo Al'ami, *Iggeret Musar* edited by Abraham Haberman (Jerusalem: Meqorot, 1945). Netanyahu's discussion of the Epistle in his *The*

Marranos of Spain, 103-6, creates a misleading impression. Al'ami's rebuke of the philosophers constitutes but a small segment in this text and cannot be studied in isolation from his critique of cantors, talmudists, and the professional classes. Most importantly, this text cannot be taken at face value for the purpose of reconstructing Judeo-Spanish history in the early fifteenth century. Any critique of society by a moralist presents a skewed picture reflecting his point of view.

41. On R. Shem Tov ibn Shem Tov, the author of *Sefer ha-Emunot*, and his critique of philosophy in the name of Kabbalah see Gottlieb, "On the Road of Shem Tov ibn Shem Tov to Kabbalah," in his *Studies in the Kabbalah Literature*, 347-56. It is important to note that R. Shem Tov's knowledge of Kabbalah was derived exclusively from books rather than from oral instruction. In the first half of the fifteenth century in Spain Kabbalah was not an active force, most likely because of the devastation of 1391. Only by the end of the century did Kabbalah begin to make inroads into Jewish education in Castile, where it was cultivated alongside the rabbinic disciplines and philosophy. See Hacker, "On the Intellectual Character of Spanish Jewry," 47-56.

42. The original version of Crescas' anti-Christian polemics in the Catalan dialect is no longer extant. It is known only in the Hebrew translation by Joseph ibn Shem Tov in 1454. For a summary of some of Crescas' arguments see Lasker, *Jewish Philosophical Polemics*, according to index.

43. *Or Adonai*, I, ii, 3. For a summary of Crescas' critique of Aristotelian physics see Herbert A. Davidson, *Proofs for Eternity, Creation and the Existence of God in Medieval Islamic and Jewish Philosophy* (New York: Oxford University Press, 1987), 249-75, 365-66.

44. See Warren Z. Harvey, "Hasdai Crescas' Critique of the Theory of the Acquired Intellect," Ph.D. diss., Columbia University 1973, 20-27, 64-103.

45. Hasdai Crescas, *Or Adonai* (Vienna, 1859. Reprint. Tel Aviv: Offset Esther, 1962), introduction.

46. See Warren Z. Harvey, "R. Hasdai Crescas and His Critique of Philosophic Happiness" (in Hebrew), *Proceedings of the Sixth World Congress of Jewish Studies* (Jerusalem: World Union of Jewish Studies, 1977), vol. 3, 143-49.

47. The writings of Crescas' students are still in manuscripts, hardly studied. Ravitzky cites several scholars who refer to Crescas during the fifteenth century, therefore indicating Crescas' immediate influence. See Aviezer Ravitzky, *Crescas' Sermon on the Passover and Studies in His Philosophy* (in Hebrew) (Jerusalem: The Israel Academy of Sciences and the

Humanities, 1988), 28-33. Ravitzky's findings would conflict with my claim that Crescas' impact was rather limited. In any case, the question is not whether Jewish scholars referred to Crescas but whether his critique of Aristotelian physics was fully adopted. To my knowledge only Yohanan Alemanno, at the end of the fifteenth century, both referred to Crescas and departed from medieval Aristotelianism.

48. See Joseph Hacker, "The Place of Abraham Bibago in the Controversy on the Study and Status of Philosophy in 15th Century Spain" (in Hebrew), *Proceedings of the Fifth World Congress of Jewish Studies* (Jerusalem: World Union of Jewish Studies, 1972), vol. 3, 151-58; Shaul Regev, "Concerning the Problem of the Study of Philosophy in 15th Century Thought: R. Joseph ibn Shem tov and R. Abraham Bibago" (in Hebrew), *Daat* 16 (1986): 57-86. The debate on philosophy and the impact of Joseph ibn Shem Tov and Abraham Bibago on David ben Judah Messer Leon is further discussed in Chapter Five below.

49. On the scope of Kabbalistic studies in Castilian Yeshivot prior to the expulsion from Spain see Hacker, "On the Intellectual Character of Spanish Jewry," 52-55. For the relative strength of Kabbalah and philosophy after the expulsion from Spain see n. 55 below.

50. See Moshe Idel, "Studies in the Thought of the Author of "Sefer ha-Meshiv: A Chapter in the History of Spanish Kabbalah" (in Hebrew), *Sefunot* 17 (= n.s. Book 2) (1983): 232ff.

51. See, for example, Joseph Albo, *Sefer ha-Iqqarim* II:11. On Abraham Shalom's use of Kabbalistic sources see Herbert A. Davidson, *The Philosophy of Abraham Shalom: A Fifteenth Century Exposition and Defense of Maimonides* (Berkeley: University of California Press, 1964), 12. On Abraham Bibago's citations from the Zohar see Allan Lazaroff, *The Theology of Abraham Bibago: A Defense of the Divine Will, Knowledge, and Providence in Fifteenth Century Spanish-Jewish Philosophy* (University: The University of Alabama Press, 1981), 57, n. 71. These philosophers commonly equated the *Sefirot* with the Separate Intellects of medieval Aristotelian cosmology.

52. See Gedalyah Negal, "The Views of Joseph Ya'abez on Philosophy and Philosophers, Torah and Commandments" (in Hebrew), *Eshel Beer Sheba* 1 (1976): 258-87; Barzilay, *Between Reason and Faith*, 133-49.

53. On Isaac Abravanel's critique of Maimonides' theory of prophecy see Alvin J. Reines, *Maimonides and Abrabanel on Prophecy* (Cincinnati: Hebrew Union College, 1970), xiii-lxxx. On Abravanel's critique of Maimonidean dogmatism see Isaac Abravanel, *Principles of Faith (Rosh Amanah)*, edited and translated by Menachem M. Kellner (East Brunswick: Associated University Presses for the Littman Library of Jewish Civilization,

1982), 17-50. Further discussion of Abravanel's critique in relation to the views of R. David ben Judah is found in Chapter Six below.

54. *Tola'at Ya'acov* was printed for the first time in Constantinople, in 1560, after the death of David ben Judah Messer Leon. Given other connections between the work of this Kabbalist and David, it stands to reason that R. David knew of his critique of Maimonides even though the book was not yet in print. For information on this scholar, an adamant adherent of Kabbalah see Gottlieb, *Studies in the Kabbalah Literature*, passim.

55. The relative strength of philosophy and Kabbalah in the Ottoman Empire during the sixteenth century is still subject to academic controversy. R. Elior views the dominant perception that Kabbalah disseminated among both the Romanyots and the Iberian exiles during the sixteenth century and began to affect Halakhic observance. See Rahel Elior, "The Struggle for the Position of Kabbalah in the Sixteenth Century" (in Hebrew), *JSJT* 1 (1981): 177-190, and her critical edition of *Galya Raza* (Jerusalem: The Hebrew University of Jerusalem; Research Projects of the Institute for Jewish Studies, 1981). Elior's assertion was contested by David Tamar in his "A Critical Edition of *Galya Raza*" (in Hebrew), *JSJT* 2 (1983): 647-50. However, Isaiah Tishby endorsed Elior's claim in his "On the Problems of the Book *Galya Raza*" (in Hebrew), *Zion* 48 (1983): 103-6. Hacker appears to side with Tamar's position, noting that while the Iberian exiles brought with them Kabbalistic manuscripts they cultivated philosophy more than Kabbalah. Hacker's claim is based on a comparison of printed texts: philosophy by far outnumbered Kabbalah. The author of *Galya Raza* himself stated that he had encountered opposition. Hacker thus concluded that Kabbalah did not replace the cultivation of philosophy during most of the sixteenth century in the Ottoman Empire. See Hacker, "Intellectual Activity," 121-2. Our position is spelled out in the conclusion of this study.

56. Very little is known on Meir ibn Verga. He apparently arrived at Salonika in 1506 with other refugees from Portugal. See Meir Benayahu, "A Source about the Spanish Refugees in Portugal and Their Departure to Salonica: The Concealment of *Sefer ha-Emunot* and Its Discovery and Information about the Ibn Verga Family" (in Hebrew], *Sefunot* 11 (1967-1973): 231-65, esp. 247-49.

57. *KH*, 16.

58. *EH*, fol. 129r.

59. *EH*, fol. 1r.

60. *EH*, fol. 2v.

61. See Chapter Two, nn. 111-112.

62. *EH*, fol. 2v: ‏ואחר שדעתי האמתי אינו כדעתו‎. The same critical distance is manifested in *Magen David*. Cf. *Magen David*, fol. 71v:

‏ושזה יהיה דעתו אראה לך זה מדבריו כדי שלא תחשוב שבאתי להפך בזכות‎
‏הרב בשקרים והמצאות, כי אין זה דרכי, בשכבר ידעת כמה פעמים אני‎
‏חולק עם הרב ברוב שרשי התורה.‎

In his last work, *Tehillah le-David*, R. David ben Judah exhibits a more critical attitude toward Maimonides, and in fact criticizes Maimonides' conception of prophecy as "alien to the views of Torah." See Chapter Six below.

63. *EH*, fol. 1V:

‏ואם כן למה נרע למשה, בעבור רבים מעמי הארץ מתיהדים, והיה שכר‎
‏טורחו כי יקום איש עברי אשר לא ראה בחכמה ג׳ דלתות וקרא בקול גדול:‎
‏"יהודים מה לכם לחכמה מצרית לשתות מי שיחור מבאר חפרוה הרועים,‎
‏שרים מבני עמנו." ומשה נגש אל הערפל חשך וענן וערפל חתולתו שמעו שמוע‎
‏מלתי ותתענג בנפש נפשכם כי משה עלה אל האלהים בשרשיו ובמופתיו‎
‏היסודיים וזאת היתה כוונתו העיקרית. לכן אמרתי לבחור דרך אמצעי בין‎
‏אלה החכמים, כמו שראיתי בזאת ההסכמה. כי ראשונה ספרתי דעת הרב‎
‏וחזקתי בראיותיו. ואח"כ ספרתי דעתי לפי מה שנ"ל שיהיה דרך התורה.‎
‏והשיבותי לראיות הרב בכבוד ובמוסר, לא בחרפות וגדופין, כדרך שעשו‎
‏אחרים, ח"ו. ולמה לי זה? אלא שלכבוד הרב רציתי להאריך בשרשיו, לגלות‎
‏דעותיו, כדי שיהיה עקר זה הספר העיוני בידך ובזכרונך בכלל, כי ראוי לכל‎
‏חכם פילוסוף לחשוק בו.‎

64. R. David expressed the same position also in *Shevah ha-Nashim*, as discussed in Chapter Three, when he defended the legitimacy of humanist curriculum.

65. R. Joseph ibn Shem Tov was another fifteenth century Jewish Philosopher who expressed a positive attitude toward the Rashba's ban on the study of philosophy. Like R. David ben Judah Messer Leon, R. Joseph ibn Shem Tov was a well-trained Aristotelian philosopher who argued for the superiority of Torah (qua wisdom) over philosophy. For a fuller discussion of his attitude toward philosophy see Regev, "Concerning the Problem of the Study of Philosophy," cited above.

66. *EH*, fol. 129r.

67. *EH*, fol. 1v:

‏ובפרט כי כוונתו היתה לשם שמים להעלות תורתנו מהבלי הספורים שלמה‎
‏תהיה בעניניה ותועלתה של החכמה העליונה.‎

68. *EH*, fol. 2r.

69. *EH*, fol. 2r:

‏שזה אני עושה לכבוד הרב ומעלתו הגדולה וחכמתו ושמועתו הגדולה‎

המפורסמת ולא בלבד בינינו אלא אפי׳ בחכמי האומות, ובפרט הנוצרים
הרחוקים מעיקרי הדת לפי התחלפות הספר ההוא מורה נבוכים אשר
בפרסום מגלה חרפתם בפ״ג מהא׳ ובפ״ע מ״מ מכבדים ומנשאים אותו לכבוד
החכמה כמו שעושים לב״ר המפרש ולאחרים.

David was correct to cite the undeniable influence of Maimonides on Christian scholasticism, especially on Albertus Magnus and Thomas Aquinas, and
the respect accorded to him. See Etienne Gilson, *History of Christian Philosophy in the Middle Ages* (New York, 1955), 649-51.

    70. *EH*, fol. 14r-v:

כי כל כונתו בחבוריו היתה לכוין התורה עם החכמה ועם המושכל כדי
להראות מעלתה ויקרה כי אינה מיוסדת בדמיון שהוא כאמת בשאר הדתות.

Maimonides criticized the Kalam views on numerous issues, including the
nature of divine attributes, the ontological status of revealed law and causality. For a detailed analysis of this critique see Harry A. Wolfson, *Repercussions of the Kalam in Jewish Philosophy* (Cambridge: Harvard University
Press, 1979), 29-40, 111-13, 178-89.

    71. *EH*, fol. 156r.

    72. *EH*, fol. 83v: כי ראה הרב שב״ס ואבוחמד עשו כן בתורתם, נתקנא
בדתנו והביאם ורמזיהם ויסודותיהם משכיתם חדרי מכל ולקח הרב מזה. Cf. ibid. fol.
82v:

כי מי שראה ספרי ב״ס גדול הפלוסופים ובפרט בפלוסופיא המזרחית, יראה
כי כל כונתו היתה לקבץ בין תורתו לפלוסופיא אשר ממנו לקח אבוחמד
תלמידו כל ההסכמות שעשה כמו שראיתי בהרבה מספריו וראיתי כי
יסודות הרב ברמזיו לקוחים כלם ממנו כי הוא כת׳ באגרת אחד כי אבוחמד
ראש כל חכמי ישמעאל עד שרוב ספר המורה לקוח מאלו השנים ר״ל ב״ס
ואבוחמד.

This statement contrasts with Pines' characterization of Maimonides' attitude toward Avicenna as

> ...the only philosopher considered as belonging to the Aristote-
> lian school with regard to whom Maimonides in his letter to ibn
> Tibbon expresses some reservations and even some distrust.

See Shlomo Pines, trans. and ed., *The Guide of the Perplexed* (Chicago: University of Chicago Press, 1963), xciii. Pines concedes that Maimonides could
have adopted Avicenna's views had he been a mere "eclectic philosopher,"
but that he did not follow Avicenna in regard to prophecy shows, according
to Pines, that Maimonides was an uncompromising philosopher for whom
philosophic truth reigns supreme. The actual wording of Maimonides in the
letter to ibn Tibbon in fact supports R. David's position rather than

Pines'. See Alexander Marx, "Texts by and About Maimonides," *JQR* 25 (1934-35): 374-81. However, R. David's uncritical identification of Avicenna and Alghazali is peculiar. Indeed, Alghazali did summarize the teachings of Avicenna's philosophy in his *Maqasid al-Falsifah (The Intentions of the Philosophers)* but he did so only in order to disprove them in his *Tahafut al-Falsifah (The Destruction of the Philosophers)*. R. David was familiar with both works, so that his presentation of Alghazali is awkward.

73. *EH*, fol. 9r: שהרב כיוון כל הפנות התוריות עם העיון והחקירה.

74. Maimonides defined Christianity as a form of idolatry; see *The Commentary on the Mishnah*, 'Abodah Zarah, 1:3 and 4. In *The Guide of the Perplexed* Maimonides flatly stated (II:35): "Thus it has been made clear that his apprehension is different from that of all those who came after him in Israel which is *a kingdom of priests and a holy nation, and in whose midst is the Lord* — and, all the more, from the apprehension of all those who came in other religious communities." This statement clearly intends to reject any claim by Christians that Jesus was a prophet superior to Moses. The same point is reiterated in Maimonides' list of Thirteen Principles, in the Seventh Principle. But the most derogatory comments about Jesus, especially the Messianic claims of Jesus, are found in the *Mishneh Torah*, Hilkhot Melakhim, 11:4. The relevant comment was omitted from most printed editions, but the recent edition of the *Mishneh Torah*, from a Yemenite manuscript by Joseph Kafah (Jerusalem, 1985), included the entire passage; see p. 771.

75. *EH*, fol. 84r:

שאין ראוי לקבל הפנות התוריות בקבלה לבד מצד התורה, אלא אחר
שקבלם בנערותו בתורה ראוי לו לעיין בחכמות המופתיות ולבאר היסודות
במופת מצד החכמה ולא יספיק לו זה לבד אלא אח"כ ישתדל בתלמודה של
תורה שהוא סתם תלמוד בפעל כדי שיקנה לקיים המצות המעשיות ההרגל
בהם ויהיו לו בקנין.

David cites *The Guide* III:54 as his prooftext. See ibid.

> The Sages, may their memory be blessed, mentioned likewise that man is required first to obtain knowledge of the Torah, then to obtain wisdom, then to know what is incumbent upon him with regard to the legal science of the Law.

76. In *Posterior Analytics* Book I, Aristotle distinguished between "demonstrative knowledge" and "dialectic." Whereas the former is necessarily true, the latter belongs to the realm of opinion. By the same token, demonstrative knowledge proceeds from "necessary basic truths," whereas dialectic reasons in a syllogistic manner from generally accepted premises. See

Edel, *Aristotle and his Philosophy* (Chapel Hill: University of North Carolina Press, 1982), 202-4.

77. Edel, ibid., 191.

78. See Aquinas, *Summa Contra Gentiles*, translated with introduction and notes by Anton C. Pegis (Notre Dame: University of Notre Dame Press, 1975), Book I:3, p. 63:

> There is a twofold mode of truth in what we profess about God. Some truths about God exceed all the ability of human reason. Such is the truth that God is triune. But there are some truths which natural reason also is able to reach. Such are that God exists, that He is one, and the like. In fact, such truths about God have been proved demonstratively by the philosophers guided by the light of natural reason.

Cf. Aquinas, *Summa Theologiae*, Ia, q. 1, a. 1.

79. *EH*, fol. 3r. David admits that he has changed the meaning of Maimonides' words by adding the distinction between "things which are by nature demonstrable" and "things which cannot be demonstrated by their very nature." Undoubtedly, David presents a tendentious interpretation of Maimonides so that he could defend him.

80. *EH*, fol. 9r. Cf. fol. 12v: וישיש עיונים שעם היותם אמיתיים אינם מבוארים במופת שזהו עיקר דרושנו. R. David's interpretation of Maimonides as a thinker who maintained the limitation of human knowledge, and who distinguished between natural and supernatural truths, reflects the impact of Aquinas. See Hava Tirosh-Rothschild, "Maimonides and Aquinas: The Interplay of Two Masters in Medieval Jewish Philosophy," *Conservative Judaism* 39 (1986): 54-66. The impact of Aquinas on the thought of David is explored in further detail in Chapters Five and Seven.

81. Medieval and modern interpreters have all tried to crack the intricate structure, so to eliminate the contradictions which Maimonides included in the text to obfuscate its teachings. Strauss offered a most detailed, though still disputed, analysis of the *Guide*'s structure. See Leo Strauss, "How to Begin to Study *The Guide of the Perplexed*," in *The Guide of the Perplexed*, edited and translated by Shlomo Pines, xi-1vi. But cf. Simon Rawidowicz, "The Structure of the *Guide of the Perplexed*", in his *Hebrew Studies in Jewish Thought*, edited by Benjamin C.I. Ravid (Jerusalem: Rubin Mass, 1969), 237-96.

82. See *Guide*, Introduction to Part One.

83. The history of Maimonidean interpretation is yet to be written. Although most research into medieval Jewish philosophy in the post-

Maimonidean era addresses Maimonidean interpretations, there is no comprehensive presentation of the Maimonidean tradition in medieval Jewish philosophy. A recent article of Aviezer Ravitzky approximates this desideratum. See Aviezer Ravitzky, "The Secrets of *The Guide of the Perplexed* Between the Thirteenth and the Twentieth Centuries" (in Hebrew), *JSJT* 5 (1986): 23-69. For earlier surveys of the Maimonidean tradition see Eliezer Schweid, *Maimonides and the Members of His Circle* (in Hebrew), edited by Dan Oryan (Jerusalem: Aqademon, 1968); Sirat, *A History of Jewish Philosophy*, 205-344.

84. Aryeh L. Motzkin, "On the Interpretation of Maimonides," *The Independent Journal of Philosophy* 2 (1979): 39-46. Maimonides instructs his addressee, Joseph ben Judah ibn Sham'un, in the Introduction to *The Guide*:

> You ought rather to learn everything that ought to be learned and constantly study this Treatise. For it then will elucidate for you most of the obscurities of the Law that appear as difficult to every intelligent man.

Though written to a specific individual, the *The Guide* addresses all Jewish intellectuals who share ibn Shamun's perplexity. The advice to study *The Guide* constantly then, creates the context in which a rationalist interpretation of the Law can take place regardless of time and place.

85. See Warren Z. Harvey, "The Return of Maimonideanism," *JSS* 42 (1980): 249-68. Harvey discusses contemporary interpretations of Maimonides by Leon Roth, Isaiah Leibowitz, and David Hartman as indicative of their own interpretations of Judaism, especially in regard to the relationship between Halakhah and philosophico-scientific speculation.

86. Davidson already raised the possibility that Maimonides deliberately obfuscated his teachings so as to make them the very subject matter of future study, but he dismissed it as a "cynical" interpretation. See Herbert A. Davidson, "Maimonides' Secret Position on Creation," in *Studies in Medieval Jewish History and Literature*, vol. 1, 16.

87. *EH*, fol. 5r: ‏וכבר ידעת שהרב מיושב בחכמות ולא הטעה עצמו בשום דרוש‎.

88. See Chapter Five below.

89. *EH*, fol. 103v:

‏ובפרט בין אלו השתי כתות כת ב"ס ואבוחמד שהרב נמשך אחריהם, וכת‎
‏ב"ר שהנרבוני היה נפשו וכל דבריו הם דברי ב"ר אשר הרב לא ראה אותם‎
‏כי לא נתפשטו בימיו כמו שזכרתי.‎

R. David's assertion that Maimonides had no access to the works of Averroës prior to completing *The Guide* is based on Maimonides' letter to Samuel ibn Tibbon.

90. *EH*, fol. 53v:

וכן קרה לרב עם הנרבוני, כי עשה עצמו נרבוני מפרש דבריו של הרמב״ם
ומהפך בכוונתו הרצויה לדעת הפך מה שכיון. ובפרט כי גדלה חכמתו
בפילוסופיא להמשיכו אחר דעות ב״ר [אבן רשד] מה שלא ראה הרב. ומדעות
ב״ר ועמוקותיו עשה לו רכב ופרשים כי כל דבריו הם דברי ב״ר מבלי תוספת
ומגרעת כמו שנר׳ למי שהורגל בהם.

Cf. fols. 31r; 34v.

91. *EH*, fol. 130r.

92. See Aviezer Ravitzky, "Samuel ibn Tibbon and the Esoteric Character of *The Guide*," *AJS Review* 6 (1981): 87-123.

83. *EH*, fol. 129r.

94. *EH*, fol. 12v.

95. *EH*, fol. 12r.

96. *EH*, fol. 12v.

97. *EH*, fol. 13v.

98. *EH*, fol. 23r: תראה איך פלפלנו בלשונו ובמלותיו וכווננו הלשונות והפרקים
בהשגתם זה על זה כמו שצוונו.

99. This date is surmised on the basis of the opening statement in
Kevod Hakhamim. See below n. 101, also consult Chapter Two, n. 2.

100. On Jewish commercial activity in Valona during the sixteenth
century see Shmuelevitz, *The Jews of the Ottoman Empire*, 130-34. On the
composition of the Jewish community see Rosanes, *A History of the Jews in
Turkey*, 1:231-38.

101. *KH*, 5. For a calculation of the relative worth of rabbinic salaries
in this period see Bonfil, *The Rabbinate*, 103-10.

102. *KH*, 5:

ולהיותי אז נחפז במצרים דרך קארפו בדוגאיות מפני ששלחו לי משם
כתבים זה שנים רבות, והיתה העיר הזאת קרובה, ועניתי ונעתרתי למבקשים
אותי משם ובאתי הנה אבילונא.

Bernfeld read "במצרים" to mean "in Egypt" and hence asserted that David
was invited to serve as a rabbi in a Jewish congregation in Egypt. Instead, I
suggest to read this word as "במצרים" [that is "in the straits"), a reference to
the straits of either the Aegean Sea or the Adriatic Sea, through which David
had to pass on his way from Salonika to Corfu. I believe that "משם" in the
passage quoted above refers to Corfu, and not to Egypt, so that David was
never invited to Egypt and never lived there.

103. *KH.* 5.

104. *KH.* 5.

105. *KH.* 5.

106. *KH.* 5. On the wars of succession to the Sultanate from 1509-1512, to which David refers to as בלבול המלכות (i.e., governmental confusion), see Michael A. Cook ed., *A History of the Ottoman Empire to 1730* (Cambridge: Cambridge University Press, 1976), 65-70.

107. On Ottoman-Venetian struggles in the Adriatic see ibid., 62-3.

108. The controversy is discussed in detail by David Tamar, "About *Kevod Hakhamim* by David ben Judah Messer Leon" (in Hebrew), *Kiryat Sepher* 26 (1950): 96-100; reprinted in his *Studies in the History of the Jews in Israel and Italy* (in Hebrew) (Jerusalem, 1970), 48-52.

109. The opinion also contains R. David's halakhic reasoning, which will not be discussed in this book.

110. *KH*, 6.

111. R. Jacob Tam changed the tense from past to future, the form most prevalent in America today. The Sephardim did not accept this change. See *Encyclopedia Judaica*, s.v. "Kol Nidre."

112. *KH*, 7.

113. *KH*, 8.

114. *KH*, 9.

115. *KH*, 12.

116. *KH*, 12-13.

117. *KH*, 16.

118. The dispute is known to us only from David's account in *Kevod Hakhamim*. For the little biographical information available on R. Meir ibn Verga see Benayahu, "A Source on the Spanish Exiles," 247-49; idem, "The House of Abravanel in Salonika," 9-13.

Benayahu conjectures that the Samuel Abravanel who supported Meir ibn Verga in Valona was the third son of Don Isaac Abravanel. However, Hacker refutes this identification by noting that this Smauel Abravanel died in 1504, and was eulogized by Joseph b. Meir Gerson. See Hacker, "On the Intellectual Character of Spanish Jewry," 39-40. Hacker published the eulogy by Joseph Gerson in *Sefunot* 12 (1978): 33-36. The Samuel Abravanel who settled in Valona was apparently another member of the House of Abravanel. Nevertheless, it stands to reason that hostility between R. David ben Judah

Messer Leon and R. Meir ibn Verga was further fueled by the Abravanel family's support of ibn Verga. As noted above, the animosity between David and the head of the Abravanel family should be understood as a feud between two Jewish aristocratic clans. David may not have appreciated the strong economic and political presence of the Abravanels in Salonika.

119. *KH*, 16.

120. *KH*, 17.

121. *KH*, 16.

122. *KH*, 28, 53, 77. The texts are cited in full in Chapter Two, n. 3.

123. *KH*, 64.

124. *KH*, 62-63. Bonfil, *The Rabbinate*, 37.

125. *KH*, 53-54.

126. *KH*, 55; see also Katz, "Ordination and Rabbinic Authority," 211.

127. Tamar, "About *Kavod Hakhamim*," already noted that R. David ben Judah Messer Leon used long sections from the Responsum of R. Joseph Colon, but he did not realize that the two rabbis held diametrically opposed views. See also Bonfil, *The Rabbinate*, 64, n. 275.

128. *KH*, 63.

129. Bonfil published this ordination writ in *The Rabbinate*, 217-19.

130. See Bonfil, *The Rabbinate*, 61-62.

131. R. David ben Hayyim Hacohen, *Sheelot u-Teshuvot* (Salonika, 1803), no. 22, and consult also Bonfil, *The Rabbinate*, 37, n. 72.

132. Katz, "Ordination," 211; Bonfil, *The Rabbinate*, 37.

133. In 1536, Emmanuel ben Refael Meltafrida, the copyist of *'Ein ha-Qore* (MS. Parma Perreau 44), mentioned David as already deceased.

134. For a detailed description and analysis of this important controversy see Jacob Katz, "The Ordination Controversy Between R. Jacob Berab and R. Levi ben Hayyim" (in Hebrew), in his *Halakhah and Kabbalah*, 213-36.

135. See Bonfil, *The Rabbinate*, 60-66.

Chapter Five

1. My discussion of the concept of faith in medieval Jewish philosophy is indebted to the insightful studies of Shalom Rosenberg. In particular, I

have consulted "The Concept of *'Emunah* in Post-Maimonidean Jewish Philosophy," in *Studies in Medieval Jewish History and Literature*, edited by Isadore Twersky (Cambridge: Harvard University Press, 1984), vol. 2, 273-307; Menachem M. Kellner, *Dogma in Medieval Jewish Thought, From Maimonides to Abravanel* (Oxford: Oxford University Press for The Littman Library, 1986). To minimize a repetition of the bibliographical information that Kellner and Rosenberg mention, I cite here only the most pertinent primary and secondary sources.

2. On Maimonides' inconsistent usage of these terms and the diverse Hebrew translations of his terminology see Rosenberg, "The Concept of *'Emunah*," 274-75.

3. Aristotle, *Topics* 100a 30-100b 21; and consult Kellner, *Dogma*, 5.

4. Kellner, ibid., 4.

5. The usage of the Hebrew word *qabbalah* during the Middle Ages was as confused as the usage of the word *emunah*. Literally, *qabbalah* means reception or receipt. Broadly speaking, *qabbalah* refers to the tradition which Moses received at Sinai consisting of the Written and Oral Torahs. However, with the emergence of the theosophic school in Spain by the thirteenth century, the term *qabbalah* was used as the proper name of a specific intellectual tradition. The Kabbalists conceived of their own teachings as authentic oral tradition originating in Sinatic revelation. As an intellectual program, Kabbalah presented itself as an alternative to Jewish philosophy even though Kabbalah derived many concepts from the teachings of the philosophers. For the sake of clarity, we will employ the term *qabbalah* as the Hebrew designation of rabbinic tradition, and Kabbalah as a proper name of the distinct historical movement which flourished in Spain during the thirteenth century.

6. The title of Saadia's work, *Kitab al-'Amanat w'al I'tiqadat (Sefer ha-Emunot ve-ha Deot; The Book of Doctrines and Beliefs)*, captures the essence of his enterprise. On Saadia's usage of the two types of beliefs see Alexander Altmann, "Translator's Introduction, Saadia Gaon, *The Book of Doctrines and Beliefs*," in *Three Jewish Philosophers*, Hans Lewy et al (New York: Atheneum, 1979), 16-20; Israel Efros, *Studies in Medieval Jewish Philosophy* (New York: Columbia University Press, 1974), 27, 31-2. Harry A. Wolfson, "The Double Faith Theory in Saadia, Averroës and St. Thomas," in *Studies in the History of Philosophy and Religion*, 1:583-618.

7. For a good introduction to Aristotle's conception of science and the division of the sciences see John H. Randall, *Aristotle* (New York: Columbia University Press, 1960), 32-58.

8. Rosenberg, "The Concept of *'Emunah*," 278.

9. Rosenberg, ibid., 284.

10. Maimonides' theory of prophecy has been a bone of contention among medieval and modern interpreters. This reconstruction of Maimonides' position, and of the differences and similarities between Maimonides and Aquinas, is indebted to Alexander Altmann, "Maimonides and Thomas Aquinas: Natural or Divine Prophecy," *AJS Review* 3 (1978): 1-19.

11. *Ibid.*, p. 7.

12. D. Blumenthal has argued that Maimonides' conception of prophecy falls under the category of "intellectualist mysticism" common in modern Islamic scholarship. Blumenthal has emphasized Maimonides' usage of the term *'ittiṣāl* (contact, connection or conjunction), and even *'ittihad* (union or identification), to describe the relationship between the human intellect and the phenomenon of prophecy. See David Blumenthal, "Maimonides' Intellectualist Mysticism and the Superiority of the Prophecy of Moses," in *Approaches to Judaism in Medieval Times* (Chico: Scholars Press, 1984), 27-51. However, Blumenthal avoids discussing the role of the Active Intellect in prophecy. According to Maimonides, the unitive experience of the prophets, including Moses, is not directly with God but with the Active Intellect. Hence, the term "intellectual mysticism" is justified in regard to Maimonides only to the extent that it involves the semidivine intermediary — the Active Intellect. See Altmann, "Natural and Divine Prophecy," 16. I believe that only by the fifteenth century, within a new conception of prophecy as direct illumination from God, did Jewish thinkers endorse intellectual mysticism to the full extent.

13. See Warren Z. Harvey, "Between Political Philosophy and Halakhah" (in Hebrew), *Iyyun* 40 (1980): 198-212.

14. N. Samuelson has shown that this is but one possible interpretation of Maimonides. Another reading is "that reason and revelation have different but overlapping ranges and that there is no qualitative difference between conclusions from either source." See Norbert Samuelson, "Possible and Preferred Relations between Reason and Revelation as Authority in Judaism," in *Studies in Jewish Philosophy* 2 (Philadelphia: Academy for Jewish Philosophy, 1981), 12-13. Both interpretations, however, are clearly rationalistic and were common among the Jewish philosophers of the thirteenth and fourteenth centuries. In the fifteenth century, Maimonides' defenders (e.g., R. Abraham Shalom, Abraham Bibago and R. David ben Judah Messer Leon) argued that Maimonides distinguished between the range of authority of reason and revelation. I suggest in Chapter Four above that a preference to one or the other interpretation of Maimonides reflects the intellectual orientation of the interpreter more than it helps resolve the Maimonidean puzzle.

15. Maimonides, *The Guide* I:72, III:54.

16. On the debates over Maimonides' true position Chapter Four, nn. 83-86 and Kellner, *Dogma*, 34-49.

17. Maimonides, *Commentary on the Mishnah*, Sanhedrin, Chapter Ten. Maimonides' list of fundamental principles is discussed in greater detail in Chapter Six below. The list is analyzed with great clarity in Kellner, *Dogma*, 10-24.

18. The entire dogmatic enterprise in medieval Judaism was but an interpretation of Maimonides' Thirteen Principles. The history of this process and the views of the various interpreters is coextensive with the evolution of the Maimonidean tradition. The subject is discussed in greater length in Chapter Six below.

19. The impact of Averroës on Jewish philosophers in the thirteenth and fourteenth centuries is undeniable, but one should be cautious of an uncritical label "Jewish Averroism." While Jewish scholars undoubtedly considered Averroës the most accurate interpreter of Aristotle and studies Aristotle through Averroës' commentaries, they did not blindly follow him. They retained their independent judgment and deviated from Averroës whenever they found his position unsuitable. More importantly, Jewish Averroism is clearly not to be identified with the so-called Double Truth Theory which was ascribed to the Latin Averroists such as Siger of Branbant and Boethius of Dachia. Averroës did not teach that what can be true in philosophy can be untrue in religion or vice versa: rather, he taught that there is one philosophical truth which can be known in different manners. See Alfred Ivry, "The Implications of Averroës' Thought for Jewish Philosophy" (in Hebrew), *Proceedings of the Sixth World Congress of Jewish Studies* (Jerusalem: World Union of Jewish Studies, 1976), vol. 3, 321-27. The same guarded attitude toward Averroës is evident in the fifteenth century in the writings of R. David ben Judah Messer Leon. On the one hand he held Averroës as second only to Aristotle; see *MD*, fol. 114r:

והאיש הזה הוא יותר גדול מכל הפלוסופים זולת ארסטו, וכמו שארסטו
הוא אשר חדש החכמה והשלימה ... כן האיש הזה פרש אותה ובארה
והשלים תועלתה ... ובד"כ אני אומר כי ב"ר הוא משנה לארסטו בחכמה
האנושית.

Despite such high esteem, R. David at times rejects Averroës' views as incompatible with the tenets of a revealed religion, especially Judaism. See, for example, *EH*, fol. 83r:

ומפני שאתה רואה בזה ב"ר שלא רצה לסבול שתהיה תורה כ"כ מעולה כמו
החכמה המופתית והפילוסופיא אלא שאדרבא יותר שפלים מדרכי החכמה,
ולא חשש המתעקש הזה לגנות תורתו כדי לבטל שרשי ב"ס ואבוחמד אויביו
הקדומים ... והאמת כי פלפולו בחכמה הגיע עד שחקים, אבל בזה הדרוש
יותר נאות דעת ב"ס ואבוחמד לכבד התורה עד שמביאנה לחכמה המופתית.

20. There is considerable confusion in modern scholarship concerning the meaning of "theology" and "philosophy" in the Jewish Middle Ages. If

"theology" stands simply for discourse about God, then there are a considerable number of medieval Jewish texts which would fall under the category of "theology." This has led Blumenthal to argue that modern scholarship has wrongly employed the term "philosophy" to denote the activity of medieval Jewish thinkers, whereas "theology" would have been more appropriate. According to Blumenthal, medieval texts dealing with topics such as

> "creation and the current scientific view of the universe, God's existence, his attributes and man's language, human free will, the role of the Torah in society, the nature of prophecy and revelation, the problem of evil, the problem of divine retribution, the nature of wisdom, God's oneness, the eschatological dimension of religious belief, miracles, the image of God in man,"

belong to the genre of theology. These topics constitute "the divine Science" as opposed to "science" which consists of knowledge about the natural world including the heavenly spheres. See David Blumenthal, "Religion and the Religious Intellectuals: the Case of Judaism in Medieval Times," in *Take Judaism for Example: Studies towards the Comparison of Religions*, edited by Jacob Neusner (Chicago: University of Chicago Press, 1983), 121-24, 139-41.

While Blumenthal's distinction may be helpful for the modern reader, the issue is more complicated than that. The problem arises from the unique status of metaphysics, or First Philosophy, as the highest body of natural philosophic knowledge. Metaphysics was the divine science for the Jewish rationalists of the thirteenth and fourteenth centuries, and they did not recognize theology as a distinct discipline apart from philosophy. That distinction appeared only in the fifteenth century under the influence of Christian scholasticism in general and Aquinas in particular. Aquinas distinguished formally between philosophy and theology in a manner similar to Blumenthal's description.

21. See Rosenberg, "The Concept of *'Emunah*," 287.

22. See Ralph Lerner and Mushin Mahdi eds., *Medieval Political Philosophy: A Source Book*, 2d. printing (Ithaca: Cornell University Press, 1978), 13-14.

23. For an excellent concise history of Christian scholasticism as a response to the challenge of Aristotelianism, see Frederick C. Copleston, *A History of Medieval Philosophy*, (New York: Harper and Row, 1974), 150-276 and the bibliography cited in 360-76.

24. For a concise survey of the main heretical movements in medieval Christianity, pertinent sources, and bibliography, see Edward H. Peters, *Heresy and Authority in Medieval Europe: Documents in Translation* (Philadelphia: University of Pennsylvania Press, 1980).

25. See David Knowles, *The Evolution of Medieval Thought* (New York: Vintage Books, 1964), 221-34.

26. See Joseph Sermoneta, "Moses ben Solomon of Salerno and Nicholaus of Giovinazo on Maimonides' *The Guide of the Perplexed*" (in Hebrew), *Iyyun* 20 (1970): 212-40.

27. I have followed Copleston in reconstructing Aquinas' position. See Fredrick C. Copleston's *A History of Philosophy* (Garden City, NY: 1985), Book 1, 302-434; idem, *Aquinas* (London: Penguin, 1957). I believe with Sermoneta that attention to Aquinas is essential to the interpretation of Jewish thinkers, especially in the fifteenth century. The impact of Aquinas should be seen as part of the profound changes that Jewish thought underwent during the fifteenth century to address the challenge of Christianity.

28. See Copleston, *Aquinas*, 67-68.

29. The following analysis of Aquinas' epistemology of faith is indebted to Timothy C. Potts, "Aquinas on Belief and Faith," in *Inquiries into Medieval Philosophy*, edited by James F. Ross (Westport, CT, 1971), 3-22.

30. Ibid., 8.

31. Ibid., 21.

32. Thomas Aquinas, *Summa Theologiae*, II-II, q. 1, a. 1.

33. Aquinas, *ST*, II-II, q. 1, a. 5.

34. On Aquinas' notion that metaphysics is natural theology see Copleston, *Aquinas*, 73-83; idem, *A History of Philosophy*, 312-23; John F. Wippel, *Metaphysical Themes in Thomas Aquinas* (Washington, DC.: Catholic University of America Press, 1984), 55-67.

35. Aquinas, *Summa Contra Gentiles*, Book I, chs. 4, 5.

36. Aquinas, *ST*, Ia, q. 1, a. 1.

37. See Copleston, *A History of Philosophy*, 314-18.

38. Aquinas, *SCG*, Book I, ch. 4.

39. Aquinas, *SCG*, Book III, chs. 39 and 48.

40. Aquinas, *SCG*, Book III, ch. 53.

41. Altmann, "Natural or Divine Prophecy," 9-17.

42. Aquinas, *De Veritate*, q. 21, a. 2. The notion of participation is crucial to Thomistic ontology and reflects the strong Neoplatonic streak in Aquinas' universe of discourse. On Neoplatonic dimension of Aquinas'

ontology see Robert J. Henle, *Saint Thomas and Platonism: Study of the Plato and Platonici Texts in the Writings of Saint Thomas* (The Hague: Martinous Nijhoff, 1956); Arthur Little, *The Platonic Heritage of Thomism* (Dublin: Golden Eagle Books, 1949). The Neoplatonic element of Aquinas' thought facilitated its acceptance by fifteenth century Jewish philosophers. In a sense, Neoplatonic ontology and epistemology mitigated the harsh naturalism of Aristotelian philosophy, and made Aristotelianism more compatible with religious concepts, sentiments, and even scriptural language. By the same token, the fusion on Neoplatonism and Aristotelianism enabled Jewish thinkers to be receptive to the Neoplatonic doctrines of Kabbalah, to the Neoplatonic world view of Abraham ibn 'Ezra and Judah Halevi (two very popular thinkers in the fifteenth century), or to return to Avicenna's philosophy. All of these trends are evident in the case of David ben Judah Messer Leon.

43. Aquinas, *ST*, II-II, q. 172, a. 1; 172, a. 2; Copleston, *The History of Philosophy*, 388-97. In his epistemology, Aquinas followed the Hellenistic commentator Themistius rather than Alexander. Themistius held that the soul is an intellectual substance and hence essentially capable of immortality; he spoke about "illumination" as the nature of intellection. As E.P. Mahoney showed, according to Aquinas, the "'illuminated' are the many potential intellects and the 'illuminating' are the many agents intellects." The ultimate source of illumination is God rather than the lowest of the Intelligences. See Edward P. Mahoney, "Themistius and the Agent Intellect in James of Viterbo and other 13th Century Philosophers (Saint Thomas, Siger of Brabant and Henry Bate)," *Augustiniana* 23 (1973): 434-38.

44. Aquinas, *SCG*, III, ch. 51.

45. See n. 42 above.

46. On the collaboration between Jewish and scholastic masters in the thirteenth century see Sirat, *A History of Jewish Philosophy*, 227.

47. In his critical edition of R. Hillel ben Samuel's *Tagmule ha-Nefesh*, Sermoneta showed the decisive dependency of Hillel on the writings of Thomas Aquinas. Sermoneta elaborated the point in his "On the Third Dissertation: *The Fall of Angels*" (in Hebrew) in *Studies in Honor of Jacob Friedman* (Jerusalem, 1974), 155-203. Sermoneta showed that, especially during the first quarter of the fourteenth century in Rome, Jewish scholars such as Judah of Rome incorporated the teachings of Aquinas into their interpretation of Maimonides, in order to make Maimonides' views more compatible with Scriptural text. See Joseph Sermoneta, "Prophecy in the Writings of R. Yehuda Romano," in *Studies in Medieval Jewish History and Literature*, vol. 2, 337-74. Sermoneta argued for the existence of a distinct "Thomistic school" in Jewish thought in his "The Scholastic Philosophic Lit-

erature in Rabbi Joseph Taitazak's *Porat Yosef* (in Hebrew), *Sefunot* 11 (=
Book of Greek Jewry 1) (1978): 135-85. Unfortunately, Sermoneta's insightful
thesis has not received due attention by contemporary scholars of Jewish
intellectual history, perhaps because modern scholars focused on Jewish-
Christian polemics rather than on Jewish-Christian scholarly dialogue.

48. For a description of this phase of the Maimonidean Controversy,
the meaning of the ban and pertinent bibliography see Chapter Four, n. 35.

49. Sermoneta, "Prophecy in the Writings of R. Judah Romano," 361, n.
39.

50. Private and public debates as well as forced sermons were major
source of Jewish acquaintance with scholastic teachings. Aquinas' *Summa
Contra Gentiles* must have figured prominently in these debates, since it was
written at the request of the Master General of the Dominican Order,
Raymond de Panaforte, as a manual for Dominican preachers. Given the
centrality of the Dominican order in the missionizing during the fourteenth
and fifteenth century, it stands to reason that Thomistic views could be
known first through oral exchanges. To answer the Christian position a
deeper understanding of scholastic theology was necessary. This could be
attained through direct access to the texts.

Although the polemical encounter had its compulsory and repressive
aspects, we need not view it exclusively as such. Some debates were con-
ducted in a friendly atmosphere, and in some cases the Jewish audience
might have actually enjoyed listening to Christian preaching. The latter point
is suggested by Isaac 'Arama, the rabbi of Qalat Ayud and leader of Aragonese Jewry in the second half of the fifteenth century. 'Arama states that "the
people of Israel would listen to Christian preachers because they were enjoy-
able." Isaac 'Arama, *'Aqedat Yizhaq* (Pressburg, 1849), introduction,
excerpted in Sarah Heller-Wilensky, *The Philosophy of Isaac Arama: In the
Framework of Philonic Philosophy* (in Hebrew) (Jerusalem: Mosad Bialik and
Tel Aviv: Dvir, 1957), 27, n. 31. The polemical encounter between Judaism
and Christian was more complex and nuanced than modern scholarship has
admitted. One way of rebutting the Christian position was to appropriate the
logic of the position to the case of Judaism. This took place in the second
half of the fifteenth century among Iberian and Italian scholars.

51. R. Isaac 'Arama openly praises the Christian theologians who
"have validated philosophy and chose its paths ... but whenever any [philo-
sophic] teaching contradicts anything from their religion, whether a root or
a branch, they would say that it is because of the shortcoming of philosophy
and its inability to comprehend divine things ... because the divine religion
is superior to philosophic inquiry ... People of my generation, watch and listen to their words because they are pleasant." Isaac 'Arama, *Hazut Qashah*
(Pressburg, 1849), excerpted in Heller-Wilensky, 69.

52. Herbert Davidson, "Medieval Jewish Philosophy in the Sixteenth Century," in *Jewish Thought in the Sixteenth Century*, 112.

53. Kellner, *Dogma*, 81.

54. A systematic analysis of fifteenth century Jewish thought is still a desideratum. To date the most comprehensive discussion is Sirat, *A History of Jewish Philosophy*, 345-412. Very enlightening are the comments of Davidson in the article cited n. 52 above; cf. Julius Guttmann, *Philosophies of Judaism*, 274-301.

55. For a detalied description of R. David's indebtedness to Abraham Bibago's *Derekh Emunah* see Chapter Four, n. 34. Bibago's work is indicative of the "conservative stance" of a Jewish philosopher who was a supporter of Maimonides as well as a very learned Aristotelian philosopher.

56. *MD*, fol. 146v.

57. *MD*, fol. 27v; R. Joseph Albo, R. Isaac 'Arama, R. Joseph ibn Shem Tov, R. Abraham Bibago, and R. Abraham Shalom all held similar views on the limitations of scientific inquiry. See Sarah Heller-Wilensky, *The Philosophy of Isaac Arama*, 59-60; Shaul Regev, "Theology and Rational Mysticism in the Writings of R. Joseph ben Shem Tov," Ph.D. diss., Hebrew University 1983, 216-19; idem, "The Rational-Mystical Trend in Fifteenth Century Jewish Thought" (in Hebrew), *JSJT* 5 (1986): 155-189.

58. *TD*, 37a.

59. *TD*, 37b-38a:

אמנם המאמינים לא יספיק להם באמונה אלא צריכין שבכח השכלי הכוסף
יכספו ויאהבו כל כך האמונה ההיא כד שיחשבו במחשבתם שימסרו בגופם
וכל אשר להם בעד קיום האמונות ההם. כי ציור השכל מקנה הידיעה
והרצון השכלי מקנה האהבה שהוא תנאי עצמי לאמונה. ולפי זה המאמין
הוא המצייר האמונה ואוהבה אהבה חזקה.

60. *ST*, II-II, q. 1, a. 2.

61. *MD*, fol. 170v.

62. *TD*, 37b.

63. *MD*, fol. 29v.

64. *TD*, 2a:

מפני שהאדם נולד משולל מכל השלמויות המוכרחים לשלמותו ולא נשלם
בשלמות האחרון בצאתו מרחם אמו כשאר בעלי החיים ... ובאורך הימים
ועזר ההשתדלות יגיע אל השלמות האחרון בהשגה.

65. *TD*, 2a-3b, is a passionate plea for study as a way of life despite the external difficulties which prevent one from doing so. R. David argued

the importance of study in *Shevah ha-Nashim* against the opponents of the secular sciences. In R. David's view, study of the sciences is crucial to the proper understanding of divine revelation leading ultimately to the knowledge of God. R. Joseph ibn Shem Tov and R. Abraham Bibago articulated the same view. See Regev, "Concerning the Problem of Philosophic Studies," cited Chapter Four, n. 48.

66. *MD*, fol. 122r; cf. ibid. fol. 27v. The same view is shared by R. Joseph ibn Shem Tov in *Kevod Elohim*, 18a-19b. For an analysis of ibn Shem Tov's position see Shaul Regev, "Theology and Rational Mysticism," 137-38. In essence, both ibn Shem Tov and R. David stressed that intellectual perfection by means of philosophic inquiry does not yield personal immortality. Only revelation does. Ibn Shem Tov's *Kevod Elohim* was an important source for the views of R. David ben Judah Messer Leon, though he frequently argued against ibn Shem Tov's position.

67. *MD*, fol. 32r.

68. *TD*, 52a; *MD*, fol. 36r. Cf. Isaac 'Arama, *'Aqedat Yizhaq*, ch. 19, 137a, and Heller-Wilensky, *The Philosophy of Isaac Arama*, 173. Isaac Abravanel, *Commentary on the Guide of the Perplexed*, II: 36, 37.

69. *MD*, fol. 28r.

70. This view comes closer to the rabbinic conception of prophecy, according to which the Written Torah and the Talmud were communicated to Moses in a miraculous verbal revelation. In the Middle Ages, this view characterizes Halevi's conception of prophecy, which clearly resonates in R. David's discussion. The fusion of Halevi's and Maimonides' views on prophecy is also characteristic of Isaac Abravanel, who was an important source to R. David notwithstanding his *ad personam* attacks on Abravanel. On Abravanel's theory of prophecy see Reines, *Maimonides and Abravanel on Prophecy*, lxxiii-lxxx.

71. On the Thomistic version of this notion see Altmann, "Natural or Divine Prophecy," 14.

72. The allegiance to Maimonidean ontology and epistemology was due to the inability of Jewish thinkers to dispense with the Aristotelian world view. Given the lack of serious alternative to Aristotle and the deep inroads Aristotelianism had made through Jewish culture and education, they could only modify the Aristotelian system from within, rather than boldly demolish it. These modifications ultimately dethroned Aristotle from his authoritative place in Jewish thought, though not until well into the sixteenth century.

73. *Hamshakhah* is a technical term in the writings of thirteenth century Kabbalists (e.g., R. 'Azriel, R. 'Ezra, R. Jacob ben Sheshet) and especially in the works of J. Joseph Gikatila. The term denotes "overflow" of

divine effluence from the supernal world to the sublunar world. See Shlomo Blickstein, "Between Philosophy and Mysticism: A Study of the Philosophical-Qabbalistic Writings of Joseph Giqatila (1248-c. 1322)," Ph.D. diss., Jewish Theological Seminary 1983, 62-78. The term appears in philosophical literature no earlier than the fourteenth century. Moses Narboni in particular employed the term *hamshakhah* in his Hebrew translation and commentary to ibn Tufayl *Hayy ibn Yaqzan*. R. David's older Iberian contemporaries R. Joseph ibn Shem Tov, R. Abraham Bibago, and R. Abraham Shalom used the same term to designate the difference between prophetic knowledge and scientific investigation. *Hamshakhah* stands for this superrationalist cognition that comes as a result of divine illumination. In this context the term "intellectualist mysticism" is clearly appropriate.

74. See William James, *Varieties of Religious Experience* (New York: Macmillan, 1961), 300. For a critical analysis of the "noetic quality" in mystical experience see Wayne Proudfoot, *Religious Experience* (Berkeley: University of California Press, 1985), 136-48.

75. Ibn Tufayl's *Hayy ibn Yaqzan (Living the Son of Wakeful)* was translated into Hebrew and commented upon by Moses Narboni. During the fifteenth century it was studied and quoted by Joseph ibn Shem Tov, Abraham Bibago, Isaac 'Arama, Isaac Abravanel, Shaul ha-Cohen, Yohanan Alemanno and R. David ben Judah Messer Leon. See Steinschneider, *HU*, 366-68, no. 210. R. David regarded ibn Tufayl's work as "the profound book which explains this matter [i.e., the conjunction between the human intellect and the Active Intellect] in the most perfect manner superior to all other books." *MD*, fols. 58r, 63v. Cf. Joseph ibn Shem Tov, *Kevod Elohim* (Ferrara, 1556. Reprint. Jerusalem, 1966?), 14b.

76. See Majid Fakhry, *A History of Islamic Philosophy*, 2d ed. (New York: Columbia University Press, 1983), 267.

77. *MD*, fol. 69r.

78. *MD*, fol. 28r.

79. *MD*, ibid.

80. See Tirosh-Rothschild, "The Concept of Torah," 97-102.

81. *MD*, fol. 34r:

> וא"כ כמו שהיה טעות בשכל לומר על הדבר שמטבעו לקבל מופת שאין לו
> מופת, כי הוא טעות לומר על הדבר שמטבעו לקבל מופת שיש לו מופת, כן
> לפי טבע הנושא וחמרו צריך שנדבר בעניני החכמה... וא"כ במציאותו ית'
> הוא טעות לומר שאין מופת עליו שטבעו הוא לקבל מופת, ובחדוש העולם
> טעות הוא לומר שיש מופת על סותרו.

R. David adopted this distinction to his defensive interpretation of Maimonides. See Chapter Four above.

82. *MD*, fol. 35r.

83. *MD*, fol. 32r.

84. *TD*, 38b-39a.

85. "Moderate fideism" is the common label given to Aquinas' synthesis of reason and faith to distinguish it from "extreme fideism." See Alvin Plantinga, "Reason and Belief in God," in *Faith and Rationality*, edited by Alvin Plantinga and Nicholas Wolterstorff (Notre Dame: University of Notre Dame Press, 1983), 87-88.

86. See Isadore Twersky, "Talmudists, Philosophers, Kabbalists: The Quest for Spirituality in the Sixteenth Century," in *Jewish Thought in the Sixteenth Century*, 431-59.

87. See Kenneth Stow, *Catholic Thought and Papal Jewry Policy 1555-1593* (New York: The Jewish Theological Seminary, 1977), 3-59.

88. See Amos Funkenstein, "Basic Types of Christian Anti-Jewish Polemics in the Late Middle Ages," *Viator* 2 (1971): 373-82.

89. *TD*, 39a; cf. *MD*, fol. 34r.

90. *MD*, fol. 31r, fol. 145r.

91. See Moshe Idel, "Differing Conceptions of Kabbalah in the Early Seventeenth Century," in *Jewish Thought in the Seventeenth Century*, 140.

92. On Renaissance theory of universal truth see Paul O. Kristeller, *Renaissance Thought and Its Sources*, 196-210. The humanist version of universal truth was itself a response to the perennial conflict of reason and faith which intensified during the Renaissance as a result of the increased knowledge of classical antiquity.

93. On the interest of Renaissance humanism in Kabbalah see Chapter Two, n. 77.

94. I concur with Bonfil that the syncretist tendencies of Renaissance Jewish scholars should be seen in the general context of Renaissance syncretism. I also endorse Bonfil's interpretation that the need to reconcile diverse modes of thought is typical to a transition period in which patterns of thought are not fully replaced by new ones so that old and new coexist. See Bonfil, *The Rabbinate*, 190. Syncretism is manifested in an eclectic style of writing.

95. R. David refers to *Sefer ha-Zohar* in *MD* fols. 7r, 19v, 154v; *EH*, fol. 67r; *TD*, 2b, 12b, 73a; *KH*, 48; *SH*, fol. 92v.

96. See Idel, "Major Currents in Italian Kabbalah," 246-49; idem, review of Robert Bonfil, *The Rabbinate in Renaissance Italy*, (in Hebrew) *Pe'amim* 4 (1980): 100-2.

97. On the mythical nature of Zoharic Kabbalah see Isaiah Tishby, *The Wisdom of the Zohar* (in Hebrew), 3d. ed. (Jerusalem: Mosad Bialik, 1971), vol. 1, 131-161; Idel, "Major Currents," 241-2.

98. *MD*, fol. 119r. A similar position was held by R. Joseph ibn Shem Tov and reflects the continuation of the Maimonidean tradition.

Chapter Six

1. R. David ben Judah Messer Leon shared this conception of theology. See *TD*, 2a-4a. R. David regards the theologian as the "wise man absolutely speaking" *(hakham be-hehlet)* while referring to a scholar who lacks the knowledge of theology as a "wise man relatively speaking" *(hakham be-qishur)*. Cf. Aquinas, *SCG* I: ch. 1; *ST*, Ia, q. 1, a. 5, a. 6.

2. On the encyclopedic tendencies of Sephardic scholars in the Ottoman Empire see Hacker, "Intellectual Activity," 107-10.

3. For the textual dependence of these three authors on Thomas Aquinas see Sermoneta, "Scholastic Philosophic Literature," cited in the previous chapter; Robert Bonfil, "The Doctrine of the Soul and Holiness in the Teachings of R. Obadiah Sforno" (in Hebrew), *Eshel Beer Sheva* 1 (1976): 200-57; Sirat, *History of Jewish Philosophy*, 388-89.

4. Shaye Cohen, *From the Maccabees to the Mishnah* (Philadelphia: The Westminster Press, 1987), 62.

5. For comprehensive surveys of Jewish dogmatism consult David Neumark, *Toledot ha-Iqqarim be-Israel* (Odessa: Moriah, 1919, 1921); Louis Jacobs, *Principles of the Jewish Faith: An Analytical Study* (New York: Basic Books, 1964); and more recently Kellner, *Dogma*, cited in the previous chapter. For a bibliographical survey of the topic see Menachem M. Kellner, "Dogma in Medieval Jewish Thought: A Bibliographical Survey," *Studies in Bibliography and Booklore* 15 (1984): 5-21. Kellner's work was closely consulted for this chapter.

6. Kellner, *Dogma*, 17.

7. On Karaite dogmatism see Abraham Halkin, "A Karaite Creed," in *Studies in Judaica, Karaitica, and Islamica Presented to Leon Nemoy*, edited by S.R. Brunswick (Ramat Gan: Bar Ilan University, 1982), 145-53.

8. See Saadia Gaon, *The Book of Doctrines and Opinions*, translated by Samuel Rosenblat (New Haven: Yale University Press, 1948), 11-12. For a modern critique of Saadia's distinction see Marvin Fox, "On the Rational Commandments in Saadia's Philosophy: A Reexamination," in *Modern Jewish Ethics* edited by Marvin Fox (Columbus: University of Ohio Press, 1975), 174-87.

9. See Joseph Dan, *Hebrew Ethical and Homiletical Literature* (in Hebrew) (Jerusalem: Keter, 1975), 47-65.

10. Kellner, *Dogma*, 34-49.

11. R. Abraham ben David (Rabad) was not familiar with Maimonides' *Commentary on the Mishnah* where Maimonides introduced the principles of Judaism. The Rabad rejected Maimonides' claim that to belief in the corporeality of God is heretical. See Rabad's gloss to Maimonides' *Mishneh Torah, Book of Knowledge*, Laws of Repentance, III, 7.

12. See R. Moses ben Nahman (Nahmanides), "Torat ha-Shem Temimah" in *Kitvey Rabbenu Moshe ben Nahman* edited by Charles B. Chavel (Jerusalem: Mosad Ha-Rav Kook, 1978), vol. 1, 7th printing, 150.

13. On the Ramah's opposition to Maimonides see Septimus, *Hispano-Jewish Culture in Transition*, 39-60.

14. Kellner, *Dogma*, 75-80; Solomon Shechter, "The Dogmas of Judaism," in his *Studies in Judaism: Essays on Persons, Concepts, and Movements of Thought in Jewish Tradition* (New York: Atheneum, 1970), 90.

15. Kellner, *Dogma*, 80-2.

16. On the centrality of the Messianic belief in the Jewish-Christian debate of the fifteenth century see Baer, *The Jews in Christian Spain*, 2:170-210.

17. For a list of the major anti-Christian Jewish philosophical treatises and a detailed analysis of the major philosophic arguments against Christian doctrine see Daniel Lasker, *Jewish Philosophical Polemics*. Although Lasker presents the philosophical argumentation as a genre in medieval Jewish literature, most of his material in fact comes from the fifteenth century. The philosophical debate with Christian scholars required detailed knowledge of Christian theology as well as familiarity with scholastic methods of argumentation and philosophical terminology. Acquiring all of these led Jews to reshape their internal formulation of Jewish beliefs.

18. Kellner noted that Duran's conception of theology is reminiscent of Aquinas' discussion in the opening of the *Summa Theologiae* (*Dogma*, 96). My claim is stronger: the entire concept of Jewish theology and in turn of Jewish dogma was indebted to Christian scholasticism, especially to Aquinas.

19. That Marranism exerted an impact on Jewish spirituality has long been recognized. However, scholars so far have focused on the seventeenth century when Marranos, who fled from the Iberian Peninsula, openly returned to their mother religion. I suggest that Marranism contributed to the spiritualization of Judaism already in the fifteenth century when Jews who remained loyal to their religion modified their self-definition in order to address the challenge of Marranism.

20. For a summary of fifteenth century Jewish dogmatism see Kellner, *Dogma*, 108-217.

21. All references to *Rosh Amanah* are to Kellner's critical edition and English translation cited Chapter Four, n. 53.

22. Abravanel, *Principles of Faith*, 205, excerpted also in Kellner, *Dogma*, 187.

23. While Abravanel continued to theorize within the conceptual framework of medieval scholasticism, he was quite receptive to Kabbalah. See Idel, "Kabbalah and Ancient Philosophy," 86-94.

24. I here follow Kellner's innovative suggestion which convincingly explains the alleged about-face of Abravanel concerning Maimonides. Most scholars have noted the discrepancy between the first twenty-two chapters of *Rosh Amanah*, in which Abravanel defended Maimonides against the critique of Crescas and Albo, and the twenty-third chapter, in which Abravanel claims that every teaching of Judaism has a status of principle. Kellner resolves this apparent discrepancy by suggesting that Abravanel defended Maimonides all along only to the extent that the principles are didactic devices for the sake of the unlearned multitude. See Kellner, *Dogma*, 191.

25. Abravanel, *Principles of Faith*, 192. Excerpted also in Kellner, *Dogma*, 184.

26. *TD*, 6a. Abravanel rejected this very scientific approach to the Torah claiming (correctly) that it reflects an adaptation to a Christian mode of thought. See Abravanel, *Principles of Faith*, 194.

27. This is the gist of Abravanel's critique of dogmatism in *Principles of Faith*, 195.

28. This picture of the universe was commonly held by all Jewish philosophers of the Late Middle Ages who adhered to the Neoplatonized version of medieval Aristotelianism. See Davidson, "Medieval Jewish Philosophy in the Sixteenth Century," 113.

29. *TD*, 6a.

30. Albo, *The Book of Principles*, I:11.

31. *TD*, 6a.

32. *TD*, 6d. The comparison of the science of theology to medicine was employed as well by Abraham Bibago, *Derekh Emunah*, III:1.

33. Albo, *The Book of Principles*, III:25.

34. *TD*, 7a.

35. For a comparison of Isaac Abravanel's objections and those of R. David ben Judah consult Kellner, *Dogma*, 279-281, note 8 and ibid. 284, n. 12.

36. See Albo, *Book of Principles*, I:3; Abravanel, *Principles of Faith*, 182.

37. *TD*, 8b.

38. Ibid.

39. Crescas' objections were summarized by Abravanel, *Principles of Faith*, 72-73.

40. *TD*, 8b-9a.

41. *TD*, 9a. Cf. Abravanel, *Principles of Faith*, 85-91.

42. *TD*, 9a.

43. See n. 11 above. Albo quoted the gloss of the Rabad on Maimonides in his *Book of Principles* I:2, Isaac Abravanel referred to it in *Principles of Faith*, 112. For a recent analysis of the Rabad's objection to Maimonides' abstract conception of God see Jerome Gellman, "The Philosophical Hasagot of Rabad on Maimonides' Mishneh Torah," *The New Scholasticism* 58 (1984): 145-69.

44. *TD*, 9b.

45. Cf. Albo, *Book of Principles*, I:4; Abravanel, *Principles of Faith*, 150.

46. *TD*, 10b based on Midrash Bereshit Rabbah, 1, 5.

47. Cf. Abravanel, *Principles of Faith*, 66.

48. Maimonides' omission of the belief in creation from the list of Thirteen Principles puzzled medieval and modern scholars. Most scholars have held that Maimonides' Fourth Principle implicitly includes the belief in creation. For a detailed discussion of the problem, and a detailed bibliography, see Kellner, *Dogma*, 57-61.

49. *TD*, 10a.

50. Cf. *Book of Principles*, I:3, and by Abravanel, *Principles of Faith*, 148.

51. *TD*, 10b.

52. Cf. Albo, *Book of Principles*, I:3; Abravanel, *Principles of Faith*, 148 and 70.

53. *TD*, 10b.

54. Ibid.

55. Cf. Crescas, *Or Adonai*, III:5:1; Albo, *Book of Principles*, III:13; Abravanel, *Principles of Faith*, 133. Whether or not the Torah will change in the Messianic future was the crux of the debate between Jews and Christians. Midrash Song of Songs Rabba I,2,4 pondered the possibility of such change. Albo cited this particular Midrash in *Book of Principles* III:19.

56. *TD*, 11a.

57. *TD*, 11a-b. On the implicit antinomianism in Maimonidean and Kabbalistic eschatology see Gershom Scholem, "The Crisis of Tradition in Jewish Messianism," in his *The Messianic Idea in Judaism* (New York: Schocken, 1971), 49-77.

58. The Messiah is a counterpart to Moses, i.e., a philosopher, king, prophet, and legislator. For an excellent exposition of Maimonides' naturalist conception of the Messianic Age see Joel L. Kraemer, "On Maimonides' Messianic Posture," in *Studies in Medieval Jewish History and Literature*, 2: 109-142.

59. *TD*, 11b.

60. R. David regarded the resurrection of the dead as a miracle. He discusses it at some length in *TD*, 57b-58a in the context of discussing the belief in miracles which R. David lists as one of the three axioms of Judaism.

61. *TD*, 11b.

62. Cf. Albo, *Book of Principles*, I:1, 44; IV:42. Bibago, *Derekh Emunah*, III:1, 101c; Abravanel, *Principles of Faith*, Chap. 3.

63. *TD*, 12a-b.

64. Abraham Bibago, *Derekh Emunah*, 99c. Consult Kellner, *Dogma*, 170-75; Lazaroff, *The Theology of Abraham Bibago*, 12-15.

65. *TD*, 36a.

66. Three modern scholars of Maimonides have attempted to solve this puzzle. Lawrence Kaplan, "Maimonides on the Miraculous Element in Prophecy," *HTR* 70 (1977): 233-56; Herbert Davidson, "Maimonides' Secret

Position on Creation," in *Studies in Medieval Jewish History and Literature*, 1: 16-40; Warren Z. Harvey, "A Third Approach to Maimonides' Cosmogony-Prophetology Puzzle," *HTR* 74 (1981): 287-301. Each of them has resolved the puzzle differently, leaving the puzzle intact.

67. For a concise exposition of the three positions on the origins of the world see Davidson, "Maimonides' Secret Position," 19-20.

68. See Alvin Reines, "Maimonides Concept of Miracles," *HUCA* 45 (1974): 243-85. According to Reines, Maimonides' exoteric "theology of creationism" stood in sharp contrast to his esoteric naturalist views.

69. For a summary of the three opinions on prophecy and their interpretation by medieval and modern scholars consult Kaplan, "Maimonides on the Miraculous," 234-36.

70. *TD*, 53b.

71. See Kaplan, "Maimonides on the Miraculous," 247-53.

72. *TD*. 40b.

73. See Davidson, "Maimonides' Secret Position," cited n. 66 above.

74. On Gersonides' view of creation from pre-existent matter see Seymour Feldman, "Platonic Themes in Gersonides' Cosmology," in *Salo Wittmayer Baron Jubilee Volume* (Jerusalem: American Academy for Jewish Research, 1975), 383-405.

75. *TD*, 40b.

76. Ibid., 40a.

77. Ibid.

78. On the centrality of the belief in creation among fifteenth century Jewish thinkers see Kellner, *Dogma*, 213-17.

79. *TD*, 40b.

80. Ibid.

81. Saadia Gaon, *The Book of Beliefs and Opinions*, Chap. 1, 40-46.

82. *TD*, 41b.

83. Ibid., 41b-42a.

84. R. David cites ibn Gabirol's enigmatic statement in *Keter Malkhut (The Royal Crown)* as the source of this doctrine:

ומחכמתך אצלת חפץ מזומן בפעל ואומן למשך היש מאין כהמשך האור הנמשך מהעין.

For a modern interpretation of this statement see S. Pines, "*'And he called out to nothingness and it was split,'* A Note on a Passage in ibn Gabirol's *Keter Malkhut*" (in Hebrew), *Tarbiz* 50 (1980-81): 339-97. Ibn Gabirol used light *(or)* as synonymous with the process of creation/emanation.

85. Midrash *Bereshit Rabbah*, Lekh Lekha, 39.

86. *TD*, 41b.

87. *TD*, 42a.

88. *TD*, 43a.

89. Ibid.

90. *TD*, 40b.

91. *TD*, 44a; cf. 92b.

92. *TD*, 42a; cf. 75a-b.

93. *TD*, 40b.

94. Ibid.

95. On the Kabbalist interpretation of creation *ex nihilo* see Scholem, *Kabbalah*, 88-105; idem, *Origins of the Kabbalah*, edited by R.J. Zwi Werblowsky and translated by Alan Arkush (Philadelphia: The Jewish Publication Society; Princeton: Princeton University Press, 1987), 421-430. Scholem noted that the Kabbalistic interpretation changed the original meaning of the belief in creation toward a pantheistic position. He suggested a pagan Neoplatonic philosopher, Scotus Erigena, as the source from which the early Kabbalists of Gerona derived their identification of creation and emanation from the essence of God. While the precise source is still unclear, the pantheism of Kabbalistic cosmology is rather evident. Since pantheism was regarded as heretical, the Kabbalists of Gerona did well to guard the creation as a mystery to be taught esoterically only. R. David's knowledge of Kabbalistic cosmology is too general to determine a precise source.

96. *TD*, 45b; cf. 72b. This doctrine was very common in the fifteenth century, probably under the influence of Kabbalah. It is discussed further in Chapter Seven below.

97. See Bracha Sack, "R. Joseph Taitazak's Commentaries," (in Hebrew) *Shlomo Pines, Jubilee Volume on the Occasion of his Eightieth Birthday* (= *Jerusalem Studies in Jewish Thought* 7) vol. 1, 341-56.

98. Averroës, *Middle Commentary on Aristotle's "Metaphysics"*, MS Paris 915, fol. 146r:

הנה הוא יתברך שמו הנמצאות כלם בצד יותר שלם וכל הנמצאות הם בצד
יותר חסר, הנה הוא היודע הנמצאות כלם בידיעה השלמה.

R. David was familiar with this text and often cited from it in his *'Ein ha-Qore*. Citing Averroës as his authoritative source, R. David states in fol. 240v:

כי הנמצאות הם עומדות ברומו של עולם בשכל השם יתברך והוא המציאות
היותר משובח האפשרי להם כי שם עומדות ברוחניות ובאחדות קצויי עד
שהוא ית' כל הנמצאות באופן רוחני ומשובח כאחד.

99. On this distinction in medieval Muslim philosophy see Emil L. Fackenheim, "The Possibility of the Universe in Al Farabi, ibn Sina and Maimonides," *PAAJR* 16 (1947): 39-43.

100. *TD*, 44b.

101. *TD*, 46b; 49b.

102. *TD*, 52b, 54b. Conversely, when Maimonides' professed position accords with the rabbinic position (as in the case of divine knowledge of particulars), R. David praises Maimonides for not following the philosophers.

103. *TD*, 51b.

104. On Maimonides' Platonic political theory see Lawrence Berman, "Maimonides the Disciple of Alfarabi," *Israel Oriental Studies* 4 (1974): 154-78; reprinted in Joseph A. Buijs, *Maimonides, A Collection of Critical Essays* (Notre Dame: University of Notre Dame Press, 1988), 195-214.

105. *TD*, 51b.

106. Ibid.

107. Maimonides, *Guide*, II:37.

108. *TD*, 53a.

109. Sarah Klein-Braslavy, "Ma'amad Har Sinai be-Mishnato shel R. Nissim ben Reuven Gerondi (ha-Ran)," *Sinai* 80 (1977): 26-37.

110. Undoubtedly, R. David's interpretation of the gathering at Sinai attests the impact of Judah Halevi's thought. See Judah Halevi, *Kuzari*, IV: 3; Yohanan Silman, "Historical Reality in the *Kuzari*," (in Hebrew), *Daat* 2-3 (1978-9): 29-42. Halevi's interpretation also affected the view of R. Nissim Gerondi see *Derashot ha-Ran le-Rabbenu Nissim ben Reuben Gerondi*, edited by Aryeh L. Feldman (Jerusalem: Makhon Shalem, 1977), 81-83.

111. Kalman P. Bland, "Moses and the Law According to Maimonides," in *Mystics, Philosophers and Politicians, Essays on Jewish Intellectual History in Honor of Alexander Altmann*, edited by Judah Reinharz and Daniel Swetchinski (Durham: University of North Carolina, 1982), 53.

112. Maimonides, *Commentary on the Mishnah*, Sanhedrin: X, Introduction; *TD*, 24b, 59b.

113. *TD*, 24b.

114. *TD*, 57a.

115. *TD*, 52a, 53b.

116. *TD*, 74b.

117. *TD*, 75a.

118. *TD*, 61b; cf. Gersonides, *Wars of the Lord*, VI: 2:10.

119. *TD*, 61b.

120. Gersonides, *Wars of the Lord*, VI: 2: 12.

121. *TD*, 62b.

122. On this basis R. David defends Maimonides in his *'Ein ha-Qore*, fol. 221v, claiming that Maimonides truly believed in the possibility of miracles. In *'Ein ha-Qore* R. David applies the claims that nature is only highly regular in order to defend Maimonides against those who claim that he did not believe in miracles.

123. This is essentially Aquinas' position. See, *SCG* Book II, Pt. III, Chap. 102.

124. Nahmanides, *Perush 'al ha-Torah*, Exod. 13: 16; and "Torat ha-Shem Temimah," 150-54.

125. *EH*, fol. 224r:

וכמו שהאריך הרמבן ונתפאר שהמציא זה הוא לבד שכן יעודי התורה נסים
נסתרים אינם מתיחסים עם המצות בטבע ... ואני רואה שגנבו מהרב
בפרסום.

R. David believed that Nahmanides derived his well-known distinction from the ending of Maimonides' Epistle on Resurrection. R. Joseph ibn Shem Tov has already noted Nahmanides' indebtedness to Maimonides on this point. See *Kevod Elohim*, 21a.

126. *TD*, 62a.; cf. Abraham Bibago, *Derekh Emunah*, 79d.

127. The origin of R. David's comment is Bibago, *Derekh Emunah*, 76b. On the dominant view among Muslim philosophers see Fazlur Rahman, *Prophecy in Islam: Philosophy and Orthodoxy* (London: George Allen and Unwin, 1958), 45-52.

128. Abraham ibn 'Ezra, *Perush 'al ha-Torah*, Num. 20:8.

129. *TD*, 63b.

130. See Aviezer Ravitsky, "The Anthropological Theory of Miracles in Medieval Jewish Philosophy," in *Studies in Medieval Jewish History and Literature*, 2: 231-51.

131. Ibid., 260.

132. *TD*, 63b. Already the rabbinic sages limited prophetic power to change the Torah. *Babylonian Talmud*, Berakhot 5a. Consult also Ephraim Urbach, *The Sages, Their Concepts and Beliefs*, translated by Israel Abrahams (Jerusalem: Magnes Press, 1975), vol. 1, 304.

Chapter Seven

1. The stylistic differences among the three works reflect both the differences in their subject matter and the evolution of R. David's cultural orientation. I have suggested that the scholastic style of *Tehillah le-David* indicates the growing impact of Sephardic scholarship on R. David ben Judah. Despite the stylistic differences among these three works they reflect a coherent conception of God to be discussed in this chapter.

2. See the discussion of these dogmas in the previous chapter.

3. *The Encyclopedia of Philosophy*, edited by Paul Edwards (New York: Macmillan, 1972) 2d. printing, s.v. "Theism."

4. *TD*, 86b.

5. That R. David employed the scholastic style indicates not only his continuity with medieval literary traditions, but also his need to systematize existing philosophic knowledge. The need for such systematization was felt primarily after the decade of expulsions that ended the fifteenth century. The continued preoccupation with philosophy does not detract from our claim that, during the sixteenth century, Jewish Aristotelianism declined as a creative force thus paving the way for the rise of Kabbalah.

6. While most scholars have recognized the Neoplatonized nature of medieval Aristotelianism, the precise nature of this phenomenon still awaits systematic analysis. Crucial to the discussion is the so-called Renaissance of Abraham ibn 'Ezra in the second half of the fourteenth century in the works of Samuel ibn Motot, Samuel Zarza, Joseph Bonfils, Shem Tov ben Isaac ibn Shaprut, and Solomon Franco. Their works, extant mainly in manuscript, are least known. For preliminary comments consult Sirat, *A History of Jewish Philosophy*, 332-44, and the bibliography in 446-7.

7. On the various strands of thirteenth century Kabbalah see Scholem, *Kabbalah*, 48-61. Scholem distinguished between five major strands of Kabbalistic thought: the Kabbalah of Gerona, the Gnostic Kabbalah of Cas-

tile, the Prophetic Kabbalah of Abraham Abulafia, the Kabbalah of *Sefer ha-'Iyyun*, and the Kabbalah of *Sefer ha-Temunah*. He viewed the *Zohar* essentially as the fusion of the first two strands. Recent research by Moshe Idel, *Kabbalah: New Perspectives* has refined Scholem's reconstruction on many points too numerous to be summarized here.

8. The precise dating of *Sefer ha-Zohar* is still debated. Scholem dated the earliest stratum of the *Zohar (Midrash ha-Ne'elam)* to 1275 and the writing of the bulk of the Zohar between then and 1286. Isaiah Tishby, on the other hand, argued that the earliest stratum of the *Zohar* was written in 1286, and the bulk was composed from 1293 until the death of Moses de Leon in 1305. See Tishby, *The Wisdom of the Zohar*, 1: 105-6. Recently, Yehudah Liebes argued convincingly that while Moses de Leon composed most of the text of the *Zohar*, the work as a whole reflects the activity of a group of Kabbalists including R. Bahya b. Asher, R. Joseph b. Shalom Ashkenazi, R. Joseph Giqatila, R. Joseph of Hamadan, and R. David b. Judah he-hasid. See Yehudah Liebes, "How was *Sefer ha-Zohar* Composed?" *JSJT* 8 (1989): 1-71.

9. R. David accepted *Sefer ha-Zohar* as an ancient Midrash and shared the reverence of Kabbalists to this text. He composed a commentary to certain portions of the *Zohar* (mentioned in *TD*, 73a) and utilized material from the *Zohar* in his sermons.

10. R. David refers by title only to Recanati's *Beur 'al ha-Torah* (*EH*, fol. 147r, 177r; *MD*, fol. 27r, *SH*, fol. 99r), but he also made use of Recanati's *Ta'amey ha-Miẓvot* (*MD*, fols. 12r-v), and his *Perush ha-Tefilot* (*MD*, fol. 2v) without specifying his source. Sometimes R. David copied Recanati's text only to reject Recanati's position later, and other times R. David reinterpreted Recanati's position by situating it in a different context. An example of the latter is R. David's use of one motif from Recanati's *Perush ha-Tefilot* in R. David's *Magen David* as noted by Idel in his "Between the Concept of Essence and Instruments," 104-6. R. David cites *Ma'arekhet ha-Elohot* in *MD*, fol. 6r, in the context of discussing the doctrine of Sefirot as the essence of God. R. David was probably familiar with two contemporary commentaries to this text composed in Italy during the 1490s: one by R. Judah Hayyat and the other by R. Reuben Ẓarfati. On these two commentaries see Ephraim Gottlieb, "The Author of the Anonymous Commentary to *Ma'arekhet ha-Elohot*" (in Hebrew), in his *Studies in the Kabbalah Literature*, 357-69.

11. Two modern scholars, Joseph ben Shlomo and Ephraim Gottlieb, have already debated whether or not David believed in the existence of Sefirot. I discussed this debate and attempted to resolve it in my "The Sefirot as the Essence of God." Sections from that article are revised and incorporated into this chapter.

12. Among the few Kabbalists active during the 1530s and 1540s in Ottoman Turkey were Meir ibn Gabbai, Hayyim ben Jacob Obadiah de

Bushal, Shlomo Alkabeẓ, Joseph Taitaẓak, and the anonymous author of *Galya Raza*. On the status of Kabbalah in the Ottoman Empire during the first half of the sixteenth century see Chapter Four, n. 55. While Kabbalah was not the dominant mode of thought among the Iberian refugees, some of them did bring Kabbalistic manuscripts and oral traditions to the Ottoman Empire.

13. The Messianic agitation among Iberian refugees during the first half of the sixteenth century is well attested, although the impact of this Messianism is still debated. Scholem argued that this Messianism was the major impulse for the rise of Lurianic Kabbalah and later the Sabbatean Movement. See Scholem, *Major Trends in Jewish Mysticism* (New York: Schocken, 1941), 244-86; idem, *Sabbatai Sevi, the Mystical Messiah*, translated by R.J. Zwi Werblowsky (Princeton: Princeton University Press, 1973), 15-124. Scholem's thesis has been widely accepted by the scholarly community until the recent challenge of Idel, *Kabbalah: New Perspectives*, 264-267. Whereas I tend to agree with Idel on the interpretation of Lurianic Kabbalah, it appears to me that there is a connection between Iberian Messianism and the consolidation of Kabbalah prior to Isaac Luria, primarily in the works of Meir ibn Gabbai and Moses Cordovero. For example, ibn Gabbai's *Derekh Emunah* is a short summary of Kabbalistic doctrine of *Sefirot* almost in a "catechismal" form. Such summary could have been written to spread the knowledge of Kabbalah for Messianic purposes. Idel himself admits that Cordovero's *Pardes Rimmonim* is a *Summa Kabbalistica* of Spanish Kabbalah; see Idel, "Major Currents in Italian Kabbalah," 250. Cordovero's systematization of Kabbalah could have been propelled by messianic impulses since he was deeply concerned with the exilic existence of Israel. See Bracha Sack, "The Exile of Israel and the Exile of the Shechinah in "Or Yakar" of Rabbi Moses Cordovero" (in Hebrew), *JSJT* 4 (1982): 157-78.

14. On R. David's interpretation of this cardinal dogma see Chapter Six above.

15. All English translations of Aquinas come from Anton C. Pegis, *Basic Writings of St. Thomas Aquinas* (New York: Random House, 1944).

16. The secondary literature on Aquinas' proofs of God's existence is too extensive to be cited in full. I have consulted in particular the following works: Etienne Gilson, *Elements of Christian Philosophy* (Garden City, 1960), 43-87, 291-300; Anton C. Pegis, "Four Medieval Ways to God," *The Monist* 54 (1970): 317-58; Joseph Owens, *St. Thomas Aquinas on the Existence of God: The Collected Papers of Joseph Owens*, edited by John R. Catan (Albany: State University of New York Press, 1986); Copleston, *Aquinas*; Anthony Kenny, *The Five Ways* (Notre Dame: University of Notre Dame Press, 1969. Reprint. 1980); David Burrell, *Aquinas: God and Action* (Notre Dame: University of Notre Dame Press, 1976). Burrell's interpretation is the most radical, claiming that Aquinas had no doctrine of God, but that he only

wished "to ascertain what logical structure true statements about God would have to have, and to determine a class of expressions which could be used of him with propriety" (p. 69). While one may not agree with Burrell, his work illuminates the "grammar" of Aquinas' metaphysics.

17. For a general introduction to the types of arguments for the existence of God, selected representative texts, and contemporary philosophical analysis see John Hick, *The Existence of God* (New York: Macmillan, 1964). On the Cosmological Argument in particular see William Lane Craig, *The Cosmological Argument from Plato to Leibniz* (London: MacMillan Press, 1980), and the secondary literature cited there. On the proofs for God's existence in medieval Jewish philosophy see Norbert Samuelson, "On Proving God's Existence," *Judaism* 16 (1967): 21-36.

18. *TD*, 71a.

19. *TD*, 71a; cf. *MD*, fol. 31v, in which R. David combines the argument from motion with the argument from efficient causality.

20. *TD*, 71a.

21. I borrowed the distinction between "vertical" and "horizontal" hierarchy of causes from Copleston, *Aquinas*, 123.

22. The claim that being has degrees makes little sense to modern philosophers, but it was an accepted principle for most medieval philosophers, especially those who exhibited strong Neoplatonic tendencies. If God is the perfection of being, and if things imitate God to the extent that things participate in the Divine Being, then things exhibit different degrees of being. Among modern neo-Thomists Etienne Gilson attempted a systematic defense of this view. He claimed that Aristotelian logic could not handle existential propositions, see Etienne Gilson, *Being and Some Philosophers* (Toronto: Pontifical Institute of Mediaeval Studies, 1949), 190. Therefore, Gilson argued that existence cannot be conceived and that it functions neither as a copula nor predicate in such propositions as "John is." According to Gilson's interpretation of Aquinas, "If I say that *x is*, the essence of x exercises through my judgment the same act of existing which it exercises in x." Ibid., 201. For a recent critique of Gilson's position see Ralph McInnery, *Being and Predication: Thomistic Interpretations* (Washington DC.: Catholic University of America Press, 1986), 173-80.

23. *TD*, 71a.

24. *TD*, 71a.

25. Aquinas, *SCG*, Book I, Chap. 13. For an analysis of the discussion in the *Summa Contra Gentiles* see Joseph Owens, "The Conclusion of the Prima Via," in his *St. Thomas Aquinas*, 154-158.

26. *TD*, 71a.

27. On Averroës' identification of God with the Unmoved Mover and with the First Intelligence see Harry A. Wolfson, "Averroës' Lost Treatise on the Prime Mover," in *Studies in the History of Philosophy and Religion*, 1: 403-4. For a summary of Averroës' metaphysics in relation to his predecessors Avicenna and Alfarabi see Herbert Davidson, "Averroës on the Active Intellect as a Cause of Existence," *Viator* 18 (1987): 191-225, esp. 192-201.

28. *TD*, 71a.

29. These two works were paraphrases of Neoplatonic texts circulating in the Middle Ages under the name of Aristotle. *The Book of Causes (Liber De Causis)* was a paraphrase of Proclous' *Elements of Philosophy*, and *The Theology of Aristotle (Theologia Aristotelis)* was a paraphrase of Plotinus' *Enneads*, Books 4, 5, and 6. These two paraphrases elaborated an emanationist metaphysics which exerted profound impact on Muslim philosophy and in turn on Jewish philosophy. On these texts and their importance for Muslim philosophy see Majid Fakhry, *History of Islamic Philosophy*, 19-30. The *Liber de Causis* was translated into Hebrew first by Zerahya ben Isaac Shealtiel Gracian (published by Alexander Scheiber, *Pseudo-Aristoteles Liber de Causis* (Budapest, 1916), and again by Judah of Rome see Steinschneider, *HU*, 263-67, no. 142. These translations were done from the twelfth century Latin version, even though the Arabic original of this work, *Kalam fi Mahd al-Khayr* was quite widely known. On the Arabic text see Richard Taylor, "'Abd al-Latif al-Baghdadi's Epitome of the Kalam fi Mahd al-Khayr (*Liber de Causis*)," in *Islamic Theology and Philosophy*, edited by Michael Marmura (Albany: State University of New York Press, 1984), 236-48. It is difficult to determine whether R. David had a direct knowledge of the *Liber de Causis* (in either Hebrew or Latin) or whether he derived his knowledge from a secondary source. One possible source was Abraham Abulafia's *Imrey Shefer*. See Idel, "The Magical and Neoplatonic Interpretations," 96-7. R. David could have known the text also from references in the writings of Thomas Aquinas. On the impact of the *Liber de Causis* on the philosophy of Aquinas see Henle, *Saint Thomas and Platonism*, 331-35.

30. See W.J. Hankey, *God in Himself: Aquinas' Doctrine of God as Expounded in the Summa Theologiae* (New York: Oxford University Press, 1987).

31. On Abraham Shalom's use of the concept Necessary Being see Herbert Davidson, *The Philosophy of Abraham Shalom*, 20-21; on Abraham Bibago's employment of the concept see Lazaroff, *The Theology of Abraham Bibago*, 10.

32. *TD*, 71a.

33. Avicenna's proof of God's existence on the basis of possibility and necessity appeared in a seminal form in the writings of Alfarabi. See *Uyun al Masai* in Alfarabi's *Philosophische Abhandlungen* edited by Friedrich Dietrichi (Leiden, 1890), 57; Alfarabi was the first Muslim philosopher to work out Aristotle's analysis of being (*Posterior Analytics*, Bk. II, Chap. 3, 90b 10; II: 7, 92b; II: 8, 93a, 6ff) to the context of Islam and to the peculiarity of the Arabic language. On Alfarabi's analysis of being see Fadlou Shehadi, *Metaphysics in Islamic Theology* (Delmar: Caravan Books, 1982), 45-69. Avicenna's proof of possibility and necessity is based on the Alfarabian distinction of essence-existence. Accordingly "existence" is a regular predicate. See Shehadi, ibid., 71-85. For an analysis of Avicenna's proof of God's existence see Davidson, *Proofs for Eternity*, 281-304.

34. On the distinction see Fackenheim, "The Possibility of the Universe," 39-41.

35. See Alexander Altmann, "Essence and Existence in Maimonides," in his *Studies in Religious Philosophy and Mysticism* (Ithaca: Cornell University Press, 1969), 115; Reprinted in *Maimonides: A Collection of Critical Essays*, edited by Joseph A. Buijs (Notre Dame: University of Notre Dame Press, 1988), 148-165.

36. Maimonides, *The Guide of the Perplexed*, II, 1.

37. Averroës, *The Incoherence of the Incoherence*, 1: 179-80. The origin of the distinction between the logical and ontological meanings of "existence" goes back to Aristotle who distinguished four meanings of being *(to on), Metaphysics* Book 4, Chap. 7, 1011b, 26, and Book 9, Chap. 10, 1051a 34-35.

38. See Davidson, *The Philosophy of Abraham Shalom*, 20.

39. See n. 27 above. The debate between Avicenna and Averroës was summarized in Gersonides, *Milhamot Adonai* (Leipzig, 1866) V:iii:12, 45d-46a.

40. Moses Narboni, *Beur 'al Moreh Nebukhim*, ed. by Jacob Goldenthal (Vienna, 1859), 9a; see Altmann, "Essence and Existence," in *Studies*, 121-22; in *Maimonides*, 157.

41. Recent scholarship has recognized the need to view Aquinas' doctrine of *esse* in the context of the philosophical debate among the Muslim metaphysicians, Avicenna and Averroës. See Joseph Owens, "The Accidental and Essential Character of Being in the Doctrine of St. Thomas Aquinas," in his *St. Thomas Aquinas*, 74.

42. The appropriate translation of Aquinas' *esse* is still disputed. Joseph Bobik, *Aquinas on Being and Essence: A Translation and Interpreta-*

tion (Notre Dame: University of Notre Dame Press, 1965), uses "being" to translate *ens* and "existence" to translate *esse*. Owens objected to this translation on the ground that it obscures the Thomistic point that "existence is the only kind of being." R. David ben Judah Messer Leon is less precise in his use of terms. The Hebrew words *heyot* and *meẓiut* appear in his writings interchangeably.

43. Owens, "The Accidental and Essential Character of Being," 74.

44. Owens, "Diversity and Community of Being," in his *St. Thomas Aquinas*, 102.

45. Ibid., 103.

46. The following rendering of the Fourth Way is indebted to Anthony Kenny, *The Five Ways*, 70. Most scholars agree that the Fourth Way is the most Platonic of the proofs of God's existence. While some contemporary scholars (e.g., Peter Geach) find it lacking in rigor, others (e.g., Etienne Gilson) regard it the most profound proof of God's existence.

47. Aristotle, *Metaphysics*, Book 2, Chap. 1, 993b 30.

48. See *EH*, fol. 37v:

כי הש"י מחוייב המציאות במוחלט אין לו אפשרות כלל וזהו מופת חותך
אצל שרשי ב"ס אע"פ שלדעת ב"ר יש להשיב בזה בשרשים חזקים אין זה
מקומו כבר ביארתים בהרחבה בלקוטי על פי' הכוונות ועל פי' המורה.

The passage indicates that R. David already reviewed the debate between Avicenna and Averroës in his glosses to Moses Narboni's commentary on Alghazali's *The Intentions of the Philosophers* and on Maimonides' *The Guide of the Perplexed*. Cf. *MD*, fol. 24r:

וכבר ידעת שזה סובב על סברתו [של הרמב"ם] שלקחו מב"ס רבו שהמציאות
מקרה לנמצא כמו שהתחיל פרק מפרקיו [מו"נ א', נ"ז] וכך אשר הטיב עליו
הנרבוני "מי יתן ולא נמצא", ושבשביל ההתחלה הראשונה היה מציאותו
מהותו וזה היה מחוייב המציאות. וזה השרש כבר ידעת הפסדו ואיך בטלו
ב"ר בשרשים וראיות חזקות באמצעי ממש"ה.

49. *EH*, fol. 53v, cited in Chapter Four, n. 90.

50. *MD*, fol. 24r:

והמציאות הממשי הוא אחד עם המהות בכל הנמצאות לא לבד בשי"ת.

51. *MD*, fol. 23v; cf. *MD*, fol. 43r:

ואמנם מצד שישתוקק כל דבר בטבע להשגת שלמותו והיה הבורא ית' רוצה
בשלמות הנמצאים שלכך נבראו ר"ל להגעת השלמות וישישו ערו בשלם

שהראשון הפשוט אשר הוא התחלת העצמים אחר שיחויב המצא אחד פשוט
בכל מאמר הוא המדידה והשעור ליתר הדברים הנכנסים באותו המאמר.

52. *MD*, fol. 23v; cf. Aquinas, *ST*, Ia, q. 95, a.1.

53. *MD*, fol. 127v.

54. *MD*, fol. 23v which is based on ibn 'Ezra's *Perush 'al ha-Torah*, Ki Tisa.

55. *MD*, ibid.:

כי כל הנמצאות אין להם מציאות אלא מצד המציאות שיש להן מהש"י ולכן
הוא כל הנמצאות באופן היותר משובח.

56. *TD*, p. 71b.

57. Ibid.

58. Rabbinic anthropomorphism has long been recognized both in the talmudic-midrashic literature as well as in the mystical literature of *Shi'ur Qomah* and *Hekhalot*. However, Idel recently suggested a new view of this anthropomorphism. According to Idel, both the talmudic-midrashic literature and the mystical literature refer to God primarily as "great" *(gadol)* or "mighty" *(gibbor, rav-koah)*. However, these two bodies of literature differ in that the former elaborated the conception of God as power, whereas the latter provided the statistical information concerning the size of the divine limbs. According to Idel, the gist of the talmudic-midrashic conception (i.e., the ability of human activity augments the power of God. In contrast, the mystical literature presented the knowledge of the divine measurements as a revelation from above. See Idel *Kabbalah: New Perspectives*, 158.

59. On the use of this formula see Arthur Marmorstein, *The Old Rabbinic Doctrine of God* (London: Oxford University Press and H. Milford, 1927-37), vol. 2, 131.

60. The impact of Maimonides on Aquinas' theory of divine attributes has long been recognized. Among the first to document Aquinas' indebtedness to Maimonides was Jacob Guttmann in his *Moses ben Maimon; sein Leben, seine Werke und sein Einfluss* (Leipzig, 1908). The relevant section on Aquinas has been reprinted in *Studies in Maimonides and St. Thomas Aquinas* edited by Jacob I. Dienstag (New York: Ktav, 1975), 225-251. Consult also Harry A. Wolfson, "St. Thomas on Divine Attributes" in *Studies in the History of Philosophy and Religion*, 2:497-524, reprinted in *Maimonides and St. Thomas Aquinas*, 1-29.

61. By a "nominalist" theory I mean the claim that universals are terms or signs standing for, or referring to, individual objects and sets of objects, but that they themselves do not exist. What exists must be an indi-

vidual and the universal cannot be that. However one defines Maimonides' view on universal, it was definitely not a "nominalist" view. We need not be concerned here whether Maimonides' view conformed to "conceptualism" (i.e., the claim that names are not directly connected with things but only via a concept) or to "moderate realism" (i.e., the claim that universals are apprehended directly by the mind, but only through the process of abstraction from material things, the nature of which they comprise).

62. Maimonides, *The Guide* I:52.

63. On the Aristotelian teleological model of causes see Edel, *Aristotle*, 61-75.

64. On Maimonides' distinction between "correlation" and "some relation" see Seymour Feldman, "A Scholastic Misinterpretation of Maimonides' Doctrine of Divine Attributes," in *Studies in Maimonides and St. Thomas Aquinas*, 58-74, esp. 62-64. Feldman claims that Maimonides forbade ascribing to God both types of attributes, and that the Christian theologians misinterpreted Maimonides when they claimed that Maimonides allowed ascribing attributes of "some relation" to God. Reprinted in *Maimonides: A Collection of Critical Essays*, 267-83.

65. Maimonides, *The Guide*, I:52.

66. See Harry a. Wolfson, "Maimonides on Negative Attributes" in *Studies in the History of Philosophy and Religion*, 2:197-99.

67. Maimonides, *The Guide* I:59, 139:

> The most apt phrase concerning this subject is the dictum occurring in the *Psalms, Silence is praise to Thee*, which interpreted signifies: silence with regard to You is praise. This is a most perfectly put phrase regarding this matter.

68. *The Guide* I:68.

69. Ibid., 166.

70. This has been the gist of R. David's defense of Maimonides in *'Ein ha-Qore*, fols. 53r. See also Chapter Two, n. 157.

71. This is Feldman's argument in the article cited in n. 64 above.

72. This appears to me to be the case. The Christian theologians whom Feldman discusses (e.g., Thomas Aquinas, Duns Scotus, and Henry of Ghent) operated within a tightly prescribed theological framework. They could accept Maimonides' philosophical analysis of attributes only to the extent that their theology permitted. To exclude from God attributes of "some relation" negates the theology of creationism. At least for Aquinas this

was impossible. On the connection between the doctrine of creation and the interpretation of divine attributes in Aquinas see Frederick D. Wilhelmsen, "Creation as a Relation in Saint Thomas Aquinas," *The Modern Schoolman*, (1979): 56 (no. 2): 107-33. By the same token Jewish theologians of the fifteenth century, among them R. David ben Judah Messer Leon, asserted the centrality of creationism, and hence interpreted Maimonides as someone who allowed the attribution of "some relation." In other words, theological needs dictated the "misinterpretation" of Maimonides.

73. Aquinas, *ST*, Ia, q. 13, a. 2.

74. See Feldman, "A Scholastic Misinterpretation," 70.

75. See Copleston, *Aquinas*, 134.

76. Aquinas, *ST*, Ia, q. 12, a. 4. The distinction between the thing signified *(res significata)* and the manner in which a thing is signified *(modus significandi)* is crucial to the entire Thomistic enterprise. See also Burrell, *Aquinas: God and Action*, 65-67.

77. Gersonides, *Or Adonai*, III:3 (Leipzig, 1866), 132-137. Consult also Harry A. Wolfson, "Maimonides and Gersonides on Divine Attributes as Ambiguous Terms," in *Studies in the History of Philosophy and Religion*, 2: 231-46. That Aquinas was indeed the source of Gersonides' view of divine attributes was suggested by Shlomo Pines, "Scholasticism after Thomas Aquinas and the Thought of Hasdai Crescas and His Predecessors" (in Hebrew), in his *Studies in the History of Jewish Philosophy: The Transmission of Texts and Ideas* (Jerusalem: Mosad Bialik, 1977), 205-7. Feldman, however, shed doubt on this assertion when he asserted that Gersonides most likely did not have a working knowledge of Latin. See Levi ben Gershom (Gersonides), *The Wars of the Lord*, edited by Seymour Feldman (Philadelphia: The Jewish Publication Society, 1984), vol. 1, 5-6. Nonetheless, Feldman did not rule out influence of Aquinas on Gersonides when he correctly suggested that the latter could have learned these ideas through oral communication.

78. Gersonides, *Milhamot Adonai*, III:3, 135. For analysis of this passage consult, Norbert Samuelson, *The Wars of the Lord: Treatise Three on God's Knowledge* (Toronto: The Pontifical Institute of Mediaeval Studies, 1977), 210-13. The passage was copied by succeeding Jewish philosophers (e.g., Abraham Shalom and Abraham Bibago).

79. On Crescas' critique of Maimonides see Chap. Five and the bibliography cited there.

80. Crescas, *Or Adonai* (Vienna, 1859) I:3, 1-6.

81. Alexander Altmann, "The Divine Attributes, An Historical Survey of the Jewish Discussion," *Judaism* 15 (1966): 56.

82. Crescas, *Or Adonai*, I:3:3, 24b; consult also Pines, "Scholasticism after Thomas Aquinas," 212. Pines suggested Duns Scotus as the possible source of Crescas' notion of Divine Goodness, but the idea could have equally come from Thomas Aquinas or another Thomistic source.

83. See Warren Z. Harvey, "Kabbalistic Elements in *Or Adonai* by R. Hasdai Crescas," (in Hebrew), *JSJT* 2 no. 1 (1982-83): 75-109; Eliezer Schweid, "Essential Attributes in the Philosophy of R. Hasdai Crescas" (in Hebrew), *Iyyun* 4 (1964): 449-67, esp. 463.

84. Schweid, ibid., 464.

85. Albo, *Book of Principles*, II:21.

86. See Davidson, *The Philosophy of Abraham Shalom*, 26-42.

87. *Neveh Shalom* III:2, 44a, cited in Davidson, ibid., 38.

88. See Lazaroff, *The Theology of Abraham Shalom*, 12-15.

89. *MD*, fol. 4v; cf., Aquinas, *ST*, Ia, q. 12, a. 4.

90. *TD*, 69b.

91. *TD*, 69b, and see n. 78 above. The translation of these two terms has been a matter of controversy. Wolfson translated them as "existent subject" and "subject of discourse" respectively (Wolfson, "Crescas on Divine Attributes," *JQR* 7 (1916): 39). In a later article he changed the translation into "subject of existence" and "subject of discourse" (Wolfson, "Maimonides and Gersonides on Divine Attributes," in *Studies in the History of Philosophy and Religion*, 2:243). For further discussion of these two terms, their sources in Aristotelian philosophy and transformation in Arabic philosophy see Feldman ed., *The Wars of the Lord*, 2:113, n. 12.

92. This position is extremely close to Crescas' notwithstanding R. David's derogatory remarks about Crescas. See *Or Adonai*, I:3:3.

93. compare *TD* III:8 with Aquinas, *ST*, Ia, q. 18, a. 3; and *TD* III:9 with Aquinas' *ST* Ia, q. 10, a. 2.

94. This notion is typically Thomistic. Cf. *ST*, Ia, q. 7, a. 1; and consult Gilson, *The Christian Philosophy of St. Thomas Aquinas*, 104; Copleston, *Aquinas*, 135-6; G.E.M. Anscombe and Peter Geach, *Three Philosophers* (Oxford: Oxford University Press, 1961), 89.

95. *TD*, 72a, 69b; cf. *EH*, fol. 20v. Isaac Abravanel also identified Crescas' notion of "essential attributes" with the Kalam's theory of attributes. Like R. David ben Judah, Abravanel rejected Crescas' theory; see Abravanel, *Commentary on "The Guide of the Perplexed"* I:51. (Whether they both understood it correctly is another matter.)

96. For Aquinas, universals exists in the divine mind as divine ideas (i.e., objects of God's thought). See Anton C. Pegis, "The Dilemma of Being and Unity," in *Essays in Thomism* edited by Robert E. Brennan (Freeport: Sheed and Ward, 1972), 177-78.

97. I suggest this term because it is usually applied to Aquinas' and Scotus' theory of universals. "Realism" recognizes the debt to Plato, and "moderate" the distinction. Plato held the theory of *universalia ante rem* (universals independent of particulars) whereas Aquinas, following Aristotle, held that universals are *in rebus* (in things). But, for Aquinas, universals exist in things because things participate in the Divine Being. In the Divine Mind, then, universals preexist as perfections.

98. See Randall, *Aristotle*, 116-123. Aristotle, *Metaphysics*, Book 7, 1028b 2 ff.

99. *MD*, fols. 5r-13v.

100. *TD*, 72a.

101. See Saadia Gaon, *The Book of Doctrines and Beliefs*, II, 5.

102. The Muslim theologians of the Kalam school were divided on the ontological status of the divine attributes. At first Muslim theologians asserted the existence of attributes in contradistinction to the Christian doctrine of the Trinity. These theologians, labeled "attributionists" *(sifatiyya)*, considered life, knowledge, and power to be real beings or "things." Against these theologians, a second group led by Wasil ibn 'Ata denied the reality of the attributes and interpreted any reference to God negatively. See Altmann, "The Divine Attributes," 42; cf. Harry A. Wolfson, *The Philosophy of the Kalam* (Cambridge: Harvard University Press, 1976), 112-43. R. David has in mind the first group. He derived his knowledge of their views solely from Maimonides' refutation.

103. *TD*, 72b.

104. Ibid.

105. Ibid.

106. Cf. Aquinas, *ST*, Ia, q. 15, a. 2; consult Anton C. Pegis, "The Dilemma of Being and Unity," 178; Copleston, *Aquinas*, 147.

107. *MD*, fol. 14r; Cf. fol. 13v:

כי היתה הצורה המושכלת אשר בנפש הסבה הראשונה אשר היא עצמותו
ית׳ סבה לדברים הנמצאים אחריו.

108. The notion that God is the "paradigm of all existents" *(defus*

ha-nimẓaot) or "exemplar of reality" *(dugmat ha-nimẓaim)* was common among Jewish theologians of the late fifteenth and early sixteenth centuries. It appears, for example, in the writings of R. Joseph Taitaẓak, R. Isaac Aderbi, and R. Shlomo Alkabeẓ. See Chapter Six, n. 96.

109. *TD*, 72b.

110. See Tirosh-Rothschild, "The Concept of Torah."

111. *TD*, 72b.

112. *TD*, 74a.

113. Ibid.

114. *TD*, 75b.

115. The distinction between personal mystical experience on the one hand, and oral reception of esoteric traditions on the other hand is clarified by Idel, *Kabbalah: New Perspectives*, 250-56. Moses de Leon, Abraham Abulafia, and Joseph Gikatila represent the first trend, and R. Abraham ben David (Rabad), R. Moses ben Nahman (Nahmanides) and R. Solomon ben Aderet (Rashba) represent the second trend. Idel has convincingly argued that Kabbalah originated first in oral transmission of esoteric doctrine, and that such oral transmission continued even after Kabbalah was committed to writing. See ibid., 20-22.

116. For a general exposition of the doctrine of *Sefirot*, see Scholem, *Kabbalah*, 105-16. For a refinement of Scholem's schematic presentation see Idel, *Kabbalah: New Perspectives*, 112-55.

117. Nahmanides and Rashba are the most noted examples of Kabbalists who were both Halakhic authorities and communal leaders. What was the precise relationship between their Kabbalistic leanings and their leadership requires further clarification. It is not yet clear to what extent Kabbalah is relevant to the standing of these persons as communal leaders. In other words, are we dealing with communal leaders who also happened to be Kabbalists, or were they scholars who commanded authority because of their unique expertise in Kabbalah? To answer this question, far more research is necessary in order to clarify the social status of these Kabbalists in their respective communities. For an early attempt to connect the rise of Kabbalah with a social shift in leadership pattern see Septimus, "Piety and Power in Thirteenth Century Catalonia," cited in Chapter Four.

118. The notable exception of this rather "conservative" trend is Abraham Abulafia and the Kabbalists associated with him, primarily Isaac of Acre. In the works of these Kabbalists, ecstatic experiences of a unitive type are common. See Idel, *Kabbalah: New Perspectives*, 59-71. Ephraim Gottlieb,

"Hearot Devequt u-Nevuah be-*Oẓar ha-Hayyim* le-Yiẓhaq de-min 'Akko," in his *Studies in the Kabbalah Literature*, 231-247.

119. See Tishby, *The Wisdom of the Zohar*, 1: 95-117, 151-161, 219-269.

120. The Kabbalists followed Judah Halevi's conception of the Hebrew language as a sacred (i.e., nonconventional) language. See Judah Halevi, *Kuzari* II:68. The Kabbalistic (and Halevi's) conception of language stands in sharp contrast to the Maimonidean conception of language as expounded in *The Guide* III:8. This difference in the conception of language distinguishes Kabbalistic from philosophic commentaries of the Scripture. While the former views the Hebrew words as expressing the essence of things, and even as expression of the divine Name itself, the latter considers the Hebrew words allegories for philosophical truths. On the Maimonidean conception of language and its impact on Maimonidean conception of language and its impact on Maimonidean interpretation of the biblical text see Shalom Rosenberg, "Biblical Exegesis in the *Guide of the Perplexed*," (in Hebrew) *JSJT* 1 (1981): 85-157, esp. 98-103. The difference between the Kabbalistic symbol and the philosophical allegory cannot be discussed here in any detail. For the best exposition of the subject to date see Idel, *Kabbalah: New Perspectives*, 200-34.

121. This description pertains to the main trend in Kabbalah − the theosophic trend of *Sefer ha-Zohar*. Our analysis does not apply to the ecstatic Kabbalah of Abraham Abulafia which lacks the symbolism of the Sefirot, and indeed considers the symbolism of the *Sefirot* a hindrance to the attainment of mystical union with God. See Idel, *Kabbalah: New Perspectives*, 201-3.

122. Despite the considerable literature, precious little is understood about the linguistic mechanism of Kabbalistic symbols. Recent attempts by literary critics, especially by adherents of Deconstruction, to write on Kabbalah should be taken with great caution, given the fact that most of these writers lack the knowledge of Hebrew and/or Kabbalistic texts. In most cases contemporary literary theories are applied not to Kabbalah but to Scholem's exposition of Kabbalah. For the fusion between literary theory and Kabbalah to be fruitful mastery of Hebrew, Kabbalistic primary sources and literary theory are required. For a first successful integration of these fields see Betty Roitman, "Sacred Language and Open Text," in *Midrash and Literature*, edited by Geoffrey H. Hartman and Sanford Budic (New Haven: Yale University Press, 1986), 159-175.

123. A typical Kabbalistic "dictionary" available in print in Joseph Gikatilah's *Sha'arey Orah* edited by Joseph ben Shlomo (Jerusalem, 1974). These "dictionaries" (still extant in manuscripts) constitute a distinct literary genre in Kabbalistic literature. Full decoding of Kabbalistic language requires the perusal of this material.

124. See Gershom Scholem, "Religious Authority and Mysticism," in *Kabbalah and Its Symbolism* (New York: Schocken, 1969), 5-31, esp. 15-21.

125. See Idel, *Kabbalah: New Perspectives*, 136-46.

126. Ibid., 176-99.

127. Idem, "Major Currents in Italian Kabbalah," 243-245.

128. On the interpretation of the *Sefirot* in *Ma'arekhet ha-Elohut* see Idel, *Kabbalah: New Perspectives*, 138.

129. *MD*, fol. 5v:

הנה מצאתי בשם ב״ר החוקר העמוק שכמו ששבח חכמי ישראל בסוף ספר
הפלת ההפלה והביא ראיה מספרי שלמה כן שבחם במקום אחר בשם
אפלטון ואמר כי אפלטון נכנס לא׳ מבני ישראל המתעסקים בחכמת
האלהות.

Compare Simon van den Bergh, trans., *Averroës' Tahafut Al-Tahfut: The Incoherence of the Incoherence*, 1: 361.

130. *EH*, fol. 186r:

והוא שהיה אומר אפלטון האלהי המכוון בדעותיו עם הקבלה.

Cf. *MD*, fol. 5v:

כי מי שיעיין בספריו [של אפלטון] יראה בהם סודות גדולים ועצומים
אלהיים, כי כל דעותיו הם דעות אנשי הקבלה האמיתית.

R. David's reference to Plato ("the divine Plato") reflects the perception of Plato among contemporary Renaissance thinkers, most notably Ficino. Among the Jewish contemporaries of R. David, Judah Abravanel employed this phrase in his *Dialoghi D'Amore*. The claim that Plato's philosophy was compatible with the Jewish tradition was also shared by R. Isaac Abravanel and his son Judah Abravanel, as noted already by Idel in "Kabbalah and Ancient Philosophy." On the possibility that R. David confused Plato with the Muslim philosopher Abu Aflah see my "Sefirot as the Essence of God," 420, n. 46.

131. *MD*, fol. 5v:

ובענין הצורות ראוי להביט כמו שאמרנו כי הוא ית׳ כולל הכל ולכן נקרא
ה׳ ית׳ צבאות כי הוא אדון צבאות מעלה ומטה ר״ל שהוא צבאות העולם
כלו וכל דין ומשפט ורחמים הם בה׳ ית׳ כי הוא פועל אותם וממנו יצאו
והוא אחד בהם על הדרך שבארנו. ועתה אוכיח היות הספירות עצם
האלהות בדברי רז״ל ואח״כ מדברי גדולי המקובלים בספר הזהר המופלא.

132. As Idel noted in "Between the Concepts of Essence and Instruments," 104-5, R. David ben Judah Messer Leon drew this analogy from

Menahem Recanati, *Perush ha-Tefillot* (MS Jewish Theological Seminary of
America 1887, fol. 137r). Meir ibn Gabbai took this analogy from R. David
ben Judah, *'Avodat ha-Qodesh* (Warsaw, 1883), 14b. Cordovero used it in
Pardes Rimonim; see ben Shlomo *Mystical Theology*, 127-34.

133. *MD*, fol. 7r:

כי הספירות הם מתאחדות בעצמות הבורא ית׳ וההתחלפות היא בערך אל
הפעולות המתחלפות המשתלשלות מאחדות הבורא לא שיהיה בו חלוף.

134. Moses Cordovero, *Pardes Rimonim* (Cracow, 1592), 22a-b; ben
Shlomo, *Mystical Theology*, 73.

135. R. David's treatment of this Zoharic passage typifies his philosophic bias. He was familiar with this passage both in the Zoharic original
אתתקן ולא אתתקן and in the translation of R. Isaac Mar Hayyim in his second letter to Isaac da Pisa where it was translated as מתקשט ואינו מתקשט. R.
David rejected *inter alia* Mar Hayyim's use of *mitqashet* ("beautified,
bedecked of jewelry"), and translated instead *metuqqan* ("perfected, fixed").
While both are acceptable (see Yehudah Liebes, "Sections of the Zohar Lexicon," (in Hebrew), Ph.D. diss., Hebrew University of Jerusalem, 1976, 197),
R. David rejected that which agrees more readily with the mythical symbolism found throughout the *Zohar*. Further, having explicated his own interpretation, he then cites Aristotle's *Metaphysics*, Book XII, for support.

136. See Harry A. Wolfson, "The History of Platonic Ideas," *JHI* 22
(1961): 3-32.

137. *MD*, fol. 22r.

138. Cf. *MD*, fol. 13r with Aquinas, *De Veritate*, I, q. 2, a. 2.

139. Cf. *MD*, fol. 13v with van den Bergh, *Averroës Tahafut al-Tahafut*,
1: 130.

140. *EH*, fol. 202v:

ובזה הצד יצייר אחדות הספירות בשכלו ית׳ שהם האלוהות כמו החדרים
והעליות וכל עניני הבית בשכל האמן שהם בצד מופשט ואחדי וכשמתחיל
לבנות אז הם מתחלקים ומתרבים שיוצאים חוץ לגשם ואינם באותו השבח
כמו שהיו בשכל האמן כן הספירות נחלקו ונאמרו י׳ כשהתחילו היצירות
הנפרדות.

141. *MD*, fol. 13r.

142. See n. 29 above.

143. The Gerona Kabbalists (e.g., R. 'Ezra and R. Jacob ben Sheshet)

interpreted *teshuvah* as the ontological process of the return of all things to their divine source. See Ephraim Gottlieb, *The Kabbalah in the Writings of R. Bahya ben Asher ibn Halawa* (in Hebrew) (Jerusalem: Kiryat Sepher, 1970), 61-2, 119-21, 233-37. They founded this interpretation upon the Biblical verse, *"ve-shavtem ish el ahuzato,"* Lev. 25:10, and made it the major tenet of their doctrine of *Shemittot*. R. 'Ezra cites for support *he-hakham*, usually a reference to a non-Jewish source, and oftentimes Aristotle. R. 'Ezra repeats a Neoplatonic concept, "Everything came from the First Cause and everything must return to the First Cause." R. David ben Judah Messer Leon, then, could and did claim that the Kabbalistic concept *teshuvah* was verified by the metaphysicians *(ha-filosofim ha-elohiyyim)*.

144. Aquinas, *Truth (De Veritate)*, I, q. 2, a. 2; compare the use Isaac Abravanel made of this Thomistic source in *Mif'alot Elohim*, 7:4.

145. See Alexander Altmann, "Moses Narboni's 'Epistle on Shiur Qoma'," in his *Jewish Medieval and Renaissance Studies*, 225-88; Alfred Ivry, "The Implications of Averroës' Thought," cited above. Ivry's conclusions are valid not only with respect to Narboni's philosophy but also with respect to that of later Jewish commentators of Averroës who depended greatly upon Narboni's works. These authors include Joseph ibn Shem Tov and his son Isaac, Abraham Bibago, and our author, David ben Judah Messer Leon, whose commentaries on Averroës are still extant in manuscript.

146. See Albo, *Book of Principles*, 2:11, 26.

147. See Lazaroff, *Theology of Bibago*, 57, where Kabbalistic texts cited in *Derekh Emunah* are listed; Abraham Nuriel, "The Philosophy of Abraham Bibago," Ph.D. diss., Hebrew University of Jerusalem, 1978, 7, 30.

148. Shalom, *Neveh Shalom* (Venice, 1574), 81b.

149. Isaac Abravanel, *'Ateret Zekenim* (Warsaw, 1894), 41b.

150. See Gottlieb, "'Or Olam'," 412-18. For analysis of the passages from *Magen David* copied in ibn Gabbai's *'Avodat ha-Qodesh* I:12, 12a-14a, see Ronald Goetchel, *Meir ibn Gabbay le discours de la Kabbale Espagnole* (Leuven, 1981), 36, 58, 152, 154, 168.

151. On the rabbinic conception of divine providence, see Urbach, *The Sages*, according to index.

152. Aristotle, *Metaphysics*, Book XII, Chaps. 9-10.

153. *The Guide* III:21, 485.

154. Davidson, *The Philosophy of Abraham Shalom*, 69.

155. *The Guide* III:20, 483:

> All the contradictions that may appear in the union of these assertions are due to their being considered in relation to our knowledge, which has only its name in common with His knowledge.

156. *The Guide* III:17, 471-74.

157. *The Guide* III:27, 511:

> [Man's] ultimate perfection is to become rational *in actu*, I mean to have intellect *in actu*; this would consist in knowing everything concerning the beings that it is within the capacity of man to know in accordance with his ultimate perfection ... the only cause of ultimate preservation.

Cf. *The Guide* III:54, 635:

> The true human perfection ... consists in the acquisition of the rational virtues—I refer to the conception of the *intelligibilia*, which teach true opinions concerning the divine things. This is in true reality the ultimate end; this is what gives the individual true perfection, a perfection belonging to him alone.

The origin of the Maimonidean position is Aristotelian epistemology which clearly prefers the general (or the universal) over the particular. See Aristotle, *Posterior Analytics* I:4, and 31.

158. Gersonides *Milhamot Adonai*, Book III; Feldman, ed. *The Wars of the Lord*, 2: 87-137. For an analysis of Gersonides' reconstruction of Maimonides' position, and the opposition to it, consult Feldman's notes and see also Samuelson, *Gersonides and God's Knowledge*, 24-46.

159. See Samuelson, ibid., 63-66.

160. Gersonides, *Milhamot Adonai*, III: 4. Feldman, *The Wars of the Lord*, 2: 117:

> [It] follows that God has all knowledge possessed by the other intelligences, for the knowledge possessed by them is related to the divine knowledge as matter is related to form.

161. On the status of the Active Intellect in Gersonides, see Samuelson, *Gersonides on God's Knowledge*, 58-9.

162. Ibid., 46-53.

163. Shlomo Al'ami's attack in *Iggeret Musar* on the "philosophers" is a typical example of the popularization of Gersonides' doctrines. See Chapter Four, n. 40.

164. See Chapter One.

165. *TD*, 79b.

166. Ibid.

167. Ibid.

168. Compare Aquinas, *ST* Ia, q. 14, arts. 1, 5.

169. Gersonides also referred to this position in *Milhamot Adonai*, III, 2; Samuelson, *Gersonides on God's Knowledge*, 113, n. 32, explains this Aristotelian view as follows:

> A knower insofar as he is a knower has the function of knowing. Excellence in knowing is knowing well. Knowing well consists in knowing truths. Consequently everything known perfects the knower as a knower.

170. *TD*, 79a.

171. Cf. Aquinas, *ST* la, q. 14, a. 5.

172. *TD*, 79a. Cf., *ST* Ia, q. 14, a. 6. A similar position is advocated by Abraham Shalom, *Neveh Shalom*, III:6, 49b; Davidson, *The Philosophy of Abraham Shalom*, 70-1.

173. Cf. Abraham Shalom, *Neveh Shalom*, XII:1, 199b; discussed in Davidson, *The Philosophy of Abraham Shalom*, 70.

174. This metaphor originated in Aristotle but over the centuries it received numerous interpretations according to the philosophic and theological needs of the interpreters.

175. *TD*, 79a; Cf., Thomas Aquinas, *ST*, Ia, q. 14, a. 11.

176. *TD*, 79a:

אתה רואי עצמותי שהמהות שלי מצוייר בך דמיון הצורה הנרשמת במראה
של זכוכית ומצד זה הציור המפותח כבודך רואה ומשיג אותי אשר נראה
מכל זה שידיעת השם ית׳ היא תלויה בעצמו בעצם ומשם נמשכת לזולת.

177. Ibid.

178. *TD*, 80a-b.

179. *TD*, 80b:

אנו אומרים שהאל וזולתו יודעים ולא יצדק בש״ית מקבילו שהוא בלתי
יודע בהחלט שכבר הנחנו שהוא ית׳ יודע אבל יצדק שהוא אינו יודע
במחשבה ועיון כידיעת האדם אלא באופן יותר נכבד מזה וזהו השתוף
הגמור שישותפו בשם לבד ולכן נאמר שכאשר יצדק עליו ית׳ אינו יודע. יובן
שאינו יודע בדרך ידיעת חלושי השכל אלא באופן כללי ומעולה.

180. *TD*, 81a. Compare *TD*, III:19, with Aquinas, *ST*, Ia, q. 22, a. 1.

181. *TD*, 81a.

182. *TD*, 81a.

183. Cf. Aquinas, *ST*, Ia, q. 22, a. 3.

184. Cf. Aquinas, *ST*, Ia, q. 22, a. 3, and *TD*, 82a:

כי ההשגחה כפי אפלטון נחלקת לג׳ מינים הא׳ ההשגחה בתולדה וביצירה
והוא שהשי״ת ברא הנמצאים באופן היותר שלם שאפשר כפי העניינים
ההכרחיים למציאותו ... הב׳ בבחינת קיום הנמצאי׳ אשר שם השי״ת בטבע
כ״א לדרוש קיומו ונצחיותו ... אמנם יש מין ג׳ שהיא ההשגחה לגמול ולענוש
פרטי האדם כפי פעולותיהם.

It is difficult to tell whether R. David misunderstood the Thomistic text, or
whether he preferred to cite Plato rather than the Church Father. R. David
had already encountered serious opposition to his practice of citing Christian
sources as authoritative.

186. On the renewed interest of Jewish thinkers in Halevi's *Kuzari* see
Bonfil, *The Rabbinate*, 186, 200, Judah Halevi's *Kuzari* exerted profound
influence on R. David, who praises the *Kuzari* as a "holy book" *(sefer qadosh)*
and claims that the book "includes all the belief of the Jewish tradition obligatory for all Jews for the sake [of attaining] holiness and purity, so that it
has to be studied prior to any other book in philosophy" *(MD*, fol. 152r). R.
David regarded the teachings of Judah Halevi as the best exposition of Jewish particularism, which he attempted to harmonize with the universalism of
Maimonides' *The Guide of the Perplexed*. See also n. 21 above.

187. *TD*, 82a:

ואומת ישראל הם מיוחדים וראשונים באלו הג׳ מיני השגחות יותר משאר
אישי המין אם בהשגחת היצירה צוה להטביל האשה במי מקוה כדי שהילד
יהיה נזיר אלהים מבטן. ואם השגחת הקיום הביאם אל הארץ הקדושה
אשר כפי מצבה ותכונתה היושבים בה בטבע מואסים הדברים המביאים
הכליון וההפסד ובקלות אוהבים הדברים המעמידים גופם ונפשם. ואם
השגחת הפעולות נתן לנו התורה והמצות להרחיקנו מן העבירות ולהקריבנו
אל הפעולות הטובות והישרות לא עשה כן לכל גוי ומשפטים בל ידעום.
הכלל העולה שכל הנמצאים בכלל נכנעים תחת השגחתו אבל לא בשווי כמו
שביארנו.

188. On the status of the Land of Israel in Kabbalah see Moshe Idel,
"The Land of Israel in Medieval Kabbalah," in *The Land of Israel: Jewish
Perspectives*, edited by Lawrence Hoffman (Notre Dame: University of Notre
Dame Press, 1986), 170-81.

189. R. David elaborated this notion in *MD*, fols. 152-176, which
serve as a summary of Halevi's *Kuzari*.

190. *TD*, 81a and cf. Aquinas, *ST*, Ia, q. 22, a. 2, *sed contra*. Compare
also *TD*, 83a with Aquinas, *ST*, Ia, q. 116, 1.

191. *TD*, 81b.

192. Aquinas, *ST*, Ia, q. 22, arts. 1 and 3; *SCG*, Book III, ch. 77.

193. On the prevalence of astrology among medieval Jewish philosophers, especially during the 14th century, see Sirat, *A History of Medieval Jewish Philosophy*, 93-97.

194. *TD*, 85a.

195. Ibid.

196. *TD*, 86a.

Conclusion

1. *TD*, 97a.

2. Ibid.

3. Ibid.

4. Alkabeẓ, *Shoresh Yishai* (Constantinople, 1561), 34b:

ראיתי אח' ממיוחדי דורנו ושמו מהר"ר דוד בן מהר"ר יהודה נוחי נפש הרבה
הפציר והפליג להפך בזכות הרב ז"ל.

5. See Gottlieb, "Or Olam," 404, n. 30.

6. *MD*, fols. 5v-14v.

7. See ben Shlomo, *The Mystical Theology*, 72-5.

8. See Chapter Seven n. 150.

9. Gershom Scholem, "Sefer Magen David ha-Nizkar be-Sefer Pardes Rimonim Mahu?," *Kiryat Sepher* 9 (1932):258.

10. A detailed study of these writers is still a desideratum. For the meantime consult Barzilay, *Between Reason and Faith*, 167-217.

Bibliography

Works by David ben Judah Messer Leon

Printed

Tehillah le-David. Constantinople. 1576.

Kevod Hakhamim. Edited by Simon Bernfeld, Berlin: Meqiẓey Nirdamim, 1899; Reprint. Jerusalem: Maqor, 1970.

Sheelah bi-Devar Limmud ha-Hokhmot. In *Divrey Hakhamim* edited by Eliezer Ashkenazi. Metz, 1844.

Manuscripts

Magen David. MS. Montefiore 290.

'Ein ha-Qore. MS. Oxford-Bodleian Reggio 41 (= Neubauer, 1263). MS Parma-Pereau 44.

Shevah Ha-Nashim. MS. Parma 1395.

Perush 'al Megilat Eikhah. MS. Paris 676.

Iggerot. MS. Firenze-Laurenziana. Plut. 88/12.

Primary Sources

Abravanel, Don Isaac, *'Ateret Zekenim*. Warsaw, 1894. Reprint. Jerusalem, 1968.

_____. *Mif'alot Elohim.* 1592. Reprint. Don Isaac Abravanel *Opera Minora:* Westmead, Gregg International, 1972.

_____. *Principles of Faith (Rosh Amanah).* Translated and edited by Menachem M. Kellner. East Brunswick: Associated University Presses for the Littman Library of Jewish Civilization, 1982.

_____. *Perush 'al ha-Torah.* 1579. Jerusalem: Hozaat Sefarim Abravanel, 1979.

_____. *Shamayim Hadashim.* Roedelheim, 1892. Reprint. Don Isaac Abravanel, *Opera Minora,* Westmead: Gregg International, 1972.

Al'ami, Shlomo (Ibn Lahmish). *Iggeret Musar.* Edited by Abraham Haberman. Jerusalem: Meqorot, 1945.

Albalag, Isaac. *Sefer Tiqqun ha-De'ot.* Edited by Georges Vajda. Jerusalem: The Israel Academy of Sciences and Humanities, 1973.

Albo, Joseph. *Sefer ha-Iqqarim (Book of Principles).* Translated and edited by Isaac Husik. 4 vols. Philadelphia: Jewish Publication Society of America, 1929-30.

Alkabez, Shlomo ben Moses Ha-Levi. *Shoresh Yishai.* Constantinople, 1561.

'Arama, Isaac ben Moses. *'Aqedat Yizhaq.* 1573. Pressburg, 1849.

_____. *Hazut Qashah.* Pressburg, 1849.

Aquinas, St. Thomas. *Basic Writings of St. Thomas Aquinas.* Edited by Anton C. Pegis. 2 vols. New York: Random House, 1944.

_____. *Summa Contra Gentiles.* Translated and edited by Anton C. Pegis. 5 vols. Notre Dame: University of Notre Dame Press, 1975.

_____. *Truth (Quaestiones Disputatae de Veritate).* Edited by R.W. Mulligan. Chicago: Chicago University Press, 1952-54.

Aristotle. *The Basic Works of Aristotle.* Edited by Richard McKeon. New York: Random House, 1941. 13th printing.

Assaf, Simhah. ed. *Meqorot le-Toledot ha-hinnukh be-Yisrael.* 4 vols. in 2. Jerusalem: Dvir, 1924-1945.

Averroës. See ibn Rushd.

Avicenna. See ibn Sina.

Bibago, Abraham. *Derekh Emunah.* 1522. Reprint. Jerusalem: Meqorot, 1970.

Boccaccio, Giovanni. *Concerning Famous Women (De Claris Mullieribus)*. Translated and edited by Guido A. Guarino. New Brunswick: Rutgers University Press, 1974.

Boksenboim Yacob. ed. *Letters of Jewish Teachers in Renaissance Italy (1555-1591)* (in Hebrew). Tel Aviv: The Chaim Rosenberg School of Jewish Studies Tel Aviv University, 1985.

Capsali, Elijah. *Seder Eliyahu Zuta*. Edited by Meir Benayahu, Aryeh Shmuelevitz and Shlomo Simonsohn. 2 vols. Jerusalem: The Ben Zvi Institute and the Hebrew University; Tel Aviv: the Diaspora Research Institute of Tel Aviv University, 1976.

Colon, Joseph. *New Responsa and Decisions by R. Joseph Colon* (in Hebrew). Edited by Eliyahu D. Pines. 2d rev. ed. Jerusalem: Makhon Or Ha-Mizrah, 1984.

Cordovero, Moses. *Pardes Rimonim*. Lemberg, 1862.

Crescas, Hasdai. *Or Adonai*. Vienna, 1859. Reprint Tel Aviv: Offset Esther, 1962.

_____. *Derashat ha-Pesah le-Rav Hasdai Crescas*. Edited by Aviezer Ravitzky. Jerusalem: Israel Academy of Sciences and the Humanities, 1988.

David ben Hayyim ha-Cohen (RADAKH). *Sheelot u-Teshuvot* (= *Responsa*). Salonika, 1803.

Del Medigo, Elijah. *Sefer Behinat ha-Dat*. Edited by Jacob J. Ross. Tel Aviv: Tel Aviv University, 1984.

Duran, Shimon ben Zemah. *Tashbez* (= *Teshuvot Shimon ben Zemah*). Amsterdam, 1738-41.

_____. *Sefer Magen Avot: Ha-Helek ha-Pilosofi*. 1785. Reprint. Jerusalem: Maqor, 1969.

Galya Raza. Edited by Rahel Elior. Jerusalem: The Hebrew University of Jerusalem; Research Projects of the Institute for Jewish Studies, 1981.

Gikatila, Joseph. *Sha'arey Orah*. Edited by Joseph Ben Shlomo, Jerusalem: Mosad Bialik, 1974.

Gerondi, Nissim ben Reuben. *Derashot ha-Ran*. Edited by Aryeh L. Feldman. Jerusalem: Makhon Shalem, 1977.

Gersonides. See Levi ben Gershon.

Hillel ben Samuel. *Sefer Tagmule ha-Nefesh.* Edited by Joseph Sermoneta, Jerusalem: Israel Academy of Sciences and Humanities, 1981.

Ibn 'Ezra, Abraham. *Perush 'al ha-Torah.* Printed in *Miqraot Gedolot.*

————. *Kitve Avraham ibn-Ezra.* Jerusalem: Maqor, 1970.

Ibn Gabbai, Meir ben Yehezkel. *Sefer Derekh Emunah.* Padua, 1562.

————. *Sefer 'Avodat ha-Qodesh.* 1566-68. Warsaw, 1883.

Ibn Rushd, Abu l-Walid Muhammad ibn Ahmad (Averroës). *Tahafut al-Tahafut: The Incoherence of the Incoherence.* Translated and edited by Simon van den Bergh. 2 vols. London: Luzac, 1954.

————. *The Epistle on the Possibility of Conjunction with the Active Intellect with Commentary of Moses Narboni.* Translated and edited by Kalman P. Bland. New York: Jewish Theological Seminary of America, 1982.

————. *Sefer Hevdel ha-Neemar be-mah she-beyn ha-Torah ve-ha-Hokhmah min ha-Devequt.* Edited by Norman Golb, "The Hebrew Translation of Averroës' Fasal Al-Maqal," *PAAJR* 25 (1956): 91-113; 26 (1957): 41-63.

————. *On the Harmony of Religion and Philosophy.* Translated and edited by George F. Hourani. E.J.W. Gibb Memorial Series, n.s. 21. London: Luzac, 1961.

————. *Drei Abhandlunger uber die Conjunction des Separaten Intellects mit dem Menschen von Averroës (Vater und Sohn).* Translated by Samuel ibn Tibbon. Edited by J. Hercz. Berlin, 1869.

————. *Beur Emza'i le-Sefer ha-Metaphisica (Middle Commentary on Aristotle's Metaphysics).* MS. Paris 915.

Ibn Sina, Abu Ali al Husain (Avicenna). *The "Metaphysica" of Avicenna (Ibn Sina): A Critical Translation, Commentary and Analysis of the Fundamental Arguments in Avicenna's "Metaphysica" in the "Danish Nama-i 'ala'l" (The Book of Scientific Knowledge).* Edited by Parviz Morwedge. Persian Heritage Series, no. 13. London: Rutledge and Kegan Paul, 1973.

Ibn Tufayl, Abu Bakr Muhammad *Ibn Tufayl's Hayy Ibn Yaqzan.* Translated and edited by Lenn E. Goodman. New York: New York University Press, 1972.

Ibn Shem Tov, Shem Tov. *Sefer ha-Emunot.* 1556-57. Reprint. Jerusalem, 1968-69.

Ibn Shem Tov, Joseph ben Shem Tov. *Kevod Elohim.* 1556-57. Reprint. Jerusalem? 1966?

_____. "The Short Commentary of Averroës' Epistle on the Possibility of Conjunction." Edited by Shaul Regev. *JSJT* 2 (1982): 38-93.

Ibn Yahya, Gedalya ben Joseph. *Shalshelet ha-Kabbalah.* 1586. Warsaw, 1881. Reprint. Jerusalem, 1962.

Isaac Mar Hayyim. "Epistles." Edited by Yael Nadav, "An Epistle of the Qabbalist Isaac Mar Hayyim Concerning the Doctrines of 'Supernal Lights'," [Hebrew], *Tarbiz* 26 (1957): 440-58; Edited by Arthur Greenup, "A Qabbalistic Epistle," *JQR* n.s. 21 (1931): 365-75.

Josippon. Edited by David Flusser. 2 vols. Jerusalem: Magnes Press, 1978-81.

Judah, Halevi. *The Kuzari [Kitab al Khazari]: An Argument for the Faith of Israel.* Translated from the Arabic by Hartwig Hirschfeld. Leipzig, 1887.

_____. *Sefer ha-Kozari le-Rabbi Yehudah Halevi.* Edited by Yehuda Even-Shmuel (Kaufman). Tel Aviv: Dvir, 1972.

Landau, Jacob. *Sefer ha-Aggur ha-Shalem.* Edited by Moshe Hershler. Jerusalem, 1970.

Levi ben Gershon. *Milhamot Adonai.* 1560. Leipzig, 1866.

_____. *The Wars of the Lord.* Translated and edited by Seymour Feldman. 2 vols. Philadelphia: Jewish Publication Society of America. 1984, 1987.

_____. *The Wars of the Lord: Treatise Three on God's Knowledge.* Translated and edited by Norbert Samuelson. Toronto: The Pontifical Institute of Mediaeval Studies, 1977.

_____. *Perush 'al Ha-Torah.* Venice, 1547.

Lerner, Ralph and Mushin Mahdi. eds. *Medieval Political Philosophy: A Source Book.* 2d printing. Ithaca: Cornell University Press, 1978.

Ma'arekhet ha-Elohut. Ferrara, 1568.

Maimonides. See Moses ben Maimon.

Messer Leon, Judah Ben Yehiel. "Letters." In *Jeschurun.* Vol. 6. Edited by Joseph I Kobak. Bamberg, 1868.

_____. "Poem." In *Jeschurum.* vol. 7. Edited by Joseph I. Kobak. Bamberg, 1872.

———. "Pesaqim." In *Divrey Rivot ba-She'arim.* Edited by David Frankel. Husiatin: Dovevey Siftey Yeshenim, 1902.

———. "Introduction to *Mikhlal Yofi.*" *MGWJ* 37 (1893): 313-14.

———. *Sefer Nofet Zufim.* Mantua, 1475-6. Reprint with introduction by Robert Bonfil. Jerusalem: Magnes Press, 1981.

———. *The Book of the Honeycomb's Flow: Sēpher Nōphet Ṣūphīm.* Translated and edited by Isaac Rabinowitz. Ithaca: Cornell University Press, 1983.

Moses ben Maimon (Maimonides). *Mishneh Torah: Ha-Yad ha-Hazakah.* Warsaw-Vilna edition with commentaries. 6 vols. New York: S. Goldman, 1955-56.

———. *Sefer Moreh Nubukhim.* Translated by Samuel ben Judah Ibn Tibbon with Commentaries by Isaac Abravanel, Asher Crescas, Profiat Duran (Efodi) and Shem Tov ben Joseph ibn Shem Tov. Jerusalem, 1959-60.

———. *Mishnah 'Im Perush Rabbenu Moshe ben Maimon.* Translated and edited by Joseph Kafah. 4 vols. Jerusalem: Mosad Ha-Rav Kook, 1959.

———. *The Guide of the Perplexed.* Translated and edited by Shlomo Pines. Chicago: University of Chicago Press, 1964.

Moses ben Nahman (Nahmanides). *Kitvey Rabbenu Moshe ben Nahman.* Edited by Charles B. Chavel. 2 vols. Jerusalem: Mosad Ha-Rav Kook, 1963-64.

———. *Perush Ha-Ramban 'al Ha-Torah.* Edited by Charles B. Chavel. 2 vols. Jerusalem: Mosad Ha-Rav Kook, 1959-60. Reprint, 1977.

Mizrahi, Elijah. *Sheelot u-Teshuvot* (= *Responsa*). Constantinople, 1640.

Narboni, Moses ben Joshua. *Beur le-Moreh Nebukhim.* Edited by Jacob Goldenthal. Vienna, 1852. Reprint in *Sheloshah Qadmoney Mefarshey ha-Moreh.* Jerusalem, 1960-61.

———. *Maamar bi-Shelemut ha-Nefesh (Treatise on the Perfection of the Soul).* Edited by Alfred L. Ivry. Jerusalem: Israel Academy of Sciences and Humanities, 1977.

Neubauer, Adolph. ed. *Medieval Jewish Chronicles* (= *Seder ha-Hakhamim ve-Qorot ha-Yamim*). 2 vols. Oxford: Clarendon Press, 1887-95. Reprint. Jerusalem, 1967.

Petrarch, Francesco. *The Triumphs of Petrarch.* Translated and edited by Ernest H. Wilkins. Chicago: University of Chicago Press, 1963.

_____. *Petrarch's Lyric Poems.* Translated and edited by Robert M. Durling. Cambridge: Harvard University Press, 1976.

Provenẓali, Jacob. *Teshuvah bi-Devar Limmud ha-Hokhmot.* In *Divrey Hakhamim* edited by Eliezer Ashkenazi. Metz, 1844.

Recanati, Menahem. *Perush 'al ha-Torah 'al Derekh ha-Emet.* Venice, 1545.

_____. *Ta'amey ha-Miẓvot.* MS. Paris 825.

Saadia ben Joseph, Gaon. *Sefer ha-Emunot ve-ha-De'ot.* Translated by Judah Ibn Tibbon. Yosefow, 1885.

_____. *The Book of Beliefs and Opinions.* Translated and edited by Samuel Rosenblatt. New Haven: Yale University Press, 1948.

Sefer ha-Zohar. Edited by Reuben Margaliot. 6th printing. Jerusalem: Mosad Ha-Rav Kook, 1989.

Schirmann, Jefim. ed. *Mivhar ha-Shirah ha-'Ivrit be-Italyah.* Berlin: Schocken, 1934.

Shalom, Abraham ben Isaac. *Sefer Neveh Shalom.* 1575. Reprint, Westmead: Gregg International, 1969.

Sforno, 'Obadia. *Or 'Amim.* Bologna, 1537.

Printed Secondary Sources

Albeck, Hanoch. "Ordination, Appointment and Court" (in Hebrew). *Zion* 8 (1943): 85-93.

Aloni, Nehemyah. "The Term 'Music' in Our Literature in the Middle Ages" (in Hebrew). *Yuval* 1 (1968): 12-35.

Altmann, Alexander. "Ars Rhetorica as Reflected in Some Jewish Figures of the Italian Renaissance." In *Essays in Jewish Intellectual History.* Hanover: University Press of New England, 1981.

_____. "Maimonides and Thomas Aquinas: Natural or Divine Prophecy." *AJS review* 3 (1978): 1-19.

_____. "Essence and Existence in Maimonides," in his *Studies in Religious Philosophy and Mysticism.* Ithaca: Cornell University Press: 1969. Reprint *Maimonides, a Collection of Critical Essays*, edited by Joseph Buijs. Notre Dame: University of Notre Dame Press, 1988.

_____. "Moses Narboni's Epistle on Shiur Qoma." In *Jewish Medieval and Renaissance Studies.* Cambridge: Harvard University Press, 1967.

——. ed. *Jewish Medieval and Renaissance Studies.* Cambridge: Harvard University Press, 1967.

——. "The Divine Attributes, An Historical Survey of the Jewish Discussion." *Judaism* 15 (1966): 40-60.

Amarillio, Abraham S. "The Great Talmud Torah of Salonika," (in Hebrew). *Sefunot* 13 (= The Book of Greek Jewry III) (1971-78): 145-68.

Amram, David. *The Makers of Hebrew Books in Italy.* Philadelphia, 1909. Reprint. London: The Holland Press, 1963.

Ankori, Zvi. *Karaites in Byzantium: The Formative Years, 970-1100.* New York: Columbia University Press, 1959.

Anscombe, G.E.M. and Peter Geach. *Three Philosophers.* Oxford: Oxford University Press, 1961.

Assaf, Simha. "Responsa and Letters by R. Moses Capsali" (in Hebrew). *Sinai* 5 (1939): 485-6.

——. "From the Hidden Treasures of the Library in Jerusalem" (in Hebrew). In *Minha le-David, Qovez Maamarim be-Hokhmat Yisrael ... R. David Yellin.* Jerusalem, 1935. Reprinted in *Meqorot U-Mehqarim be-Toledot Yisrael.* Jerusalem: Mosad Ha-Rav Kook, 1966.

Avenary, Hanoch. "The Hebrew Version of Abu L-Salt's Treatise on Music." *Yuval* 3 (1979): 7-13.

Avitsur, Shemuel. "The Woolen Industry in Salonica" (in Hebrew). *Sefunot* 12 (= *Book of Greek Jewry 2*) (1971-1978): 147-68.

Baer, Yitzhak F. *The Jews in Christian Spain.* Translated by Louis Schoffman. Philadelphia: Jewish Publication Society of America 1961-66. Reprinted 1978.

Baron, Hans. *The Crisis of the Early Italian Renaissance.* Rev. ed. Princeton: Princeton University Press, 1966.

Baron, Salo W. *The Jewish Community: Its History and Structure to the American Revolution.* 3 vols. Westport: Greenwood Press, 1972.

——. *A Social and Religious History of the Jews.* 18 vols. 2nd rev. ed. New York: Columbia University Press, 1952-80.

Barzilay, Isaac. *Between Reason and Faith, Anti-Rationalism in Italian Jewish Thought 1250-1650.* The Hague, Paris: Mouton, 1967.

Becker, Marvin B. "The Republican City-State in Florence: An Inquiry into its Origins and Survival." *Speculum* 35 (1960): 39-50.

Ben Sasson, Haim H. "The Generation of the Spanish Expulsion on Itself" (in Hebrew). *Zion* 26 (1961): 23-34.

Ben Shlomo, Joseph. *The Mystical Theology of R. Moses Cordovero* (in Hebrew). Jerusalem: Mosad Bialik, 1965.

Benayahu, Meir. "Sefer ha-Emunot by R. Shem Tov, Its Concealment and Discovery" (in Hebrew). *Molad* 5 (1979): 158-162.

_____. "Moshe Benvenest, Court Physician and Rabbi Jehudah Zarko's Poem on his Exile to Rhodes" (in Hebrew). *Sefunot* 11 (= *Book of Greek Jewry* 1) (1971-1978): 123-44.

_____. "Rabbi David ben Ban Benest of Saloniki and his Letter to R. Abraham ibn Yaish in Brusa" (in Hebrew). *Sefunot* 11 (= *Book of Greek Jewry* 1) (1971-1978): 267-97.

_____. "A Source About the Spanish Refugees in Portugal and their Departure to Salonica; the Concealment of *Sefer ha-Emunot* and its Discovery and Information about the Ibn Verga Family," (in Hebrew). *Sefunot* 11 (1971-1978): 231-65.

_____. *Marbiẓ Torah: Samkhuyotav, Tafqidav ve-Helqo be-Mosdot ha-qehilah be-Sefarad, be-Turkeyah u-ve-Arẓot ha-Mizrah.* Jerusalem: Mosad Ha-Rav Kook, 1953.

Bentov, Hayim. "Methods of Study of Talmud in the Yeshivot of Salonica and Turkey after the Expulsion from Spain" (in Hebrew). *Sefunot* 13 (1979): 39-102.

Berlin, Charles, ed. *Studies in Jewish Bibliography and Booklore in Honor of I.E. Kiev.* New York: Ktav, 1971.

Berman, Lawrence. "Maimonides the Disciple of Alfarabi." *Israel Oriental Studies* 4 (1979): 159-78.

_____. "Ibn Bajja Ve-ha-Rambam," Ph.D. diss., Hebrew University of Jerusalem, 1959.

Bickerman, Elias J. *The Jews in the Greek Age.* Cambridge: Harvard University Press, 1988.

Birnbaum, Eduard. *Jewish Musicians at the Court of the Mantuan Dukes (1542-1628).* English edition, revised and augmented by Judith Cohen. Tel Aviv: Tel Aviv University Publications of the Department of Musicology, 1978.

Bland, Kalman. "Moses and the Law According to Maimonides." In *Mystics, Philosophers and Politicians, Essays in Jewish Intellectual History in*

Honor of Alexander Altmann, edited by Judah Reinharz and Daniel Swetschinski. Durham: Duke University Press, 1982.

Blau, Joseph L. *The Christian Interpretation of the Cabbalah in the Renaissance.* Port Washington: Kennikat Press 1944. Reprint, New York: Columbia University Press, 1965.

Blickstein, Shlomo. "Between Philosophy and Mysticism, A Study of the Philosophical-Qabbalistic Writings of Joseph Giqatila (1248-c. 1322)." Ph.D. diss., Jewish Theological Seminary, 1983.

Blumenthal, David. "Maimonides' Intellectualist Mysticism and the Superiority of the Prophecy of Moses." In *Approaches to Judaism in Medieval Times.* Chico, CA: Scholars Press, 1984.

Bobik, Joseph. *Aquinas on Being and Essence: A Translation and Interpretation.* Notre Dame: University of Notre Dame Press, 1965.

Bonfil, Robert. "How Golden was the Age of the Renaissance in Jewish Historiography?" In *History and Theory: Studies in the Philosophy of History, Essays in Jewish Historiography*, edited by Ada Albert-Rapaport. Beiheft 27 (1989): 78-102.

————. "The Historian's Perception of the Jews in the Italian Renaissance, Toward a Reappraisal." *REJ* 143 (1984): 59-82.

————. "Some Reflections on the Place of Azariah de Rossi's *Meor Enayim* in the Cultural Milieu of Italian Renaissance Jewry." In *Jewish Thought in the Sixteenth Century*, edited by Bernard D. Cooperman, 23-48. Cambridge: Harvard University Press, 1983.

————. "Introduction." In *Judah Messer Leon Nofet Zufim on Hebrew Rhetoric.* Jerusalem: The Jewish National and University Library Press and Magnes Press, 1981.

————. *The Rabbinate in Renaissance Italy* (in Hebrew). Jerusalem: Magnes Press, 1979.

————. "The Doctrine of the Soul and Holiness in the Teachings of R. Obadiah Sforno," (in Hebrew). *Eshel Beer Sheva* 1 (1976): 200-57.

Bouwsma, William J. "Changing Assumptions in Later Renaissance Culture." *Viator* 7 (1976): 422-40.

————. "The Two Faces of Humanism, Stoicism and Augustinianism in Renaissance Thought." In *Itinerarium Italicum: The Profile of the Italian Renaissance in the Mirror of its European Transformations*, edited by Heiko O. Oberman and Thomas A. Brady, 3-60. Leiden: E.J. Brill, 1975.

Bowman, Steven, S. *The Jews of Byzantium 1204-1453.* University: University of Alabama Press, 1985.

Boyarin, Daniel. "Studies in the Talmudic Commentaries of the Spanish Exiles" (in Hebrew). *Sefunot*, n.s. Book 2 (17) (1983): 165-84.

Braude, Benjamin and Bernard Lewis, eds. *Christian and Jews in the Ottoman Empire, The Functioning of Plural Society*, vol. 1. New York: Holmes and Meier, 1982.

Brennan, Robert E., ed. *Essays in Thomism.* Freeport: Sheed and Ward, 1972.

Breuer, Mordekhai. "The Ashkenazic Ordination" (in Hebrew). *Zion* 33 (1978): 18-23.

_____. "The Position of the Rabbinate in the Leadership of the German Communities in the Fifteenth Century" (in Hebrew). *Zion* 41 (1976): 48-52.

_____. "'Aliyat ha-Pilpul ve-ha-Hilluqim be-Yeshivot Ashkenaz." in *Sefer Zikkaron le-Morenu ha-Rav Weinberg.* Jerusalem, 1970.

Brucker, Gene A. *Renaissance Florence.* Berkeley: University of California Press, 1969.

_____. "The Medici in the Fourteenth Century." *Speculum* 32 (1957): 1-26.

Brunswick, S.R., ed. *Studies in Judaica, Karaitica and Islamica Presented to Leon Nemoy.* Ramat Gan: Bar Ilan University Press, 1982.

Buijs, Joseph A., ed. *Maimonides: A Collection of Critical Essays.* Notre Dame: University of Notre Dame Press, 1988.

Burckhardt, Jacob. *The Civilization of the Renaissance in Italy.* Translated by S.G.C. Middlemore. New York: Harper and Row, 1958.

Burrell, David. *Aquinas, God and Action.* Notre Dame, University of Notre Dame Press, 1976.

Carpi, Daniel, ed. *Bibliotheca Italo-Ebraica: bibliografia per la storia degli Ebrei in Italia 1969-1973.* Rome: Caracci, 1982.

_____. "R. Judah Messer Leon and his Activity as a Doctor" (in Hebrew). *Michael* 1 (1972): 277-301; Reprinted in *Korot* 6 (1974).

_____. "The Jews in Padua at the Age of the Renaissance" (in Hebrew). Ph.D. diss., Hebrew University of Jerusalem, 1967.

Cassirer, Ernest, Paul Oscar Kristeller and John Herman Randall, Jr., eds.

The Renaissance Philosophy of Man. Chicago: University of Chicago Press, 1948.

Cassuto, Umberto, *Gli Ebrei a Firenze nell'eta del Rinascimento. Ha-Yehudim be-Firenze bi-Tequfat ha-Renesans*. Translated by Menahem Artom. Jerusalem: Kiryat Sepher, 1967.

_____. "The Destruction of Academies in Southern Italy during the Thirteenth Century" (in Hebrew). In *Memorial Volume for Asher Gulak and Samuel Klein*. Jerusalem: Hebrew University of Jerusalem, 1942.

_____. "Sulla Pamiglia de Pisa." *Rivista Israelitica* 5 (1908); 227-38; 6 (1909): 21-30; 102-13; 160-70; 223-36.

_____. "La Famiglia di David da Tivoli". *Ill Corriere Israelitico*, 45 (1906): 149-52; 261-4; 297-302.

Chambers, David S. *Patrons and Artists in the Italian Renaissance*. Columbia: University of South Carolina Press, 1982.

Chojnacki, Stanley. "Patrician Women in Early Renaissance Venice." *Studies in the Renaissance*. 21 (1979): 176-204.

Clark, Donald L. *Rhetoric and Poetry in the Renaissance*. New York, Columbia University Press, 1922; Reprint. New York: Russell & Russell, 1963.

Cohen, Gerson D. Review of *The Marranos of Spain*, by Ben Zion Netanyahu in *JSS* 29 (1967): 178-84.

Cohen, Jeremy. *The Friars and the Jews, The Evolution of Medieval Anti-Judaism*. Ithaca: Cornell University Press, 1982.

Cohen, Rivka. *Constantinople-Salonica-Patras, Communal and Supra Communal Organization of Greek Jewry under the Ottoman Rule (15th-16th Centuries)* (in Hebrew). Tel Aviv: Tel Aviv University Press, 1984.

Cohen, Shaye D. *From the Maccabees to the Mishnah*. Philadelphia: The Westminster Press, 1987.

Conforte, David. *Qore ha-Dorot*. Edited by David Cassel. Berlin, 1845.

Cook, Michael A. et al. *A History of the Ottoman Empire to 1730*. Cambridge: Cambridge University Press, 1976.

Cooperman, Bernard D., ed. *Jewish Thought in the Sixteenth Century*. Cambridge: Harvard University Press, 1983.

Copleston, Frederik C. *A History of Philosophy*. Book One includes Vols. I, II, III, published separately 1946, 1950, 1953, respectively. Garden City: Image Books, 1985.

_____. *A History of Medieval Philosophy.* New York: Harper and Row, 1974.

_____. *Aquinas.* London: Penguin, 1955.

Craig, William L. *The Cosmological Argument from Plato to Leibniz.* London: MacMillan Press, 1980.

Dan, Joseph and Joseph Hacker, eds. *Studies in Jewish Mysticism, Philosophy and Ethical Literature Presented to Isaiah Tishby on his Seventy-Fifth Birthday.* Jerusalem: Magnes Press, 1986.

Dan, Joseph. *Hebrew Ethical and Homiletical Literature* (in Hebrew). Jersualem: Keter, 1975.

_____. *The Esoteric Theology of Ashkenazic Hasidism* (in Hebrew). Jerusalem: Mosad Bialik, 1968.

Danon, Abraham. "The Karaites in European Turkey." *JQR* n.s. 15 (1924-25): 285-360.

David, Abraham. "New Information about Caleb Apandopolo" (in Hebrew). *Kiryat Sepher* 48 (1973): 180.

Davidson, Herbert A. "Averroës on the Active Intellect as a Cause of Existence." *Viator* 18 (1987): 191-225.

_____. *Proofs for Eternity, Creation and the Existence of God in Medieval Islamic and Jewish Philosophy.* New York: Oxford University Press, 1987.

_____. "John Philoponus as a Source of Medieval Islamic and Jewish Proofs of Creation." *Journal of Medieval American Oriental Society* 89 (1969): 357-91.

_____. *The Philosophy of Abraham Shalom: A Fifteenth Century Exposition and Defense of Maimonides.* Berkeley: University of California Press, 1964.

Day, John. "The Great Bullion Famine of the Fifteenth Century." *Past and Present* 79 (1978): 3-54.

De Benedetti-Stow, Sandra. "Due poesie bilingui inedite contro le donne de Semuel de Castiglione (1553)." *Italia* 2 (1983): 7-27.

De Molen, Richard, ed. *The Meaning of the Renaissance and Reformation.* Boston: Houghton Mifflin Company, 1974.

Dienstag, Jacob I. ed. *Studies in Maimonides and St. Thomas Aquinas.* New York: Ktav, 1975.

Dimitrowsky, Hayim. "'Al Derekh ha-Pilpul." In *Jubilee Volume in Honor of Salo W. Baron,* edited by Saul Lieberman. Jerusalem: American Academy for Jewish Research, 1975.

_____. "The Academy of R. Jacob Berab in Safed" (in Hebrew). *Sefunot* 7 (1973): 41-102.

Edel, Abraham. *Aristotle and His Philosophy.* Chapel Hill: University of North Carolina Press, 1982.

Efros, Israel. *Studies in Medieval Jewish Philosophy.* New York: Columbia University Press, 1974.

Elior, Rahel. "The Struggle for the Position of Kabbalah in the Sixteenth Century" (in Hebrew). *JSJT* (1981): 177-190.

Ellsperman, Gerhard L. "The Attitude of the Early Christian Latin Writers Toward Pagan Literature and Learning." In *Catholic University of American Patristic Studies*, vol. 82 (1949).

Encyclopaedia Judaica. 17 vols. corrected edition. Cecil Roth, ed. Jerusalem: Keter, 1971; New York: MacMillan, 1972.

Encyclopedia of Philosophy. Paul Edwards, editor in chief. 2nd printing. New York: Macmillan 1972.

Epstein, Mark A. *The Ottoman Jewish Communities and their Role in the Fifteenth and Sixteenth Centuries.* Freiburg, K. Schwarz. Series: Islam Kundlische Unterschuugen vol. 56, 1980.

Etkes, Emanuel and Joseph Salmon, eds. *Studies in the History of Society Presented to Professor Jacob Katz on his Seventy-Fifth Birthday.* Jerusalem, 1980.

Fackenheim, Emil L. "The Possibility of the Universe in Al-Farabi Ibn Sina and Maimonides." *PAAJR* 16 (1947): 39-43.

Fahy, Conor. "Three Early Renaissance Treatises on Women." *Italian Studies* 2 (1956): 30-55.

Fakhry, Majid. *A History of Islamic Philosophy.* New York: Columbia University Press, 1983.

Ferguson, Wallace K., ed. *The Renaissance: Six Essays.* New York: Harper Torchbooks, 1953.

Ferorelli, Nicola. *Gli Ebrei nell 'Italia Meridionale dall' eta romana al secolo XVIII.* 1915; Reprint. Bologna: Arnoldo Forni, 1966.

Festugiere, Andre M.J. *La Revelation d'Hermes Trismegiste.* 4 vols. Paris: Lecoffre, 1949-1959.

Fishman, Talya. "A Medieval Parody of Misogyny: Judah ibn Shabetai's 'Minhat Yehuda Sone ha-Nashim'." *Prooftexts* 8 (1988): 89-111.

Fox, Marvin, ed. *Modern Jewish Ethics.* Columbus: Ohio State University Press, 1975.

Friedenwald, Harry. "Jewish Physicians in Italy: Their Relation to the Papal and Italian States." *Publication of the American Jewish Historical Society* 28 (1922): 133-211.

_____. *The Jews and Medicine: Essays.* Baltimore: Johns Hopkins Press, 1944. Reprinted with introduction by George Rosen, New York: Ktav, 1967.

Garin, Eugenio. *Italian Humanism, Philosophy and Civic Life in the Renaissance.* Translated by Peter Munz. New York: Harper and Row, 1965.

Geffen, David. "Insights into the Life and Thought of Elijah del Medigo Based on his Published and Unpublished Works." *PAAJR* 41-42 (1973-74): 69-86.

_____. "Faith and Reason in Elijah Del Medigo's *Behinat ha-Dat.*" Ph.D. diss., Columbia University, 1970.

Gellman, Jerome. "The Philosophical Hasagot of Rabad on Maimonides' Mishneh Torah." *The New Scholasticism* 58 (1984): 145-69.

Gerber, Hayim. *Economic and Social Life of the Jews in the Ottoman Empire in the 16th and 17th Centuries* (in Hebrew). Jerusalem: The Zalman Shazar Center, 1982.

_____. "Initiative and Commerce in the Economic Activity of the Jews in the Ottoman Empire during the Sixteenth and Seventeenth Centuries" (in Hebrew). *Zion* 43 (1978): 38-67.

Gilbert, Felix. "The Renaissance Interest in History." In *Art, Science and History in the Renaissance*, edited by Charles S. Singleton. Baltimore: John Hopkins Press, 1967.

Gilson, Etienne. *Elements of Christian Philosophy.* Garden City, 1960.

_____. *The Christian Philosophy of St. Thomas Aquinas.* New York: Octagon Books, 1956.

_____. *History of Christian Philosophy in the Middle Ages.* New York: 1955.

_____. *Being and Some Philosophers.* 2nd ed. Toronto: Pontifical Institute of Mediaeval Studies, 1952.

Giustiniani, Vito R. "Homo, Humanus, and the Meaning of Humanism." *JHI* 46 (1985): 167-96.

Goetshel, Ronald. *Meir ibn Gabbay le discours de la Kabbale Espagnole.* Leuven, 1981.

Goodblatt, Moris S. *Jewish Life in Turkey in the XVIth Century as Reflected in the Legal Writings of Samuel de Medina.* New York: Jewish Theological Seminary of America, 1952.

Gottlieb, Ephraim. *Studies in the Kabbalah Literature.* Edited by Joseph Hacker. Tel Aviv: The Chaim Rosenberg School for Jewish Studies, Tel Aviv University, 1976.

_____. *The Kabbalah in the Writings of R. Bahya ben Asher ibn Halawa* (in Hebrew). Jerusalem: Kiryat Sepher, 1970.

Grabois, Aryeh. "The Hebraica Veritas and Jewish-Christian Intellectual Relations in the Twelfth Century." *Speculum* 50 (1975): 613-34.

Gray, Hanna H. "Renaissance Humanism: The Pursuit of Eloquence." *JHI* 24 (1963): 497-514.

Grayzel, Solomon. *The Church and the Jews in the Thirteenth Century.* Revised 2d ed. Philadelphia: Jewish Publication Society, 1933; Reprint. New York, 1966.

Guttmann, Jacob. *Moses ben Maimon: sein Leben, seine Werke und sein Einfluss.* Leipzig, 1908.

Guttmann, Julius. *The Philosophies of Judaism.* Translated by David W. Silverman. Philadelphia: Schocken, 1964.

Hacker, Joseph R. "Jewish Autonomy in the Ottoman Empire: Its Scope and Limits" (in Hebrew). In *Transition and Change in Modern Jewish History, Essays Presented in Honor of Shmuel Ettinger.* 249-388. Jerusalem: The Historical Society of Israel and the Zalman Shazar Center, 1987.

_____. "The Intellectual Activity of Jews in the Ottoman Empire during the Sixteenth and Seventeenth Centuries." In *Jewish Thought in the Seventeenth Century,* edited by Isadore Twersky and Bernard Septimus, 95-135. Cambridge: Harvard University Press, 1987.

_____. "On the Intellectual Character and Self-Perception of Spanish Jewry in the Late Fifteenth Century" (in Hebrew). *Sefunot* 17 (= n.s. Book 2) 1983: 21-95.

_____. "The Institution of the Chief Rabbinate in Constantinople in the Fifteenth and Sixteenth Centuries" (in Hebrew). *Zion* 49 (1984): 225-63.

_____. "The Payment of Djizya by Scholars in Palestine in the Sixteenth Century" (in Hebrew). *Shalem* 4 (1978): 63-117.

_____. "The Jewish Community of Salonica from the Fifteenth to the Sixteenth Centuries, A Chapter in the Social History of the Jews in the Ottoman Empire and their Relations with their Authorities." Ph.D. diss., Hebrew University of Jerusalem, 1978.

———. "The Place of Abraham Bibago in the Controversy on the Study and Status of Philosophy in Fifteenth Century Spain," (in Hebrew). *Proceedings of the Fifth World Congress of Jewish Studies*, vol. 3. Jerusalem: World Union of Jewish Studies, 1972.

Hale, John R. *Florence and the Medici, the Pattern of Control.* London: Thames and Hudson, 1977.

Halkin, Abraham. "The Ban on the Study of Philosophy" (in Hebrew). *P'raqim, Yearbook of the Schoken Institute for Jewish Research*, vol. 1 edited by E.S. Rosenthal. Jerusalem, 1967-68.

Harvey, Warren Z. "Kabbalistic Elements in *Or Adonai* by R. Hasdai Crescas" (in Hebrew). *JSJT* 2 no. 1 (1982-83): 75-109.

———. "A Third Approach to Maimonides' Cosmogony-Prophetology Puzzle." *HTR* 74 (1981): 287-301.

———. "Between Political Philosophy and Halakhah" (in Hebrew). *Iyyun* 29 (1980): 198-212.

———. "The Return of Maimonideanism." *JJS* 42 (1980): 249-68.

———. "R. Hasdai Crescas and His Critique of Philosophic Happiness" (in Hebrew). *Proceedings of the Sixth World Congress of Jewish Studies*, Vol. 3. Jerusalem: World Union of Jewish Studies, 1977.

———. "Hasdai Crescas' Critique of the Theory of Acquired Intellect." Ph.D. diss., Columbia University, 1973.

Hankey, W.J. *God in Himself: Aquinas' Doctrine of God as Expounded in the Summa Theologiae.* New York: Oxford University Press, 1987.

Heller-Wilensky, Sarah. *The Philosophy of Isaac Arama* (in Hebrew). Jerusalem and Tel Aviv: Mosad Bialik and Dvir, 1956.

Henle, Robert J. *Saint Thomas and Platonism. A study of the Plato and Platonici Texts in the Writings of Saint Thomas.* The Hague: M. Nijhoff, 1956.

Heyd, Uriel. "Moses Hamon Chief Physician to Sultan Suleyman the Magnificent." *Oriens* 15 (1963): 152-70.

———. "The Jewish Communities of Istanbul in the Seventeenth Century." *Oriens* 4 (1953): 294-314.

Hick, John. *The Existence of God.* New York: MacMillan, 1964.

Hirschberg, Hayim Z. "The Oriental Jewish Communities." In *Religion in the Middle East*, edited by Arthur J. Arberry, vol. 1, 146-57. Cambridge, 1969.

Hope, Charles. "Artists, Patrons and Advisers in the Italian Renaissance." In *Patronage in the Renaissance*, edited by Guy F. Lytle and Stephen Orgel. Princeton: Princeton University Press, 1982.

Horowitz, Elliot. "The Dowering of Brides in the Ghetto of Venice: Between Tradition and Change, Ideas and Reality" (in Hebrew). *Tarbiz* 56 (1987): 347-71.

Husik, Isaac. *A History of Medieval Jewish Philosophy*. New York, 1916. Reprint. Philadelphia: The Jewish Publication Society and New York: Meridian Books, 1940.

_____. *Judah Messer Leon's Commentary on "Vetus Logica"*. Leiden, 1906.

Hyman, Arthur. "The Liberal Arts and Jewish Philosophy." In *Arts Libéraux et Philosophie au Moyen Âge*, Montreal: Institut D'Etudes Medievales; Paris: Libraire Philosophique, 1969.

Idel, Moshe. *Kabbalah, New Perspectives*. New Haven: Yale University Press, 1988.

_____. "Major Currents in Italian Kabbalah Between 1560-1660". *Italia Judaica*, vol. 2. Rome, 1986.

_____. "The Land of Israel in Medieval Kabbalah." In *The Land of Israel: Jewish Perspectives*, edited by Lawrence Hoffman. Notre Dame: Notre Dame University Press, 1986.

_____. "Kabbalah and Ancient Philosophy in R. Isaac and Yehudah Abravanel" (in Hebrew). In *The Philosophy of Love of Leone Ebreo*, edited by Menahem Dorman and Zvi Levi. Haifa: Hakibutz Hameuhad, 1985.

_____. "Studies in the Thought of the Author of Sefer ha-Meshiv, A Chapter in the History of Spanish Kabbalah" (in Hebrew). *Sefunot* n.s. Book 2 (17) (1983): 185-265.

_____. "The Magical and Neoplatonic Interpretations of the Kabbalah in the Renaissance" (in Hebrew). *JSJT* 4 (1982): 60-112. English version in *Jewish Thought in the Sixteenth Century*, edited by Bernard D. Cooperman. Cambridge: Harvard University Press: 1983.

_____. "The Magical and Theurgic Interpretation of Music in Jewish Texts: Renaissance to Hasidism" (in Hebrew). *Yuval* 4 (1982): 32-63.

_____. "Between the Concept of Sefirot as Essence and Instruments in

Kabbalah in the Renaissance Period" (in Hebrew). *Italia* 3 (1982): 89-111.

_____. "The Study Program of R. Yohanan Alemanno" (in Hebrew). *Tarbiz* 48 (1979): 303-30.

_____. "The Source of the Cycle Imagery in Judah Abravanel's Dialoghi D'Amore" (in Hebrew). *Iyyun* 28 (1978): 156-66.

Ivry, Alfred. "The Implications of Averroës' Thought for Jewish Philosophy" (in Hebrew). *Proceedings of the Sixth World Congress of Jewish Studies*, vol. 3. Jerusalem: The World Union of Jewish Studies, 1976.

_____. "Moses of Narbonne's 'Treatise on the Perfection of the Soul,' A Methodological and Conceptual Analysis." *JQR* (1966): 271-97.

Jacobs, Louis. *Principles of the Jewish Faith: An Analytical Study.* New York: Basic Books, 1964.

James, William. *Varieties of Religious Experience.* New York: Macmillan, 1961.

Jewish Encyclopedia, edited by Isidore Singer. 12 vols. New York: Funk and Wagnalls, 1901-06.

Jordan, Constance. "Feminism and the Humanists: The Case of Sir Thomas Elyot's *Defense of Good Women*." In *Rewriting the Renaissance: The Discourses of Sexual Differences in Early Modern Europe.* Edited by Margaret W. Ferguson, Maureen Quilligan, Nancy J. Vickers. Chicago: University of Chicago Press, 1986.

Kaplan, Lawrence. "Maimonides on the Miraculous Element in Prophecy." *HTR* 70 (1977): 233-56.

Katz, Jacob. *Halakhah and Kabalah, Studies in the History of Jewish Religion, Its Various Faces and Social Relevance* (in Hebrew). Jerusalem: Magnes Press, 1984.

Kaufmann, David. "Leone De Sommi Portaleone (1527-92)." *JQR* o.s. 10 (1898): 446-9.

_____. "La Famille de Yehiel de Pise." *REJ* 26 (1893): 83-110 220-39.

Kellner, Menachem M. *Dogma in Medieval Jewish Thought from Maimonides to Abravanel.* Oxford: Oxford University Press, 1986.

_____. "Dogma in Medieval Jewish Thought: A Bibliographical Survey." *Studies in Bibliography and Booklore* 15 (1984): 5-21.

Kennedy, George A. *Classical Rhetoric and Its Christian and Secular Tradi-*

tion from Ancient to Modern Times. Chapel Hill: The University of North Carolina Press, 1980.

Kenny, Anthony. *The Five Ways.* Notre Dame: University of Notre Dame, 1969. Reprint 1980.

Kibre, Pearl. *The Nations in the Medieval Universities.* Cambridge: Harvard University Press, 1948.

King, Margaret L. "Thwarted Ambitions: Six Learned Women of the Italian Renaissance." *Soundings* 59 (1976): 280-304.

Kinsman, Robert S., ed. *The Darker Vision of the Renaissance.* Los Angeles: University of California Press, 1979.

Klein-Braslavy, Sarah. "Ma'amad Har Sinai be-Mishnato Shel R. Nissim ben Reuben Gerondi (ha-Ran)." *Sinai* 80 (1977): 26-37.

Knowles, David. *The Evolution of Medieval Thought.* New York: Vintage Books, 1964.

Kristeller, Paul O. "Jewish Contributions to Italian Renaissance Culture." *Italia* 4 no. 1 (1985): 7-20.

_____. *Renaissance Thought and Its Sources.* Edited by Michael Mooney. New York: Columbia University Press, 1979.

_____. "The Impact of Early Italian Humanism on Thought and Learning." In *Developments in the Early Renaissance.* Edited by Bernard S. Levey. Albany: State University of New York Press, 1972.

_____. "Paduan Averroism and Alexandrism in the Light of Recent Studies," in *Aristotelismo padovano e filosofia aristotelica.* Atti del XII congresso internazionale di filosofia, IX, Florence: 1960.

_____. "Music and Learning in the Early Italian Renaissance." *Renaissance Thought II, Papers on Humanism and the Arts.* 142-162. New York: Harper and Row, 1965.

_____. *Studies in Renaissance Thought and Letters,* Rome: Edizioni d. Storia e Letteratura, 1955.

_____. *The Philosophy of Marsilio Ficino.* Translated by Virginia Conant. New York: Columbia University Press, 1943.

_____. "Thomism and the Italian Thought of the Renaissance." In *Medieval Aspects of Renaissance Learning — Three Essays.* Edited and translated by Edward P. Mahoney. Durham: Duke University Press, 1974.

Labalme, Patricia, ed. *Beyond their Sex: Learned Women of the European Past.* New York: New York University Press, 1980.

Lasker, Daniel. *Jewish Philosophical Polemics Against Christianity in the Middle Ages.* New York: Ktav, 1977.

Lazaroff, Allan. *The Theology of Abraham Bibago: A Defense of the Divine Will, Knowledge and Providence in Fifteenth Century Spanish-Jewish Philosophy.* University: University of Alabama Press, 1987.

Lesley, Arthur M., Review of *The Book of the Honeycomb's Flow: Sēpher Nōphet Ṣūfīm* by Isaac Rabinowitz. *Prooftexts* 4 (1984): 312-16.

_____. "Hebrew Humanism in Italy: The Case of Biography." *Prooftexts* 2 (1982): 163-77.

_____. "'The Song of Solomon's Ascents' by Yohanan Alemanno: Love and Human Perfection According to a Jewish Colleague of Giovanni Pico della Mirandola." Ph.D. diss., University of California, Berkeley, 1976.

Lewis, Bernard. *The Jews of Islam.* Princeton: Princeton University Press, 1984.

_____. "The Privileges Granted by Mehmed II to His Physician." *BSOAS* 14 (1952): 551-63.

Lewy, Hans, et al. *Three Jewish Philosophers.* 7th printing. New York: Atheneum 1979.

Lieberman, Saul, ed. *Salo W. Baron Jubilee Volume.* Jerusalem: American Academy for Jewish Research, 1979.

Liebes, Yehudah. "How Was *Sefer ha-Zohar* Composed?" *JSJT* 8 (1989): 1-71.

_____. "Sections of the Zohar Lexicon." Ph.D. diss., Hebrew University of Jerusalem, 1976.

Little, Arthur. *The Platonic Heritage of Thomism.* Dublin: Golden Eagle Books, 1949.

Mahoney, Edward P., ed. *Philosophy and Humanism, Renaissance Essays in Honor of P.O. Kristeller.* New York: Columbia University Press, 1976.

_____. "Themistius and the Agent Intellect in James of Viterbo and Other Thirteenth Century Philosophers (Saint Thomas Siger of Brabant and Henry Bate)." *Augustiniana* 23 (1973): 434-38.

_____. "Nicoletto Vernia and Agostino Nifo on Alexander of Aphrodisias: An Unnoticed Dispute." *RCSF* 23 (1968): 270-71.

Marmorstein, Arthur. *The Old Rabbinic Doctrine of God.* 2 vols. London: Oxford University Press and H. Milford, 1927-37.

Martines, Lauro. *Power and Imagination, City States in Renaissance Italy.* New York: Knopf 1979.

_____. "A Way of Looking at Women in Renaissance Florence." *JMRS* 4, no. 1 (1974): 15-28.

_____. *The Social World of the Florentine Humanists (1390-1460).* Princeton: Princeton University Press, 1963.

Marx, Alexander. "R. Joseph of Arles in the Role of a Teacher and Head of a Yeshivah in Sienna" (in Hebrew). In *Jubilee Volume in Honor of Levi Ginzberg.* New York: American Academy for Jewish Research, 1946.

_____. "The Expulsion of the Jews from Spain, Two New Accounts." In *Studies in Jewish History and Booklore.* New York: Jewish Theological Seminary, 1944.

_____. "Texts by and about Maimonides." *JQR* n.s.: 25 (1934-35): 374-87.

McInnery, Ralph. *Being and Predication Thomistic Interpretations.* Washington, DC: Catholic University of America Press, 1986.

Melamed, Abraham. "Rhetoric and Philosophy in Nofet Sufim by R. Judah Messer Leon" (in Hebrew). *Italia* (1978): 7-39.

Milano, Attilio. *Storia degli ebrei in Italia.* Turin: Giulio Einaudi, 1963.

Miskimin, Harry A. *The Economy of Early Renaissance Europe, 1300-1460.* Cambridge: Cambridge University Press, 1975.

Molho, Anthony and John Tedeschi, eds. *Renaissance Studies in Honor of Hans Baron.* DeKalb: Northern Illinois University Press, 1971.

Motzkin, Aryeh L. "Elia del Medigo, Averroës and Averroism." *Italia* 6 (1-2) (1987): 7-19.

_____. "On the Interpretation of Maimonides." *The Independent Journal of Philosophy* 2 (1973): 39-46.

Murphy, James J. *Rhetoric in the Middle Ages, A History of Rhetorical Theory from St. Augustine to the Renaissance.* Berkeley: University of California Press, 1974.

Nadav, Yael. "An Epistle of the Qabbalist Isaac Mar Hayyim Concerning the Doctrine of Supernal Lights" (in Hebrew). *Tarbiz* 26 (1957): 440-58.

Nardi, Bruno. *Saggi sull'Aristotelisimo padovano del secolo XIV-XVI.* Florence, 1958.

Negal, Gedalyah. "The Views of Joseph Ya'abez on Philosophy and Philosophers, Torah and Commandments." *Eshel Beer Sheva* 1 (1976): 258-87.

Nehama, Joseph. *Histoire des Israelites de Salonique.* 7 vols. in 4 Paris—Salonique, Librairie Molho, 1935-36. Vol. 5 published by World Sephardi Federation, London; vols. 6-7 published by the Communate Israelite de Thessalonique.

Nelson, Benjamin N. *The Idea of Usury: From Tribal Brotherhood to Universal Otherhood.* Princeton: Princeton University Press, 1949. Reprint. Chicago, 1969.

Netanyahu, Ben Zion. *The Marranos of Spain from the Late XIVth to the Early XVIth Century According to Contemporary Hebrew Sources.* New York: American Academy for Jewish Research, 1966.

_____. *Don Isaac Abravanel — Statesman and Philosopher.* Philadelphia: Jewish Publication Society of America, 1953.

Neubauer, Adolph. "Petrarque a Avignon." *REJ* 10 (1885): 94-97.

_____. "Zur Frauenliteratur." *Israelitische Letterbode.* 10 (1884-85): 97-105; 11 (1899): 62-5.

Neumark, David. "Toledot ha-Iqqarim be-Israel." Odessa: Moriah 1919, 1921.

Jacob Neusner, ed. *Take Judaism for Example, Studies toward the Comparisons of Religions.* Chicago: University of Chicago Press, 1983.

Noonan, John T. *The Scholastic Analysis of Usury.* Cambridge: Harvard University Press, 1957.

O'Kelly, Bernard, ed. *The Renaissance Image of Man and the World.* Columbus: Ohio State University Press, 1966.

Owens, Joseph. *St. Thomas Aquinas on the Existence of God: The Collected Papers of Joseph Owens.* Edited by John R. Catan. Albany: State University of New York Press, 1986.

Pagis, Dan. *Change and Tradition in the Secular Poetry: Spain and Italy* (in Hebrew). Jerusalem: Keter, 1976.

_____. *Secular Poetry and Poetics of Moses Ibn Ezra and His Generation* (in Hebrew). Jerusalem, Mosad Bialik, 1970.

Pegis, Anton C. "Four Medieval Ways to God," *The Monist* 54 (1970): 317-58.

Peters, Edward H. *Heresy and Authority in Medieval Europe: Documents in Translation.* Philadelphia: University of Pennsylvania Press, 1980.

Peters, Frank E. *Aristoteles Arabus, The Oriental Translations and Commentaries on the Aristotelian Corpus.* Leiden: E.J. Brill 1968.

Pines, Shlomo. "On the Term *Rohaniyyot* and Its Origin and on Judah Halevi's Doctrine" (in Hebrew). *Tarbiz* 57 (1989): 511-540.

──────. "'And he called out to nothingness and it was split,' A Note on a Passage in Ibn Gabirol's Keter Malkhut" (in Hebrew). *Tarbiz,* 50 (1980-81): 33-97.

──────. *Studies in the History of Jewish Philosophy, the Transmission of Texts and Ideas.* Jerusalem: Mosad Bialik, 1977.

Pipano, David. *Hagor Ha-Efod.* Sofia, 1925.

Plantinga, Alvin and N. Wolterstorff. *Faith and Rationality.* Notre Dame: University of Notre Dame Press, 1983.

Plumb, John H. *The Italian Renaissance.* New York: American Heritage, 1961.

Porges, N. "Elie Capsali et sa cronique da Venisa," *REJ* 78 (1924): 21-25.

Potts, Timothy C. "Aquinas on Belief and Faith." In *Inquiries into Medieval Philosophy,* edited by James F. Ross. Westport, CT, 1971.

Proudfoot, Wayne. *Religious Experience.* Berkeley: University of California Press, 1985.

Pullan, Brian. *Rich and Poor in Renaissance Venice: The Social Institutions of a Catholic State.* Oxford: Basil Blackwell, 1971.

Rabil, Albert Jr., ed. *Renaissance Humanism: Foundations, Forms and Legacy.* 3 vols. Philadelphia: University of Pennsylvania Press, 1988.

Rahman, Fazlur. *Prophecy in Islam: Philosophy and Orthodoxy.* London: George Allen and Unwin, 1958.

Randall, John H. *Aristotle.* New York: Columbia University Press, 1960.

──────. "The Development of Scientific Method in the School of Padua." *JHI* 1 (1940): 170-206. Reprinted In *Saggi e Testi.* Padua: Editrice Antenore, 1958.

Ravitzky, Aviezer. "The Secrets of *The Guide of the Perplexed* Between the Thirteenth and Twentieth Centuries" (in Hebrew). *JSJT,* 5 (1986): 23-69.

──────. "On the Sources of the Commentary to Proverbs by Emmanuel of Rome" (in Hebrew). *Kiryat Sepher* 56 (1981): 726-39.

_____. "Samuel Ibn Tibbon and the Esoteric Character of the Guide." *AJS Review* 6 (1981): 87-123.

_____. "The Thought of R. Zerahya ben Isaac b. Shealtiel Hen and the Maimonidean-Tibbonian Philosophy in the 13th Century." Ph.D. diss., Hebrew University of Jerusalem, 1977.

Rawidowicz, Simon. "The Structure of the Guide of the Perplexed." (in Hebrew). In *Hebrew Studies in Jewish Thought,* edited by Benjamin C. I. Ravid, vol. 1. Jerusalem: Rubin Mass, 1969.

Regev, Shaul. "The Rational-Mystical Trend in Fifteenth Century Jewish Thought" (in Hebrew). *JSJT* 5 (1986): 155-89.

_____. "About the Problem of the Study of Philosophy in 15th Century Thought; R. Joseph ibn Shem Tov and R. Abraham Bibago" (in Hebrew). *Daat* 16 (1986): 57-86.

_____. "Theology and Rational Mysticism in the Writings of R. Joseph ben Shem Tov" (in Hebrew). Ph.D. diss., Hebrew University of Jerusalem, 1983.

Reines, Alvin J. "Maimonides' conception of Miracles." *HUCA* 45 (1974): 243-45.

_____. *Maimonides and Abravanel on Prophecy.* Cincinnati: Hebrew Union College Press, 1970.

Rhine, A. B. "The Secular Poetry of Italy." *JQR* n.s. 1 (1910-11): 352-54.

Rosanes, Solomon. *A History of the Jews in Turkey.* Vol. 1, Tel Aviv: Dvir, 1930; vols. 2, 3, Sofia: Defus Hamishpat, 1938-39.

Rosen, Mina. "The Activities of Influential Jews at the Sultan's Count in Istanbul in Favor of the Jewish Community in Jerusalem in the Seventeenth Century" (in Hebrew). *Michael* 7 (1982): 394-430.

Rosen, Tova. "On Tongue Being Bound and Let Loose: Women in Medieval Hebrew Literature." *Prooftexts* 8 (1988): 67-87.

Rosenberg, Shalom. "The Concept of Emunah in Post Maimonidean Jewish Philosophy" (in Hebrew). In *Bar Ilan University Year Book in Judaic Studies and the Humanities,* 22-23 (1988): 351-389; English version in *Studies in Medieval Jewish History and Literature,* edited by Isadore Twersky, Vol. 2. Cambridge: Harvard University Press, 1984.

_____. "Biblical Exegesis in the Guide of the Perplexed." in *JSJT.* 1 (1981): 85-157.

_____. "Logic and Ontology in Jewish Philosophy of the Fourteenth Century" (in Hebrew). Ph.D. diss., Hebrew University of Jerusalem, 1974.

Rosenthal, Franz J.E. "Yohanan Alemanno and Occult Sciences in *Prismata: Naturwissenschaft Geschichtliche Studien: Festschrift für Willy Hartner.* Wiesbadden, 1977.

Rosenthal, Judah. "Usury from a Gentile" (in Hebrew). In *Studies and Texts in Jewish History, Literature and Religion.* Jerusalem: Rubin Mass, 1966.

Roth, Cecil. *The History of the Jews in Venice.* Philadelphia, 1930. Reprint. New York: Shocken, 1975.

_____. *The Jews in the Renaissance.* Philadelphia: Jewish Publication Society of America, 1959.

_____. *The House of Nasi: The Duke of Naxos.* Philadelphia: Jewish Publication Society, 1947-48. Reprint. New York: Greenwood Press, 1969.

_____. *The History of the Jews of Italy.* Philadelphia: The Jewish Publication Society of America, 1946.

Roth, Norman. "The 'Theft of Philosophy' by the Greeks from the Jews." *Classical Folia* 2 (1978): 53-67.

_____. "The 'Wiles of Women' Motif in the Medieval Hebrew Literature of Spain." *Hebrew Annual Review* 2 (1978): 145-65.

Ruderman, David B. "The Impact of Science on Jewish Culture and Society in Venice with Special Reference to Jewish Graduates of Padua's Medical School." In *Gli Ebrei e Venezia Secoli XIV-XVIII,* 417-48. Venice: Editioni Comunita, 1987.

_____. "An Exemplary Sermon from the Classroom of a Jewish Teacher in Renaissance Italy." *Italia* 1 (1982): 7-38.

_____. *The World of a Renaissance Jew, The Life and Thought of Abraham ben Mordecai Farissol.* Cincinnati: Hebrew Union College Press, 1981.

Sack, Bracha. "R. Joseph Taitazak's Commentaries" (in Hebrew). In *Shlomo Pines Jubilee Volume on the Occasion of his Eightieth Birthday,* Part 1 (= *JSJT* 7 1988): 341-356.

_____. "The Exile of Israel and the Exile of the Shechinah in 'Or Yaqar' of Rabbi Moses Cordevero" (in Hebrew). *JSJT* 4 (1982): 157-78.

Samuelson, Norbert. "Possible and Preferred Relations Between Reason and Revelation as Authority in Judaism." In *Studies in Jewish Philosophy* 2 (1981): 7-15. Reprint in *Collected Essays of the Academy for Jewish*

Philosophy 1980-1985. Philadelphia: University Press of America, 1986.

———. "On Proving God's Existence." *Judaism* 16 (1967): 21-36.

Schatzmiller, Joseph. "Between Aba Mari and the Rashba — The Negotiations Preceding the Ban in Barcelona" (in Hebrew). *Mehqarim be-Toledot 'Am Israel ve-Eretz Yisrael* 3 (1975): 121-37.

Schechter, Solomon. "The Dogmas of Judaism," in his *Studies in Judaism: Essays on Persons, Concepts, and Movements of Thought in Jewish Tradition.* New York: Atheneum, 1970.

———. "Notes sur Messer David Leon, tirées de manuscripts." *REJ* 24 (1892): 118-37.

Schirmann, Jefim. *The Comedy of Betrothal by Yehudah Sommo (1527-92)* (in Hebrew). 2d ed. Jerusalem: Tarshish, 1965.

———. "Theater and Music in the Jewish Ghettos in Italy (from the 16th to the 18th Centuries)" (in Hebrew). *Zion* 29 (1964): 61-108.

Schmitt, Charles B. "Toward a Reassessment of Renaissance Aristotelianism," *History of Science* 11 (1973): 159-83. Reprint. In *Studies in Renaissance Philosophy and Science.* London: Variorum Reprints, 1981.

———. *Critical Survey and Bibliography of Studies on Renaissance Aristotelianism, 1958-69.* Padua: Editrice Antenore, 1971.

Scholem, Gershom. *Origins of the Kabbalah.* Edited by R.J. Zwi Werblowsky. Translated by Alan Arkush. Philadelphia: The Jewish Publication Society of America; Princeton: Princeton University Press, 1987.

———. *Elements of the Kabbalah and its Symbolism* (in Hebrew). Translated by Joseph Ben Shlomo. Jerusalem: Mosad Bialik, 1976.

———. *Kabbalah.* Jerusalem: Keter, 1974.

———. *Sabbatai Sevi, The Mystical Messiah.* Translated by R.J. Zwi Werblowsky. Princeton: Princeton University Press, 1973.

———. "The Crisis of Tradition in Jewish Messianism." In *The Messianic Idea in Judaism,* 49-77. New York: Schocken, 1971.

———. *On the Kabbalah and its Symbolism.* New York: Schocken, 1969.

———. *Von der Mystischen Gestalt der Gottheit.* Zurich: Rhein Verlag, 1962.

———. *Major Trends in Jewish Mysticism.* New York: Schocken, 1941.

Schweid, Eliezer. *Maimonides and the Members of His Circle* (in Hebrew). Edited by Dan Oryan. Jerusalem: Aqademon, 1968.

_____. "Essential Attributes in the Philosophy of R. Hasdai Crescas" (in Hebrew). *Iyyun* 4 (1964): 444-67.

Secret, François. "Les Kabbalists chretiens les hébraisants chrétiens," *REJ* 124 (1965): 157-77.

_____. *Les Kabbalists chrétiens de la Renaissance.* Paris: Dynod, 1964.

_____. "Qui etait l'orientaliste mithridate." *REJ* 116 (1957): 96-102.

Seigel, Jerrold. *Rhetoric and Philosophy in Renaissance Humanism, The Union of Eloquence and Wisdom, Petrarch to Valla.* Princeton: Princeton University Press, 1968.

_____. "Civic Humanism or Ciceronian Rhetoric." *Past and Present.* 34 (1966): 3-34.

Septimus, Bernard. *Hispano-Jewish Culture in Transition: The Career and Controversies of Ramah.* Cambridge: Harvard University Press, 1982.

Sermoneta, Joseph. "Prophecy in the Writings of R. Yehuda Romano" (in Hebrew). *Daat* 8 (1982): 59-86. English version in *Studies in Medieval Jewish History and Literature,* Vol. 2.

_____. "The Liberal Arts in the Jewish Community in Italy in the Fourteenth Century" (in Hebrew). In *Town and Community, Lectures Delivered at the 12th Convention of the Historical Society of Israel.* Jerusalem, 1978.

_____. "Scholastic Philosophic Literature in Rabbi Yosef Taitasak's *Porat Yosef*" (in Hebrew). *Sefunot* 11 [= Book of Greek Jewry 1] (1971-1978): 135-85.

_____. "On the Third Dissertation: The Fall of Angels" (in Hebrew). In *Studies in Honor of Jacob Friedman.* Jerusalem, 1974.

_____. "Moses ben Solomon of Salerno and Nicholas of Giovinazo on Maimonides' *The Guide of the Perplexed*" (in Hebrew). *Iyyun* 20 (1970): 212-39.

Seznec, Jean. *The Survival of the Pagan Gods, the Mythological Tradition and Its Place in Renaissance Humanism and Literature.* Translated by Barbara F. Sessions, 2d ed. Princeton: Princeton University Press, 1972.

Shehadi, Fadlou. *Metaphysics in Islamic Philosophy,* Delmar: Caravan Books, 1982.

Shmuelevitz, Aryeh. *The Jews of the Ottoman Empire in the Late Fifteenth and the Sixteenth Centuries: Administrative, Economic, Legal and Social Relations as Reflected in the Responsa.* Leiden: E.J. Brill, 1984.

Shohat, Azriel. "Taxation and its Administration" (in Hebrew). *Sefunot* 11 [=Book of Greek Jewry 1] (1971-1978): 301-39.

Shulvass, Moses A. "Hayyey he-Yehudim bi-Tequfat ha-Renesans." New York, 1955. *The Jews in the World of the Renaissance.* Translated by Elvin I. Kose. Leiden: E.J. Brill, 1973.

_____. "The Jewish Population in Renaissance Italy." *Jewish Social Studies* 13 (1951): 3-24.

_____. "Torah Study among Italian Jews in the Period of the Renaissance" (in Hebrew). *Horev* 10 (1948): 105-28.

_____. "The Disputes of Messer Leon and His Attempt to Exert His Authority on the Jews of Italy" (in Hebrew). *Zion* 12 (1947): 17-23. Reprinted in *Bi-Zevat ha-Dorot.* 56-66. Tel Aviv: Ha-'Ogen, 1950.

_____. "The Knowledge of Antiquity Among the Italian Jews of the Renaissance." *PAAJR* (1948-49): 291-99.

Shumaker, Wayne. *The Occult Sciences in the Renaissance, A Study in Intellectual Patterns.* Berkeley: University of California Press, 1972.

Silman, Yohanan. "Historical Reality in the Kuzari" (in Hebrew). *Daat* 2-3 (1978-9): 29-42.

Silver, Daniel J. *Maimonidean Criticism and the Maimonidean Controversy 1180-1240.* Leiden: E.J. Brill, 1965.

Simonsohn, Shelomo. *Ha-Yehudim be-Duksut Mantova,* 2 vols. Jerusalem: Kiryat Sepher 1962-1964. English translation, *The Jews in its Duchy of Mantova.* Jerusalem: Publications of the Diaspora Research Institute, 1977.

Sirat, Collete. *A History of Jewish Philosophy in the Middle Ages.* Cambridge: Cambridge University Press; Paris: Editions de la Maison de Sciences de L'homme, 1985.

Skinner, Quentin. *The Foundations of Modern Political Thought,* Cambridge: Cambridge University Press, 1978.

_____. "Meaning and Understanding in the History of Ideas," *History and Theory* 8 (1969): 3-53. Reprinted in *Meaning and Context: Quentin Skinner and his Critics.* Edited by James Tully. Princeton: Princeton University Press, 1988.

Starr, Joshua. "The Mass Conversion of Jews in Southern Italy (1290-1293)." *Speculum* 21 (1946): 203-11.

Steinschneider, Moritz. *Die hebräische Übersetzungen des Mittelalters.* Berlin, 1893. Reprint Graz: Akademische Druk-u. Verlagsanstalt, 1956.

———. "Zur Frauenliteratur." *Israelitsche Letterbode* 12 (1884-85): 56-62.

Stevens, Elliot, ed. *Rabbinic Authority.* New York: Central Conference of American Rabbis, 1982.

Stow, Kenneth R. "The Jewish Family in the Rhineland in the High Middle Ages: Form and Function." *The American Historical Review* 92 (1987): 1085-1110.

———. "Papal and Royal Attitudes toward Jewish Moneylending in the Thirteenth Century." *AJS Review* 6 (1981): 161-84.

———. *Catholic Thought and Papal Jewry Policy, 1555-1593.* New York: The Jewish Theological Seminary of America, 1977.

Stow, Kenneth R. and Sandra De-Benedetti. "Donne ebree a Roma nell'eta del ghetto: afett dipendenza, autonomia." *RMI* 52 terza serie (1986): 64-115.

Strauss, Leo. "How to Begin to Study *The Guide of the Perplexed.*" In *The Guide of the Perplexed*, translated by Shlomo Pines. Chicago: University of Chicago Press, 1963.

Ta-Shema, Israel. "'Al Petor mi-Missim le-Talmidey Hakhamim be-Yemey ha-Beynayim." In *Studies in Rabbinic Literature, Bible and Jewish History Dedicated to Professor Ezra Zion Melamed* (in Hebrew). Ramat Gan, 1972.

Tamar, David. "A Critical Edition of Galya Raza" (in Hebrew). *JSJT* 2 (1983): 647-50.

———. "About *Kevod Hakhamim* by David ben Judah Messer Leon (in Hebrew) *Kiryat Sepher* 26 (1950): 96-100. Reprint *Studies in the History of the Jews in Israel and Holy* (in Hebrew). Jerusalem, 1970.

Taylor, R. "Abd al Latif al Baghdadi's Epitome of the Kalam fi Mahd al-Khayr (Liber de Causis)." In *Islamic Theology and Philosophy.* Edited by Michael Marmura. Albany: State University of New York Press, 1984.

Tirosh-Rothschild, Hava. "In Defense of Jewish Humanism." *Jewish History* 3 (1988): 32-57.

———. "Maimonides and Aquinas: The Interplay of Two Masters in Medieval Jewish Philosophy." *Conservative Judaism* 39 (1986): 54-66.

———. "Sefirot as the Essence of God in the Writings of David Messer Leon." *AJS Review* 7-8 (1982): 409-25.

_____. "The Influence of Judah Halevi on the Thought of David ben Judah Messer Leon" (in Hebrew). *Proceedings of the 8th World Congress of Jewish Studies.* vol. 3. Jerusalem: The World Union of Jewish Studies, 1982.

_____. "The Concept of Torah in the Works of David ben Judah Messer Leon" (in Hebrew). *JSJT* 2 (1982): 94-117.

Tishby, Isaiah. *The Wisdom of the Zohar* (in Hebrew). 3d ed. 2 vols. Jerusalem: Mosad Bialik, 1971.

_____. "On the Problems of the Book Galya Raza," (in Hebrew). *Zion* 48 (1983): 103-6.

Toaff, Ariel. "Jewish Banking in Central Italy in the 12th-15th Centuries." In *Jews in Italy: Studies Dedicated to the Memory of U. Cassuto on the 100th Anniversary of his Birth.* Jerusalem: Magnes Press, 1988.

_____. *The Jews of Medieval Assisi, 1305-1487, A Social and Economic History of a Small Jewish Community in Italy.* Florence: L.S. Olschki, 1979.

_____. *Gli Ebrei a Perugia.* Perugia: Fonti per la storia dell'umbria, n. 10, 1975.

_____. ed. *Studi sull'ebraismo italiano in memoria di Cecil Roth.* Rome: Barulli, 1974.

Tobi, Yosef, Jacob Barnai and Shalom bar Asher, eds. *History of the Jews in the Islamic Countries.* Jerusalem: The Zalman Shazar Center, 1981.

Todorov, Tzvetan. "The War of the Words." Review of *In Defense of Rhetoric*, by Brian Vickers. *The New Republic.* January 23, 1989.

Tully, James, ed. *Meaning and Context: Quentin Skinner and his Critics.* Princeton: Princeton University Press, 1988.

Twersky, Isadore, ed. *Studies in Medieval Jewish History and Literature*, vol. 2. Cambridge: Harvard University Press, 1984.

_____. "Talmudists, Philosophers, Kabbalists: The Quest for Spirituality in the Sixteenth Century." In *Jewish Thought in the Sixteenth Century.* Edited by Bernard D. Cooperman. Cambridge: Harvard University Press, 1983.

_____. "Ha-Hinnukh ha-Yehudi be-Ashkenaz bi-Yemei ha-Beynayim." Reprint. In *Studies in Jewish Law and Philosophy.* Hebrew section. New York: Ktav, 1982.

_____. ed. *Studies in Medieval Jewish History and Literature.* Vol. 1. Cambridge: Harvard University Press, 1979.

_____. *Rabad of Posquieres: A Twelfth Century Talmudist.* Cambridge: Harvard University Press, 1962.

_____. and Bernard Septimus, eds. *Jewish Thought in the Seventeenth Century.* Cambridge: Harvard University Press, 1987.

Urbach, Ephraim. *The Tosaphists: Their History, Writings and Methods* (in Hebrew). 4th enl. ed. Jerusalem, 1980.

_____. *The Sages, Their Concepts and Beliefs.* Translated by Israel Abrahams. Jerusalem: Mosad Bialik, 1975.

Wagner, David L. ed. *The Seven Liberal Arts in the Middle Ages.* Bloomington: Indiana University Press, 1983.

Walker, Daniel P. *Spiritual and Demonic Magic from Ficino to Campanella.* London: The Warburg Institute, 1958.

Weinberg, Joanna. "Azariah De Rossi and the Septuagint Traditions." *Italia* 5 (1985): 7-35.

Wilhelmsen, Frederick D. "Creation as a Relation in Saint Thomas Aquinas." *The Modern Schoolman* 56 (1979): 107-33.

Wippel, John F. *Metaphysical Themes in Thomas Aquinas.* Washington: Catholic University of America Press, 1984.

Wirszubski, Chaim. *Three Chapters in the History of Christian Kabbalah* (in Hebrew). Jerusalem, 1975.

_____. "Giovanni Pico's Companion to Kabbalistic Symbolism." In *Studies in Mysticism and Religion Presented to Gershom Scholem on his Seventieth Birthday by Pupils, Colleagues and Friends.* Edited by Ephraim E. Urbach, R.J. Zwi Werblowsky and Chaim Wirszubski. Jerusalem: Magnes Press, 1967.

_____. "Flavius Mithridates" (in Hebrew). *Israel National Academy for Sciences Proceedings* 1 (1966): 1-10.

_____. "Flavius Mithridates' Christological Sermon" (in Hebrew). In *Yitzhak Baer Jubilee Volume.* Jerusalem: Israel Historical Society, 1960.

Wolfson, Harry A. *Repercussions of the Kalam in Jewish Philosophy.* Cambridge: Harvard University Press, 1979.

_____. *Studies in the History of Philosophy and Religion.* Edited by Isadore Twersky and George Williams. Cambridge: Harvard University Press. Vol. 1, 1973; Vol. 2, 1977.

_____. *The Philosophy of the Kalam.* Cambridge: Harvard University Press, 1976.

_____. "The History of Platonic Ideas." *JHI.* 22 (1961): 3-32.

_____. *Crescas' Critique of Aristotle, Problems of Aristotle's Physics in Jewish and Arabic Philosophy.* Cambridge: Harvard University Press, 1929.

Yerushalmi, Yosef H. *The Lisbon Massacre of 1506 and the Royal Image in the Shevet Yehudah.* Cincinnati: Hebrew Union College, 1976.

_____. ed. *Bibliographical Essays in Medieval Jewish Studies.* New York: Anti-Defamation League of B'nai B'rith, 1976.

_____. *From Spanish Court to Italian Ghetto.* Seattle: University of Washington Press, 1971.

Zarfati, Ben-Ami. *The Mathematical Terms in Hebrew Scientific Literature of the Middle Ages"* (in Hebrew). Jerusalem, 1979.

Zohori, Menahem and Aryeh Tartakover, eds. *Studies in Jewish Themes by Contemporary European Scholars.* Tel Aviv: Tel Aviv University, 1969.

Index

A

Abravanel, Don Isaac, 23, 28, 50, 51, 53, 54, 84, 89, 186, 217
  Rosh Amanah, 89, 90, 121, 146-148, 227
Abravenel, Judah, 50
Abraham, ben David (Rabad), 144, 153-154
Abulafia, Abraham, 37
Active Intellect, the, 110, 118, 174, 179, 182, 220
Aderbi, Isaac, 83, 171
Aggadah, 37-38
Al'ami, Shlomo, 87
Albalag, Isaac, 84, 164
Albo, Joseph, 84, 85, 121, 147, 149-150, 152, 205, 217
Alchemy, 16, 37, 47, 233
Alemanno, Yohanan, 29, 35, 36, 37, 42, 47, 48, 49, 51, 74
Alexander, of Aphrodisias, 84
Alfarabi, 84, 109, 110, 174, 202
Isaac, Alfasi, 19, 21, 36
Alghazali, 30, 37
Alkabez, Shlomo, 83, 171, 231
Ammoraim, 71

Analogical predication, 194
Analogy, between God and humans, 199
Anatoli, Jacob, 17, 36, 119
'Arama, Isaac, 84, 85, 88, 121, 186, 227
Aquinas, Saint Thomas, 84, 94, 106, 109, 114, 120, 124, 126-127, 131, 186, 235-236
  and Maimonides, 114-119, 200
  and Jewish philosophers, 119-121
  harmonization of reason and faith, 114-120
  on God's existence, 188-192, 194-197
  on divine attributes, 203-204
  Quaestiones de Veritate, 217
  Summa Contra Gentiles, 191, 226
  Summa Theologiae, 115, 139, 188, 191, 221, 224, 226
Aristotelian philosophy, 26, 93, 168, 198, 233
  corpus, 16
  Jewish philosophers, 6-7
Aristotelianism, 8, 39, 41-44, 114
  Jewish, 233, 237
  medieval, 88, 128, 207, 237, 238